HOUSING VOUCHERS FOR THE POOR

HOUSING VOUCHERS FOR THE POOR

Lessons from a National Experiment

Raymond J. Struyk
Marc Bendick, Jr.
Editors

An Urban Institute Book

THE URBAN INSTITUTE PRESS · WASHINGTON, D.C.

This publication was printed by Braun-Brumfield, Inc.
from type set by Typesetters, Inc.

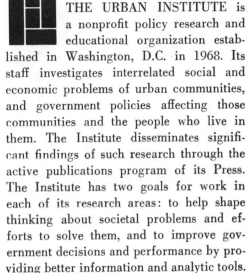 THE URBAN INSTITUTE is a nonprofit policy research and educational organization established in Washington, D.C. in 1968. Its staff investigates interrelated social and economic problems of urban communities, and government policies affecting those communities and the people who live in them. The Institute disseminates significant findings of such research through the active publications program of its Press. The Institute has two goals for work in each of its research areas: to help shape thinking about societal problems and efforts to solve them, and to improve government decisions and performance by providing better information and analytic tools.

Through work that ranges from broad conceptual studies to administrative and technical assistance, Institute researchers contribute to the stock of knowledge available to public officials and to private individuals and groups concerned with formulating and implementing more efficient and effective government policy.

Conclusions or opinions expressed are those of the authors and do not necessarily reflect the views of other staff members, officers or trustees of the Institute, or of any organizations which provide financial support to the Institute.

Contents

Tables

Page

Page

Foreword

A continuing issue in government assistance to the poor is the extent to which assistance should be unrestricted or limited to uses that society deems vital, for example, food, housing, and health care. At one extreme, government could provide "vital" goods or services in-kind. At the other extreme, a household could simply receive cash to spend on its needs as it sees them.

Since the mid-1930s, the government has responded to perceived housing needs of the poor through federal-state-local partnerships of grants-in-aid and through legal protection against discrimination. Mainly, the government augmented the supply of low-income housing by building and operating public housing projects to provide dwellings for the poor. Government has also subsidized privately built and operated low-income housing by providing mortgage-financing at below-market interest rates.

In contrast to this (supply side) approach and also since the 1930s, some policy makers and students of the subject have advocated a demand-oriented, less restrictive strategy. If poor households were given vouchers (housing allowances) to secure housing on their own, they could effectively demand housing of higher quality. Such housing allowances, advocates claimed, would be more effective and economical than the traditional governmental approach.

In 1970 Congress and the U.S. Department of Housing and Urban Development initiated an elaborate social experiment. The Experimental Housing Allowance Program (EHAP), conducted over an 11-year period, tested the feasibility of providing cash subsidies to low-income households to help them obtain adequate housing. The Urban Institute was involved with EHAP since its beginning. In this book, eight Institute researchers not only thoroughly analyze and describe the experiment but also probe the larger question of just what government strategies seem most effective in aiding the poor.

Three field operations within EHAP, the Demand Experiment, the Supply Experiment, and the Administrative Agency Experiment, examined issues raised by the use of housing allowances. Policy makers and interested observers wanted to know how allowances would affect the suppliers of housing; whether inflation would occur in housing markets; who would participate in this type of program; and how participants would respond to different payment formulas, varying levels of benefits, and minimum housing consumption requirements.

EHAP answered these questions and provided implications for other aspects of housing programs and aid to the poor. Findings were derived by analyzing the behavior of 30,000 lower-income households who participated at 12 sites across the country. Analysis showed that from the household's viewpoint, straight cash transfers to low-income households are even more beneficial and effective than are housing allowances which are loaded with government restrictions. EHAP findings also suggested that allowances provide services equivalent to other housing programs but at a lower cost.

Limited resources, red tape, and even unforeseen preferences and special needs of the poor often stymy the power of the government to aid the poor. In a world where government aid is intensely scrutinized, the authors stress that program benefits must outweigh their costs. So an effective housing program must be marked by this aim: to simultaneously improve the situation of individual households, develop communities, and enhance the vitality of the housing sector. In this broader context, the efficacy of housing allowances is less clear.

Analysis of housing programs, including housing vouchers, also indicates a need for coordinated strategies. Unfortunately, housing subsidies and community development programs have often been poorly coordinated although they frequently affect the same individuals. And importantly, housing programs must be tailored to the particular circumstances of different housing markets.

It is in indicating the need for complex and varying mixes of programs to meet the nation's housing needs that EHAP has made its most important contributions. Neither housing vouchers nor any other single, simple program can itself be a panacea.

WILLIAM GORHAM
President
The Urban Institute

Acknowledgments

This statement of findings from the integrated analysis of EHAP may be designated as the "final" report, but it is still only one of a large repertory of Urban Institute papers around the housing allowance theme produced during more than a decade of research. As with the development of all knowledge, one piece builds on another. Consequently, acknowledgments are due to those who contributed during the many years of work. Inevitably, I will miss some individuals, so my first act of appreciation (and my apologies) is to those unnamed.

The individuals who must get the most credit for EHAP are those assistant secretaries at the U. S. Department of Housing and Urban Development who literally battled to get the program funded initially and then fought to sustain the program through the long years required to keep an experiment going. Some of these individuals—Harold Finger, Michael Moskow, Charles Orlebeke, and Donna Shalala—"believed" in the notion of a housing allowance, some did not. But they all shared an interest in conducting a fair test and occasionally put their jobs on the line to protect objective research. Backing them up were a large number of HUD staff too numerous to name except for those individuals who were government technical representatives at one point or another: among them Charles Field, Jack Betz, Jerry Fitts, Marty Levine, Evelyn Glatt, Carolyn MacFarlane, Robert Causin, and Terry Connell in chronological order.

Frank de Leeuw took the initial responsibility for The Urban Institute's contribution to the analysis of housing allowances—in the late 1960s before there were experiments. But John Heinberg had the longest association with EHAP and saw the program through the long and tedious design stage. And, when other contractors were selected, Dr. Heinberg oversaw the difficult report review function along with James Zais, the deputy project manager throughout EHAP. Marc Bendick, Jr. picked up the reins as project manager on short notice and took the work through the final two years of the integrated analysis.

Other Urban Institute staff who made a major contribution to EHAP during this period included Verna Alburger, Mark Berkman, Elizabeth Bernsten, Helen Blank, Garth Buchanan, David Carlson, Joanne Culbertson, Margaret Drury, James Follain, Harriet Freid, Jeanne Goedert, John Goodman, Jr., Sam Leaman, Stephen Malpezzi, C. Reid Melton, Larry Ozanne, Ronald Sepanik, Anne Squire, Peggy Spohn, Michael Springer, Grace Taher, Cynthia Thomas, Robert Tinney, John Trutko, Joseph Valenza, Mary Vogel, and Jean Vanski. Some of their precise contributions can be found in the many individual reports of the Institute related to EHAP.

Many other individuals contributed administrative, secretarial, and clerical support to the program over the years, but Beverly Caldwell must be given a very special note of acknowledgment as the administrative secretary who saw it through. Maureen Ring also provided outstanding service as the division's administrative associate.

When it came time to put this report together, Raymond J. Struyk and David Rasmussen willingly chipped in to help the surviving EHAP trio of Jim Zais, Frank Cronin, and Anne Squire. Ray Struyk, whose time was supported entirely by the Ford Foundation grant to the Institute, served as a general editor of this final report along with Marc Bendick. Jack Goodman of the Institute's staff, Jack Lowry and his colleagues at the Rand Corporation, and HUD staff carefully reviewed the draft of this document for us. Theresa Walker skillfully edited the final manuscript.

Finally, we wish to thank our advisory panel and our colleagues who labor at the other EHAP contractors—the Rand Corporation and Abt Associates—for their constructive interactions during the long EHAP process, and we wish them our best in completing their respective tasks.

MORTON ISLER, *Director*
Housing and Communities Division

About The Authors

RAYMOND J. STRUYK, co-editor of this volume, is director of the Households and Housing Assistance Research Program at The Urban Institute. From 1977 to 1979, he was deputy assistant secretary for research at the U.S. Department of Housing and Urban Development where his responsibilities included the Experimental Housing Allowance Program. Dr. Struyk's previous books include *A New System for Public Housing; Improving the Elderly's Housing; Housing Policies for the Urban Poor;* and *The Web of Urban Housing.*

MARC BENDICK, JR., co-editor of this volume, was project manager for the Experimental Housing Allowance Program at The Urban Institute during 1978 and 1979. An institute senior research associate, Dr. Bendick is an economist specializing in problems of poverty, human resources, economic development, and the management of social assistance programs.

DAVID B. CARLSON is director of the Neighborhoods and Communities Research Program at The Urban Institute. Previously, he was deputy assistant secretary for model cities at the U.S. Department of Housing and Urban Development and a senior program advisor at the Ford Foundation.

FRANCIS J. CRONIN, an economist, is a senior research associate in the Housing and Communities Division of The Urban Institute. Besides housing, he has worked in the areas of urban energy, and environmental economics and industrial organization.

MORTON L. ISLER, has been director of the Housing and Communities Division of The Urban Institute since 1970. His wide-ranging contributions to housing research include participation in the inception of the Experimental Housing Allowance Program.

LARRY J. OZANNE, a senior research associate in the Housing and Communities Division of the Urban Institute, worked on the Experimental Housing Allowance Program from 1972 to 1980. His other research has focused on urban housing markets and housing policies.

DAVID W. RASMUSSEN is professor of economics at Florida State University and a special consultant to The Urban Institute. An urban economist, he was previously the special assistant for research at the U.S. Department of Housing and Urban Development and worked at the U.S. Department of Commerce.

ANNE D. SQUIRE is a research associate in the Housing and Communities Division of The Urban Institute. Prior to EHAP, she was involved in the Institute's studies of public housing management.

JAMES P. ZAIS was deputy project manager for the Experimental Housing Allowance Program at The Urban Institute from 1975 to 1980. Currently a senior research associate in the Institute's Housing and Communities Division, Dr. Zais is a political scientist.

PART I.

Introduction

CHAPTER 1

Policy Questions and Experimental Responses

Raymond J. Struyk

A CLASSIC ISSUE in government's provision of assistance to the poor is the extent to which the assistance should be restricted to certain uses deemed by society particularly important, normally the purchase of life's necessities food, housing, and health care, as examples. At one extreme the government could provide the goods or services in-kind; so the needy household receives food commodities, for example. At the other extreme the household simply receives cash which it spends on its priority needs as the household defines them.

Over the past 20 years in the United States, the broad trend in assistance for the poor has been away from most severe restrictions on the way in which assistance is provided in support programs. Numerous examples reflect this trend. Assistance to the poor in obtaining adequate amounts of food has shifted from the provision of a limited set of food commodities, which were collected by recipients from distribution points, to food stamps that are spendable at many locations. This permits recipients a much greater choice among foods and among vendors as well. Similarly, the provision of medical services to the needy has been evolving from a system of clinic-based service delivery agencies to a much broader choice by patients of doctors and associated facilities under Medicare. Still, the country has not been prepared to take the next major step of "welfare reform," under which the poor would simply receive cash transfers to cover their needs.

The putative virtues of allowing recipients greater choice in allocating the resources provided by government are impressive. Economists theorize that with greater flexibility recipients value each dollar of the subsidy received more highly than it is valued under systems where fixed amounts

3

of goods or services are provided. Hence, it takes fewer resources to obtain a given level of improvement in a household's perceived well-being. These economists also argue that the market is a more efficient producer of services than government because of government's "red tape," restrictive conditions, and the like. Furthermore, the greater the flexibility in resources—cash at the limit—the easier it is to divide the available resources equitably among eligible households. It is argued that under the programs with restrictions and not enough funding to serve all those eligible, a small share of those eligible receive large amounts of assistance (which they may not value greatly) while others receive nothing. Also, some households will not participate because of the restrictions on the level or type of services provided under sharply restrictive programs.

The counter arguments are also formidable. Some economists argue that the level of satisfaction that taxpayers receive depends on how the poor are helped. If the assistance is for goods and services that the taxpayers view as appropriate, then they will be more satisfied and more supportive of assistance in general. For this reason restricting or earmarking services is desirable. Political scientists, for their part, observe that the committee structure of the Congress strongly militates in favor of a piecemeal approach. Since each committee will fight to maximize the size of the programs and funding levels under its jurisdictions, the total resources going to the poor are larger than they would be if the appropriate level of aid were examined *en block* as would be the case under a purely cash transfer system. Finally, those supporting strong earmarking argue that inequities arise from inadequate funding, not from the structure of the programs themselves.

This book is about these issues, but it discusses them in the context of housing policy. More specifically, it is about an elaborate experiment to test the feasibility and efficacy of reducing the restrictions traditionally placed on government-provided housing assistance to lower-income households.

The story begins at the end of the 1960s when Americans and their elected representatives could look back on two decades of enormous progress in the housing situation of the average American. In 1950, 1 dwelling in 3 lacked full plumbing facilities, by 1970, only 1 in 20 was in this category; the percentage of units in dilapidated condition was cut from 9 to 4 percent; and the fraction of households who were homeowners had risen dramatically.[1] Still, problems remained. An increasing fraction

---

1. de Leeuw, Schnare, and Struyk [P14], table 2, p. 123. This book's bibliography is divided into four sections to help the reader more easily locate specific references. The four sections reflect the various aspects of the Experimental Housing Allowance Program and related research to date: [P] Public Policy and Housing Allowances; [E] Experimental Housing Allowance Program; [H] Household Responses to Allowances; and [C] Community, Market, and Agency Issues.

of renters were devoting over one quarter of their incomes to housing, a conventional indicator for excessive housing expenditures; and minorities were still not being accorded treatment equal to whites in the housing marketplace. Worse, the gains achieved by the majority of households had bypassed a significant number of the poor whose dwellings exhibited multiple deficiencies even though these dwellings were neither dilapidated nor lacking in plumbing facilities. Households who were both poor and members of a minority group had especially high rates of deficiencies compared to the nonpoor.

The relative housing difficulties of the poor and minorities had been matters of public concern for decades. Since the mid-1930s, government in the United States had sought to respond to the housing problems of the poor, acting through the federal-state-local partnership of grant-in-aid programs and through legal protection against discrimination. The main strategy utilized in these efforts was to augment the *supply* of standard quality low-income housing, through such means as construction and operation of public housing which provided dwellings in housing projects to the poor on a take-it-or-leave-it basis and through the subsidization of the construction of privately operated projects by provision of mortgage finance at below-market interest rates. By 1972, however, only 7 percent of the households who were income-eligible for assistance under the federal housing programs were receiving it.[2]

Also since the 1930s, however, various policy makers and researchers have advocated an alternative, *demand* oriented, less restrictive strategy to seek the same ends sought by these housing supply programs. The reasoning was deceptively simple: Lack of purchasing power is certainly one factor in the housing problems of lower-income households. If poor households were given additional purchasing power, and if they chose to spend substantial proportions of that purchasing power on housing, then they could effectively demand housing of higher quality. Additionally, since program recipients would be renting existing units, rather than living in new housing specially built as subsidized housing, lower program costs were anticipated. In this book, these demand-augmenting voucher programs are called *housing allowances*.

Serious reservations were raised, however, about supplier responses to housing demand subsidies as well as about how participants would use cash payments, whether earmarked for housing or not. If the poor have more money with which to pay for better housing, would sellers, landlords, builders, mortgage lenders, realtors, and other suppliers of housing services come forward to serve them? Or would landlords simply charge the poor more for the same units? Are markets too sluggish, poor neighborhoods

---

2. See U.S. Department of Housing and Urban Development [P81], table 9, p. 98. Figures are for households with incomes of less than $5,000 per year.

too burdened with negative conditions, and perceptions and attitudes too fixed for even adequate purchasing power to make a difference in the housing of low-income Americans?

In the closing years of the 1960s, social experiments were being tried on a number of proposed policy innovations, such as a guaranteed income approach to welfare, performance contracts in education, and national health insurance.[3] In light of the uncertainty surrounding a major shift in the structure of housing policy in the United States, some pretest of a demand-oriented program to resolve the major outstanding uncertainties seemed prudent. In 1970, Congress and the U.S. Department of Housing and Urban Development decided to invest in a social experiment on housing allowances to secure an empirical resolution to the questions at hand. This decision led to the housing allowance experimental program. The experiment focused on the following questions:

- Who would participate in a housing allowance program? What types of households (husband-wife, single parent)? Could both whites and minorities secure adequate housing and participate?

- How would participating household use their allowance payments?

- Would the quality of housing improve for participating households?

- Would a housing allowance program cause participants to change the location of their housing?

- Would landlords and homeowners rehabilitate substandard properties and increase maintenance?

- What would happen to the price of housing? Would there be significant market responses to a housing allowance program?

- What alternatives exist for administering the program?

- What are the probable costs of a nationwide housing allowance program?

The subject of this book is the conduct and the results of the experimental effort launched in 1970. The Experimental Housing Allowance Program (EHAP) tested the concept of giving low-income households cash payments with which the households themselves would secure adequate housing. In most parts of the experiment, the size of payment was determined as the difference between the cost of adequate housing in the local market and the household's reasonable ability to pay for it.

Before exploring the details of EHAP, one might ask if the findings are relevant today, a decade after EHAP's formal initiation. In 1970 the

---

3. See Ferber and Hirsch [E45].

possibility of an entitlement housing allowance program was genuine. The Nixon Administration strongly favored less government direction in the provision of adequate housing for the poor. Indeed, shortly after EHAP was launched, the administration considered proposing a full program to Congress, called Direct Cash Assistance. The Congress and the administration joined forces in the landmark housing legislation of 1974, in which a limited entitlement housing allowance program was made operational—the "Section 8 Existing" program.[4]

Currently, housing allowances, or rather an expansion of Section 8 Existing to an entitlement program, are getting another look. The Congress has become increasingly discouraged at the very high subsidies required to build new housing for the poor (Section 8 New). On average, about two households can be assisted by leasing an existing unit for each household assisted in a new unit. Moreover, there are few units in urban areas with gross deficiencies compared to the situation 20 years ago; hence, many units now occupied by lower-income households could be brought into an existing-housing program at low initial cost to the landlord and then maintained at that level.

This argument has been advanced by the National Low Income Housing Coalition in calling for an entitlement housing allowance program for very low-income households (i.e., households with incomes of less than half of the local area median family income). Under this program the modest amount of subsidized new construction, which would coexist with the existing-housing emphasis, would be reserved for moderate-income households in markets with an absolute shortage of rental housing.[5] This strategy is receiving serious consideration as the Congress deliberates about the 1980 housing bill, particularly in light of the prospective federal budget stringencies. A key element in considering such a proposal, of course, is the evidence from the Experimental Housing Allowance Program. The findings are also highly relevant because they provide important empirical information for the consideration of the earmarking issue, not only in housing but in other areas as well. This more general relevance stems from the basic facts on the responsiveness of households to certain incentives embodied in housing allowances but similar in structure to those other programs.

The actual experimental program has been enormous: to date more than 30,000 lower-income households at 12 sites across the country have received housing allowance payments, and some will still be receiving them a full decade after receiving their first payment. The total cost of the

----

4. Section 8 Existing and the housing allowances tested in EHAP are contrasted in chapter 2.

5. National Low-Income Housing Coalition [P57; P58].

experiment, including payments to households will be about $160 million. This makes it one of the largest social experiments in history.

The experiment was complicated in structure because of the many questions to be answered. Three distinct field operations were established, each focusing on a different set of questions:

- The *Demand Experiment* involved about 1,800 households in Phoenix and another 1,800 in Pittsburgh. Its goal was to illuminate the way households would react to housing allowances in terms of participation, household mobility, and housing consumption. It also probed how households' reactions and program outcomes varied under alternative forms of allowance programs involving different payment formulas, varying generosity of benefits, and minimum housing consumption requirements.

- The *Supply Experiment* involved over 16,000 households in Green Bay, Wisconsin, and South Bend, Indiana. The purpose of the Supply Experiment was to raise the level of demand for housing services within a housing market to the level likely to be attained if a nationwide housing allowance program were instituted. This permitted observation of the reactions of suppliers of housing services in terms of increase in the quantity, quality, and price of housing services. It also was designed to probe community and institutional reactions, including those of real estate brokers and mortgage lenders, to a full-scale allowance program.

- The *Administrative Agency Experiment* (AAE) involved between 400 and 900 households at each of eight sites scattered widely across the United States. This experiment emphasized the behavior of administering agencies in the "real world" of actual program operations. Thus, while the allowance programs in the other two experiments were operated by special agencies created by the research organizations, allowances in the AAE were administered by existing agencies, state or local.

Figure 1.1 indicates the location and total enrollments at each of the 12 experimental sites.

Figure 1.1 also indicates the existence of several other non-EHAP recent experiences with housing allowance-like programs outside of the experimental program itself. The findings of these other experiences are occassionally drawn on in this report. At two sites—Kansas City, Missouri, and Wilmington, Delaware—housing allowance demonstration projects were locally initiated and funded under the Model Cities program.[6] The final two sites—Seattle and Denver—are included in figure 1.1 because a

---

6. For results from these two sites see Heinberg, Taher, and Spohn [P34] and Solomon and Fenton [P75].

Figure 1.1

The Location of Field Experiences with Housing Allowances within HUD Regions

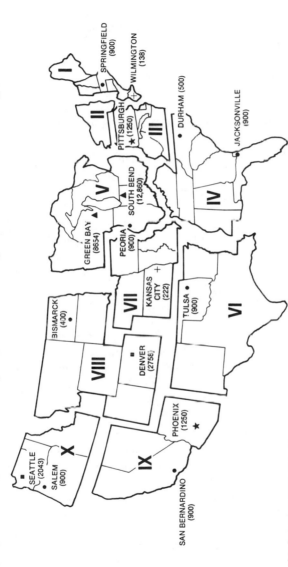

★ EHAP Demand Experiment
  (Planned number of recipient households at each site given for Demand Experiment sites)

▲ EHAP Supply Experiment
  (Total number of households authorized for payments as of February 1980 given for Supply Experiment sites)

● EHAP Administrative Agency Experiment
  (Planned number of recipient households at each site for AAE sites)

■ Income Maintenance Experiment Housing Study
  (Total number of enrolled households at each site as of 1976 given for income maintenance experiment sites)

+ Model Cities Demonstration Project
  (Total number of participating households at each site given for model cities sites)

special HUD-funded study of housing behavior was incorporated in the income maintenance experiments conducted in these two sites by the Department of Health and Human Services. Also relevant, of course, is the experience of the nationwide program, Section 8 Lower-Income Rental Assistance for Existing Housing, mentioned previously. When combined, the three operations of EHAP and these supplementary sources provide a rich and varied data base upon which to base empirical answers to a wide variety of questions which previously had been dealt with only by speculation or by theoretical reasoning.

AN OVERVIEW OF THE BOOK

This book provides serious students of housing policy (rather than technicians) with an in-depth view of the entire Experimental Housing Allowance Program, including its design, operation, findings, and policy implications. The report also provides comprehensive references to the technical papers containing the statistical studies upon which the programs results are based. This volume is not merely a summary of experiments or a parroting of the policy thoughts of others. Rather, it emphasizes the editors' and chapter authors' judgments about the technical studies and what their findings imply for contemporary housing policy in the United States. Hence, the report represents an excursion in the best sense—a tour led by knowledgeable and experienced guides.

Most of the findings from EHAP were compiled by the time this book was completed. In particular, the results from the Demand Experiment and the Administrative Agency Experiment were in hand, as were those from the collateral Seattle-Denver Income Maintenance Experiment.[7] In contrast, results from the Supply Experiment were limited to analyses of the first two years of field operations. However, even these early findings seem to have convincingly answered the questions which the Supply Experiment had been designed to answer. The decision was therefore made jointly by HUD and The Urban Institute to prepare a final report on the findings to those principal questions which had motivated the initiation of EHAP. Consequently, this volume, focusing largely on the questions listed earlier in the chapter, provides the complete story of the enormous EHAP experiment.

Chapters 2 and 3 trace the historical roots and developments of EHAP and contain a description of the overall experimental design as

---

7. All of the reports regarding specific topics addressed by the Demand Experiment were available to us. However, the final report for the entire Demand Experiment had not been drafted.

well as the design of each of the three field operations. The actual housing allowance programs operated in each field operation are outlined.

Chapters 4 through 7 detail the findings on household reactions to housing allowances. These four chapters discuss findings on program participation, household mobility induced by the programs, changes in the quality and type of housing occupied, and the change in housing expenditures associated with the allowances.

Chapters 8 through 10 review findings in three distinct areas. First the degree of dwelling upgrading associated with occupancy by allowance recipients is examined. Second, "market reactions" are reviewed; the effects of an open enrollment program on the price of housing services, both of units occupied by participants and in the market at large, are considered. Another major "market reaction" covered is the response of community leaders and residents to the introduction of an allowance program. Third, chapter 10 deals with program administration by surveying the lessons concerning administering a housing allowance program uncovered in the course of the experiments. In the final part, chapter 11 draws out the implications of the results of the Experimental Housing Allowance Program for issues in national housing policy currently being debated. Chapter 12 reviews EHAP as a social experiment and evaluates the outcomes in light of EHAP's cost.

ANSWERS TO THE INITIAL QUESTIONS

Questions about the effects of a housing allowance program were listed at the beginning of this chapter. Finding their answers was the driving force in the establishment of the Experimental Housing Allowance Program. Over the 11-year period required to execute EHAP, inevitably, some questions on this list lost prominence and others not even on the initial list became the focus of policy debate in housing and community development. Nevertheless, the answers provided to the initial questions are important, both for making policy and because the lucidity, precision, and integrity of these answers is one measure of EHAP's success.[8]

Responses to these questions are summarized as follows:

● *Who would participate in a housing allowance program?*

Participation in EHAP differed considerably from what had been anticipated. Originally, participation was predicted to be at rates similar to participation in current income-transfer programs. The Aid to Families

---

8. In chapter 12 other measures of program success are discussed and applied to EHAP.

with Dependent Children program, for example, has a participation rate in excess of 80 percent; in EHAP participation has been only 42 percent for renters and 33 percent for homeowners in the open enrollment Supply Experiment and 27 percent in the Demand Experiment, despite extraordinary outreach efforts. Of course, benefit levels were modest compared to AFDC, and for some households, "entry costs" were high. Also, there has been substantial turnover among participants in the Supply Experiment so that many more households participate at some time than are measured by "snapshot" participation rates.

There are consistent differences in participation rates among households. Households in three overlapping groups—welfare recipients, those headed by a member of a minority group, and single-parent families—participate at higher rates than households with earned income, those not headed by a member of a minority group, and husband-wife households. The elderly participate at lower than average rates, and homeowners of all household types participate at lower rates than renters.

Analysis of EHAP participation generally shows consumers responding to the incentives and constraints imposed by the program. Eligible households most likely to participate were those whose dwellings already met the housing standards imposed by the program. For these households, the housing allowance was essentially an income transfer that represented a monthly benefit available at little or no cost. In contrast, households whose dwellings initially did not meet the housing standards were less likely to participate because they were required to either upgrade their dwelling or move to one that met the standards before they could receive allowances.. Many households that did not meet the housing standards did not even look for a new unit. The failure to search, and the resulting loss of an allowance payment, was most often because of ties to the current neighborhood and the belief that a better unit could not be found. Racial discrimination, both perceived and actual, also reduced the mobility of minorities.

Among those whose dwellings initially failed to pass the program standard, households most likely to search for a different dwelling were those that had the highest gains from moving and were most dissatisfied with their current dwelling. Unfortunately, after controlling for race, income, and other factors, it was found that households in the worst housing (as measured by the EHAP program's own standards) also had the lowest rates of participation. These households would have had to make the greatest change to participate.

Participation was primarily determined by how a household perceived the benefits of the allowance payment when compared to the cost of receiving it. Not surprisingly, participation rates increased as the dollar benefit conferred by the allowance increased, but the degree of increase was modest.

● *How would participating households use their allowance payments?*

● *Would the quality of housing improve for participating households?*

Participants divided their housing allowances between the consumption of more housing and the purchase of other goods and services. However, most of the allowance payment was typically spent on non-housing items. The extent to which participants used allowances to increase housing consumption varied according to the initial quality of the unit occupied by a potential recipient and the local housing market conditions. In Pittsburgh, a tight market in which mobility is constrained, only about 10 percent of the payment was used to increase housing consumption. In Phoenix, where mobility is easier, this figure was 25 percent. Moreover, increased housing consumption was more prevalent among households living in units that failed program standards when the household enrolled in the program. Increasing housing consumption is only one goal of housing policy's concern for how households spend their resources. Another concern is rent burden, the percentage of income devoted to housing. At enrollment, rent burdens in the Demand Experiment sites averaged approximately 40 percent. Housing allowances sharply reduced recipients' contribution to rent and reduced rent burden to an average of 25 percent in the Demand Experiment sites.

Housing standards played a significant role in the consumption decisions of households as well as affecting participation. In performing repairs to pass EHAP housing standards, or in selecting a dwelling to which to move, participating households usually responded very narrowly to the program requirements. That is, they changed their housing consumption only to the extent necessary to qualify for allowances. Thus, while standards certainly altered the consumption *patterns* of those households that had to move to enter the program, there was little evidence that housing requirements resulted in more *total* housing consumption, as measured by rent expenditures or other broad indices of housing quality. Households adhered strictly to the specific items embodied in the standards. This suggests that it would be possible to increase housing consumption with more stringent standards. As noted earlier, however, such a strategy would result in a lower participation rate, particularly affecting those potential recipients in the worst housing.

Finally, it is important to observe that except for the effects on meeting specific housing standards, there were no differences in the change in housing consumption produced by the alternative types of housing

allowances tested. These include unconstrained cash payments to households, plans which based payments solely on the percentage of rents,
and those involving various types of earmarking.

- *Would a housing allowance program cause participants to change the
location of their housing?*

Mobility was not increased by the allowance payment, but those pre-
disposed to move did so earlier than they otherwise would have. Similarly,
the destinations of movers were not affected. The housing allowances
appear to have had little if any impact on the extent of income and racial
segregation, on the length of the journey to work, on neighborhood
quality, or on movement between the central city and suburbs.

- *Would landlords rehabilitate substandard properties and increase
maintenance?*

Households could qualify for payments if their enrollment units were
already standard, if the units were improved to meet the program requirements, or if enrollees moved to standard units. The fraction of
participating households using unit improvements as the means of qualifying for the program varied from a low of 2 percent of recipients in one
EHAP site to a high of 44 percent in another. The more stringent the
program standards, and hence the greater the amount of repairs needed
to pass the standard on average, the less likely improvements were to
take place. Additionally, homeowners are more likely to improve their
dwellings than renters; consequently, renters qualify more often by
moving than homeowners do.

   On the basis of the systematic data from the repair logs kept in the
Supply Experiment, we know the amount of repairs necessary to pass the
standards in this part of EHAP was generally small. The small amount
of required repairs and the high rates of repairs in the two Supply Experiment sites mirror the quality of housing stock in these sites as well as
the housing standard employed. The vast majority of dwellings were free
from major defects. The most frequent type of improvements were to meet
health and safety items in the program's standard. Hence, the most frequent action was the installation of stairway handrails, averaging $10
in out-of-pocket costs. Repairing windows and painting ceilings, floors,
and walls were also frequent. The average out-of-pocket costs per housing
unit repair were only $55 and $81 in Green Bay and South Bend, respectively, for homeowners, and $39 and $37 for renters in the two sites. Consistent with these low expenditure figures, evidence indicates that slightly
substandard units were more likely to be improved than were more seriously deficient units. The proportion of failed units that were subsequently

repaired dropped from about 88 percent for homeowners with one housing defect to 50 percent in cases with four or more defects. In the case of renters, the parallel drop was from about 70 percent to 30 percent.

Despite low levels of initial repairs to meet standards, other evidence from the Supply Experiment suggests that the program might be having a longer-run impact on maintenance activities carried on during the year by participating households. The most accurate information currently available is for homeowners.[9] Contrasting census data on cash outlays for repairs and improvements by low-income households in the North Central census region (containing Green Bay and South Bend) with similar expenditures by program participants shows that EHAP participating homeowners may be spending an average of $75 to $100 more per year on repairs and improvements. Furthermore, these data indicate that improvements made annually after enrollment are likely to be more substantial than those completed to participate in the program.

- *Would there be significant market responses to a housing allowance program? What would happen to the price of housing?*

In discussions of an entitlement housing allowance program during 1968-1972, the possible inflationary impact on housing prices was generally considered the major drawback of an allowance. Now, however, we know from the experiments that programs on the scale of those tested in EHAP —including an entitlement program in two markets—will cause little if any inflation in rents for recipients and no inflation at all in rents for others. Early results from the Supply Experiment show that the introduction of the program had no major, immediate effect on marketwide rent inflation. Furthermore, we know from all three operations that the allowance programs tested increase only marginally the demand for housing because of the relatively low participation rates and the modest earmarking of subsidies for housing consumption described earlier. Thus, it is extremely unlikely that demand pressures would ever build up sufficiently to heighten market rent inflation in areas served by allowances.

The lack of significant effects in other aspects of the housing market can also be explained by the small change in demand. Thus far, neighborhoods in the two Supply Experiment sites have undergone little change due to the program, either through household movement patterns or through dwelling improvements induced in units not directly involved in the allowance program. The types of market intermediaries and indirect suppliers important to expanding the supply of housing services have

---

9. Renters, who provide repair information for their units, did not always know the full extent of repairs done by their landlords; information has subsequently been collected from landlords on this issue, and additional analysis will be done for rental units.

not been affected by the program and have not influenced program operations. Community leaders, on the other hand, played an important role particularly in determining whether their community would participate in EHAP; in some cases they prevented housing allowances from being tested in their jurisdictions because of fears of large-scale movement of black households into the suburbs. Once the small impact of the program was demonstrated, community opposition lessened.

● *What are the alternatives for administering the program?*

The experience under EHAP has demonstrated that there are various ways to administer a housing allowance program; some ways are more cost-effective than others. Findings related to the four major administrative functions in an allowance program—outreach, enrollment, dwelling inspection, and client services—have narrowed the range of alternatives for administration.

Outreach proved particularly difficult for program managers as they tried to balance the twin goals of (a) informing the eligible population about the programs and (b) not unduly raising expectations in those sites where enrollment was limited; managers also wanted to keep application backlogs down where enrollment was unlimited. Mass media campaigns were particularly important for attracting eligibles, such as the working poor, who were not ordinarily served by other programs. Use of media, however, was expensive.

The most important aspect of enrollment is the certification of client income. Here, EHAP clearly establishes the superior accuracy of certifying income through verification with documents or third-party inquiries, rather than relying only on client-provided information. However, since full verification of every application would be costly, EHAP analysis suggests several approaches for selective use of verification. For example, verification requirements might be lowered for three groups of households —the elderly, clients with predominantly grant income, or clients with one income source—because income errors detected through verification were significantly fewer in these cases. Another promising approach, tested in the Supply Experiment, involved varying the extent of verification inversely with the amount of documentation that is initially provided by households.

Inspections of housing units were found to cost much less than anticipated, because fewer dwellings had to be inspected for each recipient and because inspection costs per unit were somewhat overestimated. The number of inspections per enrollee before qualifying for payments was small—with a site median of 1.08. EHAP also found that inspections done by participants were far less accurate than those done by professional code inspectors or trained agency staff. Code inspectors, however, were more costly.

Analysis of the effects of nonmonetary services provided to clients—such as counseling—has been particularly difficult, due to measurement problems. However, it seems clear that no strong case can be made for agencies to provide such services indiscriminately. It is likely that they will have more effect on client households who become movers in tight-market situations, and such services may also be more useful to minorities than to nonminorities. On the basis of expressed preferences and utilization of different types of services, it appears that housing market information—specifically, information on the location of available dwellings—is the only service for which there was widespread demand.

● *What are the likely costs of a nationwide housing allowance program?*

The importance that HUD attached to obtaining an answer to this question diminished sharply over the course of the experiments, as the Carter Administration's lack of enthusiasm for a universal demand-side program became known. In fact, HUD-sponsored work on this subject was discontinued in 1977; and the detailed estimates made on the basis of early experimental experience with program participation were not later carefully revised in light of more reliable and quite different longer-term EHAP experience.

The ballpark estimates given here represent crude adjustments to estimates done for 1976 via simulation using the Transfer Income Model (TRIM) at The Urban Institute.[10] In making these adjustments, Kain assumes participation rates equal to those observed after more than two years of open enrollment program operations in the Supply Experiment sites. He estimates that 6.5 million households would participate nationally at a cost of $4.4 billion in 1976 dollars.[11] Of course, this estimate assumes that the type of program administered in the Supply Experiment would be the national prototype. Participation rates and cost levels, though, would depend on the strictness of the housing standards adopted for the program, the type of outreach conducted, and other administrative decisions. Tough standards would, as noted, reduce participation and

10. These estimates are summarized in Carlson and Heinberg [E24] and detailed in Sepanik [144] and Sepanik, Hendricks, and Heinberg [E145]. The specific extrapolation of EHAP experience in TRIM was based upon seven basic program assumptions: (1) extension of eligibility to homeowners as well as to renters; (2) exclusion of households headed by students and households consisting of nonelderly single persons; (3) an assumed nationally uniform average cost of adequate housing; (4) a payment formula that provides recipient families with an amount equal to the difference between the cost of adequate, modest housing and 25 percent of their household incomes; (5) an income definition that excludes taxes and work-related expenses and that counts cash assistance from other federal programs as income; (6) an imputed return on home equity; and (7) no assets test.

11. For details of these estimates, see Kain [P39].

costs, perhaps substantially.[12] The $4.4 billion figure is, though, probably of the correct order of magnitude.

For fiscal year 1980, HUD's budget request for assisted housing programs was about $3.1 billion (in 1976 dollars) to serve some 3.2 million households.[13] Of these participating households, about 600 thousand are participants in the Section 8 Lower Income Housing Assistance Program. These participants reside in units built without government assistance and receive housing allowance-type payments. Hence, an open enrollment housing allowance (or Section 8) program would add about 6 million households to the assisted housing rolls and more than double the annual federal outlays for assisted housing. On the other hand, even at this expanded scale, assisted housing payments would still only about equal the tax losses to the federal Treasury from deduction of mortgage interest payments by homeowners; payments for an entitlement program would also constitute only 2 percent of the fiscal year 1980 federal outlays proposed to the Congress by the Carter Administration.

A WIDER VIEW

In chapter 11 of this book, EHAP findings that may influence community development, income maintenance, and current housing programs are described. The EHAP findings are examined from three perspectives: (1) benefits to the individual, (2) benefits to the community, and (3) benefits to the housing sector.

The EHAP findings just summarized have shown that individuals generally carefully weigh the benefits and costs of participating in the program, given their personal consumption preferences and the local market conditions they face. Overall, the analyses suggest that allowances, when compared to other housing programs, should be given high marks from the perspective of benefiting individuals. Allowances provide a level of housing service equivalent to other programs but at a lower cost. Likewise, allowances efficiently provide maximum increased resources to households with minimal restrictions on freedom of choice. However, from that same perspective, straight cash transfers with no attempt to earmark the

---

12. Kain estimates, for example, that use of the Demand Experiment physical standards, which were more strict than those in the Supply Experiment, would reduce program cost by about 20 percent.

13. Assisted housing programs include: all elements of the Section 8 program; the Section 235 homeownership assistance program; rent supplements; the rental housing assistance programs (e.g., Section 236); and public housing.

subsidy for housing are even more beneficial and efficient from the household's point of view.

The design of the housing allowance experiments permitted much less information to be generated about community benefits—defined in terms of improvement of the physical environment—than was generated about benefits to individuals. Benefits to community development derived from the allowance programs seem weak; but since little is known about the impacts of other housing programs along these dimensions, no comparative statements can be made.

We do know, however, that housing allowances enlist households with low housing preferences and the dwellings with the greatest deficiencies at lower rates than others. Hence, the very processes that provide for maximum freedom of choice for individual households may tend to discourage those households whose housing would improve most by participating. Hence, there may be insufficient additional housing consumption and investment to produce communitywide effects. On the other hand, there is some evidence of allowances having a preventive maintenance effect on the housing for which recipient households do qualify. Whether or not these repairs have a neighborhood effect must await further results from the Supply Experiment.

The ideal national mix of housing programs to maximally foster improved housing must depend per force on future economic conditions and the level of financial support for income maintenance and housing subsidy programs. Still, EHAP findings have implications for two of the most important connections among programs for achieving housing goals: the linkages between housing subsidies and community development programs and the case for a different mix of programs in varying housing markets.

Housing subsidies and community development programs are often poorly orchestrated despite the fact that they sometimes affect the same individuals. Furthermore, the last decade of housing program analyses make it clear that benefits to the community and to the housing sector from housing programs must be substantial compared to those from unrestricted income transfers in order to justify the higher costs of housing programs compared to cash transfers. These findings, including those from EHAP, increasingly point to developing a coordinated strategy for housing and community development programs in each locality. In light of these findings, two basic approaches for interrelating housing and community development programs are discussed in chapter 11, along with potential mechanism for extending housing subsidies to low-income homeowners.

Finally, EHAP has contributed to the evidence indicating the importance of varying the mix of housing programs in different housing markets. Findings from EHAP have already substantially improved our capability to simulate (via housing market models) the market effects of combinations of different programs—for example, combining a housing allowance with a new construction subsidy or a housing allowance and a rehabilitation subsidy. The next step is to utilize this capability in developing the nation's housing assistance plans (HAPs) and community development programs.

PART II.

Origins, Design, and Operations

CHAPTER 2

Origins of An Experimental Approach

Marc Bendick, Jr. and Raymond J. Struyk, with contributions by David Carlson

T HE POLICY instrument referred to in this report as a "housing allowance" has been discussed under many names. Common synonyms used
are rent certificates, rent subsidies, rent supplements, housing vouchers, rent
rebates, and direct cash assistance for housing. Whatever term is used,
however, three characteristics are inherent in the concept:

- It is a public assistance grant for which one of the eligibility conditions
  is low income.

- The grant is intended to be spent largely on housing, and the grant
  is usually accompanied by some attempt to "earmark" it for housing.
  In this, it differs from an unconstrained cash transfer such as a
  public assistance payment or "negative income tax."

- The household receiving the grant selects its own housing from those
  offered by the private market; the subsidy is attached to the household,
  not linked to a particular unit. In this, it differs from many conventional housing programs in which the subsidy is attainable only if
  the household lives in a particular dwelling unit.

The first part of this chapter examines the concept of housing allowances and traces its evolution through nearly half a century of policy
debate. This debate has concerned the most basic strategic issue in
American housing policy for the poor: the relative merits of a subsidy
system directed at constructing or rehabilitating housing units specifically
for poor households, in contrast to an approach involving cash subsidies
given to the households themselves to occupy existing private housing.
The Experimental Housing Allowance Program, whose design is described

in the second part of the chapter, derived its existence, its research agenda, and much of its importance from this continuing controversy. The final secton of the chapter then reviews some ex post criticisms of the experimental design, drawing the broad conclusion that the initial design was competently drawn given the information available at that time and the constraints imposed.

FORTY YEARS OF POLICY DEBATE

For more than 40 years, the federal government has intervened in the housing problems of low- and moderate-income households primarily by financing the construction or repair of specific dwellings for their occupancy. Three policy assumptions underlie this federal housing policy approach. First, the housing needs of the poor should be met primarily by new additions to the housing stock rather than by utilization of existing housing units. Second, the private market should be involved in building this housing; but, because potential profits are low, it would not do so without substantial public subsidies. Third, these public subsidies should be directed toward builders and mortgage lenders rather than toward poor households themselves.

Although this approach has prevailed in federal housing programs for many years, there have been recurring proposals for an alternative approach—that of providing cash payments directly to low-income families so that they could select their own housing from among units produced without subsidy by the private market. This central issue—whether housing subsidies should be provided to the *supplier* side of the low-income housing market—to builders and lenders—or to the *demander* side—to low-income households—has formed the context within which housing allowances have been considered.

1935-1968: Straws in the Wind

Prior to the New Deal of the 1930s, housing was considered a matter of private or local government concern. However, as soon as debate extended to the issue of federal action on housing, the housing allowance alternative formed part of that debate. Symbolically, extensive consideration of the idea of housing allowances occurred in discussions leading to the Housing Act of 1937, legislation which created the federal public housing program and marked the beginning of major federal activity in the housing field.

This public housing program was launched after two years of congressional struggle to find ways simultaneously to promote multiple objectives. These objectives included the anti-Depression goals of job creation and income generation through public spending, as well as housing-oriented goals of slum clearance and improved living conditions. Much attention focused on widespread substandard housing in both urban slums and rural areas and the need to replace it through new construction.

Formidable forces opposed the public housing program, including the U.S. Chamber of Commerce, the National Association of Real Estate Boards, and conservatives in both the House and the Senate. The alternative they most often proposed was "rent certificates" which could be used by low-income tenants for payment of rent in existing housing. Witnesses favoring rent certificates argued that the program would bring the private market into play and keep government out of the housing business, that it would be more manageable and less costly than building new housing, and that it would grant low-income households more choice. Subsidizing the utilization of existing units was a particularly attractive idea during the high-unemployment Depression era when many families who had previously been adequately housed in units they could afford lost their jobs and thus their ability to afford their current homes.[1]

On the other side of the debate, two of the nation's leading housing experts of that time—Catherine Bauer and Edith Elmer Wood—opposed rent certificates. Bauer argued that they would be administratively unworkable, while Wood held that such a program would not result in any additional housing being built for low-income families. The Senate Committee on Education and Labor finally concluded, "In dealing with the housing of families of low income, systematic [construction of] low-rent housing should be substituted for [financial] relief [including rent certificates]. This procedure will be cheaper for the government, more beneficial to business, and infinitely more desirable to those of our citizens who are now living in slums and blighted areas, both in urban and rural parts of the country." [2] Thus, the Congress opted for a housing production approach, and the rent certificate approach was shelved.

As World War II drew to a close, a special subcommittee of the Senate, chaired by Robert Taft, took a prospective look at postwar efforts in housing and urban development and again considered a program of rent certificates. However, Taft himself opposed the idea, and the final report of his subcommittee stated, "It has been argued that families should be assisted by rent certificates just as grocery stamps have been furnished to needy families. The number of families entitled to rent certificates upon any such basis would. be infinitely larger than those

1. King [P44], p. 6.
2. Semer et al. [P70], p. 95.

requiring other relief. It is not at all certain that such a plan would bring about improvements in the bad housing accommodations that now exist. In fact, the scheme might work to maintain the profitability of slum areas and, consequently, to retard their elimination. It would certainly require a detailed regulation of private rental quarters both as to condition and rent." [3]

In 1953, a presidential Advisory Committee on Government Housing Policies and Programs again considered rent certificates. The principal benefits claimed by witnesses appearing before the committee were that housing would stay in private hands; that the rental subsidy would encourage rehabilitation and construction where currently there was none; that the program would cost less than building new units under the public housing program; that the subsidy could be strictly limited to the amount and the period actually needed by any individual household; and that the stigma of receiving "housing relief" would discourage families from receiving assistance for very long.

The list of objections was at least as long: Many more thousands of families would be added to relief rolls, generating a large administrative workload; aggregate costs would be made greater than public housing (because it was assumed that all income-eligible households would be allowed to participate); the program would not add to the housing supply; and substandard housing would not be eliminated. Eventually, these objections carried the day, and the committee's report did not propose any use of rent certificates. [4]

The rent certificate concept demonstrated its hardiness a dozen years later, however, when legislation was enacted which embodied two of the main tenets of the idea—use of existing, privately owned housing for subsidized low-income occupancy (an idea incorporated in the Section 23 leased housing program) and a direct cash payment for low-income families to occupy privately owned housing (a concept embodied in the rent supplement program). Both the rent supplement program and the Section 23 program emerged from the Housing and Urban Development Act of 1965.

The rent supplement provisions of this act carried some of the potential of a housing allowance program in that the federal government was empowered to make payments directly to private landlords on behalf of eligible households. It thereby established the principle of providing income-related housing subsidies to families residing in privately owned units. However, implementation of this program has been limited and its budget appropriations have remained small. In practice, the supplements

---

3. Semer et al. [P70], p. 114.
4. King [P44], p. 10.

were restricted to occupants of units located in housing projects already receiving federal mortgage subsidies under the so-called 221(d)(3) program; this was done to "deepen" the 221(d)(3) subsidies and thereby permit very low-income families access to those units.[5] Therefore, although its concept of subsidies directed toward tenants in privately owned and managed units makes rent supplements a forerunner of housing allowances, the program itself did not function very much like a housing allowance.

In contrast to the feebleness of the rent supplement initiative, the Section 23 leasing program grew into a large and popular program and marked an important alteration in the course of federal housing policy. Indeed, this program marked the first movement in federal policy away from exclusive reliance on new construction or substantial rehabilitation. The Section 23 program permitted local housing agencies to lease privately owned and managed dwelling units and then to sublease them to low-income families at a subsidized rental charge.[6] In contrast to the traditional approach of constructing, owning, and operating specific housing projects for the poor within the public sector, the Section 23 approach restricted the agency's role to paying rent on behalf of tenants. Furthermore, the program typically utilized existing units and units which were usually scattered across many neighborhoods rather than concentrated in large housing projects. The major difference from a pure housing allowance was that the agency typically selected units to be leased rather than allowing households free choice. Additionally, the housing authority negotiated rent levels and lease provisions with landlords and sent its subsidy check directly to the landlord rather than to the household.

Despite development of the Section 23 program and the rent supplement program, federal housing policy in the late 1960s was still dominated by the traditional approach of unit-based subsidies for new construction. Not only were about 700,000 units of conventional public housing in operation by 1970, but this activity was, through 1968 legislation and appropriations, joined by several other housing production oriented programs, including a lower-income homeownership program (Section 235) and a multifamily rental housing program (Section 236). By the close of 1970, these programs had placed some 1.6 million units into the production pipeline, the highest volume of subsidized housing production in the nation's history.[7]

1968-1970: A Willingness to Experiment

Despite rapid expansion of the unit subsidy approach, the mid-1960s

---

5. See Semer et al. [P70], p. 120.

6. See de Leeuw and Leaman [P13].

7. Aaron [P2], Appendix A.

were times of introspection in housing policy and willingness to examine alternatives. In addition to the new policy directions foreshadowed by the rent supplement program and the Section 23 program, the loosely structured Model Cities program was initiated in 1966, on the heels of War on Poverty legislation. At the same time, two presidential task forces embarked on far-ranging examinations of housing and community development issues—the President's Committee on Urban Housing (the Kaiser Committee) and the National Commission on Urban Problems (the Douglas Commission). A third task force, the President's Commission on Income Maintenance (the Heineman Commission) examined problems of the public assistance system and included housing as part of its agenda.

The Kaiser Committee's mandate was to analyze existing housing programs and their impacts upon households and markets, focusing on lower-income families. Among the recommendations in its 1968 report was one calling for testing the housing allowance approach through an experimental program.

The Kaiser Committee's espousal of housing allowances stemmed largely from the increasing difficulty of the public housing program in finding decent sites for large housing projects and a concern for the consequent "ghettoization" of the poor and minorities. The committee also stressed that an "allowance system offers the opportunity for the free market to operate in its traditional fashion" and also that "widespread distribution of housing allowances to poor families should reduce the economic dependence on slum housing and shift the demand upward for standard units. In response to this shift in demand, suppliers of housing would be induced to produce more standard housing, either by upgrading slum properties or through new construction. . . ."[8]

Despite these positive predictions, the committee did not recommend a full-scale national program but rather an experimental one. There were three reasons for this limited recommendation. First, the committee perceived a need in the short term to stimulate new construction and felt that the conventional project subsidy approach would best accomplish that result. Second, the committee was concerned that a massive allowance program "would be likely to inflate the costs of existing housing considerably, at least in the short run. . . . Consequently, any large-scale housing allowance system would have to be introduced gradually. . . ." Finally, the committee feared that without "strong programs of consumer education and vigorous attacks on racial discrimination" an allowance system could have adverse results.[9]

---

8. President's Committee on Urban Housing [P66], p. 14.
9. President's Committee on Urban Housing [P66], p. 71.

The housing allowance recommendation was not the most prominent proposal made by the Kaiser Committee and did not in itself draw much attention. However, the committee's report was issued in December 1968, a month after the election which replaced the Democratic presidency of Lyndon Johnson with the Republican administration of Richard Nixon. High officials of the incoming administration—particularly those in the Office of Management and Budget—brought with them long-standing ideological doubts concerning the appropriateness of direct government provisions of housing such as in the public housing program. One direction they favored for housing policy was promotion of low-income homeownership through the Section 235 program. The idea of housing allowances offered to them another possible policy alternative consistent with both their desire to break with past trends and with their goals of increasing utilization of the private market in public programs.

One HUD official who developed an interest in allowances was under secretary Richard Van Dusen. Another was Malcolm Peabody, Jr., then deputy assistant secretary for equal opportunity. Peabody was convinced, by the Kaiser Committee report and other sources, that allowances would be preferable to conventional public housing or to any construction subsidy if for no other reason than that allowances would prevent large concentrations of the poor and lead to more racially and economically integrated housing.[10] Peabody became involved in initiating housing allowance demonstrations under the auspices of the Model Cities program, and a demonstration was launched during the summer of 1970 in Kansas City, Missouri, with another following soon after in Wilmington, Delaware.[11]

Another HUD official who became an effective advocate of the idea of giving housing allowances experimental consideration was Harold Finger, then assistant secretary for research and technology. Finger became familiar with work of housing researchers which suggested the possible efficiency and effectiveness of the allowance approach. At the same time, as a research manager, he was impressed by the large-scale social experiments with "negative income taxes" then under way under the auspices of the Office of Economic Opportunity and was interested in implementing similar techniques. Within the policy councils of HUD, Finger played a crucial entrepreneurial role in translating theoretical notions of housing allowances into an operational research program.

During the summer of 1970, the proposed Housing and Urban Development Act of 1970 was debated in Congress, and authorization for

---

10. See Peabody [P63].

11. Results of these demonstrations are reported in Heinberg, Spohn, and Taher [P34]; Solomon and Fenton [P75].

an experimental housing allowance program was inserted into it. HUD had not asked for this authorization because it believed that the bill's proposed provisions for general research authority were broad enough to cover allowance experiments. There was also concern that if allowances were singled out for special attention, the experiment might be stopped by the White House.[12] Nevertheless, a bill mandating the experiments was introduced by Senator Edward Brooke, largely at the urging of Malcolm Peabody.

In hearings on the 1970 legislation, the Brooke proposal was seldom addressed, as the legislation contained many other complex and controversial provisions. However, several urban experts did discuss cash assistance approaches to housing subsidies. Robert C. Embry, then commissioner of housing and community development for the city of Baltimore, testified that the ". . . proposal to provide rent subsidies in private housing . . . is extremely desirable. It fosters full utilization of existing properties, it does not encourage concentration of low income families, and it avoids the many barriers to racial integration that have effectively thwarted such efforts. . . . I am convinced that this approach is the only valid program to house low income families . . . that can achieve a dramatic and significant impact."[13] Embry's enthusiasm was echoed by Cushing Dolbeare, an advocate of low-income housing, who told Senator Brooke that "a housing allowance proposal . . . would encourage people to keep standard units on the market and rent them to low income families." She did warn, however, that such a program would be costly if it covered all eligible housholds. She also expressed concern about limiting an experimental program to communities where there are sufficient vacancies in the stock of standard housing ". . . because I don't think there are any such communities today."[14] The Housing and Urban Development Act of 1970 was passed on New Year's Eve, 1970, carrying a mandate for housing allowance experiments in its Section 504.[15]

1970-1975: Policy Does Not Wait for Experimental Results

While the foregoing discussions concerning housing allowances *per se* were proceeding, a related and more publicly visible debate was address-

12. The Nixon Administration's Family Assistance Plan, a comprehensive overhaul of welfare programs, was being developed at the same time under the direction of Daniel Patrick Moynihan of the White House staff. Moynihan had circulated a memo requiring that departmental proposals concerning any income maintenance programs (which would include housing allowances) be cleared through his office. It was widely believed in HUD that Moynihan would have vetoed an allowance proposal.

13. U.S. Senate [P80], p. 798.

14. U.S. Senate [P80], p. 1039.

15. P.L. 91-609, Section 504; 12 USC1701Z-3.

ing the problems of the then-existing HUD production-subsidy programs.[16] This debate created an atmosphere of dissatisfaction with current housing policies in which the idea of a radical shift of subsidy strategy became plausible. At the same time, the specfic criticisms launched against existing HUD programs created an agenda of objectives which, it was hoped, housing allowances could better achieve.

One criticism launched against the unit-subsidy programs was that of horizontal inequity, arising from "deep" subsidies in combination with limited funding. Horizontal inequity exists when two equally needy families receive different amounts of assistance. Because the cost per housing unit was very high for new construction programs, only a limited number of housing units could be provided within available federal housing funds each year, and therefore only a small proportion of all income-eligible families could receive housing assistance. In 1973, about 1 income-eligible household in 12 was receiving large housing subsidies by occupying units subsidized by HUD programs; the remaining 11 out of 12, often equally needy, received nothing.[17]

A related criticism of the HUD production-subsidy programs concerned the high cost per unit produced. As of 1972, the average annual cost per unit of Section 236 subsidized housing, including rent supplements, was $1,901, with outlays extending over a 30-year period.[18] This situation arose in part from the focus of these programs on new construction rather than utilization and preservation of the existing housing stock.[19]

Critiques of HUD's unit-based approach to housing subsidies also cited the issue of freedom of choice, which brought into play general concepts of consumer sovereignty and free enterprise which, as we have mentioned, had particular appeal in a Republican administration. Under a housing allowance program, to a much greater extent than under conventional public housing, households could express their personal preferences with respect to the characteristics of their housing units, their locations, and their landlords, rather than simply accepting the limited choice presented by the public sector.[20]

A final problem, perhaps not inherent in the unit-subsidy programs but frequently associated with them, was administrative corruption and

---

16. Much of this debate is summarized in reports from the National Housing Review carried on during the summer of 1973. See U.S. Department of Housing and Urban Development [P81, P82]; Weicher [P88].

17. See, for example, Aaron [P2]; Weicher [P88]; and U.S. Department of Housing and Urban Development [P81].

18. U.S. Department of Housing and Urban Development [P81], p. 116.

19. See Smolensky [P72]; Eisenstadt, Gueron, and Lowry [P21].

20. For example, the influential conservative economist Milton Friedman spent three pages in his widely read book *Capitalism and Freedom* to argue for replacement of the public housing program by cash transfers [P23], pp. 178-180.

related difficulties in program control. Even setting aside the cases of outright fraud, there appears to have been widespread problems of gross inefficiency in how programs were implemented. For example, the cost per unit of public construction was running more than twice the cost of private market construction, even for units of equivalent quality. It was problems of corruption and inefficiency rather than more complex issues of inequity or ideology which caught the public's attention and created political pressure for dramatic policy action.

In January 1973, after the housing allowance experiments had been legislatively mandated but a few months before the first field operations actually got under way, President Nixon proclaimed a moratorium on all of HUD's major housing assistance programs. The programs affected constituted virtually all of the rent-subsidy programs for which allowances might have been cast as a substitute: conventional public housing (including the Section 23 program of leased public housing); mortgage insurance and interest subsidies for low-income homeownership (Section 235); mortgage insurance, interest subsidies, and operating subsidies for multifamily rental housing (Section 236); mortgage insurance for multifamily rental housing (Section 221(d)(3)); and direct loans for housing for the elderly and handicapped (Section 202).[21] The president cited as reasons for the freeze the fact that the suspended programs benefited only a small number of those who needed assistance, that they provided windfall profits and tax shelters to investors, that they drove up development costs, and that they produced housing which low-income families could not afford.

The Nixon Administration then engaged in an ambitious review of the suspended programs, and in September 1973, President Nixon announced his support for "a better approach" than the conventional one of unit subsidies, an approach which he called Direct Cash Assistance.[22] "This plan," he said, "would give the poor the freedom and responsibility to make their own choices about housing—and it would eventually get the Federal government out of the housing business." Moreover, Nixon averred that "of the policy alternatives available, the most promising way to achieve decent housing for all of our families at an acceptable cost appears to be direct cash assistance." He also announced that the moratorium would be lifted for the Section 23 leased housing program which, he said, "can be administered in a way which carries out some of the principles of direct cash assistance." The Nixon Administration was

---

21. Rural housing programs of the Farmers' Home Administration would presumably also fall into the category, but they were not included in the moratorium.

22. The Democratic candidate in the 1972 presidential election, Senator George McGovern, also had advocated allowances during the campaign.

in the process of drafting a specific Direct Cash Assistance proposal for submission to Congress when President Nixon resigned 11 months later.

Congress, in the meanwhile, was not idle in the period following announcement of the moratorium but rather forged a new direction for housing policy largely on its own initiative. With passage of the Housing and Community Development Act of 1974, the Section 23 program was to be phased out; and a version of a housing allowance program emerged as part of the new Section 8 Lower Income Rental Assistance program.[23] The Section 8 program spans within itself the full range of demand-side subsidy and supply-side subsidy approaches. Its existing housing component directly embraces the housing allowances concept,[24] but the program also includes a new construction component and a rehabilitation component, which are unit-based housing production subsidies. The existing housing component dominated Section 8 activities in the first years of the

---

23. Very early EHAP results were used in developing some aspects of Section 8 operations. These included development of a Section 8 Existing handbook, a major portion of which was claimed to have been developed on the basis of the experience of the Administrative Agency Experiment; work on housing quality requirements in Section 8; and design of the shopping incentive feature of Section 8, which was also said to have benefited from Administrative Agency Experiment findings. See Khadduri [P41] for a discussion of the shopping incentive in Section 8.

24. The Section 8 Existing program offers rent subsidies very similar to those of most of the housing allowances experimented with in EHAP. Thus, to participate, the household must be income-eligible and live in a unit which meets certain minimum physical standards. There are, however, five important differences:

1. In Section 8, the household cannot participate if it spends more than the "fair market rent" (FMR) for a unit, the FMR being an amount selected to represent the cost of a unit meeting the minimum standards. In EHAP there is no limitation, but the government will pay only the difference between the FMR and 25 percent of income. Thus, Section 8 households can search for units only within a smaller segment of the housing stock.

2. Under Section 8, landlords receive rental payments in two pieces: the subsidy payment directly from the government agency and the household's share from the tenant. In EHAP, by contrast, the agency sends its subsidy check to the participating household who then deals with the landlord.

3. While the Supply Experiment in EHAP includes both owners and renters, Section 8 is currently limited to renters.

4. While EHAP does not exclude households renting new units, it does not directly promote new construction. Section 8 does so by entering into long-term lease agreements with developers.

5. In Section 8, the income eligibility for the program is determined with reference to the median family income of the area: A family of four, for example, can have no more than 80 percent of the reference income. In EHAP, the income cut off was approximately four times the fair market rent.

For an evaluation of early Section 8 Existing housing experiences, see Drury, Lee, Springer, and Yap [P19]. For a comparison of EHAP and Section 8, see Zais, Goedert, and Trutko [P95].

program—because existing units could be brought into a new program more rapidly than could units which required time to be constructed. After only a few years of the program's existence, however, the production-oriented components are coming to absorb most of the program's funds (e.g., over 85 percent of total program expenditures during 1979).[25] The upshot of the Section 8 experience is thus that the demand-oriented approach to housing subsidies is only one aspect—and perhaps an increasingly minor aspect—of the Section 8 approach.

Questions Left Unanswered

During the 40 years in which the idea of housing allowances has been part of public policy debate, each era has judged the utility of housing allowances in terms of the needs of its own times. During the 1930s, job creation through public works construction was a key goal of public policy, a goal with lower priority during the 1970s and 1980s. The existence of slum housing—housing stock of poor quality—was also a more pressing and widespread reality in the 1930s than it is in the 1970s. On the other hand, freedom of choice in housing was not a great concern during 1930s but was a primary selling point for housing allowances during the 1960s. Also during the late 1960s and early 1970s, there was an increasing tendency to evaluate housing programs from the point of view of benefits to individual households (using criteria such as horizontal equity) rather than in terms of the program's impacts on the housing stock of a neighborhood and other community aspects which economists label externalities. Indeed, the set of public problems for which housing allowances might be suggested as a policy instrument is still evolving. For example, the possible role of housing allowances in prevention of displacement in revitalizing neighborhoods will perhaps be a policy concern of major importance during the 1980s, although it has not been in the past.

Housing allowances have continued to play a major role in debates concerning housing policy, despite changes in the criteria by which programs were judged, changes in the set of housing programs seen as an alternative to allowances, changes in the definition of the nation's housing problems, and changes in political administrations. Allowances have clearly been a flexible and durable idea. At the same time, because a housing allowance approach is quite different in structure and concept from most

25. At the same time, some of the Section 8 Existing slots are being used to financially shore up housing units or projects initially subsidized under the former Section 235 or 236 programs. This situation of tying a demand-side subsidy to a supply-side one is reminiscent of the fate of the rent supplement program, discussed earlier in this chapter.

of the housing programs with which HUD has dealt in the past, considerable uncertainty remained, even after 40 years of discussions, concerning what the effects of an allowance program would actually be. In such a situation, investment in a social experiment to obtain direct empirical information seemed a sensible action.

A COMPLEX RESEARCH DESIGN

Given the range and complexity of issues raised during policy debates, the congressional authorization to experiment with housing allowances presented an ambitious but unstructured mandate. During the period from January 1971 through March 1972, HUD designed and set in motion the EHAP program, working jointly with The Urban Institute as technical advisors. The vast majority of work under EHAP was encompassed within the Demand, Supply, and Administrative Agencies Experiments which are described here. Additional work on market effects of allowances, involving econometric analyses and development of simulation models, was also sponsored; this work and its results are outlined in chapter 9.[26]

Development of the Demand Experiment

The attention of researchers and research managers charged with designing the housing allowance study, focused first on the issues and approaches which eventually evolved into the Demand Experiment. That is, thinking centered on questions of how households would react to allowance payments, in terms of their decision whether or not to participate in the program, their use of housing allowance purchasing power to upgrade their level of housing consumption or for other consumption objectives, and the possible use of the portability of allowance payments to integrate new neighborhoods. Intertwined with these questions concerning households' reactions to allowances were questions of the appropriate design of an allowance subsidy program, concerning decisions on such questions as the level and form of subsidy payments and the imposition of various types of minimum housing consumption requirements. The design for the Demand Experiment, developed to explore these issues, had three key features: households as the unit of analysis; multiple treatment groups,

---

26. Collateral analyses of the housing consumption effects of welfare payments was later added to the overall EHAP project. The plans for this work are described in Mathematica Policy Research [E104]. Some early findings of this effort are given in Ohls and Thomas [H103] and in chapter 5 of this book.

including a control group; and a low density of experimental recipients scattered within large housing markets.

The household was selected as the basic unit whose behavior would be observed over time and analyzed. This decision made sense in preference to studying the behavior of individuals separately, since most housing decisions are made jointly within a household.[27] It also made sense relative to studying household behavior more aggregately—as did the Supply Experiment—because it permitted not just description of houehold reactions but behavioral explanation.

Once it was decided to study household behavior, one key question which had to be answered was, How long does it take for a household to finally adjust housing consumption after a change of circumstances such as the sudden addition of purchasing power provided by the allowance program? Census data showed high average mobility rates for low-income renters, but economic theory suggests that households might react only quite slowly. Three years was selected as an appropriate period for which to guarantee payments.

To generate the variety of observations necessary to estimate household reactions to allowances, the design of the Demand Experiment featured the presence of a wide variety of alternative treatment groups, or alternative versions of housing allowances, each version administered to a different group of households. As chapter 3 will discuss in detail while describing each of the 19 treatment groups included in the Demand Experiment, these alternative treatments varied among themselves in two ways. One way was by representing different concepts of housing allowances: an allowance basing its payments on a proportion of the household's rental expenditures versus an allowance basing payments on a household's income, or an allowance requiring that the household occupy decent quality housing before receiving payments versus one with no minimum housing consumption requirements.[28] The other way in which the treatments varied was simply in their degree of generosity; for example, an allowance making subsidy payments as a proportion of a household's actual rental expenditures could reimburse 20 percent of those expenditures or 60 percent. Researchers needed to (a) observe the reactions of households to allowance programs of different types and degrees of generosity; (b) estimate separately the effects of specific features of an allowance program's design, such as the presence or absence of minimum housing consumption re-

---

27. On the other hand, it reduces the ability of the experiment to observe household splits and the formation of new households. This aspect of the experimental design is discussed at length by Watts [E173].

28. For the pre-EHAP state of the art in comparing such alternatives, see de Leeuw, Leaman, and Blank [E36].

quirements; and, (c) estimate basic descriptive characteristics of household behavior such as the changes in the demand for housing in response to increased incomes or lower price of housing.[29]

Among the multiple treatment groups involved in the Demand Experiment, one particular group of households deserves special attention: the *control group.* A control group is a set of households as similar as possible to households receiving benefits under the experimental program but who receive no benefits. In any social experiment, important methodological problems are posed by the objective of determining whether observed changes in the behavior of recipients of the experimental treatment are due to the treatment itself, as opposed to changes which would have occurred over time even in the absence of the treatment. In the case of housing allowances, for example, we know that some proportion of all households move each year. In order to know how much mobility is induced by allowance payments, we must subtract from the total mobility observed for experimental households the amount of moving behavior these households would have engaged in if they had not received allowance payments. A control group, because its members are as similar as possible to the households participating in the experimental program, may be used to represent the behavior that the experimental households would have exhibited were they not participants.

It was the decision to include a control group in the design of the Demand Experiment which made this study a true experiment rather than simply a demonstration project. In the latter type of study, a public program is implemented on a trial basis and the behavior of recipients may be observed, but no precise estimates can be made of exactly what effects were due to the program.

By including both multiple treatment groups and a control group, the designers of the study had prepared the way for obtaining highly accurate estimates of households' reactions to allowances. One further threat to this goal remained, however. This threat was the possibility that accurate measurement of household reactions would be obscured by simultaneous reactions of the housing market to those household reactions. Suppose that we are interested in estimating the extent to which increases in income are associated with increases in the purchase of housing services. Presumably, we would like to know the answer to this question while holding all other circumstances constant. One of these crucial other circumstances is the price of housing. If a large proportion of all households in a housing market were suddenly given housing allowance payments and allocated most of their increased purchasing power toward housing, then the

---

29. These are the income and price elasticities of the demand for housing, defined more carefully in chapter 5.

aggregate demand for housing would exhibit a sudden and dramatic increase. Economic theory suggests that this increase in demand would generate an increase in price, to the extent that the increases were not accompanied by a corresponding increase in the available supply of housing services. The rise in the price of housing would tend to reduce the demand for housing generally and partially reduce the increase in the demand for housing created by allowance recipients' increased purchasing power. If we were seeking an accurate estimate of the income effect of the allowance alone, we would be misled by the simultaneous effect of price and income.

To avoid these problems, it was decided to conduct the Demand Experiment among a relatively small number of households scattered widely across very large housing markets. As Appendix B discusses in detail, the markets selected were Phoenix (with an SMSA population of 967,000) and Pittsburgh (with an SMSA population of 2,400,000). The probability that these markets could absorb the additional demand represented by a few hundred households receiving housing allowances without any price change or other market reaction was further enhanced by selecting two cities with relatively high rental vacancy rates.[30]

The Debate Over the Supply Experiment

While the Demand Experiment was carefully designed to generate accurate estimates of household behavior and to pick "optimal" design features for a national housing allowance program, it could not address a set of questions which, to many policy makers, were much more central to the housing allowance debate. These key questions—questions whose answers could "make or break" the feasibility of a housing allowance program— involved the reactions of markets to an allowance program, the very effects which the Demand Experiment had been designed to avoid. Opponents of housing allowance proposals had argued that the principal reaction to an allowance program would be rapid inflation in the rents charged to recipients with virtually no positive effect on the quality of housing services received by program recipients in either the long run or the short run. Many of these predictions were derived from anecdotal reports of the experiences of recipients of public assistance shelter payments, who often lived in seriously substandard housing despite these payments,

---

30. As table B.1 in Appendix B shows, the vacancy rates in the Demand sites were 7.2 percent in Phoenix and 5.8 percent in Pittsburgh in 1970. The latter value was in the upper one third of the vacancy rate distribution for all SMSAs with populations over 500,000, while the former was in the middle one third of the distribution.

and of elderly Social Security recipients who often saw their rents rise each time their Social Security payment increased.[31] It was this contention —that allowances would create windfall profits for landlords with no benefit to recipients—which was the key assertion which would have to be disproved if allowances were ever to be seriously considered for implementation.

Two alternative research strategies were proposed for investigating this matter. One approach was to rely on computer simulation models of urban housing markets. Using these models, the effects of housing allowances on prices and supply of housing could be simulated for a wide range of cities, both large and small, at relatively low cost. It was eventually decided to invest in extensive computer simulation studies of housing allowances, and modeling efforts at the National Bureau of Economic Research and at The Urban Institute were funded. As noted earlier, the findings of these studies are reviewed in chapter 9.

However, the research managers developing the EHAP research program felt that these studies by themselves would not be sufficiently credible to overcome hesitations about allowances, particularly those concerning inflation or exploitation of recipients. Before policy makers could be expected to support a national housing allowance program, it was felt that they would have to see it demonstrated in a full-scale field trial in which the effects of the program on the cost of shelter and on the quality of dwellings were carefully monitored.

To meet this requirement EHAP acquired a second field component, called the Supply Experiment. This research activity contrasted to the Demand Experiment in several key ways, each motivated by differing research objectives.

The first of these differences was that the Supply Experiment was designed to deliver to the housing market a substantial "shock" of rapidly increased demand. The Demand Experiment had specifically avoided this effect by involving only a relatively small number of households scattered within two large housing markets. The Supply Experiment, in contrast, was set to take place in two relatively small housing markets and to offer enrollment to all income-eligible households in those two communities. Thus, the reaction of a market to a "full-scale" program could be observed.

The second way in which the two experiments differed was that while the Demand Experiment was a study of households, the Supply Experiment was a study of housing markets to be monitored by examining the experience of dwelling units. As Appendix A describes in more detail, dwelling units were sampled and then monitored over time, not the households living

---

31. See, for example, Gans [P24]; Hartman and Keating [P30].

in those dwellings.[32] Dwelling rents, or more accurately the price per unit of housing services, and their physical condition were the key responses to be observed. The sample included both units occupied by program recipients and units never directly touched by the program, because the effect on both was of interest.

A third characteristic of the Supply Experiment is that no control group was embodied in the design, and no alternative treatments were tried. All households at the two experimental sites who were eligible for the program received benefits under a single program design. No dwellings were declared ineligible to form a control group, and there were no control markets. Thus, the Supply Experiment is most precisely characterized as a demonstration project, not an "experiment" in a formal sense. The implication of this characterization is that, while effects of the program can be observed and measured, we have far less assurance that the changes observed following introduction of the program were due to the program itself and not to some other factors changing at the same time. The fundamental design concept, based on the available econometric evidence, was that the "demand shock" would be sufficiently large and market effects so dramatic that they could be identified through only general comparison to other housing markets and broad national and regional economic conditions.

The final important way in which the Supply Experiment differed from the Demand Experiment was in duration. To forecast accurately the effects of a permanent program of housing allowances, researchers needed to observe the behavior of the subject of their study long enough for it to "come to equilibrium"—that is, to fully adjust to the presence of an allowance program. Low-income households, researchers felt, would indicate the full extent of their adjustment if they offered allowance payments for three years, and this duration was therefore selected for the Demand Experiment. But the object of study in the Supply Experiment—housing markets—was assumed to adjust more slowly than would individual households. First, households have to adjust to allowances to generate the demand stimulus to which the market would then adjust. Then, in accommodating this stimulus once developed, housing markets must adjust a capital stock—housing units—which are long-lived, with only a small percentage change at the margin each year by which to make the adjustments. Furthermore, if adjustment by a building supplier involved a large capital outlay, then the adjustment would only take place if the economic incentives—the additional demand stimulus provided by allowances—were to continue for long enough to justify the investment. In

---

32. Households participating in the Supply Experiment were also studied to some extent, mainly through household records of the operating agency.

consideration of these factors, the designers of the Supply Experiment required that payments should continue for 10 years, while research and monitoring would cover the first 5 of these years.

While these four design features of the Supply Experiment were selected to enable it to obtain the information being sought while staying within reasonable budget constraints,[33] they did generate a number of consequences which will be apparent as readers proceed through this book. The most obvious of these consequences is that not all the results of the Supply Experiment are yet available, even 10 years after the legislation authorizing the Experimental Housing Allowance Program. This delay reflects both the long-term horizon of the study itself—that data are still flowing in—and the long delays (some of them inherent) in processing the massive body of data generated by a study saturating two entire metropolitan areas, even relatively small ones.

The second effect of the design choices is that considerable controversy surrounds the issue of the generalizability of Supply Experiment findings. Green Bay and South Bend were selected to be different from each other in terms of such aspects as racial composition, growth rate, and vacancy rates. Table 2.1 shows vacancy and racial composition figures for the two sites and for central South Bend compared to the rest of South Bend. These separate figures are presented for South Bend because of the sharp differences in the two geographic segments.[34] Still they are quite similar to each other in a number of ways, the most important of which are that both the sites are medium-sized cities and both are located in the Middle West.[35] This lack of size variation and other design criticisms are reviewed in the next section of this chapter.

The Administrative Agency Experiment: A Bridge to the Real World

Whatever their strengths and weaknesses, the Demand Experiment and the Supply Experiment, designed as just described, constituted the research agenda for the Experimental Housing Allowance Program originally drafted by HUD's research managers. When these plans were reviewed by then-HUD Secretary George Romney, however, he insisted on one important change. He felt that because the two experiments outlined would be run by contractors through agencies created especially for the experimental program, too little information would be generated on how allow-

---

33. The cost of the Supply Experiment is described in chapter 12.

34. Appendix B discusses the process by which these sites were selected.

35. In 1974 the Green Bay area had 170,000 inhabitants and in 1975 the South Bend area had 240,000.

Table 2.1

Characteristics of the Housing Market at the Supply Experiment Sites, 1973-1974 [a]

Area	Number of Habitable Units	Average Vacancy Rate (percentage)	Annual Turnover per 100 Units	Average Vacancy Duration (weeks)	Proportion of Households Headed by a Minority in 1970
			Rental Housing [b]		
Green Bay SMSA	14,700	5.1	65.6	4.0	—
South Bend SMSA	16,400	10.6	57.4	9.6	10.6
Central South Bend	8,000	12.3	59.5	10.7	16.2
South Bend area outside of central city	8,400	8.9	55.3	8.4	0.7
			Homeowner Housing [c]		
Green Bay SMSA	31,700	.8	7.4	5.6	—
South Bend SMSA	57,000	2.4	9.9	12.6	5.1
Central South Bend	13,600	4.2	8.5	25.7	9.3
South Bend area outside of central city	43,400	1.9	10.2	9.7	0.5

Source: Rand [E93], p. 19.

a. 1973 in Green Bay and 1974 in South Bend.
b. Excludes mobile home parks, rooming houses, farmhouses, and federally subsidized dwellings.
c. Excludes mobile homes.

ance programs would actually operate in "real world" housing agencies. Romney insisted that allowances be given a field trial outside of a "hothouse" research situation.

To satisfy this requirement, a third major component of EHAP was created, the Administrative Agency Experiment (AAE). Like the Supply Experiment and unlike the Demand Experiment, it involved no control groups and therefore was a demonstration project rather than a true experiment. However, unlike both the Demand and Supply Experiments, the allowance programs in the AAE were to be administered by actual ongoing public agencies for their two-year durations. Abt Associates, the research contractor involved in the AAE (as well as the Demand Experiment), monitored the behavior of these agencies but did not actually operate the program.

The AAE was conducted at eight sites, selected to represent a wide variety of operating environments and to demonstrate the feasibility of administering housing allowances through a variety of public agencies. One of the policy questions to be addressed was whether a public agency other than a housing agency could effectively administer a housing allowance program. To examine that question, the eight agencies involved with AAE were systematically varied among four types of agencies: two local housing authorities, two public welfare agencies, two state agencies responsible for housing programs, and two county or metropolitan governments. It is important to note that these agencies were not randomly selected but rather were chosen from a set which HUD field offices rated as clearly competent.[36]

A few key characteristics of the eight AAE sites are displayed in Appendix table B.3. They range from rural areas to major cities; from areas with low rental vacancy rates to some with vacancy rates over 10 percent; from areas having almost no minorities in their population to those with almost 40 percent. Each is drawn from a different HUD administrative region.

A second purpose of the AAE component of EHAP was to learn about the "best" way to structure a number of administrative tasks that were key to successfully operating a housing allowance program: income certification, outreach to attract participants, services to help those enrolled in the program find adequate housing, and housing inspection. Both the *quality* of the accomplished task (e.g., the extent of errors in certifying incomes) and the *cost* of different approaches were of interest. The classic experimental approach to structuring this design would have been to have a very large number of sites and to systematically vary administrative practices among them while controlling for different types of ad-

---

36. For a further description of agency selection, see Appendix B.

ministrative agencies. An alternative design approach, and the one adopted, was to give the administering agencies wide latitude in performing these functions and to analyze, to the degree possible, the comparative effectiveness of the resultant approaches. This "naturalistic design" permits a variety of approaches to be tried, but it does so at the cost of making it impossible to completely isolate the effects of specific administrative practices from other factors such as the conditions in the local housing market or the general structure and mission of the agencies involved.

A final research objective for the AAE was to test the degree of community acceptance of a housing allowance program. This test was necessarily quite crude given the design, but it was thought that serious problems of rejection, should they be encountered, could nevertheless be detected.

The selection of agencies in the Administrative Agency Experiment—both the choice of sites and the choice of those with good track records—was consistent with an important political objective for persons within HUD who were supporters of the idea of housing allowances: to demonstrate convincingly that housing allowances were "workable" across a wide variety of market conditions and when delivered by diverse agencies. Furthermore, multiple sites would help to generate a supportive constituency for the program.[37] Attaining this objective was seen as very important to ultimate program enactment.

CRITICISMS OF THE DESIGN

During the late 1970s, the availability of the results of the experiment has permitted a good deal of "Monday morning quarterbacking" about the original design of the individual experiments. We would be remiss not to indicate these criticisms, since some of their themes will be heard again in later chapters reviewing the results. At the same time, these criticisms should be taken to be what they are: *after the fact* reviews nearly a decade after some of the decisions were made. Much can be gained for future work from these comments, and it is in this spirit that they are discussed.

Demand Experiment

Three broad criticisms have surfaced concerning the Demand Experiment, the first two of which are closely related.[38] The first is based on the premise that housing consumption decisions are driven by major life-events, such

---

37. AAE sites, jointly with the sites from the Demand and Supply Experiments, cover 8 of 10 HUD regions.

38. These criticisms are discussed at greater length in Watts [E173].

as marriage, divorce, and the birth and aging of children. It follows that an experimental design is flawed if it introduces a moderate economic stimulus to households and monitors its effects for only two years and only for the "major" portion of households surviving intact over the period. It is further limited if it is restricted exclusively to renter households, since it thereby misses the major housing consumption changes that accompany the shift from rental tenure to homeownership. The latter aspect of the argument carries less force, given the low rates at which low-income households have in fact been able to attain homeownership in the 1970s.[39] The general point, though, is well taken.

The second criticism is that the experiment was simply too short: payments for only three years may not have been sufficient time to convince households to alter consumption choices. Given the high average mobility rates of low-income renters, this argument has less force when first considered. On the other hand, a substantial portion of renters have long tenures; and it may be this group whose participation is underrepresented in a short experiment.[40]

It is not clear how the experiment could have been designed to combat these problems. Indeed, the consensus seems to be that a greater understanding of housing consumption and events in the life cycle is needed, quite aside from the experiments.

A third criticism is that too many distinct treatments, that is, alternative payment formulas were attempted with the inevitable reduction in the number of observations per treatment. Consequently, treatment groups often had to be combined for analysis. Hence, for example, separate behavioral relationships for racial groups were generally not estimated. While this criticism has merit, it does not challenge the validity of the results that were obtained.

One point not raised is worth noting. There is general agreement that the basic results—within the limits just noted—would not be demonstrably improved by adding more sites, since the basic findings were quite consistent across the two sites. More information could have been achieved with large samples at the two sites that were included, but this is quite a different matter.

Administrative Agency Experiment

As a piece of research, the AAE has been the most criticized component of EHAP. In particular, five criticisms have been heard.[41] By far the most

---

39. See Follain, Katz, and Struyk [C24].
40. Goodman [H43].
41. An amplified discussion is in Kershaw and Williams [C47].

frequent refrain is against the "naturalistic design" as opposed to a controlled variation or experimental design. The choice is said to have sharply curtailed the amount which could be learned about administrative efficiency. A second problem is that the design monitored a modest number of administrative practices out of a somewhat larger set. Third, because the program demonstrated in each site was one of the extremely limited enrollment—400 to 900 participants per site—the range of agency experience was necessarily limited. For example, outreach levels were geared to attracting the target number of participants rather than informing the entire population who would have been eligible to participate in an entitlement program. Fourth, the short duration of the program caused biases. As an example, administering agencies might take easy-to-enroll households rather than devote the energy needed to enroll a cross-section of those eligible.[42] Fifth, the administering agencies were not randomly selected but rather were chosen from a group recommended on the basis of their competence. This procedure means that even if all of the agencies successfully fielded the program (which they did), it would provide scant assurance that the typical agency involved in a national program could do as well.

These criticisms must be viewed in light of the underlying purpose of the demonstration, the feasibility of a different design, and the fact that the experiment did have systematic variation along one, and perhaps the most important dimension—type of administrative agency. As to purpose, the broad objective evident after the rhetoric has been cut away is that HUD needed to build a political constituency for a major shift in housing policy. One way to do this was to place "model programs" that worked without major mishap in a number of jurisdictions. This strategy had the advantage of making a prima facie case for its workability when a national program was to be considered. Viewed in this way, the *research* objective of the AAE should be restated to be that of learning as much as possible, given the design constraints imposed by its *political* role.[43]

The case for a naturalistic design is further strengthened by the consideration that, at the time the AAE design was selected, there was simply too little information available to choose intelligently among "treatments" if a controlled variation approach had been taken. Putting a program in motion at a set of agencies, with broad budget restrictions and output requirement, and then observing whatever superior practices naturalistically emerge might then be a fruitful strategy even in the absence of other constraints.[44] In fact, this is the way in which the current national

---

42. Actually, the facts do not support such a contention. See chapter 10.
43. These arguments are expanded in Hamilton [C30].
44. This point is argued more fully in Porter [C87].

housing allowance program (the Section 8 program) was launched, with guidance based in part on AAE findings. One could argue as well that limited enrollment and start-up times are consistent with the way in which a program actually begins operations in the real world. Nevertheless, it is true that these characteristics did cause the AAE to produce only a moderate amount of information applicable for an open enrollment housing allowance program, were such a program to be considered.

Supply Experiment

One putative design limitation of the Supply Experiment was the lack of control sites. In other words, sites which were very similar to each of the two program sites were *not* chosen for detailed monitoring of market changes over the life of the experiments, especially changes in the price of housing services. Absence of the control sites has meant that market effects must be analyzed against general economic trends and historical information for the two Supply Experiment markets.

To understand the reasons for selecting an experimental design without control sites, we must remember that at the time the Supply Experiment was designed, the expectation widely held in the research community was that introduction of an entitlement allowance program would produce a massive increment in the demand for housing in the low-income housing markets of the sites. When—as we shall see in chapter 9 —a smaller increment to demand was actually encountered, measurement problems became more acute. In effect, the caliper available was too large for the job at hand. But it is unclear that a paired site approach —with a carefully monitored similar nonexperimental site paired with each Supply Experiment site—would have been a genuine improvement, given the difficulties of finding truly similar pairs of metropolitan areas and of holding constant, or changing in parallel, all factors besides the introduction of the allowance. On the other hand, the approach could very well have provided at least somewhat better measurements of market phenomena than actually have been obtained.

The other design limitation frequently discussed for the Supply Experiment was its inclusion of only two experimental sites.[45] This was a problem in a *political* sense because it limited the prima facie credibility of the results. Since no direct observation was available on a big city, could one be sure that the same results would occur there? It could also have been a *substantive* problem: If the results had turned out to be highly

---

45. The Comptroller General [E27; E28] criticized all three experiments on sample size and composition, but he particularly expressed concern about the Supply Experiment. For more on the concern of site representiveness, see Appendix B.

sensitive to specific market conditions, it would definitely have been a problem. As it is, with the observed small extent of market effects, there is only relatively minor lingering doubt as to whether the results apply with equal force to the full range of housing markets. As a design matter, however, this fortuitous outcome could not have been anticipated. Yet the options permitted in the design stage were sharply limited. As noted earlier, free of cost constraints one would have tested the program in a statistically valid sample of markets. But cost constraints severely limited both the number of markets that could be included and the size of those selected.

Housing Quality Standards

A further general design issue raised about EHAP in a number of forums has concerned the range of variation in minimum housing standards which the dwelling to be occupied by would-be participants had to pass. In particular, it has been asserted that use of a higher dwelling quality standard in the Supply Experiment might have produced a greater incremental demand and hence price effect.[46]

Two observations are relevant. One, it is unclear how the use of *more* standards, as compared to a *different* one, would have been implemented within a site.[47] Two, the extent of change in demand stimulus which would result from shifting to a tougher physical standard in the Supply Experiment is speculative, given that participation rates were found to be sensitive to the range of standards employed in the Demand Experiment.[48] To accommodate a design which varied standards systematically within the Supply Experiment, assuming one standard per site, would have entailed an increase in the number of sites and would certainly have been prohibitively expensive under the original design constraints. Limited to a single standard, the logical choice was to pick one from the set of realistic candidates for a national program.

Judging EHAP's Design: A Summary

Our judgment is that the initial EHAP experimental design was generally solid, given the state of knowledge at that time, the resource constraints under which the experiment was designed, the genuine possibility that a national entitlement housing allowance program would be given serious political consideration very soon, and the need for a record of experience with a housing allowance program that would have substantial face

---

46. The strongest advocate of this position is Kain [P39].
47. Watts [E173], p. 38.
48. This evidence is reviewed in chapter 4.

validity to Congress and other public decision makers. Admittedly, this judgment is couched within a powerful set of qualifiers; but these qualifiers do little more than reiterate the set of constraints under which the design was developed.

It might be well to illustrate the role of these constraints with the hypothetical exercise of asking how the design would ideally have been changed if one or more of these constraints had not been present. If a full entitlement program had been seen as a remote possibility and a gradually phased-in limited entitlement program—similar to the Section 8 rental assistance payments program—seen as the more likely future policy trend, then the need for the Supply Experiment as designed would have been sharply reduced. An alternative design featuring the development of a longitudinal data base with which to study supplier behavior, along with the development of housing market simulation models, could have been preferable for analysis of market effects. But politically this course might still have been rejected: even faced with the evidence from operation of full entitlement programs in two markets, which have produced little inflation in the price of housing services, there are today important political figures and organizations who remain unconvinced that much smaller demand-side subsidies are not causing localized inflation.

This is not to say that with today's knowledge—that of a decade later than 1970—and today's quite different political circumstances, the designs would not be changed and could not be improved. Quite the contrary. But judged within the context of its own time, the EHAP design does seem to respond adequately, and even creatively, to a very complex interacting set of technical and political circumstances.

With the overall EHAP design and its individual components firmly in mind, we can now proceed to a description of the execution of the design in the form of operational programs, data gathering, and production of analytic results. We will return to the experimental design in the final chapter of the report and review it in light of the new information EHAP has generated for policy analysis.

CHAPTER 3

The Three Experiments

Marc Bendick, Jr. and Anne D. Squire

T HIS CHAPTER describes the three major field operations of EHAP, the times and places they occurred, and the policies and procedures by which they operated. The description begins with the Demand Experiment, followed by the Supply Experiment and the Administrative Agency Experiment. These descriptions focus on the experiments as operational programs, as seen from the perspective of recipients and administrators. In contrast, Appendix A examines the three experiments from the point of view of the researcher and discusses the data gathering and research procedures. The programs as described here represent the experimental stimulus to which households and housing markets reacted.

THE DEMAND EXPERIMENT

The basic design for the Demand Experiment was developed by the Stanford Research Institute and subsequently expanded and implemented by Abt Associates, Inc.[1] Abt was responsible both for administering the allowance program and for analyzing its effects. Approximately 1800 households participated at each of two experimental sites: Maricopa County, Arizona (which includes the city of Phoenix) and Allegheny County, Pennsylvania (which includes the city of Pittsburgh).[2] At each site, Abt established a special office to administer the program independently from any existing public angency.

Eligibility and Enrollment

Three factors governed eligibility in the Demand Experiment:

---

1. See U.S. Department of Housing and Urban Development [E166], p. 13.
2. Appendix B discusses the process by which these two sites were selected.

- *Income and assets.* To be eligible, a household's monthly adjusted income [3] had to be less than four times the estimated cost of standard housing at its site.[4] (See table 3.1) [5] The household's assets had to be less than $5,000 (if the household head was younger than 62) or $10,000 (if 62 or older).

- *Household composition.* Households were eligible if they were composed of two or more related individuals of any age, except if the household head was a full-time student. Single-person households were eligible only if the person was age 62 or older or if he was handicapped, disabled, or displaced by public action such as an urban renewal project.

- *Residency.* Only renters, not homeowners, were eligible to participate in the Demand Experiment. They had to reside within the boundaries of Maricopa County (for Phoenix) or Allegheny County (for Pittsburgh). Households living in government-subsidized housing (such as public housing) were ineligible unless they moved to a nonsubsidized unit.

Not all households in Phoenix and Pittsburgh who fulfilled these criteria could receive housing allowance benefits, however. Only a set of households randomly selected from among those residing in certain low-income census tracts at the two sites were offered a chance to participate.[6] No general publicity about the allowance program was distributed, and the first contact between the program and households was initiated by the agency. An interviewer went to the homes of the selected households and informed them that they had been randomly chosen for participation in a housing survey. The interviewer then administered a "screening interview" to determine if the household was eligible for the program in terms of the criteria described. At this time, households were not told that they were being considered for a program which would make payments to them.

Households' responses to these initial questions were reviewed at the experiment's site office, and each household appearing program-eligible

---

3. Adjusted income was defined as gross income minus federal and state income taxes and Social Security taxes, minus $300 annually per earner for work-related expenses. Other specific deductions were also allowed.

4. This estimated cost of standard housing, called C*, is used in calculating the payment levels for some treatment groups in the Demand Experiment, as well as for determining eligibility. The process by which it was determined is discussed later in this chapter.

5. Table 3.1 presents the income eligibility limits for the two Demand Experiment sites, as well as for the sites in the Supply Experiment and Administrative Agency Experiment.

6. The process of selecting these tracts and households is discussed in Appendix A.

Table 3.1

Maximum Net Annual Income Limits for Eligibility by Household Size for Each EHAP Site in the First Year of Program Operation

Site	1	2	Household Size 3-4	5-6	7-8	9+
Demand Experiment (1973)						
Phoenix	$5,500	$6,950	$8,150	$10,100	$12,250	$12,250
Pittsburgh	4,550	5,300	6,250	7,200	8,650	8,650
Supply Experiment [a] (1974)						
Green Bay	$4,320	$5,520	$3,960	$7,680	$8,640	$10,080
South Bend	4,320	5,520	6,480	7,200	7,680	7,680
Administrative Agency Experiment (1973)						
Bismarck	$4,400	$5,200	$7,000	$7,800	$8,500	$9,000
Durham	4,800	5,500	6,900	7,500	8,000	8,500
Jacksonville	4,800	5,520	6,250	6,750	7,050	7,300
San Bernardino	3,600	5,050	6,250	7,450	8,200	8,750
Salem	4,800	4,800	6,240	8,160	9,600	10,320
Peoria	4,800	6,200	7,300	8,300	9,200	9,900
Springfield	4,800	5,500	6,900	8,000	8,600	9,100
Tulsa	3,360	4,560	6,000	7,200	9,120	9,120
Average (unweighted)	$4,477	$5,468	$6,723	$7,778	$8,790	$9,220

Sources: Kozimor [H65], p. 8; Abt Associates, Inc. [E11], p. 16; Dickson [C16], p. B-7.

a. These figures represent four times annual C*, minus four times $10 for each month. No actual income limits were set in the Supply Experiment. Income eligibility rested solely on the amount of income necessary to yield the minimum payment ($10) for each treatment group.

was randomly assigned to 1 of 19 treatment cells within the experiment.[7] These households were then reinterviewed (in what was called the Baseline Survey) and subsequently were sent letters explaining the experiment and the benefits which the allowance program would offer them. The letters invited them to attend individual interviews at the site office for enrollment.

When a member of a household appeared for his enrollment interview, site staff asked further questions to insure that the household was actually eligible for allowance benefits. The staff also described the rules of the program (in the treatment cell to which that household had been assigned) and provided an estimate of the monthly benefits the household would receive if it chose to participate. Households were also informed that they must respond to various special reporting requirements, surveys, and inspections associated with the research aspects of the experiment.

If the household decided to enroll in the allowance program, the site office completed the enrollment process. As an application, the household filled in an initial household report form. Income, household composition, and job status information on the form were then verified by the agency staff.[8] A housing evaluation was performed on the unit occupied by the household at the time of application, and a final calculation of benefits was made. Finally, a formal letter of acceptance was sent to the household, along with the first benefit check and the following month's household report form. The process of sending a monthly check and receiving a report form in return continued for each household until the end of the program 36 months later, unless the household became ineligible sooner.

The period during which these events occurred is indicated in figure 3.1, and the average value of monthly allowance benefits received by participating households is presented in table 3.2. As the table indicates, the monthly payments to the average household ranged across the two sites and among treatment groups from \$38 to \$95 per month and averaged from 10 to 14 percent of the recipients' incomes.[9]

---

7. The assignment process was not entirely random, in that extra-low income limits were set for assignment to some treatment cells. Without such a procedure, many households in these cells would have been entitled to a small subsidy or none at all, due to their high incomes. See Friedman and Kennedy [H37], p. A-11.

8. Generally, third-party verification was used in the Demand Experiment. See chapter 10 for a discussion of this procedure.

9. These payments somewhat overstate the net value of these payments to those households who received both housing allowances and food stamps. Allowance payments were counted as income in determining eligibility and payment levels in the Food Stamp program, so receipt of a housing allowance led to lower benefits in that program. However, other public assistance programs, including Aid to Families with Dependent Children and Social Security retirement benefits, did not perform a similar benefit reduction.

Figure 3.1

Operating Periods for the EHAP Sites

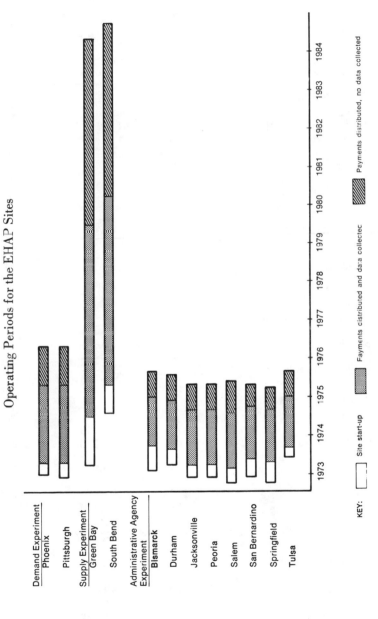

Sources: Abt Associates, Inc. [E15]; Rand [E129]; Temple et al. [E150]; individual AAE Agency final reports: [E20, E37, E66, E101, E141, E142, E152, E154].

Table 3.2

Average Monthly Housing Allowance Payments and Participant Incomes
at Twelve EHAP Sites

Site	Average Monthly Payment per Recipient Household	Average Annual Participant Income	Ratio of Monthly Payments to Monthly Income
Demand Experiment [a]			
Phoenix			
Housing gap minimum standards	$55		
Housing gap minimum rent	63		
Housing gap uncon-strained	95		
Percentage of rent	53		
All recipients	$59	$5,100	.14
Pittsburgh			
Housing gap minimum standards	$38		
Housing gap minimum rent	42		
Housing gap uncon-strained	52		
Percentage of rent	44		
All recipients	$43	$5,000	.10
Supply Experiment [b]			
Green Bay			
Renters	$77	$4,348	.21
Homeowners	67	4,973	.16
All recipients	$72	$4,612	.19
South Bend			
Renters	$93	$3,152	.35
Homeowners	67	4,209	.19
All recipients	$78	$3,782	.25
Administrative Agency Experiment [c]			
Bismarck	$72	$3,000	.29
Durham	74	2,400	.37
Jacksonville [d]	78	2,772	.34
Peoria	85	3,700	.27

Table 3.2—Continued

Average Monthly Housing Allowance Payments and Participant Incomes
at Twelve EHAP Sites

Site	Average Monthly Payment per Recipient Household	Average Annual Participant Income	Ratio of Monthly Payments to Monthly Income
Salem	84	2,800	.36
San Bernardino	84	2,900	.35
Springfield	89	3,000	.36
Tulsa	72	2,700	.32
All recipients	$80	$2,932	.33

Sources: Wallace [E172]; Rand [E129]; and U.S. Department of Housing and Urban Development [E169].
a. As of the second year of operation.
b. As of September 1976.
c. As of first year.
d. Weighted average for first and second enrollment periods.

In terms of assistance provided to households other than these payments, the general approach implemented in the Demand Experiment relied heavily on the ability of households receiving allowances to fend for themselves in the private housing market. Households were responsible for selecting their own housing unit, insuring that it passed housing quality requirements (if any were imposed on their treatment group), and negotiating their own lease and payment arrangements with landlords. The housing allowance agency sent its monthly allowance check to the households, and the household was responsible for all rent payments to the landlord.[10]

The only major exception to this "hands off" approach to clients' decisions and actions was represented in the Demand Experiment by "housing information sessions" provided to enrolled households at the beginning of the program. In the envelope with its first monthly payment, each recipient household received an invitation to attend five different

---

10. As noted in chapter 2, HUD's Section 8 rent supplement program for existing housing operates very much in the spirit of housing allowances, but it stops short of this degree of reliance on client action. In that program, the landlord signs an agreement between himself and the local housing agency administering the program, and the agency sends its monthly subsidy check directly to the landlord, with the recipient household then supplementing that check with a payment of his own for the balance. For a comparison between this approach and the EHAP system, see chapter 10 of this report and also Zais, Goedert, and Trutko [P95], pp. 55 to 58.

sessions in which information was provided on the housing allowance program and on the general housing market. The sessions were conducted by the Urban League, under contract to Abt, and about one third of those invited chose to attend. The housing allowance office staff mailed printed material on the topics covered to all households who did not attend.

Nineteen Treatment Groups

The process just outlined was followed for all households enrolled in the Demand Experiment. However, the programs in which each household found itself participating varied widely in terms of the requirements the household had to meet to receive benefits and the way benefits were calculated. Within the Demand Experiment, 19 distinct treatment cells were established, and each household was permanently assigned to one. These 19 cells represented combinations of more and less generous payments and different forms and degrees of housing consumption requirements. Figure 3.2 depicts these cells and the number of households receiving benefits under each. The most basic distinction among the treatments was between those involving a "housing gap" formula for determining benefit payment, those involving a "percentage of rent" formula, and those representing a "control group."

Housing Gap Treatment Groups

As its name implies, a housing gap formula calculates the housing allowance payments to which a household is entitled as the difference between what the household is presumed able to pay for shelter and the presumed cost of adequate housing in that household's community. The formula is

$$P = C^* - bY \qquad (3\text{-}1)$$

where

P = maximum potential allowance payment amount

C^* = the estimated cost of acceptable quality housing for a household of a certain size and composition

b = fraction of the household's income the household is expected to contribute toward its housing costs

Y = the household's program-defined income.

P is the maximum potential payment because households were never reimbursed for more than their total actual expenditures for rent (plus utilities, if paid separately); hence, a household's payment might be less than the payment specified by this formula. In the Demand Experiment, 12 of the 19 treatment cells represented various forms of housing gap treatment. The variation among them involved alternative levels of benefits and alternative housing consumption requirements.

One way the level of benefits was varied was through use of alternative values for the variable C*, the estimated cost of acceptable quality housing for a household. At each of the Demand Experiment sites, a panel of local housing experts was convened to estimate the rental cost of standard quality housing units appropriate for households of different sizes. The figures they established, designated C*, are presented in the first lines of table 3.3. (Other lines in the table indicate the values for C* adopted later to adjust for inflation.) Once C* had been established, the various housing gap treatment cells offered allowances of different degrees of generosity by varying the proportion of C* used in calculating households' payments within the equation 3-1. As panel A of figure 3.2 indicates, the three values of C used for the various housing gap treatment cells were 80 percent of C*, 100 percent of C*, and 120 percent of C*.

The second variable in equation 3-1 which was manipulated to vary the generosity of allowance benefits was b, the proportion of a household's income the household was expected to contribute toward its rental expenses. As the left-hand column in panel A of figure 3.2 indicates, this variable was also set at three different levels: 15 percent of income, 25 percent of income, and 35 percent of income; the lower this proportion, the higher the monthly allowance payment which a household would receive. The monthly payment an individual household would receive was influenced both by the level of C and b assigned to the treatment cell in which the household found itself and by the income level of that individual household.

Eleven of the 12 housing gap treatment cells offered allowance payments to households only as long as the household occupied a unit meeting some sort of minimum housing consumption requirement. One set of these requirements, utilized in those treatment cells marked one through five in figure 3.2, required that the housing unit pass specific agency-dictated minimum physical quality standards and occupancy standards. The standards addressed such topics as the allowable number of occupants per room, the presence of adequate light, heat, plumbing, and ventilation, and the sound condition of walls, roofs, and floors.[11] Conformity with these standards was monitored by inspections of the housing unit made at the initial enrollment in the program, at one-year intervals thereafter, and at any time the household moved. Inspections performed to determine eligibility for benefits for housing gap-minimum standards households

---

11. The details of these standards are presented in Appendix C.

Figure 3.2

Treatment Cells and Sample Sizes in the Demand Experiment [a, b]

A. Housing Gap Treatments (P = C — bY)

b Value	C Level	Housing Requirements			
		Minimum Standards	Minimum Rent Low = 0.7C*	Minimum Rent High = 0.9C*	Unconstrained
b = 15% of income	100% of C*	CELL 1 81 households			
	120% of C*	CELL 2 63 households	CELL 6 58 households	CELL 9 60 households	CELL 12 103 households
b = 25% of income	100% of C*	CELL 3 77 households	CELL 7 89 households	CELL 10 88 households	
	80% of C*	CELL 4 82 households	CELL 8 79 households	CELL 11 78 households	
b = 35% of income	100% of C*	CELL 5 75 households			

B. Percentage of Rent (P = aR)

a = 60%	a = 50%	a = 40%	a = 30%	a = 20%
CELL 13 49 households	CELL 14 190 households	CELL 15 179 households	CELL 16 176 households	CELL 17 111 households

C. Controls (no payments)

With Housing Information	Without Housing Information
CELL 18	CELL 17
296 households	307 households

D. Sample Sizes, All Treatments

Treatment	Phoenix	Pittsburgh	Both Sites
Housing gap-minimum standards	174	204	378
Housing gap-minimum rent	207	245	452
Housing gap-unconstrained	40	63	103
Percentage of rent	298	407	705
Controls	282	321	603
Total	1301	1240	2241

Source: Adapted from Kennedy and MacMillan [H64], p. A-11.
a. Sample sizes refer to households that were active, although not necessarily receiving payments, after 2 years.
b. Symbols are defined in the text.

Table 3.3

Values of C*, the Estimated Standard Cost of Adequate Housing, at the Twelve EHAP Sites

	Number of Persons in Household					
Site	1	2	3-4	5-6	7-8	9+
Demand Experiment						
Phoenix						
May 1973-January 1975	$125	$155	$180	$220	$265	$265
February 1975-January 1976	135	165	190	235	280	280
Pittsburgh						
April 1973-January 1975	105	120	140	160	190	190
February 1975-January 1976	115	130	150	170	205	205
Supply Experiment						
Green Bay						
June 1974-March 1976	$100	$125	$155	$170	$190	$220
April 1976-April 1977	125	145	175	195	210	230
May 1977-April 1978	130	155	185	205	220	245
May 1978-December 1979	140	170	200	235	265	300
South Bend						
December 1974-August 1976	100	125	145	160	170	170
September 1976-						
August 1977	115	140	160	175	185	185
September 1977-						
December 1978	120	150	175	180	190	190
January 1979-						
December 1979	130	160	190	195	205	205
Administrative Agency Experiment						
Bismarck						
July 1973-April 1976	$ 90	$120	$155	$195	$230	$230
Durham						
July 1973-May 1976	100	115	145	175	190	190
Jacksonville						
April 1973-August 1974	100	115	135	155	185	205
September 1974-July 1977	115	125	150	180	200	220
Peoria						
April 1973-January 1976	100	130	155	195	225	235
Salem						
March 1973-December 1975	100	125	155	195	225	235
San Bernardino						
May 1973-March 1976	95	125	150	190	225	225
Springfield						
April 1973-February 1976	110	125	155	185	220	240
Tulsa						
August 1973-June 1976	90	115	145	170	210	210
Average	$111	$134	$160	$187	$214	$223

Sources: Rand [E130]. p. 22, table 2.3. AAE data from *Payment Initiation Form Codebook, Appendix III*, table III-1. Demand data from *HADE Codebook for Non-Interview Data*, p. 62.

were done by the same staff and involved a shortened version of the same checklist used in the periodic inspections done for research purposes on the housing unit occupied by each household in the Demand Experiment, whether or not payments to households were conditional on meeting minimum housing standards.

In contrast to these five "minimum standards" housing gap treatment groups, six "minimum rent" housing gap treatment groups used a more indirect method of insuring minimum levels of housing consumption. Households receiving payments in these treatment groups were required to maintain at least a specified level of rental expenditures, under the assumption that housing units commanding certain levels of rent would automatically provide housing of certain levels of quality. As figure 3.2 indicates, three of these treatment groups, called "high minimum rent" treatments, required households to spend at least 90 percent of C* monthly, while the remaining three treatment groups, called "low minimum rent," required households to spend at least 70 percent of C*.

The final housing gap treatment cell, number 12 in figure 3.2, was designated the "unconstrained" treatment group. Households in this group were free to choose whatever housing they wished to occupy, constrained by neither minimum rent requirements nor minimum standards of housing quality. The behavior of this group thus established a baseline against which the effects of the housing consumption requirements could be measured.

Percentage of Rent Treatments

Five treatment cells in the Demand Experiment received payments under a formula quite different from any of the "housing gap" programs just discussed. Households under this alternative approach, called a "percentage of rent" plan, received an allowance which was calculated as a fixed fraction of their actual rental payments and thus represented simply a price discount on housing. The formula by which their payments were calculated was

$$P = aR \qquad\qquad (3\text{-}2)$$

where

P = allowance payment amount

a = the proportion of rent reduced

R = the household's actual rental expenditures

There were five treatment cells which applied this formula, numbers 13 through 17 in panel B of figure 3.2. These cells implemented five different levels of rent reduction (or value for the variable "a") : 20 percent, 30 percent, 40 percent, 50 percent, and 60 percent of rent. No housing consumption requirements, either of a "minimum standards" or of a "minimum rent" type, were imposed on these households. Monthly payments to minimum rent household averaged $63 in Phoenix and $42 in Pittsburgh (table 3.2).

Control Groups

The final two treatment cells, numbers 18 and 19 in panel C of figure 3.2, represented "control groups" in this experiment. Households in these cells were selected at the same time and through the same procedures as the households in the other treatment groups, and they were similar to the households in the other cells in terms of their economic and social characteristics. During the 36 months of the Demand Experiment, they were subjected to the same periodic interviews and housing inspections to monitor their behavior. However, unlike the households in the other treatment groups, these households did not receive housing allowance benefits. Instead, they were only given a small payment for cooperating with periodic data gathering: $10 for each monthly report and $25 for each periodic interview.

The only difference between the two control group cells concerned attendance at housing information sessions. Households in treatment cell 18 were invited to attend the agency's housing information sessions, and their attendance was encouraged by paying them $10 for each session they did attend. In contrast, households in treatment cell 19 were excluded from attending these sessions. The objective of this rule was to permit measurement of the effects of the information sessions in the absence of allowance payments.

THE SUPPLY EXPERIMENT

The Supply Experiment was designed, operated, and evaluated by the Rand Corporation. Field operations were conducted at two sites: Brown County, Wisconsin (which includes the city of Green Bay) and St. Joseph County, Indiana (which includes the city of South Bend) ; and at each site Rand established a nonprofit housing allowance office (HAO) to administer the program independently from any existing government agencies.[12]

---

12. During the first five years of Supply Experiment operations, while research data were being collected, Rand maintained strict control over HAO operations. An

In contrast to the Demand Experiment and the Administrative Agency Experiment, which each served only renters, eligibility in the Supply Experiment was extended to both renters and homeowners. Furthermore, no enrollment limits were set in the Supply Experiment, but rather enrollment was open to all eligible households on an "entitlement" basis.[13] This feature permits an estimate to be made of how many households would elect to participate in such an open-ended program.

To inform potentially eligible households of the availability of this new form of public assistance, the HAOs conducted extensive outreach and publicity campaigns at the start of their programs. These efforts began in June 1974 in Green Bay and December 1974 in South Bend, using radio, television, and newspaper advertisements and stories; contacts with civic, fraternal, and religious organizations; and establishment of referral channels from other housing and social service agencies. These general efforts were curtailed after a large backlog of applications had been compiled.[14]

Households interested in applying for housing allowances could submit an application by phone or mail. Elderly or handicapped applicants could request that an HAO staff member come to their home to fill out the application form. The eligibility criteria by which the agency judged these applications were similar to those employed in the Demand Experiment:

- *Income and assets.* To be eligible, a household's monthly adjusted income[15] had to be less than four times C^*, the estimated cost of standard housing at its site. Assets (including homeowner's equity, if any) had to be less than $20,000 if the household head was under 62, or $32,500, if 62 or older.[16]

- *Household composition.* Initially, these requirements were identical to those in the Demand Experiment. In August 1977, consistent with

additional five years of allowance payments are guaranteed, however, so that behavior during the first five-year research period could be assumed to reflect a long-term program. During this second five-year period, Rand has relinquished control of the HAOs to the localities. Unlike the site offices in the Demand Experiment, which were closed once the experiment was concluded, the Green Bay and South Bend HAOs have become permanent agencies independent of their Supply Experiment origins.

13. Actually, an implicit maximum was established by funding levels, but this never became a practical constraint.

14. Chapter 10 provides a general discussion of outreach practices and their effectiveness.

15. Adjusted income is defined as gross income minus a $300 exemption per dependent and each secondary wage earner; a 5 percent standard deduction (10 percent for elderly-headed households); and other, less important, specific deductions.

16. Beginning in mid-1978 asset limits were indexed.

changes in congressional legislation, eligibility was extended to all
single-person households so long as they met all other requirements
and so long as they did not constitute more than 10 percent of all
enrollees at each site.

- *Residency.* Recipients had to reside within the boundaries of Brown
  County (for Green Bay) or St. Joseph County (for South Bend). Households already residing within these boundaries prior to the initiation
  of the Supply Experiment were given preference over those who moved
  in after the program began. Both homeowners and renters were
  eligible.

Actual compliance of households with these requirements was verified by
the allowance agency staff before payments were initiated to the household.

After determining a household's eligibility for the allowance program,
HAO staff calculated the subsidy benefits to which the household would be
entitled. This calculation was done using the "housing gap" formula
presented in equation 3-1, with the value of C equal to the value of C*
given for each site in table 3.3 and "b" set at 25 percent of the household's
adjusted gross income. As in the Demand Experiment, subsidy payments
could not exceed the household's actual level of housing expenditures.
This payment calculation is, of course, identical to that in one treatment
cell of the Demand Experiment, the cell numbered three in figure 3.2. As
table 3.2 indicates, monthly payments of the two sites averaged $61 and
$80 for renters and $46 and $48 for homeowners. The payments were
equivalent to between 10 and 28 percent of recipients' incomes.

The Supply Experiment's treatment for all households further paralleled the Demand Experiment's treatment cell three in requiring as a
condition for receiving allowance payments that a household occupy a
housing unit which passed the agency's minimum housing quality standards. Initial compliance with these standards was monitored by the
agency's inspection staff at the time of application. The minimum standards
imposed by the Supply Experiment were devised by Rand and were not
the same as those imposed in the Demand Experiment.[17]

As chapter 4 will discuss in more detail, as of September 1978—
when the programs were in approximately steady-state operations—
approximately 3,400 households in Green Bay and 5,800 households in
South Bend were receiving monthly payments.[18] The programs were thus
significantly larger than either the Demand Experiment or Administrative Agency site operations.

---

17. Appendix C provides an overview of these standards and a summary comparison of them among the three experiments.

18. See Rand [E130], p. 16, table 2.1.

Payments to a homeowner household were initiated as soon as their income-eligibility was certified and their housing unit had passed inspection. Payments to renter households started as soon as these two conditions were met and the HAO had received a copy of the tenant-landlord lease.[19] Once a household began to receive benefits, its housing unit was reinspected annually and at any time the household moved. The household's income and family size were recertified every six months by mail-in questionnaires. Households were also required to visit HAO offices annually to recertify income and asset information. More frequent assessments could be requested if income changed by more than $40 per month or if household size changed.

As in the Demand Experiment, the Supply Experiment's monthly housing allowance payment check was sent directly to the recipient household, and it was the household's responsibility to deliver its rental payment to landlords or mortgage payments to mortgage holders. No legal relationships existed between the HAO and either mortgagor or landlord, only between the agency and the household. Indeed, in theory, the landlord or mortgagor need never have known that the household was receiving allowance payments. The household was entirely responsible for itself: making its own decision concerning where to live; negotiating rents, repairs, and other occupancy conditions with the landlord; and obtaining the landlord's signature on the lease. As in the Demand Experiment, the agency's role in the Supply Experiment in providing services to recipient households was, by deliberate experimental policy, limited.

There were two major exceptions to this "hands off" policy in terms of HAO intervention in the housing choices of households.[20] One exception arose when a client household appeared to the HAO staff incapable of functioning in the housing market (due, for example, to limited mental

---

19. Payments to households in both the Supply Experiment and the Administrative Agency Experiment were funded under HUD's Section 23 leased housing program, and the requirement for a written lease arose from a provision in Section 23. Furthermore, prior to an amendment to the Section 23 program in October 1975, payments to homeowners in the Supply Experiment required that they sign a lease-leaseback agreement with HUD, a complexity which may have discouraged some homeowners from enrolling. Because payments to households in the Demand Experiment were funded directly through HUD research funds, no lease requirement was necessary in that program, and none was imposed.

20. In both the Demand Experiment and the Supply Experiment and in many of the sites of the Administrative Agency Experiment, the operating agency made clear to the members of its staff that they were not to provide counseling, "steering," or advice on how to deal with the housing market. Nevertheless, it is probable that at least some of this informal advising did occur, for example, during enrollment interviews or during housing inspections. The inability to exercise perfect control over the treatment, particularly in interpersonal interactions, is a recurring problem in social experiments, just as it is in operating programs.

capacity or physical frailty). In these cases, the HAO encouraged the household to enlist a friend or relative to deal with the HAO and the housing market for them, or the HAO referred the client household to other private or public social service agencies in the community and then cooperated with that agency in processing that household. The second exception was that, starting in December 1976, the HAO in South Bend produced weekly summaries of housing units available for rent in their communities and made these summaries available to households searching for new units. The HAOs initially attempted to conduct group information sessions. One session, covering program rules and procedures, was offered to program applicants, and three further voluntary sessions were offered to enrollees. These latter sessions covered both specific program information and general advice on such topics as how to make housing and neighborhood choices, how to purchase a home, how to finance and arrange for home improvements, and what to do in case of encountering discrimination. However, poor attendance forced their elimination. HAO staff continued providing some of this information on an individual basis.

Payments under the Supply Experiment will be provided for a total of 10 years, of which only the first 5 were a research period during which data were collected. At the end of the research period, administration of the program was turned over to local agencies who will determine how long applicant households will be accepted into the program. Only households enrolling at the very beginning of the program could receive benefits for the full 10 years, however, since the entire program will cease in 1984.

THE ADMINISTRATIVE AGENCY EXPERIMENT

Abt Associates, Inc., designed the Administrative Agency Experiment, monitored its operation, and analyzed its outcomes. However, in contrast to the role played by the Rand Corporation in the Supply Experiment and by Abt itself in the Demand Experiment, Abt did not create special agencies to operate the AAE housing allowance program at each site. Rather, HUD contracted directly with existing local public agencies at each site to administer housing allowances along with their other ongoing programs. The eight sites where the Administrative Agency Experiment was conducted, and the local operating agencies involved, are listed in table 3.4.

The research focus in the Administrative Agency Experiment was on exploring alternative ways to implement a housing allowance program.

Table 3.4

Sites, Operating Agencies, and Numbers of Recipients in the
Administrative Agency Experiment

Site	Agency	Number of Recipient Households [a]
Bismarck, North Dakota	Social Service Board of North Dakota	367
Durham, North Carolina	Durham County Department of Social Services	483
Jacksonville, Florida	Jacksonville Department of Housing and Urban Development	300 541 [b]
Peoria, Illinois	State of Illinois Department of Local Government Affairs, Office of Housing and Buildings	835
Salem, Oregon	Housing Authority of the City of Salem	870
San Bernardino, California	San Bernardino County Board of Supervisors	776
Springfield, Massachusetts	Commonwealth of Massachusetts Department of Community Affairs	861
Tulsa, Oklahoma	Tulsa Housing Authority	825

Source: U.S. Department of Housing and Urban Development [E165], p. 96.
  a. Represents figure after one year of program operations at each site.
  b. Second figure for Jacksonville represents second enrollment period.

Each of the eight operating agencies was given broad discretion in designing its administrative procedures for such functions as outreach, enrollment and eligibility determination, and housing inspection. The practices adopted by the agencies varied widely, and the following discussion is therefore necessarily quite general.

Enrollment began at each of the sites during the spring or summer of 1973 and continued for 9 to 13 months, at which time enrollment limits had been reached. The only exception to this pattern occurred in Jacksonville, where recruitment of program participants proved difficult, and a second enrollment period was opened for an additional 10 months starting in September of 1974.[21]

As in the Supply Experiment, each AAE agency ran a publicity and outreach campaign to inform potential recipients in their communities

21. For discussion of the Jacksonville experience, see chapters 4 and 9 of this book and Wolfe and Hamilton [C124].

of the newly available form of benefits. However, like the Demand Experiment and unlike the Supply Experiment, the AAE agencies had target recipient levels, ranging from 400 to 900 per site. Many of the AAE agencies were therefore reluctant to unleash massive publicity campaigns which, they feared, would elicit more applicants than could be served and create resentment when applicants had to be turned away. Nevertheless, agencies experimented with a variety of outreach techniques, ranging from mass media advertising (both paid and free "public service" ads) to door-to-door canvassing in low-income neighborhoods. Agencies also experimented with special outreach techniques to reach particular groups of potential enrollees such as the elderly and the working poor.[22]

Households were allowed to file applications for housing allowance benefits in a number of ways. Each of the eight agencies operated a central office where the majority of applications were taken. Most of the agencies also operated additional temporary application offices located in low-income neighborhoods or at other satellite locations. Some agencies also allowed applications to be submitted by mail, by telephone, or by interviews conducted in applicants' homes.

To receive AAE housing allowance payments, households had to fulfill eilgibility requirements similar to those in the other two experiments as follows:

- *Income and assets.* Households' net annual income[23] had to be less than limits established for each site. Table 3.1 states these limits; the median values across the eight sites for a family of four was $6,575. Additionally, six of the eight sites imposed asset limits, each selecting its own level.

- *Household composition.* As in the Demand Experiment, households were eligible if they were composed of two or more related individuals of any age, except if the household head was a full-time student or a member of the armed forces. Single-person households were eligible only if the person was age 62 or older or if he was handicapped, disabled, or displaced by public action.

- *Residency.* Again as in the Demand Experiment and unlike the Supply Experiment, only renters, not homeowners, were eligible. Households also had to reside within the boundaries established at each site (a marketwide area, generally); and households occupying publicly subsidized housing such as public housing were ineligible unless they moved.

---

22. Chapter 10 discusses the outreach techniques used in more detail.

23. The definition of net income is gross income minus: a $300 exemption per dependent and each secondary wage earner; a 5 percent standard deduction (10 percent for elderly-headed households) ; and other specific, but less important, deductions.

Information provided by clients in their applications was verified by agency staff in ways which varied from site to site and is discussed in chapter 10.

Because each AAE agency was authorized to serve only a limited number of enrollees, not all applicants could be accommodated. Each agency selected households to be enrolled from among its applicants either randomly or by a first-come, first-served rule. However, because one of the requirements of the experimental design was that each agency should gain experience serving all major groups of persons eligible for the program, these selection processes were operated separately, with separate quotas, for such groups as the working poor, the elderly, large families, the very poor, and minorities. The demographic characteristics of program participants in the AAE therefore were the product of deliberate agency policy rather than of the number of applications received.[24]

For those households selected to participate in the AAE, the level of housing allowance benefits to which they were entitled was calculated using the same formula as for all households in the Supply Experiment and households in treatment cell three in the Demand Experiment. That is, benefits were calculated with equation 3-1, with "b" set at 25 percent of program-defined income and the value of C^* shown for each site in table 3.3. As in both other experiments, a household's subsidy could not exceed its actual monthly rental expenditure.

Also as in the Supply Experiment and in treatment cell three of the Demand Experiment, eligibility for housing allowance benefits was conditional on households' occupying units which passed agencies' minimum housing quality standards. Both the level and nature of these standards and the mode by which inspections were implemented to enforce them varied among the eight AAE agencies.[25] Four agencies utilized primarily agency staff or trained professionals to conduct inspections, while the other four agencies primarily allowed households to inspect their own units using an agency-provided checklist.[26]

Enrollees had 60 days following enrollment to locate a suitable unit and have it inspected by the agency. Households who failed to find a unit within this time forfeited their rights to participate in the program. For some households, an additional 60-day search period was allowed. Households whose units were undergoing repairs which had not been completed within that time also were often granted time extensions.

Payments to households in the AAE were initiated as soon as house-

---

24. Appendix B presents data on program-eligible households and households who enrolled in the AAE.

25. The standards are described in Appendix C.

26. Chapter 10 discusses the effectiveness and costs of these alternatives.

hold income and other eligibility conditions were verified and the dwelling unit passed inspection. As table 3.2 indicates, the average monthly benefit level ranged across the eight sites from $72 to $89. Each household was entitled to payments for 24 months from the time of its enrollment, provided that both the household and its housing unit continued to meet program eligibility requirements. Housing units were reinspected and the household's income and other eligibility conditions were reexamined after one year of program participation.

As in the Demand Experiment and the Supply Experiment, administering agencies in the AAE established no contractual relationship with landlords and sent monthly allowance checks directly to recipient households.[27] Also as in the other two experiments, AAE agencies operated group information and counseling sessions for households at the time of enrollment. However, attendance at these sessions, which had been voluntary for households in the other two experiments, was mandatory for participants in the AAE. In further contrast to the other two experiments, some of the AAE agencies elected to provide fairly extensive and intensive assistance to enrolled households in their housing search process, their negotiations with landlords concerning rents and unit maintenance, and even concerning social service needs of the households independent of their housing needs. The policies adopted by various agencies are briefly summarized in chapter 10.

DIVERSITY AND CONSISTENCY

Table 3.5 summarizes some of the key aspects of program design and operation among the three experiments as they have been described in this chapter. As the table illustrates, the three experiments exhibited a pattern of similarities and differences which can perhaps best be described as coordinated diversity.

One aspect on which the three experiments differ is the most central aspect of the experimental treatment, the housing allowance subsidy itself. Of the three experiments within EHAP, only the Demand Experiment involved multiple treatment groups subjecting different groups of recipients to different subsidy formulas and program requirements. The Supply Experiment and the Administrative Agency Experiment each operated under a single method of calculating benefits, and to promote comparability across the experiments, that formula was the same for both of those experiments and also identical to treatment cell three in the Demand Experi-

---

27. Two AAE agencies, San Bernardino and Tulsa, elected to use two-party checks made out in the name of both the household and the landlord.

ment. For this reason, treatment cell three is referrd to as the "design center" of this experiment. Despite the central role which this name implies, however, it should be borne in mind that only a small number—77 households—out of all Demand Experiment recipients received the design center treatment.

Comparing the three experiments on aspects of their operations other than subsidy calculations is more problematic. The three experiments offered benefits for different periods of time, to persons recruited by different methods, whose eligibility was verified and recertified in different ways, and who were subject to housing consumption requirements of varying stringency. In many cases, the diversity of treatments arose out of a desire to tailor the procedures in each experiment to the specific research objectives of each study. In other cases, the diversity arose simply out of the difficulty of maintaining consistency among independent operations. Whatever the origins of these differences, however, their cumulative effect is that it would be misleading to think of the three experiments as implementing the "same" program. Rather, the three experiments represent 3—and sometimes as many as 12—variations around the same general concept of housing allowances.

Given these variations, we should not expect the empirical findings concerning the effects of housing allowances to be identical in all sites. Rather, we should expect that results will systematically differ in ways which can be explained and reconciled according to how and where the programs were operated. As succeeding chapters will illustrate, this sort of explicable, consistent diversity is exactly what was observed.

Table 3.5

Key Program Design Elements in the Experimental Housing Allowance Program

Design Elements	Demand Experiment	Supply Experiment	Administrative Agency Experiment
Number of sites	Two	Two	Eight
Administrative agent	Abt Associates, Inc. site office	Housing allowance office established by the Rand Corporation	Eight public agencies: two each of four types
Scale of program	1,800 households at each site	Open enrollment	300-900 households at each site
Payment of formula	Housing gap (12 groups), Percentage of rent (5 groups), Control households (2 groups)	Housing gap	Housing gap
Definition of household unit	Households of two or more related individuals; elderly, disabled, or handicapped single persons	Households of two or more related individuals; elderly, disabled, or handicapped single persons	Households of two or more related individuals; elderly, disabled, or handicapped single persons
Tenure eligibility	Renters	Homeowners and renters	Renters
Estimate of rent for adequate housing (C*)	Panel of experts; percentage variations of this estimate tested	Rent survey and panel of experts	Panel of experts

Table 3.5—Continued

Key Program Design Elements in the Experimental Housing Allowance Program

Design Elements	Demand Experiment	Supply Experiment	Administrative Agency Experiment
Household contribution rate (b)	b = .15 (1 group) b = .25 (10 groups) b = .35 (1 group)	b = .25	b = .25
Income definition	Gross income minus federal, state, and social security taxes and $300 annually per earner for work-related expenses; other specific deductions	Gross income minus $300 exemption per dependent and each secondary wage earner; 5% standard deduction (10% for elderly); other specific deductions	Gross income minus $300 exemption per dependent and each secondary wage earner; 5% standard deduction (10% for elderly); other specific deductions
Rent definition	Gross rent or contract rent plus formula-based allowance for utilities paid by household	Gross rent or contract rent plus formula-based allowance for utilities paid by household	Gross rent or contract rent plus formula-based allowance for utilities paid by household
Housing requirements (form of earmarking)	Minimum standards (5 groups); Minimum rent (6 groups); None (8 groups)	Minimum standards	Minimum standards

Source: Adapted from Carlson and Heinberg [E24], pp. 54-55.

PART III.

Household Responses

CHAPTER 4

Participation in the Experimental Housing Allowance Program

Francis J. Cronin

T HIS CHAPTER discusses the levels, patterns, and determinants of participation in the Experimental Housing Allowance Program. Both the actual outcomes—how many and what types of households participated—and the process of becoming a participant are considered.

The salient findings on participation from EHAP are as follows:

Based on the experience in the open enrollment program in the Supply Experiment

- Approximately 56 percent of all eligible renters and 40 percent of all eligible homeowners enrolled.

- Approximately 55 to 75 percent of all enrolled renters and 83 percent of all enrolled homeowners qualified for subsidies.

- Total participation rates, that is, the rates at which eligible households became payment recipients, were low in the open enrollment program: 42 percent for renters and 33 percent for homeowners.

- Turnover among eligibles, enrollees, and recipients was substantial and depended, in large part, on local economic conditions; hence, a much larger share of all eligble households participate at various points than at a given point in time.

Based on the experience of the three field operations

- Households in the overlapping groups of welfare recipients, minorities,

79

and female-headed households generally became allowance program recipients at higher rates than other households, including the elderly and the working poor.

Based on the experience of the Demand Experiment which included control households

● Participation was, in the aggregate, highly responsive to real net gain; benefits favorably influenced households' decisions at all stages, while the housing standards imposed by the program were most important in discouraging households whose housing did not meet the standard at enrollment.

Understanding the participation process as documented in EHAP—as well as the outcomes—is important for several reasons. First, at the household level, participation is the conduit through which households obtain the program's benefits. At the neighborhood level, participation links public concern and potential improvements in the housing stock and neighborhoods.

Second, the composition of the participating population affects both the distribution of program outcomes (e.g., improved housing versus rent burden reduction) and the distribution of program benefits among households of differing characteristics. With respect to the former, the interaction of program housing requirements and the stock of local housing determines the proportion of enrolled households which pass standards at enrollment. For those passing, at least in the short run, the allowance simply reduces rent burden. With respect to equity, if some groups are more reluctant than others to enroll in housing programs or if some types of households have more difficulty in finding units that meet program standards, there could be an inequitable distribution of program benefits throughout the low-income population.

Third, program costs are determined in large measure by the rate of participation, the composition of participants, and the rate of attrition. The rate of participation strongly affects aggregate transfer costs and, given the eligible population, per recipient administrative costs. The composition of participants affects administrative costs because some groups require a higher level of services to achieve participation, and some remain in the program for shorter periods. The rate of attrition affects per recipient administrative costs by influencing the number of participants among whom administrative costs are spread.

The chapter begins by discussing the actual process of participation, that is, enrolling and then receiving a subsidy. Overall enrollment and participation rates among the experiments and within the sites of each experiment are presented. Enrollment and participation rates in the Demand and Supply Experiments are examined by household demographic, economic, and tenure characteristics. Factors that influence the rate at which eligible households become enrollees and the rate at which enrollees become payment recipients are examined. Finally, the dynamics of participation in an open enrollment program are briefly analyzed. Topics such as the time path of participation and turnover among the eligible and the enrolled populations are also discussed.

THE PROCESS AND PATTERNS OF PARTICIPATION

The Process of Participation

Becoming a participant entails two distinct steps: enrollment and becoming an allowance recipient. Enrollment includes various outreach methods to inform eligible households of the program (and their eligibility) and to encourage them to enroll. Enrollment is ended when applicant households are certified as program eligible, that is, when applicant households pass eligibility checks on household income, tenure, and household composition. To receive an allowance, enrolled households must reside in units meeting the applicable program housing requirements.

Enrollment policies and procedures differed significantly among the three field operation according to an operation's in EHAP focus—household, market, or agency. The Demand and Supply Experiments were designed to gain an understanding of the participation process from the view point of the household and from the standpoint of the housing market, respectively. The Administrative Agency Experiment, by contrast, was designed to examine the effects of varying administrative procedures on participation.

In the two Demand Experiment sites, samples of households were selected on the basis of preliminary "screener" surveys; each household within the samples was individually contacted, given an explanation of the program, and offered the opportunity to enroll. The information provided to the household during this interview was more extensive than is true of typical approaches to enrolling households. The objective of such a procedure, however, was to develop a controlled sample, statistically representative of the eligible population. In the Supply Experiment, on the other hand, enrollment was open to all eligible households (both renters and homeowners) over a five-year period, with payments to continue for an additional five-year period after the end of enrollment for households remaining eligible. The program was widely and continuously publicized, but application had to be initiated by the household.

The agencies in the Administrative Agency Experiment were limited by their budgets in the total number of recipients they could enroll; and they were encouraged to enroll different types of households (e.g., elderly or minority households) so that the resultant mix would approximate the composition of the eligible population. To accomplish this, each agency placed certain controls on the enrollment process, including the methods and intensity of outreach.[1]

Patterns of Enrollment and Participation

Since enrollment procedures and objectives varied among the three experiments, it is not surprising that enrollment outcomes also differed. As shown in table 4.1, the Administrative Agency Experiment's enrollment rates have little comparability with the rates for the other experiments. There are two reasons for this. First, the estimates of eligible households are subject to more error than in either of the other two experiments.[2] Second, limits were placed on the number of recipients at each site. The former difference helps explain the high variance across the eight sites; the estimates range from a low of 10 percent in Jacksonville and San Bernardino to a high of 47 percent in Salem. The latter difference helps explain the generally lower rates observed in the Administrative Agency Experiment, that is, a median rate of 22 percent.

On the other hand, enrollment rates of renter households in the four sites of the Demand and Supply Experiments are quite similar, as are the enrollment rates of homeowners in the two Supply Experiment sites. In the Demand Experiment, enrollment averaged 51 percent; for comparable households in the Supply Experiment, the rate averaged 56 percent. In fact, the results are highly consistent—with the rates in the four sites ranging between 49 and 57 percent. Rates for homeowners in the two Supply Experiment sites were equally consistent: 42 percent in Green Bay and 39 percent in South Bend. These figures are for the fourth year of program operation in Green Bay and the third year in South Bend and are thought to represent steady-state rates.

---

1. See chapter 10 and MacMillan and Hamilton et al. [C63].

2. Estimates of eligibles in the Demand Experiment are exact since an eligible household is defined as one offered the possibility of becoming a program participant; estimates of eligibles in the Supply Experiment are based on extensive sampling. In the Administrative Agency Experiment, on the other hand, estimates of eligibles are based on 1970 Census data. These data were four years old at the time (and analysis in the Supply Experiment has indicated significant changes in the eligible population in only two years), could not be classified exactly to eligibility criteria (e.g., wealth limitation), and, in some cases, lacked geographical comparability with program jurisdictions.

Unlike enrollment rates, which indicated fairly comparable rates by tenure among the experiments, participation rates show a much higher variance among the experiments, most of which appears related to the stringency of program standards.[3] Within the experiments, participation rates show a high degree of comparability; most of the differences at this level appear related to local housing conditions and special circumstances. In the Administrative Agency Experiment, the experiment generally considered to have the least stringent standards on average, the mean participation rate is 53 percent.[4] Excluding the two extremes, the six remaining rates vary from 46 to 66. In the Demand Experiment, the experiment with the strictest housing standards, the participation rate averages 27 percent. The mean participation rate for renters in the Supply Experiment is 42 percent. Part of the difference between the Demand and Supply Experiments is the greater stringency with which standards were imposed in the Demand Experiment. For homeowners in the Supply Experiment, the mean participation rate is 33 percent, significantly below the rate for renters.[5] Finally, note the difference between Green Bay and South Bend. The generally better condition of the housing stock in Green Bay is partially responsible for this result.

A number of factors—outreach, level of payments, and housing requirements—influenced the rate at which households enrolled in the programs. The role of these salient factors is discussed in the next section.

The entries in table 4.2 reveal the net effect of these factors for families distinguished by ethnicity, sex of head, and population group—elderly-headed households, welfare recipients, and working poor. Note that the samples used here are not the same as those underlying the figures in table 4.1; most importantly the data from the Supply Experiment in table 4.2 are from an earlier point in time. When examining renters in the Demand and Supply Experiments, data show welfare recipients enrolled at high levels, the elderly at low levels, and the working poor at moderate levels. Likewise, households headed by a minority or by a female

---

3. These participation rates are lower than those for programs such as AFDC (See Bendick [H12]). Explanations for this are offered under "Factors Affecting Participation" where the determinants of successfully making the step from enrollee to recipient status are discussed. The constrained nature of the subsidy in EHAP (i.e., imposing a housing standard), the higher nominal value of benefit levels in AFDC, and differences in eligible populations render difficult comparison between these two programs.

It should also be noted that the definition of participation used in this book employs a more comprehensive definition of the eligible population than that used in the Demand Experiment.

4. Participation rates in the Administrative Agency Experiment are defined as the proportion of *selected applicants* receiving a payment.

5. Participation rates in the Supply Experiment mask a good deal of turnover, implying that a larger number of households participate at some time.

Table 4.1

Enrollment and Participation Rates at the Twelve EHAP Sites

Experiment/Site	Specific Experiment Approach	Estimated Number of Eligible Households [a]	Number of Households Enrolled [b]	Enroll-ment Rate (percentage)	Number of Households Receiving a Payment [c]	Partici-pation Rate (percent-age)
Administrative Agency Experiment	Limited publicity, participant-initiated applications, ceiling on number of recipients, limited enrollment period, renters only.					
Bismarck		2,176	569	26	430	74 [d]
Durham		5,620	1,231	22	516	46
Jacksonville		17,429	1,696	10	339	21
Peoria		5,235	2,064	39	935	54
Salem		5,232	2,434	47	948	55
San Bernardino		19,745	1,926	10	822	64
Springfield		17,572	2,334	13	851	63
Tulsa		8,734	1,850	21	915	66
Mean				17		53
Demand Experiment [e]	Individually contacted households, one-time enrollment offer, renters only.					
Phoenix		989	524	53	273	28
Pittsburgh		1,157	563	49	300	26
Mean				51		27
Supply Experiment Renters	Continuous publicity, participant-initiated applications, open enrollment, renters and homeowners.					
Green Bay		3,696	2,122	57	1,775	48
South Bend		4,717	2,549	54	1,770	38
Mean				56		42

Homeowners					
Green Bay	7,729	3,266	42	2,835	37
South Bend	15,081	5,820	39	4,718	31
Mean			40		33

Sources: AAE, Temple et al. [E150]; Demand, Kennedy et al. [H63]; Supply, communication from Rand, January 14, 1980.

a. Estimates of the eligible populations in the three experiments employ varying procedures. In the Administrative Agency Experiment, estimates of the eligible population are based on 1970 Census data. Limitations in applying program eligible criteria to the Census data mean that the estimates are approximations. (For a discussion of how these estimates were derived, see Mac-Millan [C63].) In the Demand Experiment, estimates are based on the number of households contacted regarding enrollment. In the Supply Experiment, estimates are based on the number of eligibles calculated from experimental surveys during the fourth year of program operations in Green Bay and the third year in South Bend. (The net change in eligibles from baseline to the current period of operations is less than 5 percent in each tenure-site class.)

b. The entries for the Administrative Agency Experiment indicate the number of *applicant* households initially deemed eligible. Not all of these households were enrolled due to some being found ineligible and ceilings on the number of potential recipients requiring agencies to select only some eligible applicants. In the Demand Experiment, entries are for households accepting the initial enrollment offer. In the Supply Experiment, entries are for households enrolled during the fourth year of program operations in Green Bay and the third year in South Bend.

c. In the Administrative Agency Experiment, the entries are for households who received a subsidy before the expiration of their enrollment period. (Recall that enrolled households typically had no more than 60 days in which to find housing that met housing standards.) In the Demand Experiment, the entries are for households who received a payment at any time during the first year of program operations. In the Supply Experiment, the entries are for households currently receiving a payment during the fourth year of program operations in Green Bay and the third year in South Bend.

d. In the Administrative Agency Experiment, the participation rate is defined as the proportion of *selected applicants* (applicants offered enrollment) who received a subsidy before the expiration of their enrollment period.

e. The entries are for households enrolled in housing gap plans 1 through 9.

Table 4.2

Participation Rates by Household Group in the Two Housing Allowance Experiments

	Population Group [a]			Sex of Head		Race/Ethnicity [b]	
	Elderly	Welfare	Working Poor	Male	Female	Minority	Non-Minority
Demand [c]							
Percentage of eligibles who enrolled	43	77	54	53	61	62	56
Percentage of enrollees who became recipients	35	52	58	51	50	43	54
Percentage of eligibles who became recipients	15	40	31	27	31	27	30
Supply [d]							
Renters							
Percentage of eligibles enrolled	39	72	50	38	68	74	49
Percentage of enrollees who became recipients	80	70	68	67	73	62	73
Percentage of eligibles who became recipients	31	50	34	25	50	46	36

Homeowners							
Percentage of eligibles enrolled	23	39	35	20	36	46	25
Percentage of enrollees who became recipients	88	76	80	81	84	76	84
Percentage of eligibles who became recipients	20	30	28	16	30	35	21

Source: [E45], p. 29; Carlson and Heinberg [E24], pp. 11, 17.

a. Households are characterized as elderly if the head is 65 years of age or older; welfare, if they receive any income from welfare and are nonelderly; working poor, if they are neither elderly nor welfare households.

b. Households that are headed by a black, Spanish-American, Oriental, or Native-American individual.

c. The entries for enrollment are for those households offered enrollment n housing gap plans 1 through 9. For analytic purposes, households are also excluded with incomes above the eligibility income used for plans 4, 9, and 11. The entries for participation are for those households receiving a payment at the end of the first year of program operations.

d. The entries are based on the number of households enrolled as of June 1976 in Green Bay (24 months of open enrollment) and December 1976 in South Bend (21.5 months). Entries for minority renters and homeowners and for welfare homeowners reflect fewer than 200 households enrolled in each category in Green Bay. Entries for participation are for the proportions of households ever enrolled who ever received a payment.

enrolled at higher rates than other types of households. The enrollment gaps among these groups are striking in the Supply Experiment sites compared to the experience in the Demand Experiment Sites. The same broad patterns also hold for owner-occupant households in the two Supply Experiment sites.

The rate at which enrolled households become recipients varied considerably among sites and experiments. The figures in table 4.2 for the "percentage of enrollees who became participants" provide the essential information. They show the percentage of enrolled households achieving recipient status in the two Demand Experiment sites to be significantly lower than in the Supply Experiment. At the end of the first year, the average participation rate in the Demand Experiment for welfare recipient enrollees required to meet housing quality standards was 52 percent. In the Supply Experiment, by contrast, the average rate was 70 percent for renters and 76 percent for homeowners. One important reason for the lower rate in the Demand Experiment appears to be the more stringent housing standards used in this experiment.[6]

Minority households generally had less success in becoming recipients in all three experiments. Minority families generally had to do more to achieve recipient status. Because their housing conditions at enrollment were frequently worse than nonminority families, more minorities found it necessary to move or upgrade their units in order to receive payments. Elderly families and homeowners in the Supply Experiment sites, on the other hand, had relatively high rates of achieving recipient status once enrolled, presumably because of the good condition of their housing.

Finally, the net effect of enrolling and receiving a payment—the percentage of eligible households who actually receive payments—is shown in the rows labeled "percentage of eligibles who became recipients." Substantial variance in the outcome for specific groups of households is indicated. In the open enrollment programs at the Supply Experiment sites, the overlapping groups of welfare recipients, female-headed households, and households headed by minorities have high participation rates. By contrast, the elderly- and male-headed households participated at low rates, 31 and 25 percent respectively. Similar patterns emerge for homeowners in the Supply Experiment sites, although with lower average participation rates and smaller variances among household types. These figures indicate that certain groups believed disadvantaged in the market —for example, minorities and welfare recipients—are able to successfully use housing allowances.

---

6. Standards in all three field operations are described and compared in Appendix C.

FACTORS AFFECTING ENROLLMENT

The Effectiveness of Outreach

Agencies participating in the AAE had to enroll 400 to 900 recipients, generally representative of the eligible populations in their areas. Outreach was geared to meeting this objective.

Most agencies in the AAE had difficulty in generating a sufficient number of eligible applicants to fulfill their goal. Except for Salem, the agencies received from 8 to 53 percent fewer eligible applications than had initially been thought necessary to insure a representative sample for the eligible population. Elderly households and the "working poor" (low-income households earning at least part of their income) were underrepresented among applicants, while households receiving welfare and other grant income were consistently overrepresented.[7] In fact, the initial application rate from eligibles was generally so low that most agencies responded by intensifying their outreach efforts to generate increased applications and reach the desired number of recipients.

Much of the agencies' outreach consisted of contacts with social service agencies and community organizations. About a quarter of the applicants were referred by such organizations, and these applicants were highly concentrated among minorities and welfare recipients.[8] The other major type of outreach was use of the mass media—television, radio, newspaper, and pamphlets—which attracted over a third of the applicants. The people responding to media sources were much more representative of the eligible population, although the unrepresentative patterns persisted among them. Several agencies that attempted to target their outreach activities to the underrepresented groups met with some success. More commonly, however, the introduction of targeted campaigns produced results indistinguishable from the effects of merely intensifying outreach: more members of both the underrepresented and the overrepresented groups applied.[9]

---

7. In fact, enrollees in the Administrative Agency Experiment were not representative of the eligible populations. See MacMillan and Hamilton [C63] and Appendix A.

While the planned number of applicants varied greatly among the sites (e.g., from 1200 to 4200), the actual number of eligible applicants was fairly constant except for the two smallest agencies, Bismarck and Durham. The latter two agencies received 569 and 1231 applicants, respectively. All other agencies received approximately 2000 applications from eligibles (i.e., from 1696 to 2434).

8. See Hamilton, Budding, and Holshouser [C31], p. 11.

9. Targeted outreach throughout the enrollment period, as opposed to brief campaigns responding to unrepresentative patterns, were more effective. Jacksonville (in its second enrollment period) and Tulsa targeted outreach to the working poor and achieved quite representative proportions of applicants from that group.

Given the personalized outreach methods used to inform potential enrollees in the Demand Experiment and the bias and constraints present in the estimates of enrollment rates in the Administrative Agencies' sites, the most policy-relevant enrollment experience for an open-enrollment program is that of the two Supply Experiment sites, where the program was available to all eligible households with no restrictive time constraints on the enrollment period. Outreach in these two sites was conducted primarily through the media and direct mail. Advertising and media publicity were the sources of information cited by about 50 percent of all Supply Experiment applicants.[10] Analysis of outreach results indicated, however, that advertising could convey only the simplest messages; and attempts to provide households with enough data to determine their own eligibility were generally unsuccessful.[11] By the end of the second year of operations, about 75 percent of all household heads in South Bend had at least heard about the program.[12]

Two conclusions from this discussion might be drawn. First, site operations have shown fairly convincingly that the community's awareness of a housing program and the rate of application can both be increased through outreach. But the results give only slight confirmation to the hypothesis that the mix of eligible applicants could be altered by outreach strategies, particularly in the short run. Based on this first conclusion and the propensity of particular types of eligibles to enroll early— most obviously those already in welfare programs who have more information available to them—a second conclusion emerges concerning the equity of limited-entitlement programs: unless steps are taken from the start to achieve a mix of applicants with members of all household groups, the program may distribute benefits quite unevenly among the groups constituting the eligible population. Of course, other programs may "overserve" these other groups, so that parity across groups is achieved. Still, this characteristic of a limited enrollment allowance program is an important finding.

The Impact of Payment Levels and Housing Requirements

In brief, housing requirements and subsidy levels have little effect on enrollment. The effects of subsidy levels and the type of housing requirement on enrollment have been examind for households in the Demand Ex-

---

10. Racial minorities and welfare recipients were the least and the elderly the most media-oriented of all applicants.

11. Rand [E130], p. 153.

12. Rand [E129], p. 22.

periment analyses.[13] Acceptance rates increase very slightly as the size of the payment increases. Acceptance rates in Phoenix increase 8 percentage points as the payment increases from an average of $50 per month to an average $93 per month. A similar but even weaker relationship holds in Pittsburgh.

There appears to be only a slight difference in the acceptance rates between programs with no housing requirements and programs with minimum requirements; but no apparent difference exists among the acceptance rates for the programs with standards. In Phoenix, programs without requirements have an average acceptance rate about 6 percentage points higher than those with requirements. Among the latter, however, the rates vary by only 3 percentage points. Quite similar patterns are found in the data for Pittsburgh.[14]

Households at the acceptance stage apparently responded to the program's potential subsidy as an unconstrained grant, due possibly to a lack of understanding of the requirements or an "I'll worry about that later" attitude.[15] Certainly, a given dollar amount for the subsidy (the potential gain) is more clearly understood than a quick description of, say, the minimum standards requirement. Interestingly, even in the easily understandable plans requiring minimum rent payments, rates of acceptance were not affected. It may be that, even when requirements were understood, households tended to be unwilling to foreclose their options at this stage.

FACTORS AFFECTING PARTICIPATION

The more important factors influencing whether or not a household was successful in achieving recipient status after enrolling are reviewed here. These include the gain perceived by the household from

---

13. The data presented in Kennedy and MacMillan [H64] should be used for cross-experimental comparisons only with care. Eligible households are defined as a *subset* of all households contacted regarding enrollment; in particular, only households completing the enrollment interview (i.e., received an estimate of their allowance payment) are classified as "eligible." Estimates of enrollment rates in the Supply Experiment, on the other hand, are based on *all* eligible households, whether or not they know they are eligible, let alone their potential subsidy. In fact, outreach efforts in the Supply Experiment aimed at providing households with the data to determine their eligibility were unsuccessful.

14. See Kennedy and MacMillan [H64], pp. 2-13, 2-14.

15. To date, no analysis has examined the relationship between the household's decision to enroll and the *household's* perceived value of the subsidy (i.e., the income equivalent variation of the subsidy) as is described in "Factors Affecting Participation" for the household's decision to participate.

becoming a recipient, the program's housing requirement, market conditions (among them the average mobility in a site), and minority status. The patterns are described here factor by factor; for example, the role of the size of the potential payment offered is considered in and of itself. Hence, while low-income households may be found to be highly attracted by the larger subsidy offer, they may be repelled by the housing requirements. The combined effect of all these factors are the participation rates for specific household groups which were presented previously.

The Gain from Participation

An economic view of the household's decision to participate in a housing allowance program is based on the assumption that a household acts rationally in its own self-interest—in other words, a household attempts to maximize its well-being given its resources and the constraints it faces. As we shall see, viewing EHAP in this context yields insights on the impact of program features on household behavior.

In essence, a housing allowance offers a household additional resources (e.g., for households in housing gap programs—additional income) if the household is income-eligible for the program and successfully meets the housing requirements imposed by the program. The household must evaluate whether receipt of the subsidy payment increases its well-being sufficiently to compensate for the bother (costs) of meeting the requirement if that household would not normally meet the requirement.

Like an income maintenance program, the housing allowance program standardizes the benefits to eligible households of a given size and income. However, this standard treatment is affected by the housing requirement. The household's evaluation of its gain may vary if it fails to meet the housing requirement and would not do so even if it were to obtain the subsidy payment. For such a household, the real value of the subsidy may be substantially less than the nominal payment.[16] In addition, the cost of meeting the requirement varies by the household's pre-program housing condition. If the household's dwelling unit fails to pass program standards, the household must either upgrade or relocate to a unit which passes standards. Either option may entail substantial costs.

The difference between the nominal value of the subsidy and the value the household attaches to the subsidy is determined by the house-

---

16. In this case, the household would likely be made just as well off with a smaller unrestricted cash grant as it would be if it passed the housing requirement and received the subsidy. In essence, the program would require the household to consume an amount of housing different from the amount it would freely choose to consume. The greater this difference, the smaller the unrestricted cash grant that would make the household just as well off. Economists refer to this cash grant as the income equivalent variation. See Cronin [H23; H31].

Table 4.3

Households' Average Evaluation of the Subsidy Offer as a Percentage of the Nominal Subsidy by Site, Type of Subsidy, and Type of Housing Requirement

	Phoenix	Pittsburgh
No Housing Requirement		
Unconstrained	1.00	1.00
Percentage of Rent	.91	.92
Housing Requirement		
Minimum rent low	.98	1.00
Minimum rent high	.91	1.00
Minimum standards	.82	.97

Source: Cronin [H23], pp. 24, 25, 40.
Sample: All enrolled households paying full market rents in nonsubsidized rental housing.

hold's preference for housing and the difference between the government's mandated level of housing consumption and the houshold's desired amount of housing consumption. The greater the difference between the government's view and that of the household, the less the household values the subsidy.

Applying the economic model of household behavior discussed in the note at the end of this chapter, estimates of the household's evaluation of the allowance offer have been made. Table 4.3 presents the results by site, type of subsidy, and type of housing requirement. By definition, unconstrained payments are valued at 100 percent of their face value; percentage of rent payments, while not having a housing requirement, change the market's price of housing and cause the household to be only as well off as it would be with an unconstrained payment of about 8 percent less.[17] Households in programs with housing requirements attach less and less value to the subsidy as the stringency of the housing requirement increases. The lowest valuation is for households in Phoenix under the minimum standards requirement plan; they value the offer at only 82 percent of its face value.[18]

---

17. The distortion caused by a price rebate and its implications are discussed in Cronin [H23].

18. Relative to estimates of the average value placed on subsidies by participants in production-oriented programs, the EHAP figures, on average, are extremely high (i.e., the subsidies are efficient). Estimates of the average value attached to the subsidy by participants in production-oriented programs range from 33 to 90 percent with an average of 69 percent. See Cronin [H23], p. 39.

Table 4.4

The Proportion of Households Constrained by the Program and the Households' Average Evaluation of the Subsidy by Housing Requirement, Race of the Household Head, and Household Size in Phoenix

Housing Requirement and House- hold Size	Nonminority		Minority	
	Proportion Constrained	Average Subsidy Value for Constrained Households	Proportion Constrained	Average Subsidy Value for Constrained Households
Low minimum rent				
1	0	N.A.	.75	.99
2	0	N.A.	.64	.99
3-4	0	N.A.	.59	.94
5-6	0	N.A.	1.00	.92
7 or more	0	N.A.	1.00	.84
High minimum rent				
1	.22	1.00	1.00	.37
2	.27	1.00	.66	.83
3-4	.16	.98	.84	.69
5-6	1.00	.96	.91	.75
7 or more	1.00	.94	1.00	.50
Minimum standards				
1	.61	.98	.89	.74
2	.22	.98	.86	.79
3-4	.64	.97	.87	.55
5-6	.95	.96	1.00	.55
7 or more	1.00	.76	1.00	.13

Source: Cronin [H23], pp. 22, 25.
Sample: All households enrolled in housing gap treatment plans 1 through 11 paying full market rents in nonsubsidized rental housing.

The stringency of the housing requirement can affect certain groups more adversely than others. Table 4.4 presents the proportion of households constrained by the program and the average household evaluation of the subsidy offer by housing requirement, race of the head of household, and household size for housing gap households in Phoenix. With only one exception, a higher proportion of minority households at each household size is constrained by the program; and, without exception, minority households constrained by the program place a lower value on the subsidy than do nonminority households.[19] The combination of these two factors results in an average subsidy value of only 56 percent for all minority households under the minimum standards plan in Phoenix.

With respect to household size, larger households of both racial groups are constrained by the program at higher rates than are small households; and, larger households constrained by the program generally value the subsidy at lower rates than do smaller households. For example, viewing the minimum standards plan, the average value placed on the subsidy by all nonminority households of seven or more persons is 76 percent; for all similar minority households, the average value attached to the subsidy is only 13 percent.

The explanation behind the lower valuation by minorities and large households is the poor quality of housing initially occupied. A large increase in housing consumption would be required to conform with program standards—contrary to "revealed preferences." Of course, current "preferences" are determined in part by discrimination and other factors which constrain the housing choices of these groups.

First-year participation results for Demand Experiment households enrolled in one program—the housing gap program with housing requirements—are presented here within the benefit-cost framework just described.[20] Initially, outcomes for households participating at any time during the first year are discussed; then outcomes for households which failed to qualify at enrollment are presented.

The proportions of enrolled households participating at any time during the first year are depicted in figure 4.1 by site, by the value of the

---

19. The lower value placed on the subsidy by minority households in Phoenix results from the housing requirement being relatively further from the predicted amount of housing minority households would freely select than is the case for nonminority households. For example, for constrained households of seven or more persons, the estimated cost of the housing requirement is 32 percent more than an estimate of what nonminority households would desire to spend; for minority households, however, the figure is 101 percent.

The value minority households attach to the subsidy may be biased downward. If minorities have been unable to freely select their housing in the past, the data employed to predict the amount of housing "preferred" by minorites may give a misleading indication of the "true" preferences of minorities.

20. Due to the individualized outreach procedures employed in the Demand Experiment (designed to attract a representative sample of eligible households; see "Factors Affecting Enrollment"), participation outcomes for enrolled households can be viewed as the response to the eligible population only to the program features tested. Due to the short duration of the Demand Experiment, however, households should be more responsive to program features during the program's initial stage. (Chapter 8 discusses potential sources of experimental contamination.) In addition, one year should be long enough to allow households capable of being influenced by the program to react. Some results for the two years are presented here. For other results, see Kennedy and MacMillan [H64].

Figure 4.1

The Proportion of Enrolled Households Participating during the First
Year by Site, by Households' Evaluation of Benefits, and by Program
Housing Requirements

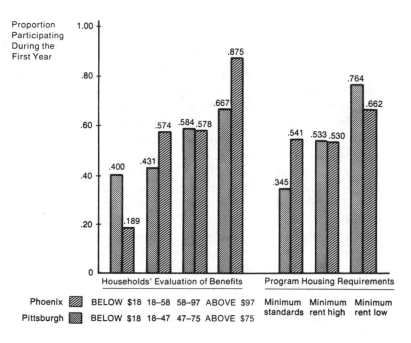

Sample: Households paying full market rents (i.e., not related to landlord,
not working in lieu of rent, not living in subsidized housing) and
enrolled in housing gap plans with housing requirements, excluding
households which terminated for nonprogram reasons (e.g., moved
out of the area).

subsidy to the households, and by the type of housing requirement.[21] The
question of the responsiveness of housholds to program benefits can be
answered without reservation: the proportion of households participating
increases steadily as the size of the benefit increases. In Phoenix, 19

21. Both of these relationships are statistically significant and similar to those
depicted in figure 4.1 when tested within a multivariate model of dichotomous choice.
Variables included in the model are program benefits; type of housing requirement;
the household's normal probability of moving; household size; household income; and
the sex, race, and age of the head of household. See Cronin [H31].

percent of the enrolled households evaluating the subsidy at $18 or less per month participate; 88 percent of the enrolled households evaluating the subsidy at $95 or more per month participate. While not quite as dramatic, the pattern for Pittsburgh is just as clear: of households evaluating the subsidy at $18 or less, 40 percent participate; of households evaluating the subsidy at $75 or more per month, 67 percent participate.[22]

Program housing requirements also have the expected impact—as the requirement becomes more stringent, the proportion of households participating falls. As shown in the right-hand panel of figure 4.1, participation rates are highest under the weakest requirement—the low minimum rent requirement—and lowest under the toughest, that is, the minimum physical standard. Although not shown in the figure, participation also falls off as the number of dwelling deficiencies rises under a minimum standards approach.[23]

While highly informative, the outcomes displayed in figure 4.1 are strongly influenced by preenrollment housing conditions—households passing standards at enrollment need not react to program features. Household reactions to variations in program features are more clearly demonstrated by viewing the participation outcomes for only those households failing housing requirements at enrollment. These households must explicitly react to program features if they wish to participate.

Data on the participation rates of Demand Experiment enrolless who failed housing requirements at enrollment disaggregated by households' evaluation of the benefits and by the type of housing requirement are displayed in figure 4.2. Once again, households are seen to be highly responsive to the real gains from participation: in both sites, a steadily increasing proportion of households participate as the gain increases.[24]

The pattern of participation by type of housing requirement is surprising. In neither site does the variation in the stringency of housing standards appear to have an important effect on the probability of households eventually participating once households fail to qualify initially. Thus stringency of housing standard acts as an initial screening mechanism, channeling subsidies to households who already reside in program-acceptable units. While the standards appear to have little if any impact on participation after enrollment, their total effect can be substantial, as inferred from the patterns reviewed in the first section of this chapter.

The effects of housing standards can be viewed more broadly by con-

---

22. At an average payment of $97 per month, the predicted probability of participating in Pittsburgh is 75 percent.

23. This is documented in chapter 5, using data from the Supply Experiment.

24. This relationship remains statistically significant when tested in the multivariate model of dichotomous choice discussed above.

Figure 4.2

The Proportion of Enrolled Households Which Failed Standards at Enrollment but Participated During the First Year by Site, by Households' Evaluation of Benefits, and by Program Housing Requirements

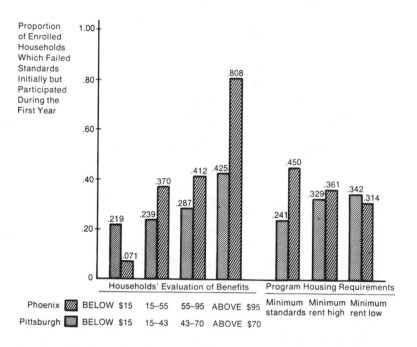

Sample: Households paying full market rents (i.e., not related to landlord, not working in lieu of rent, not living in subsidized housing) and enrolled in housing gap plans with housing requirements, excluding households which terminated for nonprogram reasons (e.g., moved out of the area).

sidering data from all three experiments shown in table 4.5. At enrollment, less than 50 percent of all households in each experiment passed the minimum standards housing requirement. In fact, only 17 percent of households in the Demand Experiment qualified for payments at enrollment. Across all 12 sites, the percentage of households qualifying for payments ranged from a low of 6 in Jacksonville to a high of 60 in Bismark.

By the end of two years, approximately half of the recipients of allowances had already met the requirements at enrollment, ranging from 34 to 70 percent across 11 of the sites. In Jacksonville, however, only 19

Table 4.5

Percentage of Households Meeting Housing Requirements at Enrollment

		Enrolled Households Meeting Requirements at Enrollment	Recipients Meeting Requirements at Enrollment
Demand Experiment			
Pittsburgh		15%	36%
Phoenix		19	34
Supply Experiment			
Green Bay	renters	52	57
	owners	50	56
South Bend	renters	41	44
	owners	49	56
Administrative Agency Experiment			
Salem		39	46
Springfield		27	38
Peoria		36	56
San Bernardino		29	35
Bismarck		60	70
Jacksonville		6	19
Durham		32	45
Tulsa		30	35

Source: U.S. Department of Housing and Urban Development [E165].

percent of the recipients had met the relatively stringent housing requirements at enrollment. For the other recipients, the principal path to qualification varied among the experiments. In the Demand and Administrative
Agency sites, most met requirements by moving. The high degree of
qualifying through mobility in the former was prompted by the stringent
standards and the difficulty of upgrading failed items (principally light
and ventilation failures); among the AAE sites, the limited time period
in which to qualify may have precluded significant upgrading.

In the Supply Experiment, on the other hand, most of those not meeting requirements at enrollment met them by upgrading their units rather
than by moving. This was true of both renters and owners. The dominance
of upgrading in place may be attributed to (a) the less stringent standards and the greater ease of upgrading failed items (the most common
defect being missing hand railings); and (b) the much longer period for
enrollment; in effect, a household, if eligible, could enroll at any time
during the five-year enrollment period.[25]

25. Dwelling deficiencies and upgrading are discussed further in chapter 8.

In summary, if housing requirements are difficult to meet, then a small portion of those receiving payments will be households that were able to meet the requiremnts initially—about a third in the Demand Experiment compared with more than half in the Supply Experiment. The rest will be mostly those households that are more mobile and able to move to units that meet the requirements.

The Impact of Services [26]

Supportive services are administrative activities intended to help enrollees become recipients and improve the quality of their housing. As detailed in chapter 10, varying services were offered across the three experiments and among the eight sites in the Administrative Agency Experiment. Among the services provided, information services were found to make a difference in program outcomes. Evidence from the AAE suggests that shoppers who face a strict standard in tight and segregated markets were aided in their housing search by program information and housing information sessions. This may indicate that the need for services inheres in the housing standard. Agency information on where to search also helped to explain which of the experimental households who were not required to meet the standard did so in the Demand Experiment.

Site Factors Affecting the Role of Achieving Recipient Status [27]

Besides program features like housing requirements and payment levels, several site specific factors were important contributors to the patterns of achieving recipient status. First, the condition of housing at the sites is associated with rates at which enrollees became participants. This was demonstrated most vividly in the two Supply Experiment sites, where uniform housing standards were applied to units in both Green Bay and South Bend. The overall failure rate for preenrollment dwellings for renters and homeowners in Green Bay (through September 1976) was 49 percent, compared to a 56 percent rate in South Bend. In addition, units in South Bend averaged more critical defects causing failures. This reflects the generally poorer condition of South Bend's housing stock.

A second factor is differential site mobility rates; the effect of higher rates is to help overcome a high failure rate at enrollment and increase the probability of achieving recipiency status. Substantial variation exists

---

26. This section is based on Bernsten [H13].
27. This discussion is taken from Carlson and Heinberg [E24].

across metropolitan areas and should be taken into account along with the state of the local housing stock.[28]

The final factor concerns the tightness of the housing market and the extent of residential segregation. An extreme example is Jacksonville in the Administrative Agency Experiment, where the low vacancy rate for inner-city rental housing and a racially segmented market for lower-rent housing was combined with two other elements previously mentioned— a high rate of units not meeting broad standards of decency, and strict housing standards in the program—to produce relatively low rates of households achieving recipiency status, particularly among blacks.

Household Mobility Rates

If the household fails requirements initially but would normally have moved in the absence of the allowance program, the household is much more likely to meet requirements during the year and receive a subsidy. In effect, the household must evaluate the program benefits relative to only the *incremental* costs of finding a unit passing standards, not total moving costs.[29] The left-hand panel of figure 4.3, using data from the first year of the Demand Experiment for households in programs with physical standards, shows that as the normal probability of moving increases so does the proportion of households participating.[30] At the lower range of probability of moving, the proportions of households participating are around 40 percent; at the upper end, the proportions are 65 to 80 percent.[31] The same very strong pattern, illustrated in the right-hand panel of the figure, holds for households whose dwellings failed the physical inspection at enrollment.

THE DYNAMICS OF PARTICIPATION

Up to this point our discussion has considered a static participation process, that is, viewing households at one or more points in time and examin-

---

28. See Goodman [H44].

29. That is, if the household has decided to move anyway, it has decided to bear the costs of searching and moving, loss of length-of-tenure discount and information capital, and any psychic costs. The gains from the program would then be compared with only the extra costs induced by the program.

30. Since receipt of a subsidy may decrease the probability of moving (households may not wish to jeopardize their payments by moving to a unit not passing standards), this relationship may actually be understated in figure 4.3.

31. The relationship shown in the figure is significant when tested in the multivariate model of dichotomous choice discussed earlier.

Figure 4.3

The Proportion of Enrolled Households in the Demand Experiment Participating in the First Year by Site, by Households' Normal Probability of Moving, and Whether a Dwelling Passed Physical Inspection at Enrollment

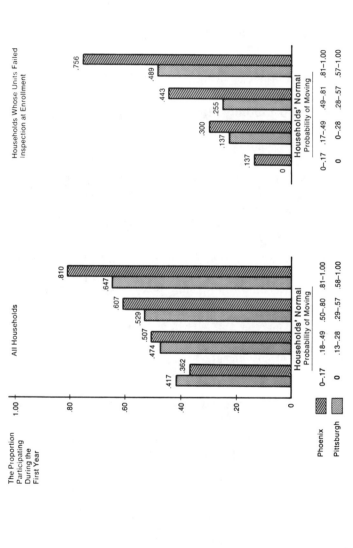

Sample: Households paying full market rents (i.e., not related to landlord, not working in lieu of rent, not living in subsidized housing) and enrolled in housing gap plans with housing requirements, excluding households which terminated for nonprogram reasons (e.g., moved out of the area).

ing the determinants and outcomes of their attempts to become participants. Now, we briefly examine the dynamics of the participation process,
that is, changes in the pools of eligibles, enrollees, and participants. Data
from the Supply Experiment are employed.[32]

Initially, about 20 percent of all households in each Supply Experiment site were eligible, but turnover in the pool of eligibles has been rapid;
it has fluctuated with local economic conditions. In an analysis of survey
records for nonmoving households using 1974 and 1975 data for Green
Bay, it was found that 10 percent of those surveyed had changed their
eligibility status. Of the households initially eligible, 26 percent had become ineligible; of this 26 percent, 76 percent reported earnings as their
main source of income. Of the households initially ineligible, only 4 percent became eligible; of this 4 percent, 68 percent reported earnings as
their main source of income. Eligibility changes for households supported
by welfare payments (all of whom were initially eligible) were almost
nonexistent. The net effect of this turnover during the first program year was
to decrease the eligible population by 11 percent. More recent estimates,
based on data for a longer time period and on more sophisticated analysis,
indicate that the turnover in the eligible population is about 20 percent
per year and that the size of the eligible population is stable over several
years.[33]

Much of the first year's turnover was linked to changes in local economic conditions. For example, households who became eligible after
being laid off during the 1973-1974 recession lost their eligibility when
they were rehired and their income rose. Abrupt changes in incomes,
especially among young couples with children, are therefore the primary
causes of changes in the pool of eligibles. Indeed, for such households,
housing allowances have been characterized as "a kind of supplemental
unemployment insurance tiding the family over a few months of hard
times." [34] While the households which received such "tiding over" are,
doubtless, grateful for the assistance, the use of housing allowance payments as supplemental unemployment insurance is an expensive and in-
efficient means to distribute unemployment payments.

During the first year of the program, enrollment in both sites grew
rapidly (figure 4.4). Total enrollment grew less rapidly during the second
year due to terminations; by the end of the second year, nearly 30 percent of all those ever enrolled had terminated, either voluntarily or in-

---

32. This discussion is based on data in the Fourth Annual Report of the Supply
Expriment. See Rand [E129], pp. 51-56.

33. Communication from Rand to U.S. Department of Housing and Urban
Development, March 13, 1980.

34. Rand [E129], p. x.

Figure 4.4

Current Enrollment and Participation Status: Housing Allowance
Programs in the Green Bay and South Bend Sites

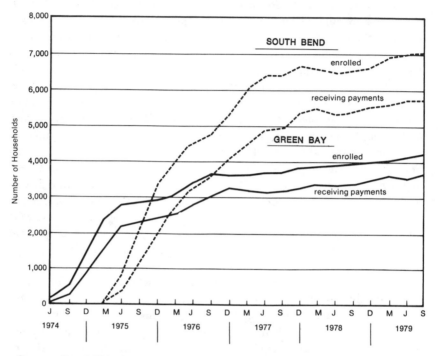

Source: Rand [E131], p. 18.

voluntarily. The major reason for termination was the loss of income
eligibility usually discovered at semiannual recertifications. Once again,
young couples with children had the highest termination rate. While the
program's period of operation is still rather short to make a final estimate,
the life expectancy of an enrollment is at least 18 months. As the time of
program operations lengthens, this estimate could increase.

Figure 4.5

Graphical Representation of the Income Equivalent Variation of a
Constrained Subsidy Offer

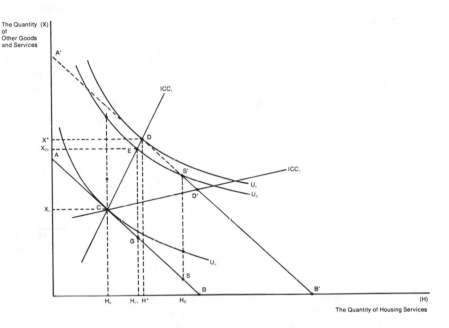

A NOTE ON THE HOUSEHOLD'S EVALUATION OF
A CONSTRAINED SUBSIDY

From the household's viewpoint, the decision to accept an offer of a housing subsidy conditional upon the household meeting a housing requirement
can be structured in a benefit-cost framework. With respect to benefits, a
household's perceived gain from accepting the government's offer can be
measured by the Hicksian income equivalent variation.[35] The income
equivalent variation (IEV) is the unrestricted cash grant that would
place the household on the same indifference curve it would attain were
the household to accept the subsidy and its associated constraints.

The income equivalent variation is depicted graphically in figure 4.5
for the case of an income-conditioned housing subsidy. In time period 0
the household maximizes its utility at C on indifference Uo, given its
income constraint AB and the relative prices of housing and other goods
and services. The household consumes Ho of housing and Xo of other

---

35. See Hicks [H59].

goods and services. In time period 1, the household is offered a subsidy AA' if it meets the housing consumption requirement Hc. In effect, the household's postsubsidy budget constraint becomes ASS'B' if it consumes at least Hc of housing. How much the household values the subsidy (SS') depends on the distortion from the household's income consumption curve (ICC) created by accepting the subsidy.

For example, if the household already consumes Ho $\geqq$ Hc or would normally consume H* $\geqq$ Hc upon receipt of the subsidy and adjustment by the household, the income equivalent value of the subsidy equals the nominal value of the subsidy. The latter case is depicted by the household response labeled ICC_2 (indifference curves other than Uo are not depicted for this household). With the subsidy-augmented budget constraint ASS'B', this household would, in equilibrium, locate at D' with H(D') $>$ Hc.

If, however, the household does not already consume Ho $\geqq$ Hc and would not consume H* $\geqq$ Hc upon the receipt of the subsidy and adjustment, the household compares alternative commodity bundles and selects the bundle which maximizes its utility. Such a case is depicted by the household response labeled ICC_1. With the subsidy-augmented budget constraint and unrestricted choice (i.e., the imaginary budget line A'B') the household would locate at D consuming H* $<$ Hc. To evaluate the constrained offer (ASS'B' H* $\geqq$ Hc), the household compares the utility maximizing position under the constraint (S') with the utility received from its initial commodity bundle (C). If u(S') $\geqq$ u(C) the household would accept the constrained position, in the absence of transactions cost and uncertainty. In the case of acceptance, the household would consume Hc of housing and (Y + S − PhHc)/Px of other goods and services, where Y is household income, S is the subsidy, PhHc is the expenditure on the required level of housing, and Px is the price of other goods and services.

Behavior is, however, neither certain nor costless. In the presence of the substantial costs of relocation together with the uncertainty associated with moving, the household would likely evaluate the benefits of participation (i.e., accepting the subsidy and locating at S') and compare these with the associated costs. In terms of figure 4.5, the IEV of the subsidy offer for the household identified by ICC_1 is GE. That is, an unrestricted cash grant of GE would make the household as well off as a subsidy of SS' coupled with a housing requirement of Hc. As can be seen, for the constrained household the IEV is less than the subsidy SS', and the transfer efficiency of the subsidy (i.e., nominal value of the subsidy divided by the household's evaluation of the subsidy's value) is GE/AA').

CHAPTER 5

Mobility

Francis J. Cronin and David W. Rasmussen

H OUSING ALLOWANCES constrained by program standards require that many eligible households move in order to participate. As a result, residential mobility is a key determinant of participation and the program's impact on housing quality. In fact, most of the households who passed the standard after initially failing in the Demand Experiment did so by moving. On the other hand, evidence from the Supply Experiment suggests that failing the housing requirement is not as important as how the standard is failed. The greater the number of housing deficiencies in a unit occupied at enrollment, the more likely the family is to seek housing elsewhere or leave the program. Those households living in units at the time of program enrollment which have a single deficiency, as defined by the program's standards, are quite likely to repair the unit. Hence, mobility is especially important for the most poorly housed.

While mobility is important as a route to program participation, some people also viewed program-induced mobility as a mechanism that would expand the residential opportunities of the poor. Freedom of residential choice was touted by the President's Committee on Urban Housing as one of the most compelling reasons for a housing allowance program.[1] This aspect of allowances, however, provided fuel for both advocates and opponents of such a program. Reducing residential segregation of the poor and minorities was seen as a benefit by program advocates, while detractors feared a mass migration of the poor that would disrupt suburbs and accelerate the decline of central cities. Because none of the programs within EHAP intentionally "steered" households to specific locations and because aspects of neighborhood quality were not included in housing standards, the experiment makes it possible to resolve this controversy. The results seem definitive. Housing allowances—when adminis-

---

1. See President's Committee on Urban Housing [P66].

tered in this "passive" way—have little if any impact on locational choice, economic or racial concentration, or neighborhood quality.

This chapter first describes the role that mobility plays in changing housing conditions. How housing allowances affect decisions to search and move, locational choice, and the effect of program services on mobility are analyzed. Finally, costs to mobility, particularly the costs of discrimination, are analyzed.

THE ROLE OF MOBILITY IN ALTERING HOUSING CONDITIONS

Moving is often the only way for households to adjust their housing consumption to new needs or circumstances.[2] More specifically, moving plays a crucial role in the response of households to housing programs with minimum housing requirements. Given the condition of the local stock of housing, the stringency of program housing standards determines the number of units which initially fail requirements. As figure 5.1 indicates, at the time of initial enrollment in the housing allowance program, between 47 percent and 82 percent of the rental dwellings nominated by enrollees at four sites in the Demand and Supply Experiments failed to pass minimum physical housing standards necessary for the household to qualify for the receipt of a subsidy. To receive allowance payments, households failing such standards are required to upgrade their current unit to standards or to move to an acceptable unit.

These routes to becoming eligible for housing allowance subsidies are not equally available to all households. Renters, in particular, are constrained in their ability to upgrade units due to contractual relationships with their landlords; and they may have to move in order to alter substantially their consumption of housing. Eligible homeowners in the Supply Experiment, on the other hand, may be unable or unwilling to move in the short run. If sufficient incentives to undertake minor rehabilitation are not offered to owners of deficient units, many may never qualify for benefits. Obviously, resistance to making major changes in housing consumption will be even greater. One simple index of the severity of a unit's deficiency is the number of items failed during program inspection. As table 5.1 indicates, the percentage of households either moving or terminating from the program at the two sites increases as the number of failures reported in the dwelling unit increases. In South Bend, for example, an increase from one item failure to four or more item failures results

---

2. For reviews of the general area of mobility, see Weinberg et al. [H128], Quigley and Weinberg [H108], and Goodman and Vogel [E50]. For a discussion and application of a generalized theory of mobility, see Cronin [H29].

Figure 5.1

Percentage of Enrolled Households under a Minimum Physical Standards
Program Whose Unit Failed Inspection at Enrollment at Four EHAP Sites

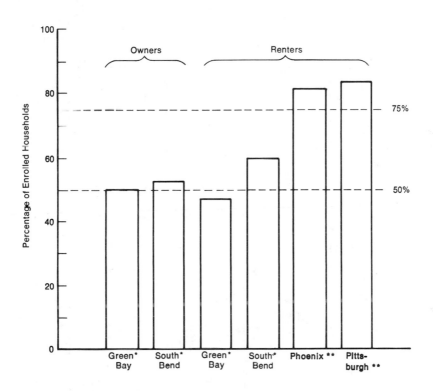

Source: * From Rand memo dated March 26, 1980.
          ** Urban Institute analysis of Demand Experiment data.

among renter enrollees in an increase from 11 percent to 17 percent
in households moving and an increase from 16 percent to 26 percent in
households terminating enrollment. The response among homeowners
is essentially to terminate enrollment at higher rates as the number of
item failures increases.

A substantial majority of renter households whose units initially
failed inspections under programs with housing standards eventually
qualified by moving. At Demand Experiment sites—Pittsburgh and
Phoenix—where especially stringent requirements were imposed, 75 percent of all such households who qualified by the end of the second year

Table 5.1

Enrollee Responses to Initial Evaluation Failures, Supply Experiment

Number of Defects	Green Bay						South Bend					
	Number of Enrollees	Enrollee Action after Initial Failure					Number of Enrollees	Enrollee Action after Initial Failure				
		Repair (%)	Move (%)	Terminate (%)	Total (%)			Repair (%)	Move (%)	Terminate (%)	Total (%)	
Homeowners												
1	422	87	1	12	100		825	88	(a)	12	100	
2	213	81	0	19	100		324	78	1	21	100	
3	91	67	1	32	100		136	63	2	35	100	
4+	89	46	3	51	100		170	51	3	46	100	
All	815	79	1	20	100		1,455	79	1	20	100	
Renters												
1	517	67	16	17	100		544	73	11	16	100	
2	266	60	17	23	100		290	55	17	28	100	
3	133	52	18	30	100		171	52	16	32	100	
4+	135	31	36	33	100		274	32	30	38	100	
All	1,051	59	19	22	100		1,279	57	17	26	100	

Source: HAO records through June 1976 for Green Bay and December 1976 for South Bend; McDowell [C61], table 2.3.
a. Less than .5 percent.

after initially failing standards did so by moving (figure 5.2). It is also important that the overall percentage of success through moving increases in the second program year at both sites. This might reflect the fact that households able to upgrade do so rather quickly, while households having to move to qualify for benefits may respond over a longer period of time. This is consistent with the findings reported in chapter four.

Another way of viewing the importance of mobility is by examining the experience of stationary households. Of households active at the end of two years who had failed standards initially and remained in their failed dwelling, only 21 percent in Phoenix and 12 percent in Pittsburgh met standards.

Moving in and of itself, however, is not a sufficient condition for passing requirements. Over half of the households initially failing requirements, who moved over a two-year program period, moved to units which also failed to pass (figure 5.3). Several hypotheses are consistent with this finding: (1) some households had a poor understanding of program requirements; (2) some households were unable to find program-acceptable units with reasonable effort or at rents they could afford; and/or (3) program requirements did not correspond to household preferences for housing features. This latter possibility is particularly relevant since requirements dealt only with objective, interior physical features, not with neighborhood, exterior of the dwelling, or subjective features.

Furthermore, for households moving into program-acceptable units, the changes in housing conditions have been significant. Table 5.2 lists the percentage of recipient-renter households at each of the 12 EHAP sites who qualified in-place and those who qualified by moving. For each group, the exhibit also shows the average rent at enrollment and the percentage increase in rent as the household moved from being an enrollee to a recipient. Using rental expenditures as a very crude proxy for the level of housing services consumed, we see that (1) prior to enrollment, mover households were consuming substantially less housing than stayer households; and, (2) substantial increases in consumption occurred for mover households once they qualified.[3] Consumption increases for movers ranged from 32 percent in Green Bay to 76 percent in Jacksonville, while increases for stayer households ranged between 1 percent and 10 percent, reflecting mainly the normal price increases in local housing markets during the period covered (i.e., three months to two years). Using control households in Pittsburgh and Phoenix to gauge the extent of actual program-induced increases in rent after one year, it is estimated

---

3. The loss of length-of-tenure discounts for mover households could account for some of this increase. To the extent that this is the case, the increases in rent may overstate increases in the actual amount of housing services consumed.

Figure 5.2

Percentage of All Households [a] Who Passed Housing Standards (after
Initially Failing) Who Did So by Moving

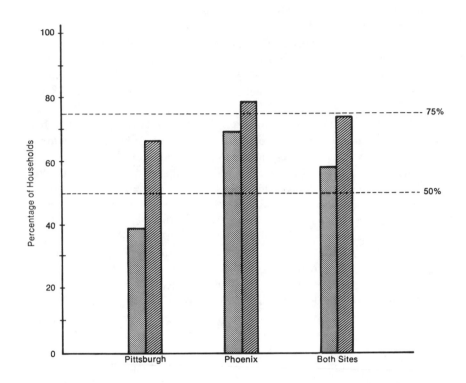

Source: Urban Institute analysis of Demand Experiment data.

    a. Only active households enrolled in allowance programs with a hous-
ing gap payment formula and housing quality standards are included.
Households enrolled over income eligibility limits are excluded.

Figure 5.3

Percentage of Households [a] Initially Failing Requirements Who Moved to Units Which Also Failed to Pass Requirements at Two EHAP Sites

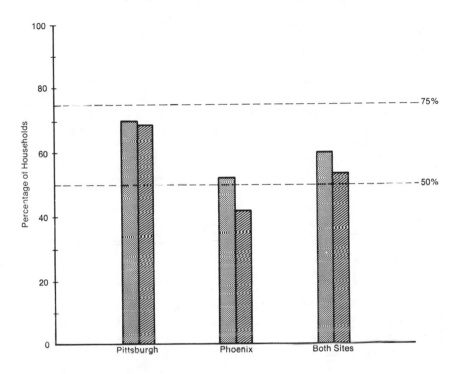

KEY.

First   Second
year   year

Source: Urban Institute analysis of Demand Experiment data.

a. Only active households enrolled in allowance programs with a housing gap payment formula and housing quality standards are included. Households enrolled over income eligibility limits are excluded.

that for households under a housing requirement program who moved and qualified after moving, the program-induced increase in rent was 16 percent in Pittsburgh and 30 percent in Phoenix.[4]

From a policy-making perspective, it is important to note in table 5.2 the site differences in the paths to qualification. The percentage of households moving to become recipients ranged from 19 in Bismarck to 58 in Jacksonville. Factors associated with such differences include the following:

1. The normal pattern of mobility in an area; that is, the higher the normal rate, the more likely households are to qualify by moving;

2. The condition of the local stock of housing; that is, the worse the stock, the higher the incidence of failure and the higher the number of households required to move;

3. The stringency of the housing standards; that is, more strict standards raise the initial failure rate and the number of households required to move; and,

4. The tightness of the market; particularly for affordable, program-acceptable units in the areas searched by low-income households, that is, the tighter the market, the lower the mobility rate because it is harder to find an acceptable unit.

The sharp differences in these conditions from city to city imply that a housing allowance program will affect mobility and participation differentially across markets. A national program should therefore be flexible to accommodate particular local conditions. For example, a housing allowance program that applied a stringent housing standard in a market with generally poor housing for low-income households, a tight market for program-acceptable units, and extensive discrimination against minorities would probably encounter low program participation. Such an extreme case was experienced in the Jacksonville allowance program, with results consistent with these expectations.[5]

THE IMPACT OF PROGRAM FEATURES ON MOBILITY

Prior to EHAP, analysis on intraurban household mobility was framed in terms of the household's attempt to overcome housing "dissatisfaction or stress" and to maximize satisfaction with the place of residence.[6]

---

4. Increases in consumption are explored further in chapter 7.

5. Wolfe and Hamilton [C124].

6. See MacMillan [H80]; Brown and Longbrake [H17]; Clark and Cadwallader [H20]; Speare [H115]; Speare [H116]; and Wolpert [H135, H136].

Empirical findings are often inconsistent with the assumption that dissatisfaction is the prime cause of household mobility: researchers repeatedly find that not all "dissatisfied" households search while some satisfied households do. An alternative paradigm, developed largely by economists, has been tested using data from the Demand and Supply Experiments.[7] This model is based on the proposition that decisions to move are generally made in an economically rational way: The expected benefits of a move are compared to the costs. Under housing allowances the gains are the net present value of benefits associated with living in a unit that provides an optimal level of housing services given the possibility of receiving a housing allowance. The costs, which must be subtracted from the gross expected benefits, include out-of-pocket costs of searching and moving, loss of length-of-tenure discounts, loss of "information capital" for out-of-neighborhood movers, and psychic costs.

Households may, therefore, choose not to participate in a program that appears to offer an attractive subsidy. Even if a household is "dissatisfied" with its current dwelling, that is, would benefit by a move to its preferred dwelling, it may not do so because the costs of the search and move more than offset these gains. In this light, instantaneous adjustment by all households to a constrained housing allowance is unlikely, a finding that is entirely consistent with low short-run income and price elasticities of demand for housing that are described in chapter 7.

Because control groups are necessary to investigate the program's impact on mobility, only Demand Experiment data are used in this analysis. Members of alternative treatment groups in the Demand Experiment faced different incentives to move. Households in the percentage of rent and unconstrained groups had a clear incentive to move because the allowance payments made it possible to afford better housing. However, they were not required to move. Households in the housing gap treatment group had, in some instances, an additional incentive to move: meeting program standards in order to receive payments. For households not meeting the standards at enrollment and whose landlords would not make repairs, moving was the sine qua non for receiving the allowance. Offsetting these incentives to move were disincentives. First, housing allowances would mean that some households who had moved into better units would be unable to afford dwellings if payments were stopped. Second, housing gap households meeting the standards at enrollment had a disincentive to move since a change of residence raised the danger of not meeting the standards in the new units with a consequent loss of subsidy. Estimates of program-induced mobility will, therefore, be biased down-

7. See, for example, Cronin [H26]; McCarthy [H76]; Hanushek and Quigley [H52]; Goodman [H46]; Friedman and Weinberg [H38].

Table 5.2

Mobility and Gross Rent Increases [a] of Renter Recipients in Programs with Housing Quality (Physical) Standards

Site	Movers			Nonmovers		
	Percentage of Site Recipients	*Average Rent at Enrollment*	*Percentage Rent Increase*	*Percentage of Site Recipients*	*Average Rent at Enrollment*	*Percentage Rent Increase*
Administrative Agency Experiment						
Bismarck	19%	$ 99	48%	81%	$121	3%
Durham	38	102	45	62	120	2
Jacksonville [b]	58	100	76	42	138	8
Peoria	30	109	46	70	125	1
Salem	48	112	44	52	136	1
San Bernardino	44	119	42	56	133	2
Springfield	42	130	40	58	144	3
Tulsa	40	107	47	60	127	2

Demand Experiment [c]						
Pittsburgh	29	108	42	71	121	7
Phoenix	53	130	39	47	150	6
Supply Experiment						
Green Bay	28	144	32	72	148	10
South Bend	28	135	34	72	148	5
Unweighted Mean	38	116	45	62	134	4

Source: Carlson and Heinberg [E24], p. 24.

a. Rent increases from enrollment to recipient status. Data on postenrollment reflect time of first payment in the Administrative Agency Experiment (generally no more than three months after enrollment), one year of program participation in the Demand Experiment, and approximately 2 years of program operations in the Supply Experiment (2 years in Green Bay, 1 year and 9 months in South Bend). The average period of enrollment for Supply Experiment households is about 11 months.

b. The entries refer to the first enrollment period only.

c. These entries are for only those participants required to meet program housing quality standards, housing gap plans 1-3, 10 and 11. They refer to those households that received allowance payments 1 year after enrollment.

ward because households are not likely to adjust totally to a short-term experiment and some mobility effects cannot be estimated.

In order to better understand the impacts of specific features of the program design on the mobility of program households, the following discussion deals separately with (1) the decision to search; (2) the relationships among satisfaction, housing adequacy, and search; (3) the decision to move; and (4) the locational decision, including changes in neighborhood quality. On balance, the program appears to have had no significant effects on the overall mobility of households in Pittsburgh. In Phoenix, the program appears to have had a statistically significant but marginal impact on the overall mobility of households. But even in Phoenix it appears that the rate at which experimental households move is largely governed by their preexperimental behavior.

The Decision to Search

The results of multivariate analysis using two years of Demand Experiment data indicate that the decision to search is positively related to dissatisfaction with the dwelling unit and/or neighborhood, a predisposition to move, previous mobility, a change in marital status, and a change in the number of children in the household. Significant factors that reduce mobility are age, positive feelings toward neighbors, and having basic facilities in a unit.[8] The relationship between search and dissatisfaction (with unit and/or neighborhood) is particularly strong. The tabulation in table 5.3 illustrates this relationship; in Pittsburgh 37 percent of the households who were satisfied with both their unit and their neighborhood searched for a new unit, while 77 percent of households who were dissatisfied with both their unit and their neighborhood did so.

This apparently robust relationship, however, is mitigated by what appears to be a high degree of inertia and/or place attachment among households in the program. Large numbers of households, even with the prospect of a housing payment, did not even search. Households who had been offered allowance payments and who were living in housing initially failing standards were no more likely to search than comparable nonprogram households in such housing (i.e., those initially failing standards).

Table 5.4 presents the reasons cited by households who did not search during the first year for not doing so. Two important points stand out. First, a large number of these households cited items suggesting a strong degree of place attachment: "reasons connected with neighborhood" or "didn't feel I'd find a place I'd like as much as present unit." Second,

8. MacMillan [H80], p. 75.

Table 5.3

Percentage of Households Searching by Unit and Neighborhood
Satisfaction

		Pittsburgh	
		Neighborhood	
		Satisfied	Dissatisfied
Dwelling Unit	Satisfied	37%	56%
		(601)[a]	(115)
	Dissatisfied	65%	77%
		(178)	(127)

		Phoenix	
		Neighborhood	
		Satisfied	Dissatisfied
Dwelling Unit	Satisfied	53%	66%
		(604)	(86)
	Dissatisfied	71%	81%
		(167)	(104)

Source: Weinberg et al. [H128], p. 26.
a. Sample size in parentheses.

over half of those households in both sites cite "financial reasons." This
is a surprising result, for prior to the experiment it was thought that
housing allowances would remove the financial impediments to mobility.
These responses suggest that over the short term, monthly housing allowance payments will not induce substantial search among many eligible
households. An analysis of direct cash assistance "up front" to offset moving costs was not included in the experiment.

Satisfaction, Standards, and Search

As noted, program housing standards in EHAP—as in past housing
programs—concentrated on "objective" measures of housing; subjective
elements were not considered. But the subjective elements are clearly important; findings from Phoenix and Pittsburgh indicate that approxi-

Table 5.4

Reasons Cited for Not Searching by Households Somewhat Dissatisfied
or Very Dissatisfied with Their Housing Unit and Their Neighborhood

Reason	Pittsburgh	Phoenix
"Didn't feel I'd find a place I'd like as much as present unit"	38%	39%
Reasons connected with neighborhood	53	39*
Financial reasons	53	52
Other reasons	29	22
Total number of respondents	(34)	(23)

Source: Weinberg et al. [H128], p. 27.
Note: Percentages add to more than 100 percent because of multiple responses.
* Chi-square statistic comparing percentage citing reasons between households fully dissatisfied (i.e., dissatisfied with both unit and neighborhood) and
all other households (not shown) significant at the 0.05 level.

mately 50 percent of all households who were living in units not meeting
program standards at enrollment were fully satisfied with their housing.
Given this finding, it is particularly important to examine the relationship among satisfaction, dwelling condition, and mobility in greater detail.
Unfortunately, it is complex and does not yield to a simple summary.

Results from an analysis of first-year data indicated that a higher
percentage of *households residing in nonstandard housing* units (defined
by objective measures) search than did those in standard units (table
5.5). This is especially true for households living in overcrowded conditions.[9] Households do *not*, however, automatically consider relocating
just because a housing program identifies their dwelling unit as nonstandard. An examination of the reasons for not searching offered by
households in nonstandard dwellings reveals great similarity with the
reasons given by households in standard dwellings. Furthermore, a large
percentage of households offered satisfaction either with the dwelling unit
and/or the neighborhood as the reason for not searching. Many households, even in "objectively" defined nonstandard housing, express some
form of place attachment. Also, once again a high proportion of households
listed financial reasons.

Still, housing conditions seem to make a difference even *for households satisfied with both their housing unit and their neighborhood.* Table

---

9. Multivariate analysis confirms that perceived overcrowding is an important incentive to search. See MacMillan [H80], p. 74.

Table 5.5

Search Rates by Housing Conditions at Two EHAP Sites

	Pittsburgh		Phoenix	
Housing Adequacy	Percentage Searching	Sample Size	Percentage Searching	Sample Size
Crowding				
Overcrowded [a]	65%	(185)	73%	(279)
Not overcrowded	46 [c]	(781)	57 [c]	(684)
Physical Condition of Unit				
Living in nonstandard unit [b]	53	(755)	63	(751)
Living in standard unit	41 [c]	(311)	57	(291)

Source: Weinberg et al. [H128], p. 29.

a. Overcrowded households are defined to be those with more than two persons per bedroom.

b. Physically nonstandard units are defined as those which fail to meet the physical requirements associated with the minimum standards portion of the experiment. Note that this latter definition is applied to all households, and not only to minimum standards households.

c. Significant difference between living condition groups at .05 level or higher.

5.6 shows that households in nonstandard housing were in fact more likely on average to search than those in standard dwellings.

The Decision to Move

Housing allowances as administered in the Demand Experiment had a variable but generally positive effect on the mobility of program participants. After controlling for other factors, in Phoenix the probability of moving was found to be 10 percentage points higher for allowance recipients than for the control group—a statistically significant difference. Recipients in Pittsburgh were also more likely to move than the control group, but this is not statistically significant.[10] These differences by site held consistently across most of the various treatment groups. Further, the size of the allowance payment had virtually no effect on mobility; but the small impact it did have was statistically significant in Phoenix.[11]

With the aid of hindsight, these results are not surprising. In a review of the literature on residential mobility, Rossi claims that the principal

10. MacMillan [H80], chapter 4.

11. Cronin [H26] has similar findings on the relationship between the amount of housing search and the real gain to the household from the subsidy offer.

Table 5.6

Search Rates for Households Initially Satisfied with Their Housing Unit and Neighborhood, by Housing Conditions

Housing Adequacy	Pittsburgh		Phoenix	
	Percentage Searching	Sample Size	Percentage Searching	Sample Size
Crowding				
Overcrowded [a]	51%	(85)	65%	(130)
Not overcrowded	36 [c]	(458)	.8 [c]	(421)
Physical Condition of Unit				
Living in nonstandard unit [b]	40	(406)	54	(417)
Living in standard unit	31 [c]	(220)	49	(181)

Source: Weinberg et al. [H128], p. 31.

a. Overcrowded households are defined to be those with more than two persons per bedroom.

b. Physically nonstandard units are defined as those which fail to meet the physical requirements associated with the minimum standards portion of the experiment. Note that this latter definition is applied to all households, and not only to minimum standards households.

c. Significant difference between living condition groups at .05 level or higher.

forces that cause moves are independent of variables affected by the provision of allowance payments:

> In aggregate over time, the amounts of moving appear to be very stable, changing with glacial speed rather than responsive to identifiable short term trends in the larger economy or in the housing market.[12]

Because allowances slightly changed the underlying determinants of mobility, the effect of allowances on mobility might best be interpreted as accelerating moves that would have been made otherwise. Of course, when households do move, a housing allowance is likely to increase their consumption of housing.

Locational Choice

The Supply Experiment offers some data on the locational choices of relocating allowance recipients, but without control households it is only suggestive. These data show some shift from declining residential neigh-

---

12. Rossi [H111], p. 15.

borhoods to areas that offered better housing and services.[13] Also, examination of the origin and destinations of enrollees' moves shows some deconcentration of blacks and some movement of whites from the neighborhoods with most blacks. But analysis of the data for South Bend (the only Supply Experiment site with a sizable minority population) suggests that moves did not involve households migrating from the central city to the suburban ring.

Data from two years of the Demand Experiment provide the only direct evidence on the impact of the program on the locational decision. Atkinson, Hamilton, and Myers[14] analyze these data, and they too find a slight tendency of allowance households to move to neighborhoods where minority and low-income households were less concentrated than in original neighborhoods. In this analysis the measures of low-income and racial concentration were, respectively, the proportion of households with annual incomes of less than $5,000 and blacks as a percentage of the total population. However, when compared with the control group, the movement pattern of participating households was not significantly different. This result held for both blacks in Pittsburgh and Spanish-Americans in Phoenix. It did not change when various subgroups, defined by income and age, were analyzed or when multivariate analysis was employed. Housing allowances do not appear to improve those neighborhood characteristics of recipients' housing.

Given that the program had virtually no impact on the degree of economic and racial concentration experienced by participants, it is not surprising that it had no effect on other neighborhood characteristics of recipients' residences. Multivariate analysis was conducted to discern the program's impact on four other measures of the quality of neighborhood chosen by recipient households: rent-quality index; crimes against persons; crimes against property; and a neighborhood hedonic index.[15] Both experimental and control households that moved show some improvement on the quality indicators, but differences between them are small and generally insignificant. In some cases, the control households show more improvement than those in the experiment.

A fact consistent with these findings is that the program has no impact on the distance moved, journey to work, or movement from the central city to the suburbs. Commentators on the impact of housing allowances on mobility and location are unanimous in the conclusion that such effects are virtually nonexistent. This conclusion is in line with the

---

13. See Rand [E129].
14. See Atkinson et al. [H5].
15. This is a measure of the share of rent attributable to the value of neighborhood attributes. See Atkinson et al. [H5].

low income and price elasticities of the demand for housing reported in chapter 7. Further, other analysis of the search process has shown that friends or relatives are a widely used and highly effective way to find housing.[16] To the extent friends live in the same neighborhood or one of similar income and racial composition, this method of search is not likely to generate mobility that alters residential patterns in neighborhoods. Finally, minimal program effects on mobility virtually dictate that housing allowances will not have a significant impact on location and neighborhood quality.

The Effects of Supportive Services on Mobility and Locational Choice

With the important exception of the favorable effects of providing highly specific information on the location and availability of units, there appears to be no discernible effect of supportive services on the rate of mobility and/or locational choice decisions.[17]

Evidence from the eight sites of the Administrative Agency Experiment, in which services varied widely across sites, indicates that services related specifically to finding a unit were generally used by movers more than nonmovers, by out-of-neighborhood movers more than movers in general, and by blacks more than whites (table 5.7). In each case, the group who faced the greater difficulties in moving used services more often.

Without a control group in the AAE it is impossible to estimate the impact of services per se on the mobility and locational choices of program households. However, the relatively high rate of service usage by households moving out of a neighborhood compared to nonmovers or within-the-neighborhood movers, suggests a possible role for services. Such moves outside of current neighborhoods may be particularly difficult for low-income households, and especially so for minorities. The bifurcation of most urban areas into segregated housing markets constrains the perceived and actual housing opportunities of minorities. Segregation does this in part by limiting the development of informal, interpersonal-information networks, possibly the most effective source of search/move information due to its low-cost and low-risk nature. Provision of specific dwelling unit information by a housing agency partially compensates for such constraints.

---

16. See Cronin [H26]; McCarthy [H76]; Vidal [H126].

17. Supportive services are provided to program households by administrative agencies to assist such households in qualifying for subsidies. In EHAP, such services included program information, housing information, assistance in locating units and dealing with landlords, and equal opportunity support, among others. See chapter 10 for a more complete discussion.

Table 5.7

Percentage of Searchers in the Administrative Agency Experiment Using Agency Housing Services, by Locational Decisions and Race

Location Decisions	Agency Housing Service Provided									
	Provided List of Available Units		Called Landlords or Agents		Took Enrollee to Look at Unit		Looked at Unit for Enrollee		Gave Transportation Assistance	
	White	Black	White	Black	White	Black	White	Black	White	Black
Stayed	30%	46%	0%	15%	0%	14%	0%	7%	0%	14%
Moved within neighborhood	27	56	2	17	2	17	2	11	0	11
Moved outside neighborhood	45	66	13	31	5	23	7	26	7	36
Total	37%	60%	8%	26%	3%	20%	4%	20%	4%	28%

Source: Holshouser et al. [C35], p. E-38.

However, the exact association between out-of-neighborhood moves by participants and services provided by agencies is difficult to determine. Households may have decided to move outside their neighborhood and then sought information from the agencies; on the other hand, they may have been helped by agency information to decide to move out of their neighborhood. In either case, an agency's provisions of such services may have an enabling effect.

Evidence from the Tulsa site suggests the potential, in particular market situations, for agency informational services to have a particularly strong effect on locational choice. Moves in Tulsa by white-recipient households were highly dispersed throughout the area, a pattern consistent with the behavior of white households in other sites. However, locations chosen by black households were highly concentrated. The area most often chosen by blacks was one in which large numbers of standard units were available. Agency counselors assisted 49 percent of black households in the selection of housing, as opposed to only 9 percent of white households. The staff's knowledge of certain areas and landlords, together with the perception by black households that they would be accepted in these areas, contributed to a pronounced concentration of locational choices by black movers.[18]

BARRIERS TO MOBILITY

Barriers to mobility must be analyzed because of the key role mobility plays in households' adjustment from substandard to standard dwellings and because of the negligible effect of allowances on mobility. Costs of search and moving are obvious barriers to mobility. As noted, these costs are several. Loss of tenure discounts and information capital appear inevitable and are not of policy interest. Of greater interest is discrimination which can raise both psychic and search costs. Table 5.8 shows the proportion of Demand Experiment households that searched for housing and reported some form of discrimination. Discrimination is widespread.[19] In Pittsburgh 53 percent of white households and 60 percent of black households reported some form of discrimination. Discrimination in Phoenix was considerably lower, ranging from a low of 28 percent for black households to a high of 39 percent for Spanish-Americans.[20] In

18. These client services are discussed further in chapter 10.

19. McCarthy [H76] reports much lower levels in the smaller Supply Experiment sites. Minorities in these cities may know the market well enough to avoid discrimination and therefore report encountering less discrimination.

20. The fact that the Pittsburgh housing market is tighter than that of Phoenix may contribute to this differential between sites.

Table 5.8

Patterns of Discrimination Reported, by Race/Ethnicity

Type of Discrimination	Percentage of Households Reporting Discrimination				
	Pittsburgh		Phoenix		
	White	Black	White	Black	Spanish-American
Any type of discrimination	53%	60*	31	28	39*
Age	15	16	14	8	9
Sex	7	11	2	2	1
Marital status	20	18	7	5	3
Source of income	27	42*	7	15	8
Race/ethnicity	3	21*	1	15*	8*
Children	44	48	24	11*	30
Receipt of a housing allowance [a]	1	1	1	0	2

Source: Vidal [H126], p. A-46.
a. This question was only asked of experimental households.
* Statistically significant from whites at the .10 level or higher.

both sites discrimination against race and ethnicity is statistically significant but low relative to discrimination against children. A recent study sponsored by the Department of Housing and Urban Development[21] used black and white testers to evaluate the level of discrimination. Although black testers often did not perceive that they were being discriminated against, a comparison with treatment afforded the white tester often revealed differential treatment. The evidence from this study generally points to the subtlety of the discriminatory practices used by landlords and real estate brokers. This, in turn, suggests the level of discrimination by race and ethnicity reported in table 5.8 to be downward biased.

Discrimination against minorities should both raise the costs and lower the effectiveness of search. Cronin[22] used multivariate analysis to show the effect of these higher costs: Minorities search more days, search in fewer neighborhoods, and visit fewer dwelling than their nonminority counterparts. The cost of housing search is reduced by car ownership, and differences in mode of transportation used by minorities and nonminorities are significant. During the first six months of the Demand

21. See Wienk et al. [II131].
22. See Cronin [H26].

Experiment, 42 percent of nonminority searches usually used their own car, as opposed to 23 percent for minorities. Minorities more frequently walked and used public transportation than did nonminorities. Although it is difficult to assess the relative importance of discrimination and mode of transportation on the search pattern of minorities, it is clear that they face significant barriers not faced by nonminorities.

As noted earlier, households reported more discrimination against children than any other form. Forty-four percent of white searchers in Pittsburgh and 24 percent in Phoenix reported discrimination against children. The results of multivariate analysis support the claim of discrimination: Larger households spend more days searching in more neighborhoods and look at more dwellings. The high proportion of households reporting discrimination against children, despite its significance in multivariate analysis, is probably not as important quantitatively as racial and ethnic discrimination. In multivariate analysis, race has a much higher impact on extending the search time and restricting the area of search than does household size. In short, although more households complain about discrimination against children than complain of racial and ethnic discrimination, the available data show minorities searching longer than do large households to overcome discrimination.

CHAPTER 6

Consumption Responses to Constrained Programs

Francis J. Cronin

A S A HOUSING program, the primary goal of housing allowances is to improve housing consumption among the eligible population. To be effective it must raise actual housing consumption—not simply raise rents, for example—and must raise consumption above any normal improvement unrelated to housing allowances. In addition, the improvement must be greater than that generated by an equal unconstrained income grant. Otherwise, the additional costs associated with the housing focus of an allowance program could be eliminated with no diminution of housing quality among eligibles. This chapter analyzes how housing allowances change housing consumption among the eligible population.[1]

The discussion in this chapter relies on results from the Demand Experiment. The presence of a control group in this experiment permits the impact of the allowance payment to be distinguished from general trends and behavior of households not in the program. Further, a group receiving unconstrained payments permits a comparison between earmarked and unearmarked subsidies with respect to improving the housing conditions of eligible households.

The more salient findings are as follows:

● The imposition of physical housing standards caused more of the pro-

---

1. The topic of inducing participants to become homeowners is not examined in this chapter for several reasons. First, since homeowners are eligible only in the Supply Experiment, the lack of a control group makes impossible an assessment of experimental inducement of homeownership. Second, the numbers of renters becoming homeowners is quite small; during the first four years of the Supply Experiment only 250 households did so. See Shanley and Hotchkiss [H114]. Third, it is not apparent from the data now available for renters becoming homeowners that these households increased their housing consumption.

gram's participating households to live in units meeting the standards than happened when similar households received unconstrained cash grants; similar effects were not found for minimum rent requirement programs.

- Households whose units pass program standards at enrollment have higher rents both at enrollment and after two years than households whose units initially fail but who later become recipients; those with units that initially passed also had much higher housing expense burdens.

- Among households subject to some form of housing requirement, the significant increases in housing expenditures and consumption that are observed are for households who eventually participate but are in units at enrollment that do not meet program standards.

- Overall, the average increase in housing consumption for recipients whose units had to pass physical standards is not greater than the average increase for unconstrained households. As noted, however, unconstrained households occupy units that are less likely to pass the program's physical housing standards.

- More generally, the average increase in the consumption of housing services is insensitive to the type of plan under which payments are made—unconstrained grants, rebates computed as a percentage of rents, or plans involving minimum rents or physical standards.

- Households in plans with minimum rent requirements increase expenditure significantly more than the corresponding increase in services received.

ALLOWANCES AND MEETING MINIMUM HOUSING STANDARDS

The kind and extent of housing consumption responses observed within EHAP are the result of interactions between the particular "carrot and stick" (i.e., allowances and housing requirements) approaches employed. Households do respond, in fact, to variations in program subsidies and constraints. For example, households in housing gap programs with requirements were induced to meet their particular housing requirements more often than they would have normally and more often than they would have with an unconstrained income transfer. These outcomes are depicted in table 6.1.

An important finding in chapter 4 was that the proportion of households passing requirements decreases as the stringency of the re-

Table 6.1

Percentage of Housing Gap, Unconstrained, and Control Households
Meeting Housing Requirements at Two Years after Enrollment [a]

	Housing Gap Households	Unconstrained Households	Control Households
	Phoenix		
Minimum rent low requirement	77	67	51
Minimum rent high requirement	50	41	33
Minimum standards requirement	56	46	36
	Pittsburgh		
Minimum rent low requirement	85	76	75
Minimum rent high requirement	52	48	44
Minimum standards requirement	45	23	28

Source: Friedman and Weinberg [H39], p. S-2.
a. Definition of types of allowance programs is in chapter 3.

quirements increases. Table 6.1 indicates, however, that the proportion of households still enrolled (i.e., active) two years after enrollment and passing standards is higher for households in programs with housing requirements than would normally be the case for households in subsidy programs without requirements (i.e., that for unconstrained households). In Phoenix, for example, 56 percent of housing gap households active at two years after enrollment passed minimum standards requirements. The comparable figures for unconstrained and control households are 46 and 36 percent, respectively.

Table 6.2 presents additional results on the effect of the allowance offer on the probability of passing standards of housing adequacy by analyzing three different standards using a multivariate probabilty model which controls for factors other than treatment group (e.g., household stage in the life cycle).[2] The minimum standards requirement just considered is a somewhat limited measure of housing quality because of its dichotomous nature and because it does not discriminate among the quality of passing and failing units. Consequently, two additional measures have been developed to give a more complete picture; they define

2. See Friedman and Weinberg [H39], p.226.

"minimally adequate" and "clearly inadequate" housing. To develop these two measures, 78 individual rating items for the main rooms in the dwelling were selected;[3] each item was intended to measure a serious housing problem or deficiency. Six of these items were classified as questionable; in defining a serious problem they did, though, provide enough information to exclude a dwelling from the "at least minimally adequate" category; but they were not used in classifying a unit as clearly inadequate.

The remaining 72 items were grouped into four categories:

Physical condition. Items related to the structural soundness of the dwelling unit and the condition of walls, ceilings, and floors.

Basic housing services. Items that measure the availability of plumbing and kitchen facilities, heating equipment, and electrical service.

Health and safety hazards. Items pertaining to adequate fire exits, the presence of unvented space heaters, and the presence of rats.

Other indicators. A residual category that includes items relating to ceiling height and windows.

Within each of these categories, items were rated as sufficient or ambiguous depending on whether the item by itself clearly identified a serious housing problem.

The individual indicators were then used to determine the unit's rating as follows:

Any dwelling unit that failed either a sufficient or an ambiguous item was excluded from the "at least minimally adequate" category.

A dwelling unit that failed 1 or more of the 47 sufficient indicators and contained at least one serious housing deficiency was classified as clearly inadequate.

A dwelling unit that failed 1 or more of the 25 ambiguous items was classified as clearly inadequate only if the evaluator's overall rating provided independent confirmation of the existence of serious problems. If the evaluator's overall rating indicated unsoundness or a need for major repairs or renovation, the unit was classified as clearly inadequate. Otherwise, it was classified as ambiguous.

The additional measures, along with the program minimum standards, provide a range of possible standards against which to judge dwelling condition.[4]

---

3. Living room, bath, and first bedroom.

4. For a further description and application of these alternative measures, see Budding [H18]; much of the description in the text is taken directly from this reference.

Table 6.2

Effect of the Allowance Offer on the Probability of Passing Various Measures of Housing Adequacy

| | Pittsburgh | | | Phoenix | | |
| | Change in the Probability of [a] | | | Change in the Probability of [a] | | |
Household Group	Meeting Minimum Standards [b]	Living in Minimally Adequate Housing	Living in Clearly Inadequate Housing	Meeting Minimum Standards [b]	Living in Minimally Adequate Housing	Living in Clearly Inadequate Housing
Unconstrained	+1	+8	−3	+8	+10	−22**
Minimum rent low	+4	−2	+1	+4	+5	−12**
Minimum rent high	−1	−4	−6	+4	+6	−11*
Minimum standards	+20**	+4	−2	+28**	+11*	−14**

Source: Friedman and Weinberg [H39], p. 227.
Sample: Housing gap households active and meeting requirements and unconstrained households active at two years after enrollment, excluding those with enrollment incomes over the eligibility limits and those living in their own homes or in subsidized housing.
  a. Measured in percentage points at two years after enrollment relative to control households, at means of the other independent variables.
  b. For households not meeting minimum standards at enrollment.
  * t-statistic of logit coefficient significant at 0.05 level.
  ** t-statistic of logit coefficient significant at 0.01 level.

As can be seen in table 6.2, the minimum standards requirement does significantly increase the probability of a household passing minimum standards in both sites. In addition, in Phoenix, the minimum standards requirement significantly increases the probability of living in minimally adequate housing and reduces the probability of living in clearly inadequate housing. While none of the other requirements in either site significantly increases the probability of passing minimum standards, all of the requirements in Phoenix significantly reduce the probability of living in clearly inadequate housing. What do we conclude about the effectiveness of the requirements? As detailed next, the imposition of a particular standard does increase the probability of a program-eligible household meeting the requirement (i.e., either minimum rent or minimum standards) but does not result in a greater consumption of housing services as measured in a more general way.

ALLOWANCES AND MORE GENERAL MEASURES OF HOUSING CONSUMPTION

Analyses in preceding chapters showed that the consumption response to a housing allowance should be influenced by the process of becoming a participant and by mobility behavior. The condition of the household's preenrollment dwelling crucially influenced the probability of participation. Likewise, the interaction of preenrollment dwelling condition and varying housing requirements can clearly influence housing consumption by determining the mix of households who need do nothing to receive payments and those who must change their behavior to receive payments. Further, although differences in housing requirements did not influence the probability of participation among those units not qualifying at enrollment, it may be that variations in housing requirements influence the kind and extent of housing consumption change.

The role of preenrollment housing condition and postenrollment mobility as factors influencing consumption responses are depicted in tables 6.3, 6.4, and 6.5. Each table presents the change in housing expenditures for all enrolled households at the end of two years by type of housing requirement and by mobility of households. The tables differ in that table 6.3 gives these data for all households while the other two differentiate households by the program-defined condition of their housing at the end of two program years.

Several general points emerge from this thicket of figures. First, viewing all households (table 6.3), a much larger increase in rents for movers

Table 6.3

Change in Housing Expenditures from Enrollment to Two Years after Enrollment, by Treatment Type and Mobility in Phoenix and Pittsburgh: For All Households

	Stayers				Movers			
	Housing Expenditures				Housing Expenditures			
	At Enroll-ment	At Two Years	Percentage Change	Sample Size	At Enroll-ment	At Two Years	Percentage Change	Sample Size
PHOENIX								
Control [a]	$125	$132	6	129	$133	$159	20	127
Unconstrained	145	151	4	16	128	175	37	21
Percentage of rent	127	134	6	111	135	179	33	169
Minimum rent low	118	130	10	31	128	173	35	58
Minimum rent high	117	128	9	31	130	185	42	62
Minimum standard	120	127	6	73	130	170	27	90
PITTSBURGH								
Control [a]	S113	127	12	201	$121	147	21	101
Unconstrained	106	119	12	37	109	145	33	22
Percentage of rent	114	130	14	243	114	156	37	142
Minimum rent low	110	123	12	78	107	143	34	44
Minimum rent high	112	128	14	72	115	159	38	39
Minimum standard	110	121	10	116	108	142	31	77

Source: Friedman and Weinberg [H39], pp. A-69 through A-74; [H38], pp. A-98, A-99.
Sample: Households active two years after enrollment excluding those with enrollment incomes over the eligibility limits and those living in their own homes or in subsidized housing.

a. See chapter 3 for description of plans.

Table 6.4

Change in Housing Expenditures from Enrollment to Two Years after Enrollment by Treatment Type and Mobility in Phoenix and Pittsburgh: For Households Who Met Requirements at Two Years

	Stayers				Movers			
	Housing Expenditures				Housing Expenditures			
	At Enroll-ment	At Two Years	Percentage Change	Sample Size	At Enroll-ment	At Two Years	Percentage Change	Sample Size
PHOENIX								
Did Not Meet at Enrollment								
Minimum rent low	$114	$135	18(10)[a]	3	$100	$173	73(80)[a]	24
Minimum rent high	—	—	—(7)	—	128	213	66 64)	28
Minimum standard	127	131	3(2)	20	129	188	46(37)	44
Met at Enrollment								
Minimum rent low	$147	$160	8(4)[a]	16	$158	$183	16(14)[a]	26
Minimum rent high	189	197	4(3)	7	179	204	14(9)	11
Minimum standard	144	155	8(7)	16	157	181	15(12)	11

PITTSBURGH

Did Not Meet at Enrollment

Minimum rent low	$100	$119	19(19)[a]	12	$ 87	$138	59(55)[a]	15
Minimum rent high	103	139	35(26)	9	121	175	45(60)	29
Minimum standard	114	126	11(20)	9	115	156	36(25)	27
			Met at Enrollment					
Minimum rent low	$123	$135	10(12)[a]	50	$122	$152	25(16)[a]	27
Minimum rent high	146	161	10(9)	21	106	180	70(11)	17
Minimum standard	126	141	12(14)	32	118	136	15(16)	6

Source: Friedman and Weinberg [H39], pp. A-69 through A-74; [H3£], pp. A-98, A-99.

Sample: Households active two years after enrollment excluding those with enrollment incomes over the eligibility limits and those living in their own homes or in subsidized housing.

a. Percentage change in expenditures between enrollment and two years after enrollment for control households of similar status.

Table 6.5

Change in Housing Expenditures from Enrollment to Two Years after Enrollment, by Treatment Type and Mobility in Phoenix and Pittsburgh: For Households Who Did Not Meet Requirements at Two Years

| | Stayers | | | | Movers | | | |
| | Housing Expenditures | | | | Housing Expenditures | | | |
	At Enrollment	At Two Years	Percentage Change	Sample Size	At Enrollment	At Two Years	Percentage Change	Sample Size
					PHOENIX			
				Did Not Meet at Enrollment				
Minimum rent low	$ 80	$ 90	13(7)[a]	12	$108	$133	23(15)[a]	6
Minimum rent high	96	108	13(7)	24	104	128	23(14)	21
Minimum standard	105	113	8(6)	37	112	140	25(15)	30
				Met at Enrollment				
Minimum rent low	—	—	—	—	131	157	20(20)[a]	2
Minimum rent high	—	—	—	—	171	139	—19(—19)	5
Minimum standard	—	—	—	—	192	169	—12(13)	5

PITTSBURGH

	Did Not Meet at Enrollment				Met at Enrollment			
Minimum rent low	$ 75	$ 83	17(12)[a]	16	$ 62	$ 68	10(1)[a]	2
Minimum rent high	97	109	12(13)	42	97	110	13(14)	10
Minimum standard	100	109	9(11)	62	100	134	34(24)	40
Minimum rent low	—	—	—	—	—	—	(—27)[a]	—
Minimum rent high	—	—	—	—	—	—	(—28)	—
Minimum standard	—	—	—	—	129	144	12(5)	4

Source: Friedman and Weinberg [H39], pp. A-69 through A-74; [H38], pp. A-98, A-99.
Sample: Households active two years after enrollment excluding those with enrollment incomes over the eligibility limits and those living in their own homes or in subsidized housing.
a. Percentage change in expenditures between enrollment and two years after enrollment for control households of similar status.

than for stayers is seen across the various programs.[5] In addition, this increase is larger for program movers than for movers in the control group. To the extent that expenditures correspond to housing services, table 6.3 supports the view that moving is the primary way for renter households to increase housing consumption.[6]

Second, among plans with a housing requirement, rent increases are relatively larger under the minimum rent standards. However, more detailed analysis finds that the increases in rent in the minimum rent program are not generally associated with a proportional increase in housing services.

Third, among those *stayers* who met requirements at the end of two years (table 6.4), households in all groups meeting standards at enrollment have higher expenditures than those failing at enrollment in similar groups. Of course, this would be expected for minimum rent programs. Similarly, it is not surprising for minimum standards programs since expenditures, on average, bear some relationship to quality. However, this differential in rent between those initially qualifying and those initially failing but who qualified later is still present at two years. This seems largely attributable to a higher preference for housing among those initially qualifying.

Among movers, patterns of rents at enrollment are very similar to those discussed for stayers. Of course, the rent changes are larger for the movers than for the stayers. The data in table 6.4 show no consistent pattern of large differences between experimental and similar control households for those meeting requirements at two years after enrollment. (Figures for control households are shown in parentheses in the table.) On the other hand, greater differences in expenditures between experimental and control households are apparent for households failing requirements at both points in time (table 6.5). Moreover, movers who lived in passing units before moving and substandard units afterwards generally had susbtantial reductions in rents.

Do the changes and patterns observed for expenditures hold up when we switch our focus to the consumption of *housing services?* These issues can be addressed using a "hedonic function," an analytic tool that statistically relates rental expenditures to the attributes of the dwelling unit, its neighborhood, and its general location to determine the "quantity"

---

5. The loss of length-of-tenure discounts for movers probably accounts for some of the increase in expenditures observed for these households.

6. Cronin [H23], p. 16, shows that in all cases (i.e., by site, race, and household size) the average rent of households passing program minimum standards exceeded the average rent of households failing minimum standards at enrollment.

of "housing services" flowing from the units.[7] Tables 6.12, 6.13, and 6.14, placed at the end of this chapter, present the data on housing services in a format identical to that used in presenting data for housing expenditures in tables 6.3, 6.4, and 6.5.

While the change in services is generally less than that for expenditures, several general patterns observed previously still hold. In particular, the larger changes in consumption for movers versus stayers and the higher level of consumption of households qualifying at two years who also qualified at enrollment compared with those of households qualifying at two years but not at enrollment are repeated.

There are, however, some differences. Among all households (table 6.12), both for stayers and for movers, the large increases in expenditures for minimum rent programs relative to controls are not associated with corresponding increases in services. The same pattern of smaller increases in housing services relative to expenditure increases is also present for minimum rent households when the data are grouped by participation status. In fact, the unconstrained movers have the largest increases in housing services. Hence, it appears that minimum rent plans encourage poor shopping on the part of recipients.

With this overview in mind, we now turn to generally confirmatory results in the same area, based on more rigorous analysis. Specifically, the procedure relies on a multivariate model which controls for selection biases present in some of the experimental groups and more precisely contrasts the responses of any group of allowance recipients with the subset of control households most similar to them. Estimated impacts on housing consumption per recipient in various treatment groups are presented in tables 6.6, 6.7, and 6.8. Households are classified on the basis of their preenrollment housing consumption and postenrollment mobility behavior. Changes in both housing expenditures and services are presented. In addition, for each classification and treatment group, the table presents the proportion of the allowance payment used for changes in housing expenditures and services above "normal," that is above the increase by similar control households.

Table 6.6 presents the results for all recipient households two years after enrollment by treatment group and site. A key finding is the difference in the effects of allowances on consumption between the two sites that is described below. To date no satisfactory explanation for this divergence has been found.

---

7. For a discussion of hedonic indices and the results of their use in the Demand Experiment, see Merrill [H89].

Table 6.6

Estimated Experimental Effect on Housing Expenditures and Services and the Proportion of the Allowance Used for Increased Expenditures and Services above Normal: All Households Meeting Requirements Two Years after Enrollment

	Percentage Change In [a]		Proportion of Payment (above normal) Used For [b]	
	Expenditures	Services	Expenditures	Services
Pittsburgh				
Unconstrained	2.6	3.4	5.7	6.7
Percentage of rent	8.0	3.0	14.0	4.1
Minimum rent low	—3.6	0.0	—7.8	0.0
Minimum rent high	8.5*	0.9	23.3	2.2
Minimum standards	4.3	3.1	8.6	5.5
Phoenix				
Unconstrained	16.0**	12.6**	19.0	15.4
Percentage of rent	8.0	—1.0	23.7	1.7
Minimum rent low	15.7	11.0**	25.5	17.7
Minimum rent high	28.4**	18.0**	41.3	25.5
Minimum standards	16.2**	10.2**	27.4	17.2

Source: Friedman and Weinberg [H39], pp. 137, 139-141, 146, 167, 169, 170, 172-176; [H38], pp. A-94, A-103, A-126.

Sample: Households active and meeting requirements at two years after enrollment, excluding those with enrollment incomes over the eligibility limits and those living in their own homes or in subsidized housing.

a. Mean percentage change for percentage of rent; median percentage change for all others.

b. Computed as the estimated change in rent due to the allowance divided by the mean payment.

* t-statistic based on estimated experimental effect (i.e., predicted normal expenditures or services from a regression using controls minus actual expenditures or services) significant at the .05 level.

** t-statistic based on estimated experimental effect (i.e., predicted normal expenditures or services from a regression using controls minus actual expenditures or services) significant at the .01 level.

No tests of significant differences have been computed for the percentage-of-rent plan.

Unconstrained payments and some allowance plans have pervasive and significant impacts on both expenditures and services in Phoenix. For each measure, households in the high minimum rent program show the largest expenditure increase, although the change for services (above normal) is substantially below the change for expenditures. In Pittsburgh, only high minimum rent households significantly increase their housing expenditures, but not the housing services they obtain.[8]

As noted earlier, minimum rent households appear to increase their expenditures substantially more than they do their consumption of housing services.[9] In addition, note that minimum standards households increase their consumption of housing services slightly less and their expenditures slightly more than do unconstrained households.

When the targeting efficiency of the subsidy—the proportion of the payment used to increase expenditures above normal—is examined one finds much lower targeting in Pittsburgh than in Phoenix. But in both sites targeting is generally greater under the plans involving high minimum rent and physical standards than for controls.[10] Overall, the broad effects of earmarking appear to be slight.

Preenrollment housing condition is important in explaining consumption responses among recipient households. Table 6.7 presents consumption responses and targeting efficiency by initial housing condition for households that eventually met the housing requirements. Both the significance and the magnitude of the impacts of treatment group vary by initial housing condition. Hence, there is greater consistency in the findings for the two sites in this respect than in other areas. Households in dwellings initially failing the standard generally increase expenditures significantly. However, only in Phoenix does this result in an increase in housing services consumed. All the targeting of the subsidies to both increased expenditures and consumption of housing services above normal is generally much greater for households in units not meeting standards at enrollment than for those meeting the standard at enrollment. Thus, confirming the less rigorously derived results presented earlier, significant increases in housing consumption are essentially a phenomena for households initially not meeting program standards.

Table 6.8 presents the impact of postenrollment mobility behavior for recipient households initially failing requirements. No statistically significant increase in housing services is apparent in Pittsburgh for movers or stayers. While the same is true for stayers in Phoenix, impacts are again generally significant and pervasive for the movers at that site. An

---

8. Friedman and Weinberg [H39], pp. 218, 223.
9. Friedman and Weinberg [H39], pp. 218, 223.
10. The exception is for services in Pittsburgh.

Table 6.7

Estimated Experimental Effect on Housing Expenditures and Services and the Proportion of the Allowance Used for Increased Housing Expenditures and Services above Normal: All Households Meeting Requirements Two Years after Enrollment, by Preenrollment Housing Condition

	Percentage Change In [a]		Proportion of Payment (above normal) Used For [b]	
	Expenditures	Services	Expenditures	Services
Pittsburgh				
Households That Met Requirements at Enrollment				
Minimum rent low	2.4	0.5	5.7	0.0
Minimum rent high	4.6	—0.7	13.7	—1.7
Minimum standards	1.1	0.8	2.3	1.6
Households That Did Not Meet Requirements at Enrollment				
Minimum rent low	8.7	—0.9	15.4	—1.5
Minimum rent high	15.8**	3.1	38.8	6.8
Minimum standards	7.5*	5.6	14.2	9.5
Phoenix				
Households That Met Requirements at Enrollment				
Minimum rent low	—1.2	2.5	—2.7	5.4
Minimum rent high	7.4	4.2	15.4	8.4
Minimum standards	—0.7	8.2+	—2.1	22.7

important exception, however, is the lack of a significant increase in housing *services* among movers in the minimum standards programs, although they do choose units meeting program standards.

The differential response in terms of increased housing consumption between households qualifying at enrollment and those failing is im-

Table 6.7—Continued

Estimated Experimental Effect on Housing Expenditures and Services and the Proportion of the Allowance Used for Increased Housing Expenditures and Services above Normal: All Households Meeting Requirements Two Years after Enrollment, by Preenrollment Housing Condition

	Percentage Change In [a]		Proportion of Payment (above normal) Used For [b]	
	Expendi-tures	Services	Expendi-tures	Services
Households That Did Not Meet Requirements at Enrollment				
Minimum rent low	42.0**	20.2**	41.7	21.7
Minimum rent high	42.6**	26.0**	50.0	30.0
Minimum standards	23.6**	10.5*	32.8	14.9

Source: Friedman and Weinberg [H39], pp. 139-141, 146, 173-175, 222.

Sample: Households active and meeting requirements at two years after enrollment, excluding those with enrollment incomes over the eligibility limits and those living in their own homes or in subsidized housing.

a. Mean percentage change for percentage of rent; median percentage change for all others.

b. Computed as the estimated change in rent due to the allowance divided by the mean payment.

+ t-statistic based on estimated experimental effect (i.e., predicted normal expenditures or services from a regression using controls minus actual expenditures or services) significant at the .10 level.

* t-statistic based on estimated experimental effect (i.e., predicted normal expenditures or services from a regression using controls minus actual expenditures or services) significant at the .05 level.

** t-statistic based on estimated experimental effect (i.e., predicted normal expenditures or services from a regression using controls minus actual expenditures or services) significant at the .01 level.

portant for policy making. From the perspective of improving the housing conditions of eligible households, there is no point in increasing the consumption of households that already pass standards. On the other hand, such households may live in standard housing only because they devote

Table 6.8

Estimated Experimental Effect on Housing Expenditures and Services and the Proportion of the Allowance Used for Increased Housing Expenditures and Services above Normal: All Households Meeting Requirements Two Years after Enrollment Which Failed at Enrollment, by Postenrollment Mobility Behavior

	Percentage Change In [a]		Proportion of Payment (above normal) Used For [b]	
	Expenditures	Services	Expenditures	Services
	Pittsburgh			
Movers				
Minimum rent low	5.4	—5.0	9.7	—8.2
Minimum rent high	21.9**	10.7	62.6	25.9
Minimum standards	9.9+	2.7	20.5	5.1
Stayers				
Minimum rent low	7.5	—0.9	—	—
Minimum rent high	4.2	—5.1	—	—
Minimum standards	—0.5	2.7	—	—
	Phoenix			
Movers				
Minimum rent low	33.1**	21.2*	35.4	22.9
Minimum rent high	36.1**	20.5*	46.0	25.1
Minimum standards	27.1**	9.5	38.2	13.7
Stayers				
Minimum rent low	12.4	3.7	—	—
Minimum rent high	—	—	—	—
Minimum standards	3.9	4.0	—	—

Source: Friedman and Weinberg [H39], pp. 181-183, 190-192, 195-197, 204-206, 209-211, 213-215.

Sample: Households active and meeting requirements at two years after enment, excluding those with enrollment incomes over the eligibility limits and those living in their own homes or in subsidized housing.

a. Mean percentage change for percentage of rent; median percentage change for all others.

b. Computed as the estimated change in rent due to the allowance divided by the mean payment.

  + t-statistic based on estimated experimental effect (i.e., predicted normal expenditures or services from a regression using controls minus actual expenditures or services) significant at the .10 level.

  * t-statistic based on estimated experimental effect (i.e., predicted normal expenditures or services from a regression using controls minus actual expenditures or services) significant at the .05 level.

 ** t-statistic based on estimated experimental effect (i.e., predicted normal expenditures or services from a regression using controls minus actual expenditures or services) significant at the .01 level.

Table 6.9

Mean Rent Burden at Enrollment and at Two Years After Enrollment in Phoenix, by Treatment Group and Housing Requirement Status at Enrollment: For Households Meeting Requirements Two Years after Enrollment

	Mean Rent Burden [a]			Reduction for Similar Controls	Sample Size
	At Enroll-ment	At Two Years	Mean Reduc-tion [b]		
All Households That Met Requirements at Two Years					
Controls	.35	.34	—.01	—	256
Unconstrained	.40	.24	—.16	—	26
Percentage of rent	.37	.27	—.10	—	282
Minimum rent low	.41	.25	—.16	—	55
Minimum rent high	.42	.30	—.12	—	54
Minimum standards	.39	.22	—.17	—	70
Did Not Meet Require-ments at Enrollments					
Minimum rent low	.38	.24	—.14	+.12	20
Minimum rent high	.37	.25	—.12	+.05	24
Minimum standards	.36	.20	—.16	—.03	43
Met Requirements at Enrollment					
Minimum rent low	.43	.26	—.17	—.03	35
Minimum rent high	.51	.31	—.20	—.07	17
Minimum standards	.48	.30	—.18	—.03	20

Source: Friedman and Weinberg [H-39], A-86 through A-88; [H-38], p. A-96.
Sample: Households active at two years after enrollment, excluding those with enrollment incomes over the eligibility limits and those living in their own homes or in subsidized housing.
a. Rent burden at two years is computed as (rent-payment at two years)/income.
b. In percentage points.

a large proportion of income to housing at the expense of other goods and services.

ALLOWANCE EFFECTS ON RENT BURDENS

Rent burden is defined as the ratio of rental expenditures to household income; as such, it provides a useful measure for examining the extent to which households initially passing the standard were "housing poor." Tables 6.9 and 6.10 present the rent burdens at enrollment and two years after enrollment by treatment group for recipient households. In

Table 6.10

Mean Rent Burden at Enrollment and at Two Years after Enrollment in
Pittsburgh, by Treatment Group and Housing Requirement Status at
Enrollment: For Households Meeting Requirements Two Years after
Enrollment

	Mean Rent Burden [a]			Reduction for Similar Controls	Sample Size
	At Enroll- ment	At Two Years	Mean Reduc- tion [b]		
All Households That Met Requirements at Two Years					
Controls	.33	.29	—.04	—	388
Unconstrained	.39	.23	—.16	—	49
Percentage of rent	.36	.23	—.13	—	290
Minimum rent low	.39	.24	—.15	—	85
Minimum rent high	.42	.30	—.12	—	54
Minimum standards	.39	.22	—.17	—	80
Did Not Meet Require- ments at Enrollment					
Minimum rent low	.31	.22	—.09	+.04	20
Minimum rent high	.37	.30	—.07	+.07	23
Minimum standards	.37	.20	—.17	—.04	25
Met Requirements at Enrollment					
Minimum rent low	.41	.25	—.16	—.05	65
Minimum rent high	.46	.29	—.16	—.08	31
Minimum standards	.42	.24	—.18	—.06	47

Source: Friedman and Weinberg [H-39], A-86 through A-88; [H-38], p. A-96.
Sample: Households active at two years after enrollment, excluding those with
       enrollment incomes over the eligibility limits and those living in their
       own homes or in subsidized housing.
   a. Rent burden at two years is computed as (rent-payment at two years)/
income.
   b. In percentage points.

Phoenix, enrollment rent burdens ranged from 35 to 42 percent—fairly excessive by the conventional standard of 25 percent. At the end of two years, however, the reduction in rent burdens for households receiving payments was substantial, ranging from 12 to 17 percentage points as compared to 1 percentage point for control group households.[11] The resultant rent burden for recipients ranged from 22 to 30 percent. In addition, there was a similar reduction for unconstrained households and minimum standard households (16 and 17 percentage points, respectively).

When households are stratified by preenrollment housing status, households meeting requirements at enrollment are seen to have higher rent burdens than those failing standards. For the former, rent burden ranges from 43 to 51 percent; for the latter, from 36 to 38. Furthermore, the change in rent burden above normal (mean reduction minus the change for similar control households) is substantially greater for those households initially failing standards than for those passing. For example, among low minimum rent households in Phoenix (table 6.9), those not meeting standards at enrollment had a reduction above normal of 26 percent (i.e., their own reduction of 14 percent minus the change for similar control households of 12 percent) versus 16 percent for those passing standards at enrollment. Households meeting standards at enrollment still had higher rent burdens after two years than did households failing at enrollment: a range of 26 to 30 percent for the former versus a range of 20 to 25 percent for the latter. Still, both groups were much less deprived at two years.

Finally, it is clear that allowances affect recipients differently depending on initial housing conditions. For households passing standards initially, the payments are used on other goods and services, as witnessed by reduced rent burdens; for households failing standards initially, payments *for recipients* are used to increase their housing consumption and to reduce rent burden. Households passing standards do not increase their

---

11. This large reduction is, in part, due to the definition of rent burden used. The definition of rent burden employed in the analysis treats the subsidy payment as reducing rent and not as part of income. Since rent burden is defined as rent/income, the numerator is greatly reduced while the denominator is held constant. If the subsidy payment were treated as an addition to income, which would be more appropriate for comparisons of housing allowances with unconstrained payments, the reduction in rent burden would be significantly less.

housing consumption and, in fact, are not expected to do so. The justifications for enrolling such households in housing programs are to relieve financial deprivation due to excessive rent burden (which could also be achieved by unconstrained payments) and to foster keeping the dwellings they occupy up to standards.[12]

After two years, the main difference between households failing standards at enrollment but eventually participating in the program and unconstrained households is that the former groups "consume" more of the requirements—either minimum standards component or higher rents—than do households receiving unconstrained payments. There appears to be a modest difference in the total housing consumed by households initially failing standards and eventually enrolling compared to unconstrained households. This is an important distinction if society is more concerned about certain aspects of housing—for example, the presence of complete plumbing and proper ventilation and the absence of rats and fire hazards—than whether the total housing consumed, including simply occupying more rooms, meets some minimum. On the other hand, meeting the standards must be weighed against differences in participation: *all* unconstrained households receive payments; only eligible housing gap households *passing* requirements receive payments.

IS THERE A PARTICIPATION-CONSUMPTION TRADE OFF?

While housing requirements such as minimum standards have not been shown to induce a greater consumption of housing services, as defined by a hedonic index, than do unconstrained transfers, policy makers may have particular interest in eliminating certain deficiencies. These items may or may not be picked up in a hedonic index for several reasons —lack of data, an item may not be highly valued by the market, or problems of statistical estimation. Even if they are not valued by the market, the items constituting the minimum standards requirements are measures of the condition of the dwelling and could reflect "decent, safe, and sanitary" housing conditions.

---

12. Chapter 8 examines the topic of the extent of maintenance effects.

As discussed, recipient households with a minimum standards housing requirement have a statistically significant higher probability of meeting the minimum standards requirement than do unconstrained households. Further evidence indicates that recipient minimum standards households, when viewed against unconstrained households, are significantly more likely to pass several of the minimum standard components in both sites two years after enrollment.[13] We also know, however, that unconstrained households become recipients at a much higher rate than minimum standards households. Nonrecipient households experience virtually none of the housing improvement that recipients enjoy. We now turn to the relationship between unconstrained and earmarked housing allowances in the extent of housing improvement experienced among the *eligible* population as defined by changes in the number of minimum standards deficiencies eliminated.[14]

Table 6.11 presents the average number of minimum standards-defined deficiencies *eliminated* per *active* enrollee two years after enrollment, by the type of housing requirement imposed.

Although only two figures for Pittsburgh are statistically significant, enrolled households in both sites in the unconstrained program had a larger number of deficiencies eliminated than did households in any other program over the two-year period. It should also be noted that the number of deficiencies eliminated for minimum standards households may be biased upward due to the higher attrition rate for minimum standards households whose unit failed requirements at enrollment.

More sophisticated analysis has indicated, however, that the rankings presented in table 6.11 may change.[15] There may be an important participation-consumption per participant trade off that significantly influences the total impact of a housing allowances program on the housing stock. While this is one of the most important policy issues surfacing from EHAP, it is also one of the least examined. With only one exception,[16]

---

13. See Goedert [H40], p. 60.

14. By definition, since we already know that unconstrained households increase their consumption of housing services just as much as minimum standard recipients, the improvement among eligible households in an unconstrained program is twice as great, or more, than among minimum standards eligibles.

15. See Goedert [H40].

16. See Goedert [H40].

Table 6.11

Average Number of Minimum Standard-Defined Deficiencies Eliminated per Active Enrollee Two Years after Enrollment, by Site and Type of Housing Requirement

Housing Requirement	Phoenix	Pittsburgh
Unconstrained	1.41	.33*
Minimum rent low	.93	—.15*
Minimum rent high	1.02	.15
Minimum standard	1.34	.17

Source: Goedert [40], p. 63.

Sample: Enrollees active at two years after enrollment, excluding those with incomes over the eligibility limits for the program.

Note: These numbers were derived by subtracting the total number of components failed at two years after enrollment from the total number of components failed at enrollment by all enrollees still active after two years and dividing the resultant differences by the number of enrollees still active after two years.

* t-statistic of the difference between the mean of unconstrained and minimum rent low household, significant at the .05 level using a two-tailed test.

the issue has received little attention. While the methodological problems are substantial (e.g., self-selection and interdependencies among individual standards) the benefits of more research on this issue may be significant.

Table 6.12

Changes in Housing Services from Enrollment to Two Years after Enrollment, by Treatment Type and Mobility in Phoenix and Pittsburgh: For All Households

	Stayers				Movers			
	At Enroll-ment	Housing Services At Two Years	Percentage Change	Sample Size	At Enroll-ment	Housing Services At Two Years	Percentage Change	Sample Size
				PHOENIX				
Control [a]	$131	$135	3	121	$127	$156	23	108
Unconstrained	146	154	5	15	125	166	33	18
Percentage of rent	115	118	3	232	133	157	18	134
Minimum rent low	124	132	6	32	127	160	26	42
Minimum rent high	131	139	6	31	132	157	19	52
Minimum standard	129	136	5	63	128	156	22	65
				PITTSBURGH				
Control [a]	$114	$116	2	181	$114	$126	11	92
Unconstrained	106	108	2	33	105	131	25	19
Percentage of rent	115	118	3	232	111	128	15	121
Minimum rent low	112	113	1	72	106	119	12	34
Minimum rent high	113	114	1	67	113	125	11	34
Minimum standard	112	113	1	112	106	121	14	67

Source: Friedman and Weinberg [H39], pp. A-78 through A-83; [H38], pp. A-127, A-128.
Sample: Households active two years after enrollment, excluding those with enrollment inccmes over the eligibility limits and those living in their own homes or in subsidized housing.
a. See chapter 3 for description of plans.

Table 6.13

Changes in Housing Services from Enrollment to Two Years after Enrollment, by Treatment Type and Mobility in Phoenix and Pittsburgh: For Households Who Met Requirements at Two Years

	Stayers				Movers			
	Housing Services		Percentage Change	Sample Size	Housing Services		Percentage Change	Sample Size
	At Enrollment	At Two Years			At Enrollment	At Two Years		
PHOENIX								
Did Not Meet at Enrollment								
Minimum rent low	$106	$115	8(5)[a]	2	$111	$154	39(57)[a]	18
Minimum rent high	—	—	—(—1)	—	127	174	37(48)	25
Minimum standard	138	145	5(5)	20	124	170	37(43)	31
Met at Enrollment								
Minimum rent low	150	159	6(2)[a]	16	147	174	20(13)[a]	19
Minimum rent high	170	177	4(2)	7	160	181	13(9)	10
Minimum standard	155	164	6(1)	12	150	169	13(—1)	9

PITTSBURGH

Did Not Meet at Enrollment

Minimum rent low	$113	$111	−2(2)ᵃ	11	$ 94	$116	23(21)ᵃ	10
Minimum rent high	113	115	2(5)	8	107	128	20(22)	16
Minimum rent standard	116	122	5(−1)	20	110	132	20(27)	25

Met at Enrollment

Minimum rent low	$116	$119	3(2)ᵃ	46	$115	$123	7(6)ᵃ	22
Minimum rent high	134	132	−1(1)	21	127	134	6(7)	10
Minimum rent standard	128	126	−2(2)	31	121	135	12(6)	6

Source: Friedman and Weinberg [H39], pp. A-78 through A-83; [H38], pp. 9-127, A-128.
Sample: Households active two years after enrollment, excluding those with enrollment incomes over the eligibility limits and those living in their own homes or in subsidized housing.
a. Percentage change in services between enrollment and two years after enrollment for control households of similar status.

Table 6.14

Changes in Housing Services from Enrollment to Two Years after Enrollment, by Treatment Type and Mobility in Phoenix and Pittsburgh: For Households Who Did Not Meet Requirements at Two Years

	Stayers				Movers			
	Housing Services				Housing Services			
	At Enroll-ment	At Two Years	Percentage Change	Sample Size	At Enroll-ment	At Two Years	Percentage Change	Sample Size
PHOENIX								
Did Not Meet at Enrollment								
Minimum rent low	$ 97	$104	7(4)[a]	14	$104	$131	26(25)[a]	3
Minimum rent high	120	128	7(3)	24	119	120	1(24)	16
Minimum standard	112	119	6(3)	31	114	127	11(19)	20
Met at Enrollment								
Minimum rent low	—	—	—	—	$116	$134	16(—3)	2
Minimum rent high	—	—	—	—	169	107	—37(13)	1
Minimum standard	—	—	—	—	169	160	— 5(12)	5

PITTSBURGH

Did Not Meet at Enrollment

Minimum rent low	$ 98	$ 98	0(1)[a]	15	$ 72	$ 92	28(8)[a]	2
Minimum rent high	101	104	3(1)	38	107	106	−1(8)	8
Minimum standard	102	103	1(3)	61	99	109	10(9)	33

Met at Enrollment

Minimum rent low	—	—	—	—	—	—	—(4)[a]	—
Minimum rent high	—	—	—	—	—	—	—(0)	—
Minimum standard	—	—	—	117	117	130	11(1)	3

Source: Friedman and Weinberg [H39], pp. A-78 through A-83; [H38], pp. A-127, A-128.

Sample: Households active two years after enrollment, excluding those with enrollment incomes over the eligibility limits and those living in their own homes or in subsidized housing.

a. Percentage change in services between enrollment and two years after enrollment for control households of similar status.

CHAPTER 7

Household Responsiveness to Unconstrained Housing Allowances

Francis J. Cronin

THE EFFECTIVENESS of allowance programs designed to improve the housing of low-income renter households depends on the type of subsidy and housing requirements, the response of eligible households to the incentives and constraints, and the response of landlords to increased demand. Household responses to unconstrained income supplements and price reduction subsidies are explored in this chapter. Knowing how households change their housing consumption when given a simple income supplement or a subsidy in the price of housing is essential to understanding the effectiveness of various government housing policies.

Economists have developed a concept called the income elasticity of demand to measure how households respond to changes in income. Of particular interest for housing policy is the income elasticity of demand for housing, which measures how households change their demand for housing when incomes change. The income elasticity of demand for housing is defined as the percentage change in housing consumed divided by the percentage change in income.[1]

---

1. If the quantity of housing consumed does not change at all when income changes, the income elasticity of demand is zero. If a housing allowance program provides an income supplement equal to 20 percent of household income, a zero income elasticity tells us that the quantity of housing consumed will not increase. If the income elasticity of demand for housing is 1, a 20 percent increase in income results in a 20 percent increase in housing consumption. And, of course, if the ·percentage change in housing consumption exceeds the percentage change in income, the income elasticity is greater than 1. For example, if the 20 percent increase in household income results in a 30 percent increase in housing consumption, the income elasticity

Just as the income elasticity of demand is useful to analyze a housing allowance that supplements income, the price elasticity of demand is crucial to evaluate an allowance that reduces the price of housing. In principle, the two concepts are parallel: the price elasticity of demand for housing is the percentage change in housing consumption divided by the percentage change in the price of housing.[2]

The basic finding of the chapter is that all the studies using EHAP data indicate a minimal response to housing allowances in the short run: demand is income and price inelastic. Consensus is elusive for the long run because estimates range from highly inelastic to unitary elastic for both income and price. Using the most defensible elasticity estimates, we compare effects of income supplement and price reduction programs.[3] The latter appear more generally effective in increasing housing consumption, targeting program funds to housing, and reducing rent burden. Some evidence from the Demand Experiment casts doubt on the applicability of this conclusion for low-income households. Also, imposing housing standards to constrain an income supplement program reduces but does not eliminate the advantage of price reduction programs.

Some of the discussion in the next two sections is fairly technical; the policy implications of the findings are explained in the final two sections of the chapter.

PRE-EHAP VIEWS OF HOUSEHOLD DEMAND

The first elasticity estimates of specific interest are those done in the 1960s and early 1970s which embodied Milton Friedman's permanent income

---

is 1.5 (30/20 percent). When the ratio of the percentage change in housing consumption over the percentage change in income is between zero and 1, we say demand is inelastic. When the ratio is 1, we say demand is of unitary elasticity. Values greater than 1 are called elastic.

2. As before, if the price elasticity of demand is less than 1, it is referred to as inelastic; if 1, as unitary elastic; and if greater than 1, as elastic. Since a decline in the price of a good usually causes consumers to buy more, the sign of the price elasticity is negative. Economists, however, often ignore the sign and refer to the price elasticity in terms of its absolute value. The importance of this concept is clear. When the price elasticity of demand is high, a housing allowance that subsidizes the price of housing will have a marked effect on housing consumption; as the elasticity falls to zero, so does the program's impact on housing consumption. New evidence on the size of the income elasticity and the price elasticity of housing demand have been produced employing the data gathered within the Demand and Supply Experiments.

3. The potential effectiveness of supply-oriented versus demand-oriented housing policies in increasing consumption of housing depends on the relative magnitudes of the supply and demand elasticities (the latter to the extent that the supply of housing is less than perfectly elastic). For a discussion of the relative effectiveness of these programs in terms of their elasticities, see Weicher [P88], p. 483.

hypothesis that posited that consumption is related to past and expected income as well as current income. Several studies reported income and price elasticities greater than 1;[4] others showed the demand for housing to be relatively inelastic with respect to income and price.[5]

De Leeuw, in work undertaken as part of HUD's pre-EHAP design analysis, reviewed and attempted to reconcile the available evidence from cross-sectional analyses.[6] He concluded that the income elasticity of home-owners varied between 1.25 and 1.46, while for renters the income elasticity was about .80 and the price elasticity was about —.70. Armed with these estimates, anticipating the effect of the EHAP on housing expenditures was straightforward. For example, consider an unconstrained housing allowance of $50 per month that is given to a family with a monthly income of $400. The family rents a unit for $100 per month and has an income elasticity of demand for housing of .8. The subsidy causes the family to increase its housing expenditures by $10—fully 80 percent of the subsidy would be spent on goods and services other than housing. This estimated effect is based on the conventional economic paradigm of household behavior—a paradigm that, as shown next, would necessarily overestimate the impact of the EHAP on housing consumption.

Conventional economic models of residential location and housing consumption focus primarily on comparative static analysis with little regard for the difficulties of adjusting, over an extended time period, from one equilibrium to another.[7] These models derive equilibrium patterns of residential location and housing consumption—patterns such that without changed conditions households have no incentive to alter behavior. Households are assumed to operate in a world of perfect information and zero transactions costs; therefore, changes in any of the determinants of the demand for housing (e.g., a housing allowance subsidy) would lead to full adjustment on the part of households by the next period. Some people began to think of the adjustment period itself as being short, when in fact the modelers themselves saw it as far from instantaneous.

However, as explained in chapters 4 and 5 the costs associated with the mobility process are fairly substantial and, unlike the gains from relocation which accrue through time, are suffered in large part at the

---

4. See Muth [H98]; Reid [H109]; Winger [H133]; Uhler [H123]; Paldam [H103]; Houthakker and Taylor [H62]; in the case of price elasticity, Lee [H68] for elasticity results exceeding 1.

5. See Houthakker [H61]; Leser [H71]; Lee [H67, H68]; Muth [H98, H99]; and Maisel, Burnham, and Austin [H82].

6. See de Leeuw [H32].

7. Alonso [H3]; Muth [H98].

time of a move.[8] When they recognize these relocation costs, households may select a housing bundle in response to current circumstances and expected changes in housing prices, income, neighborhood, and housing needs. Instantaneous adjustment certainly is unlikely.

In fact, work undertaken at about the time of the design of EHAP attempted to model the dynamic adjustments of households. Phlips estimated long-run income and price elasticities greater than 1 (in absolute value), but highly inelastic short-run elasticities (i.e., .17 for income and —.05 for price).[9] Earlier analysis had indicated a slow adjustment on the part of households to changes in their determinants of housing demand—in fact, results suggested that it would take seven years for 90 percent of the adjustment to be completed.[10]

The middle 1970s saw a wave of studies that found the *current* income elasticity of renter households to be less than .5.[11] As noted, higher values were obtained when researchers employed proxies for permanent income.[12] As de Leeuw had done earlier, Polinsky and Ellwood attempted to correct the econometric inadequacies of prior studies and concluded that the income elasticity is about —.7.[13]

Whether the pre-EHAP consensus with respect to the size of the income and price elasticities was correct or slightly too high was not crucial to the experimental design. What was crucial, however, was the acceptance of the conventional model of household behavior—behavior in a known and frictionless environment with its implied quick and full adjustment to changed circumstances. When transaction costs and uncertainty are recognized, the real net benefits of a housing allowance, particularly for

---

8. For a discussion of the benefits and costs of intraurban relocation, see Cronin [H29]. Chapter 5 discusses the issue of mobility within EHAP.

9. Philips [H104]. Similarly, Weiserbs [H130] also estimated elastic long-run elasticities and highly inelastic short-run elasticities (i.e., .24 for income and —.12 for price).

10. Lee [H68].

11. See Barton and Olsen [H11]; Brown [H14]; Carliner [H19]; Fenton [H35]; Kain and Quigley [C44]; Lee and Kong [H70]; Li [H72] and Straszheim [H118]. For a discussion of estimates made after 1970, see Mayo [H86].

12. For example, using a measure of permanent income, Carliner [H19] found income elasticities of .52 and .63 for renters and homeowners, respectively; and Lee and Kong [H70] obtained values of .70 and .87. Estimates of the price elasticity were higher (in absolute value). For example, Barton and Olson [H11]; Brown [H14]; Lee and Kong [H70]; and Straszheim [H118] report values ranging from —.53 to —.69. Carliner [H19] reports a value of —.80 while Fenton [H35] reports —1.28.

13. See Polinsky and Ellwood [H106].

14. As we shall see below, the difference between a unitary and a somewhat inelastic elasticity has little long-run consequences for the concerns of public policy.

households constrained by the experiment, may be small. Households, if they react at all, will probably do so only with a lag. As noted in chapter 2, these complications may not have been fully perceived in the design of payment structure and the length of experimental payment in the Demand Experiment.

ESTIMATES OF HOUSING DEMAND ELASTICITIES USING EHAP DATA

The results of the eight studies that have used data from the Demand or the Supply Experiments to estimate income and price elasticities of demand for housing are reviewed here. First examined are the static analyses, and then the dynamic estimates that distinguish short-run from long-run elasticities are presented.

Table 7.1 presents results from four studies using data from the Demand Experiment and based on static specifications. Two studies—those by Mayo and by Friedman and Weinberg—employ experimental data from the percentage of rent treatment groups. The former employs the first-year experimental data, while the latter employs both the first- and second-year experimental data. The other two studies—by Cronin and by Hanushek and Quigley—employ data collected from the baseline survey on the housing and household characteristics of potentially eligible households before the expirements begin.[15]

The estimates of the static income elasticity are consistently inelastic. Current income elasticities range from .11 to .37. "Permanent" income elasticities, in which income is measured as average income for two or three years, always exceed their corresponding current estimates and range from .33 to .44. Estimates of the price elasticity differ more widely but are nevertheless consistently inelastic. Those employing EHAP data range from —.11 to —.24; those based on preexperimental data range from —.53 to —.67.

Inferences of demand elasticity based on a static specification of household responses to the experimental rebate may, in fact, be mis-

---

15. See Mayo [H86]; Friedman and Weinberg [H38]; Cronin [H25]; and Hanushek and Quigley [H51]. Use of preexperimental information and, to a lesser extent, data on control households removes the possibility of experimental contamination. Mayo [H86] and Friedman and Weinberg [H38] employ a log-linear specification with the experimental rebate term used to identify the price of housing. Cronin [H25] employs a linear expenditure specification. The actual distribution of rental expenditures at baseline is employed to estimate the expenditure on the "subsistence" level of housing and, thus, all system parameters.

Table 7.1

Income and Price Elasticities: Static Estimates from the Demand
Experiment Sites

	Pittsburgh		Phoenix	
	Income Elasticity	Price Elasticity	Income Elasticity	Price Elasticity
Mayo [H86][a] [c]				
Current income	.32	—.11	.26	—.24
Average income				
(two year)	.34	—.11	.40	—.23
Friedman and Weinberg [H38][a] [d]				
Current income	.29	—.16	.37	—.24
Average income				
(three year)	.33	—.18	.44	—.23
Hanushek and Quigley [H51][e] [f]				
Current income	.14	N.A.	.24	N.A.
Cronin [H25][b] [e]				
Current income				
Nonminority	.11	—.64	.19	—.67
Minority	.13	—.53	.24	—.60

Note: All estimates are for the entire sample of households (movers and nonmovers). When only movers are analyzed, resulting elasticities are generally larger in absolute value.

a. Log-linear specification.

b. Linear specification.

c. Sample consists of households in the percentage of rent and control groups over the first year of the experiment.

d. Sample consists of households in the percentage of rent and control groups over the second year of the experiment.

e. Sample consists of households responding to the baseline survey.

f. Omits the price of housing.

leading. Household responses within a three-year experiment like the Demand Experiment may be inhibited by the normal inertia and the perception of a short time horizon created by the experiment. That is, households may normally respond to changes in the determinants of their demand for housing with a time lag. In addition, the tendency of experimental households to limit their response may predominate due to the short duration of the change in income or in the price of housing. As already noted, a limited response is more likely when substantial repairs or a move is required to become eligible for an allowance. Without such a re-

Table 7.2

Income Elasticities: Static Estimates from the Supply Experiment Sites [a]

	Green Bay	South Bend
Mulford [H94][b]		
Owners	.51	.40
Renters	.22	.15
Mills and Sullivan [C70][c]		
Owners	.76	N.A.
Renters	.20	N.A.

a. Estimates based on 3 annual observations. Three-year average annual income employed; log-linear specifications employed; no price term included.
b. Sample based on respondents to the Tenant and Homeowner Survey. Only nonmoving households sampled.
c. Sample based on enrollees. All households employed (i.e., moving and not moving).

quirement, the subsidy, if received, acts largely as a general income grant to be spent on other goods and services. Further, if the household expects not to be able to afford the higher quality housing after the program ends, participation may also require a second move. All of these factors argue against the general applicability of the elasticity results reported in Mayo and in Friedman and Weinberg which are based on experimental data.[16] They may, though, be taken as lower bounds to the true parameters.

Results from estimating static specifications from Supply Experiment data are presented in table 7.2. The same model specifications are employed by Mulford and by Mills and Sullivan, and both use three-year average annual income as a proxy for permanent income.[17] Mulford, however, employs data from the Supply Experiment's Tenant and Homeowner Survey which tracks dwelling units. Therefore, only nonmoving households are included in Mulford's analysis—a possible source of downward bias. Mills and Sullivan employ data from the administering agency's files on recipient households including both movers and nonmovers. As can be seen, both studies estimate a much larger elasticity for homeowners than for renters.

Dynamic estimates of income and price elasticities using Demand Experiment data are displayed in table 7.3. Each estimate is based on a

16. Reinforcing this conclusion is the fact that the larger elasticities (in absolute value) reported by Cronin (−.53 to −.67) were the product of a specification that constrains the price elasticities to be inelastic (i.e., less than 1).

17. Both the Mulford [H94] and the Mills and Sullivan [C70] studies employ a log-linear specification and omit explicit considerations of the price of housing.

Table 7.3

Income and Price Elasticities: Dynamic Estimates

	Pittsburgh		Phoenix	
	Income Elasticity	Price Elasticity	Income Elasticity	Price Elasticity
Mayo [H86][a c g]				
Long run	.26	—.07	.14	—.31
Short run	.39	—.11	.29	—.63
Friedman and Weinberg [H38][a d]				
Short run	.30	—.20	.27	—.22
Long run	.37	—.24	.39	—.31
Hanushek and Quigley [H55][e f]				
Short run	N.A.	—.12	N.A.	—.16
Long run	N.A.	—.64	N.A.	—.45
Cronin [H24][b d g]				
Short run				
Percentage of rent	.23 .23	—.09 —.24	.21 .17	—.25 —.29
Housing gap	.22	—.39	.13	—.32
Long run				
Percentage of rent	.54 .61	—.10 —.55	.97 .72	—1.00 —1.00
Housing gap	.68	—1.00	.47	—1.00

a. Sample consists of households in the percentage of rent and control treatment groups.

b. Sample consists of households in all treatment groups stratified by type of subsidy (i.e., percentage of rent or housing gaps). For households in the latter, only households passing the housing requirements (and thus, unconstrained by the program) are included.

c. Includes movers over the first year of the experiment.

d. Includes movers over the first two years of the experiment.

e. Includes movers and stayers over the first two years of the experiment.

f. Current income employed.

g. Average income employed.

different specification and/or data set.[18] The table shows that short-run estimates of both the income and the price elasticities are very inelastic. Short-run income elasticities range from .14 to .30; short-run price elas-

18. To date, no Supply Experiment data have been used to estimate dynamic elasticities. Except for Hanushek and Quigley [H55], who use moving and stationary households, the results are based on households which moved and could thus be expected to adjust toward equilibrium. Mayo [H86] and Cronin [H24] both employ average annual income, the former over a two-year period and the latter over a three-year period, as a proxy for permanent income. Mayo [H86] and Friedman and Wein-

ticities range from —.07 to —.31. Long-run estimates, by contrast, show considerable diversity.

Long-run results by Mayo and by Friedman and Weinberg are quite similar to their static estimates. The single exception to this pattern is a much higher long-run price elasticity (—.63) in Phoenix reported by Mayo. Their estimates of long-run income elasticities range from .29 to .39; excluding the Phoenix observation just cited, long-run price elasticities range from —.11 to —.31. Employing their indirect method, Hanushek and Quigley find somewhat higher long-run price elasticity, estimates ranging from —.45 to —.64[19]

All of these estimates are probably too low because they are based on household responses to a price discount and subject to the downward biases that result because households may not respond instantaneously or fully to the program. Further, the results reported by Hanushek and Quigley may be additionally biased downward by the use of current income and a static specification for desired rental expenditures.

Cronin[20] presents short-run elasticities which might overcome the limitations from using observed experimental responses.[21] His short-run elasticities are similar to the others—income elasticity ranging from .13 to .23 and price elasticity ranging from —.09 to —0.39. However, his long-run estimates are substantially above the results reported by the

---

berg [H38] employ a log-linear specification, relating rental expenditures to income, the rent-discount term, and rental expenditures lagged one period. Hanushek and Quigley [H52] employ baseline data to estimate a static specification of desired housing expenditures using current income. This specification is then employed in an indirect estimation of the price elasticity. The adjustments by households over time in response to initial deviations (i.e., desired versus actual expenditures) and to changes in deviations induced by the price-discount term are used to infer the value of the price elasticity.

Cronin [H24] employs a specification of the linear expenditure system which is made dynamic by allowing the "minimum level" of housing consumption (i.e., the displacement term for housing in the Stone-Geary utility function) to change with previous housing consumption. That is, the demand for housing is made dynamic in a manner consistent with incorporating habit formation into the utility maximization process. In order to specify a price of housing, Cronin employs a hedonic price function developed by Merrill [H89]. Therefore, after appropriate changes in their budget constraints, both housing gap and percentage of rent households can be used in the estimation. In order to minimize experimental influences, only housing gap households unconstrained by housing requirements are employed in the estimation. Theoretically, these households should treat the subsidy as they would ordinary income, although households may view the subsidy as transitory.

19. See Mayo [H86]; Friedman and Weinberg [H38]; Hanushek and Quigley [H52].

20. See Cronin [H24].

21. Again, see footnote 18 for a description of this procedure.

others—income elasticities ranging from .47 to .97 and price elasticities ranging from −.10 to −1.00. Three out of the four estimates of long-run price elasticity are −1.00; the only estimate below unity is obtained for percentage of rent households in Pittsburgh—a finding consistent with the hypothesis of a limited response to the experimental offer and the lower mobility rate in Pittsburgh.

Although the data collected from the Demand Experiment are probably the best available (and likely to be so for quite some time), several deficiencies mar their usefulness. First, only renter households are included. Thus, homeowners and households switching tenure from rental to homeownership are excluded.[22] In fact, the tenure switch (in both directions) in combination with life-cycle changes may be the crucial link in accurately estimating income elasticities. Second, the experimental period is short run—three years for payments and two years for data collection. As discussed, household adjustments may occur with a lag and over a much longer period. Third, the enrollment process is closed. Thus household changes, such as divorce and children leaving, which cause changes in the demand for housing, cannot be adequately modeled. Fourth, only low-income households are included. Since only a minority of these households have strong labor-force attachments and established commuting patterns, the conventional Alonso-Muthian model of urban household behavior involving simultaneous determination of location, commuting, and housing demand may not be applicable. Finally, only two sites are included. While the basic findings are fairly consistent between the sites, the differences in dynamic behavior (e.g., in mobility) cannot be easily resolved.[23]

In summary, several estimates from EHAP have indicated that the demand for housing is very inelastic with respect to both price and income. Others suggest this is true in the short run, but the long-run income elasticity is about .6 or .7—close to Polinsky and Ellwood's [24] estimate of .8 that was synthesized from recent non-EHAP studies. Price elasticity estimates from EHAP vary greatly and surround the Polinsky and Ellwood synthesis estimate of −.7. Despite the richness of the experimental data, it is unlikely that more precise estimates will be forthcoming, given the data deficiencies just noted.

---

22. A small number of renter households in the Demand Experiment did become homeowners after the start of the experiment.

23. To resolve such differences, a longer-run period would be necessary. It is possible that data from The Urban Institute's "supply comparability panel" could be used to examine these issues. The section of Appendix C on the Supply Experiment explains the potential role of the comparability panel.

24. See Polinsky and Ellwood [H106].

EVALUATING HOUSING POLICIES: THE ROLE OF ELASTICITIES

Housing allowances under EHAP took the form of an income supplement or a price reduction subsidy. A program of income supplements—that is cash payments without minimum housing requirements—works by increasing the recipients' demand for housing by raising their income. The accomplishment of the policy goal of increasing recipients' housing consumption is measured by the income elasticity of demand, when unconstrained housing programs are being considered. This measure of household responsiveness to an allowance program is also useful to analyze other policy goals such as reducing the rent burden of eligible households and the extent to which program funds are in fact spent on housing. Subsidies that reduce the price of housing to program recipients work through two mechanisms: (a) an effective increase in income because of the lower price of housing and (b) a decrease in the price of housing relative to other goods and services that encourages program participants to purchase more housing. The price elasticity of demand indicates how such a program will affect housing consumption, the targeting of program funds to housing, and the change in rent burden. In this section the income and price elasticity estimates reviewed previously are used to analyze the efficacy of alternative income or price subsidy housing allowance programs.

Income Supplement Programs

The relationship between expenditures on housing and various subsidy levels for alternative income elasticities is shown in figure 7.1. Initially, the hypothetical family depicted in the figure has a monthly income of $400 and pays $100 per month in rent. A zero income elasticity means that an income subsidy will not cause any increase in housing expenditure; the entire allowance would be spent on other goods and services. Even when the income elasticity of demand is 1, the change in expenditure is not dramatic; a subsidy of $150 raises monthly housing expenditures by $37.50. With the average monthly subsidy in EHAP being around $50, an elasticity of 1 suggests increased housing consumption of only $12.50.[25] Of course, due to lags in household response to an income supplement, the actual average initial change in housing expenditures under an allowance would be smaller. If the Demand Experiment's highest short-

---

25. An income elasticity of unity implies that the same proportion of additional income will be spent on housing as the household is currently spending on housing (e.g., .25 in figure 7.1).

Figure 7.1

Housing Consumption and the Income Elasticity of Demand for a
Household with an Income of $400 per Month

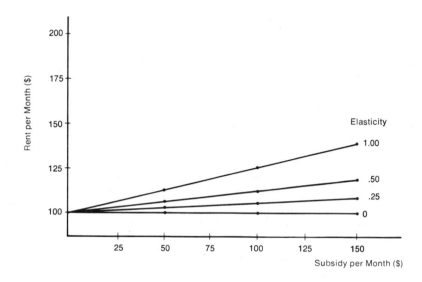

run income elasticity (.30) were used to estimate the response during the
experiment, a $3.75 increase in housing expenditures per month would
result from a $50 subsidy. Based on the long-run results just reported,
something less than one fourth of any housing allowance program funds
would be spent on housing. Moreover, the experimental evidence suggests
households take a considerable time to adjust to changed circumstances:
estimated adjustment is 90 percent complete after *seven* years in Pittsburgh
and 79 percent after the same period in Phoenix.[26]

The elasticity estimates can also be translated into implications for
a household's rent burden. Table 7.4 shows the relationship between
income elasticity and rent burdens for alternative subsidy to income ratios.
When the income elasticity of demand is greater than 1, housing expenditures rise more rapidly than income; hence, postsubsidy rent burden increases with the subsidy-income ratio when the elasticity exceeds 1.
Conversely, the postsubsidy rent burden falls as the subsidy-income ratio
rises when the income elasticity is less than 1. By definition, rent burden
remains constant when the elasticity is one. For a given subsidy to in-

<hr>

26. These results are based on the dynamic specifications estimated in Cronin
[H24].

Table 7.4

The Relationship between the Income Elasticity of Demand and Postsubsidy Rent Burden [a]

Income Elasticity	Subsidy as A Percentage of Income		
	12.5	25.0	37.5
1.50	.2652	.2795	.2932
1.25	.2575	.2643	.2707
1.00	.2500	.2500	.2500
0.75	.2427	.2364	.2309
0.50	.2357	.2236	.2132
0.25	.2289	.2115	.1969
0	.2222	.2000	.1818

a. Preprogram rent burden is 0.25.

come ratio, the rent burden increases with the size of the elasticity. Assuming a subsidy about $600 per year—the average in EHAP and a 12.5 percent income subsidy for a household with a $4,800 income—table 7.4 shows that the rent burden with the subsidy ranges from 22.2 percent of income to 26.5 percent as the income elasticity rises from zero to 1.50. Thus, the goals of targeting program funds to housing and reducing rent burden are mutually exclusive: a high-income elasticity raises both targeting and rent burden. In considering the trade off between targeting program funds and rent burden, it is important to remember that rent burdens in excess of 40 percent are common among eligible households.

Price Reduction Programs

Percentage of rent versions of housing allowances employed in the Demand Experiment are essentially price reduction programs, since the subsidy is directly tied to the amount spent on housing. Figure 7.2 shows the relationship between housing expenditures and various levels of price reductions for alternative price elasticities. As with an income supplement program, a zero elasticity means that housing expenditures will not change when the price is subsidized. When the price elasticity is —1.00, housing expenditure rises from $75 to $150 with a 50 percent price subsidy.[27] Figure 7.2 shows that expenditures on housing increase with the

27. Usually a price elasticity of —1 is associated with constant total expenditures instead of the rising expenditures shown in figure 7.2. For households to maintain constant out-of-pocket expenditures, they must double their housing expenditures since the program gives them a 50 percent rebate on the amount spent on housing.

Figure 7.2

Housing Expenditures and the Price Elasticity of Demand

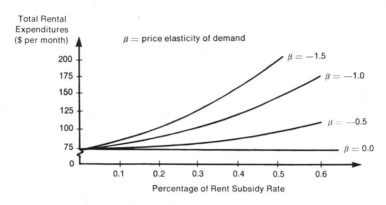

Source: Mayo [H86], p. 30.

absolute value of the price elasticity for a given price discount or, alternatively, with increases in the price discount for a given price elasticity.

The extent to which price subsidies are spent on housing depends on the price elasticity of demand for housing. When the price elasticity exceeds 1 (in absolute value), the household devotes all of the subsidy and part of its own income to increased housing consumption. For lower elasticities, less of the subsidy is devoted to housing. Table 7.5 summarizes the proportion of the subsidy that is spent on housing for

Table 7.5

The Relationship between the Price Elasticity of Demand and
Subsidy Targeting

Price Elasticity	Percentage of Rent Subsidy Rate		
	.2	.4	.6
—1.50	1.42	1.34	1.25
—1.25	1.22	1.18	1.14
—1.00	1.00	1.00	1.00
— .75	.77	.80	.83
— .50	.53	.56	.61
— .25	.27	.30	.34
.00	.00	.00	.00

Source: Mayo [H86], p. 32.

various elasticities and three price subsidies. By reading across a row, one can see that for a given price elasticity the degree of targeting the subsidy on housing increases with the size of the subsidy for a price elasticity less than 1 and decreases as the price discount increases when the elasticity is greater than 1.

As in the case of income supplement programs, the goals of targeting program funds to housing and decreasing rent burden are conflicting. Table 7.6 shows that rent burden varies directly with the absolute value of the price elasticity. This is not surprising. Since a household with an elasticity greater than 1 increases housing expenditure by more than the subsidy, rent burden must increase. Similarly, rent burden is consistent when the price elasticity of demand is 1 and falls when elasticity is less than 1.

COMPARING INCOME SUPPLEMENT AND PRICE REDUCTION PROGRAMS

We are now in a position to use the elasticities to compare the relative merits of the two basic versions of housing allowances without minimum consumption requirements with respect to changed consumption, targeting of program funds, and changes in rent burden. With respect to changes in consumption and targeting, for any plausible value of the income elasticity of demand, only a fraction of the subsidy will be spent on housing. If the "true" income elasticity were 1.0, a figure somewhat higher than most estimates, a household that spends 40 percent of its preprogram income on housing would devote 40 percent of the subsidy on housing. In sharp contrast, allowances that lower the price of housing are better targeted and increase the consumption of housing more effectively. When the price elasticity of demand is −1, a figure obtained in several estimates using EHAP data, the entire allowance is used to increase consumption. Even if the price elasticity were −.5, a value lower than the consensus estimate, such a program targets over 50 percent of the allowance, as shown in table 7.5. Whether the actual change in housing consumption is greater under the price subsidy depends on the size of the income subsidy and the rate at which rents are reduced.

A result favorable to price subsidies is also found when the programs are compared with respect to rent burden. Neither allowance program changes the rent burden of recipients when the income and price elasticities are 1 and −1 respectively. When the elasticities are less than 1, rent burden falls. Depending on the size of the subsidy relative to income,

Table 7.6

The Relationship between the Price Elasticity of Demand and
Postsubsidy Rent Burden [a]

Price Elasticity	Percentage of Rent Subsidy Rate		
	.2	.4	.6
—1.50	.2795	.3228	.3953
—1.25	.2643	.2740	.2843
—1.00	.2500	.2500	.2500
— .75	.2365	.2200	.1988
— .50	.2236	.1938	.1580
— .25	.2115	.1705	.1258
0	.2000	.1500	.1000

a. Preprogram rent burden is 0.25.

rent burden falls between 3 and 8 percent for the household depicted in table 7.2 when the income elasticity is .75. The effect of the price elasticity of demand on rent burden depends on the size of the price discount. Table 7.6 shows that for price discounts ranging from 20 to 60 percent a price elasticity of —.75 lowers rent burden from 5 to 20 percent. Not only is a price subsidy the most effective in targeting program funds to housing for plausible estimates of the elasticities; it also lowers rent burden to a greater extent. Even with rather large changes in the estimated price and income elasticities from the "best" estimates of —.7 and .7, respectively, the conclusion that price reduction programs are more effective than income supplements would not be altered.

Another way to compare these policies is to analyze which option is preferred by the recipients rather than which is preferred by the donors. Households will purchase more housing under the price reduction program than under an equal unconstrained income grant. Unconstrained income supplement programs raise the purchasing power of eligible households which is divided between housing and all other goods. The reduced price of housing programs raises purchasing power but also lowers the price of housing relative to all other goods—a change that leads households to choose more of the cheaper housing. Households that are offered a price reduction subsidy of a given value may be just as well off with a somewhat smaller income supplement that does not bias consumption in favor of housing. The difference between the value of the price reduction subsidy and an income supplement that would make recipient households just as well off is one measure of program inefficiency.

Economists have investigated the extent of the inefficiency generated by a price reduction program compared to an unrestricted cash grant. Aaron and von Furstenberg [28] simulated both the inefficiency of price reduction subsidies and the percentage increase in real income generated by such programs. Their estimates show the extent of inefficiency to be sensitive to the size of the price reduction: the estimated inefficiency ranges from 4.3 percent to 15 percent of the subsidy when the price reduction is 20 percent; when the subsidy reduces price by 50 percent, inefficiency ranges between 13.9 and 37.5 percent. Based on an analysis of EHAP data, Cronin [29] finds that inefficiency normally varied between 5 and 15 percent.

Although some inefficiency is inherent in price reduction programs, this does not necessarily imply that price reduction programs are inferior to income supplement programs. If the increase in housing generated by price reduction programs (compared with the income supplement) provides sufficient social benefits to compensate for the inefficiency induced by the price distortion, such programs could be justified on economic efficiency grounds.

The economic virtues of price discounts are countered by three potentially serious problems in their use to improve the housing of low-income families. First, a subsidy of this form appears to invite collusion of tenants and landlords to raise rents and split the increased subsidy. No evidence of this was found in the Demand Experiment, but there are still those who believe that the very structure of the subsidy would make its widespread adoption politically impossible. Second, the income elasticity with which price subsidies are compared reflects the change in housing consumption that results from an unconstrained income supplement. The imposition of standards, whether in the form of minimum rent or physical requirements, results in a significant increase in housing expenditures among households whose dwellings do not meet requirements at enrollment but who eventually qualify to receive payments.[30] Still, the magnitude of the increase from earmarking is not enough to reverse the broad findings.

The third potential problem is that the price subsidies implemented in the Demand Experiment, that is, the percentage of rent plans, produced no greater housing consumption on average than did the unconstrained cash payments. While this is partially explainable by the fact that most of the percentage of rent plans yielded smaller subsidies than did the unconstrained plan, there is certainly no guarantee that price subsidies in

---

28. See Aaron and von Furstenberg [P3].

29. See Cronin [H24].

30. This finding itself is qualified by the fact that expenditures apparently increased more than actual housing services. See chapter 6 for details.

this form given to low-income households would cause the significant increase in housing consumption described. (Recall that the price elasticity underpinning that discussion was based on a variety of evidence, some of it external to EHAP.)

Hence, the overall conclusion is that on the basis of the available evidence, price elasticities appear to be superior to income supplements as a means of improving the housing of the poor. This evidence is not strong enough, however, to recommend its adoption over unconstrained grants or grants earmarked for housing.

PART IV.

Landlord, Market, and Agency Responses

CHAPTER 8

Repairs and Maintenance on the Units Occupied by Allowance Recipients

James P. Zais

ONE IMPORTANT way that housing programs are evaluated is by their impact on the housing stock. Some programs primarily affect the housing units which are occupied by participants in the program, while other programs may have a wider impact by affecting housing production, utilization, and prices for nonparticipants' housing as well. When the housing allowance experiments were being planned, it was widely thought that allowances would cause both upgrading of units occupied by participants and changes in the price and quality of housing of nonparticipants. This chapter deals with the effects of housing allowances on the condition of units occupied by participants in the program while the following chapter will discuss impacts on the price of housing and on the rest of the housing market.

STUDYING EFFECTS ON THE HOUSING STOCK

Questions of a housing allowance's impact on the physical condition of housing units must be distinguished from questions of changes in the housing condition or housing consumption of participants, analyzed in chapter 6. Participants could experience improvements in their housing conditions by moving to better units, in which case neither units being moved to nor units being vacated will necessarily undergo physical improvements. It could happen that the housing consumption of participants will have been increased but the physical stock of housing remains

179

unchanged. Only for stationary households will changes in dwelling condition necessarily be the same as the housing improvement experienced by participants.

Depending on the criteria chosen for evaluating a program such as housing allowances, improvement in the housing conditions of participants might be considered important while improving the physical stock of housing might not be considered important. As discussed in chapter 2, the emphasis given in housing policy debates to benefits to participants has fluctuated over time; when this emphasis is strong, stock impacts receive only secondary attention. There are, however, important reasons why such stock impacts should be taken into account.

First, public concern over the quality of the housing stock has existed for many years in response to substantial real need. The number of units believed to require repairs, of course, varies depending on the measures used. The nation's annual housing goals in 1968 were developed on the basis of dwellings classified by the Census as "dilapidated" or lacking plumbing. Using these standards, several observers have concluded that the number of deficient dwellings has decreased dramatically in the postwar period.[1] If, however, a measure is used which recognizes that inadequacies of operation and maintenance are also important aspects of housing quality, then the number of units defined as inadequate is both larger and probably not declining as rapidly. Furthermore, if one uses the more detailed data on unit condition generated through the EHAP experiments themselves, a greater proportion of inadequate units is found than is found when analyses relying on data available from the Census are used.[2]

Because residential units are durable and provide services over a long period of time, substandard or deteriorating units can affect the housing conditions not only of current occupants but of future occupants as well. High levels of mobility in contemporary American society and a high rate of household formation increase the legitimacy of public concern about the stream of services provided by a housing unit beyond the tenure of its current residents. Public investment in improving the existing housing stock may be an efficient way to increase the housing consumption of families who occupy the improved units in succession.

A second reason for public policy makers to be concerned about the condition of the housing stock is that the level of upkeep and maintenance of individual units is closely related to the condition of neighborhoods. As neighborhoods experience decline, investment in individual housing units is discouraged. Conversely, revitalization of neighborhoods is in-

---

1. See Levine [P46]; Weicher [P88].
2. See Budding [H18].

extricably tied to investment in the existing stock. Given the fact that many of the households in these "fragile" neighborhoods are eligible for assisted housing programs, the potential role of housing programs in fostering revitalization is evident.

Recently, a national trend toward increased investment in the existing stock has been detected.[3] Annual expenditures for housing upkeep and improvement in the United States have been estimated to total more than $131 billion in 1977; the value of such expenditures is well over 50 percent of that of new housing construction.[4] The goal, of course, is to stimulate more of this private activity in areas of actual or incipient decline.

Despite the importance of understanding the condition of the housing stock and what influences it, the terminology used to discuss physical changes to housing units varies considerably, and there is little agreement on what particular terms mean. Everyday housekeeping activities, for example, can keep a property in shape and prevent deterioration that would necessitate major expenditures sooner than life expectancy would otherwise require. Such activities include waxing floors, cleaning windows, or picking up debris. Some analysts label such activities as *maintenance*, although others, including the Bureau of the Census, reserve this term for more substantial improvements such as painting, floor sanding, or furnace cleaning.

Perhaps a more generally agreed upon definition is that for *repairs*. In normal usage, this term includes activities which fix broken parts of housing units, activities which are directed toward upkeep of a property rather than its expansion. Examples include clearing clogged drains, caulking, and repairing light switches. Some repairs are most easily and economically accomplished through minor replacements. For example, a leaky roof might best be remedied through replacement of several shingles, or a nonworking electrical outlet might just as easily be replaced as repaired. For this reason, and because of the limited expense involved, such partial replacements are also classified as repairs.

None of these activities, however, constitutes what are thought of as capital investment in a property. Such investments come in the form of *major replacements* or *additions and alterations*. Major replacements apply to whole systems such as heating, plumbing, or electrical systems; a complete reroofing, unlike the replacement of several shingles, would also be considered a major replacement. Additions and alterations are investments which expand or alter the size or usage of the unit; installation of indoor plumbing where none existed would be considered an alteration, but adding a room normally would be classified as an addition. Capital

---

3. These trends are described in James [C38].
4. See U.S. Bureau of the Census [C112].

improvements, including major replacements, are normally assumed to increase the life of a unit and to increase its market value.

Although different levels of financial outlay are implicit in the categories of activities described, some authors prefer a definition of improvements based explicitly on costs. Grigsby and Rosenberg, for example, defined ordinary maintenance as all activities involving expenditures of less than $300 and "modest rehabilitation" as involving expenditures of between $300 and $7,500.[5] Similarly, the "moderate rehabilitation" component of HUD's Section 8 lower-income rental assistance program defines such rehabilitation as involving a minimum of $1,000 per unit.[6]

As we now turn to an examination of the housing repair actions associated with EHAP, we will repeatedly see that these repairs are extremely modest in scope compared to the scale of activities envisioned in these definitions.

INITIAL REPAIRS TO PASS STANDARDS

The Probability of Repair

This examination begins by considering those housing improvements made on units which were unable to pass program standards at the time of initial inspection.[7] Improving a unit and having it reinspected was one of several ways to qualify for payments, and figure 8.1 indicates the percentage of recipients whose housing failed its initial inspection but which eventually passed inspection after subsequent repairs. As the figure indicates, the percentage of recipients qualifying through improvements varied considerably among the 12 EHAP sites. Nearly one third of renter households who ultimately qualified for allowance payments at Supply Experiment sites did so after initial failure and subsequent unit improvements. On the other hand, as few as 2 to 4 percent of program recipients at some Administrative Agency Experiment sites used this means of qualifying. In looking at these data, keep in mind that different standards

---

5. See Grigsby and Rosenberg [P27].

6. See U.S. Department of Housing and Urban Development. [C114].

7. Chapter 10 discusses the housing inspection process as it operated in the EHAP experiments, while Appendix D describes the standards applied.

It is conceivable that a housing allowance program with widely publicized standards might induce housing improvements even before an individual household's application and housing unit inspection. Indeed, in the Supply Experiment sites, there is evidence that some anticipatory improvement behavior occurred. In the main, however, improvements were made after an inspection turned up deficiencies.

Figure 8.1

Percentage of Housing Allowance Recipients Whose Housing Unit Failed Initial Inspection and Who Subsequently Had the Unit Pass Inspection after Repairs

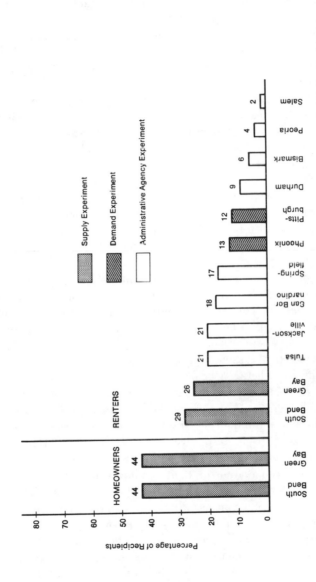

Sources: Supply sites derived from Rand [E130], p. 19; Demand Experiment sites from Merrill and Joseph [H91], p. 12; Administrative Agency Experiment sites from Abt Associates, Inc. [E10], p. 85.

were used to inspect units in the various experiments, and in the Administrative Agency Experiment several methods of inspection were used, including inspection by the would-be participant.

It is reasonable to suppose that the probability of choosing to improve one's unit in order to qualify for payments will depend on housing market circumstances, such as the average condition of the housing stock and vacancy rates. If the stock is old and in considerable disrepair, unit improvements will tend to be expensive, compared to a housing market where most units would require only minor repairs. On the other hand, in a housing market characterized by high turnover rates and high mobility rates, moving would be a more likely response than it would be in a market where finding a new unit would involve extensive search efforts and higher rent. The EHAP experience indicates, however, that these choices can be very complex. There appears to be no simple relationship between those market characteristics one would expect to have an impact on housing choice and the proportion of recipients who improve their dwellings in order to qualify for payments.[8] In part, of course, this is due to the influence of variations in program administration, as discussed below.

Figure 8.1 indicates the likely importance of some of the factors operating in the Demand and Supply Experiments. The figure indicates that one factor—tenure—is of particular importance in affecting an individual household's decision whether or not to repair. In Green Bay and South Bend, where owner-occupied units were eligible for the program and subject to the same minimum physical standards as rental units, a clear difference between homeowners and renters can be seen. About 44 percent of homeowner recipients' units at each site initially failed inspections, and their owners made physical improvements in order to qualify for payments, while the comparable numbers for rental units were 29 percent and 26 percent, respectively, at the two sites. Homeowners could decide for themselves whether a unit should be fixed, while renters usually required the cooperation of their landlords in order to have their unit improved. A situation in which the renter would be the primary beneficiary of the allowance payments while the landlord bore the primary cost of the repairs in order to qualify for payments is one in which tenant-landlord cooperation might not be forthcoming. Furthermore, as discussed in detail in chapter 5, moving is often far less preferable for homeowners; if a homeowner's unit is judged deficient, improvement may be the only viable way for him to qualify for payments.

---

8. At the market level, rank order correlations between the percentage of recipient households improving units and site characteristics thought important to the behavior of participants in the program proved to be low and insignificant. The site characteristics analyzed in this regard were those discussed by Goedert [E49].

In addition to tenure, comparison of the results for the Demand and Supply Experiments in figure 8.1 indicates the probable importance of the stringency of the program standard in determining the extent to which improvements are a chosen course of action. As part of EHAP research, a special test was conducted directly comparing the stringency of the standards imposed in these two experiments. This test demonstrated empirically that the standard used in the Demand Experiment was more stringent than that used in the Supply Experiment.[9] It is important to note that the greater stringency was tougher standards in the areas of adequate light and ventilation in bathrooms, replacing or installing electrical wall outlets, and broader application of the standard for condition of wall, ceiling, and floor surfaces in the Demand Experiment.

Seemingly because of the more stringent standard, less than half as many units in the two very different Demand Experiment housing markets eventually passed inspection after having initially failed inspection as did the units in the Supply Experiment under its less stringent standard. Given the similarities within each experiment, it appears that application of different standards is a major determinant of whether or not households find it reasonable to improve their units. The more stringent the standard, the more upgrading will be required on average for a failed unit to pass standards, and the less likely it is that households will elect this route to allowance eligibility.

Improvements Undertaken

What improvements were made to pass standards? The most detailed information on this subject comes from the two Supply Experiment sites.[10] When a unit failed its initial inspection, the agency provided a specific list of the deficiencies the inspection had uncovered to the household applying for allowance benefits. Table 8.1 indicates the various types of improvements which took place between the time a unit failed its initial inspection and the time it was reinspected in a second attempt to pass standards. The table also presents the average out-of-pocket expenditures associated with each type of improvement. The nature of improvement actions was similar for Green Bay and South Bend, so we can consider them together.

The table clearly indicates that the majority of unit improvement

---

9. This work is summarized in Appendix C and presented in detail in Valenza [E170].

10. Repair logs were kept in the Supply Experiment but not in the Demand Experiment. The Demand Experiment's strength, however, is that its design includes a control group. The evidence comparing allowance recipients with control households on likelihood of improving to pass standards is discussed below.

Table 8.1

Housing Improvements Made to Units Initially Failing Inspection,
Green Bay and South Bend

| Improvements | Percentage of All Improvements | | Average Out-of-Pocket Cost [a] |
	Owner-Occupied Units	Rental Units	
Install handrails	29%	17%	$10
Repair windows	10	15	9
Paint or repair ceilings, floors, or walls	9	10	42
Pry open windows	9	7	(c)
Repair major systems [b]	6	11	17
Replace or install windows	6	4	9
Paint or repair fences, porches, or accessory structures	3	5	18
Install curtains or partitions	3	4	5
Repair vents, vent fans, or vent pipes	3	3	2
Repair plumbing fixtures	3	2	12
Install vents, vent fans, or vent pipes	3	2	26
Repair or connect appliances	2	4	8
Pick up litter or broken glass	2	3	(c)
Other (no category more than 3%)	18	18	
Total	100%	100%	$16
Total number of improvements	3435	5545	5953

Source: Derived from special tabulations provided by the Rand Corporation. Includes repairs reported to the housing allowance offices between January 1976 and June 1977. Cost figures are based on a reduced set of records because of missing data items.
  a. Does not include value of unpaid labor.
  b. Major systems include the furnace, heating system, plumbing system, and electrical system. Repairs in this category include replacement and installation of electrical fixtures and outlets.
  c. Less than $1.00.

activities were of a repair and maintenance nature, but installations were also important. The average out-of-pocket cost involved in making installations was low, indicating that only a minor improvement occurred in the dwelling. The most expensive improvements were painting and repairing ceilings, floors, and walls, at $42 for the average action. Some improvements, such as prying open windows or picking up broken glass or litter, involved little or no cash outlays. The overall average cost of each improvement activity undertaken was only $16.

    The most frequent improvement for both rental units and owner-occupied units was installation of handrails. The Supply Experiment standards required a handrail for stairs with six or more consecutive steps. Items relating to stairs and railings constituted the greatest percentage of defects in enrollees' dwellings, 29 percent and 17 percent of the improvement activities for homeowners and renters, respectively. The installation of handrails was not a costly undertaking, averaging $10 in out-of-pocket costs; and the significance of a handrail in altering the overall quality of housing services received by the occupants of the house must reasonably be judged as marginal.

Most of the actions in table 8.1 reflect the overriding importance of health and safety elements in the particular standards imposed in the Supply Experiment. Besides handrails, the condition of windows received considerable attention in making improvements. Proper window condition was typically involved in meeting requirements for adequate light or ventilation. Actions to correct deficiencies ranged from installation and replacement of windows (4 to 6 percent), repair of windows (10 to 15 percent), or simply prying them open (7 to 9 percent). The out-of-pocket cost of all these types of actions on windows averaged only $9.

In addition to these repairs associated with "health and safety" provisions of the Supply Experiment's standards, some improvement actions of lesser frequency addressed the workability of unit features assumed necessary to provide a minimum level of housing services. In most cases, these included the repair, rather than the installation or replacement, of plumbing fixtures (bathtubs, sinks, showers). In some cases, major systems (furnace, heating, plumbing, and electrical systems) were repaired. However, the out-of-pocket costs of these actions averaged only $17.

One common improvement action—the installation of curtains and partitions—arose almost exclusively in direct reaction to the occupany standard imposed by the Supply Experiment and the way it was administered. When units did not have the required number of rooms or the privacy demanded by the program's occupancy standard, installation of curtains and partitions to subdivide rooms was allowed by the housing allowance agency as a means of meeting the requirement.[11]

The installation of both curtains and handrails clearly illustrates the *standard-specificity* of many of the improvements. Most of the actions responded directly to the specific items listed by the inspector as the reasons for failure, and their primary intention seemed to be achieving eligibility for allowance payments. No general upgrading of housing con-

---

11. While this was generally a minor task, the standard requires, for example, that each new "room" have its own light, heating source, and window. Hence, the spaces subdivided for a small outlay were ideally suited to such a division.

ditions, or even "piggybacking" of related voluntary repair actions onto repairs mandated by standards was typically observed.

Improvement Actions per Unit

Thus far, we have considered the individual repair actions undertaken to pass program standards. Although these actions were usually minor repairs costing very little, it could be that, when added together, the total number of actions taken on individual units constitutes substantial change to those units. Table 8.2 addresses this possibility by showing the total number of improvements undertaken *per unit* for all units undergoing some repairs in the Supply Experiment; it also shows the cash outlay involved. Figures for Green Bay and South Bend are displayed separately here because results were somewhat different between the two sites. As in table 8.1, the information in the table refers to units which failed an initial inspection, received some kind of repair action, and were subsequently reinspected.[12]

As table 8.1 shows, most housing units underwent one or two repair actions. Renter-occupied units underwent a slightly greater number of repairs in both sites, but across sites and tenure groups, the average number of repairs ranged only from 1.6 to 1.9. Only a small proportion of households completed four or more repairs (5 to 7 percent for homeowners, 8 to 9 percent for renters). Using the number of repairs as a rough indicator of the extent of improvements, we are once again led to conclude that major repairs or renovation of units were not at all typical of the actions undertaken on EHAP units after they failed inspections.

Since more than one repair action was taken on the average unit, the average amount spent on a dwelling was higher—over three times higher —than the $16 *per action* average cited. Indeed, average per unit outlays varied but are not consistent with the average number of repair actions taken. Homeowner households in South Bend, for example, spent the highest amount of any of the groups identified in table 8.2, an average of $81 per unit, but their average number of repairs was smallest of the groups shown in the table. These confusing average figures, in fact, are distorted by a small number of units undergoing major rehabilitation. If the median cost figures are used as a better measure of typical behavior than the mean in situations with a few observations very different from

---

12. The figures presented here are based on those dwellings for which full data are available, about two thirds of all units. The total cost of repairs for the excluded units is higher than for those included in our figures. Hence, the overall values reported are slightly downward biased. On the other hand, the sample employed has permitted us to examine the cost of individual repairs, which would not be possible using the full sample.

Table 8.2

Housing Improvement Actions per Unit, for Units Undergoing Improvements after Initially Failing Inspection, Green Bay and South Bend

	Percentage of Units			
	Owner-Occupied Units		Rental Units	
	Green Bay	South Bend	Green Bay	South Bend
Number of actions per unit				
1	57%	69%	57%	58%
2	27	19	24	20
3	9	7	11	13
4+	7	5	8	9
	100%	100%	100%	100%
Mean	1.7	1.6	1.8	1.9
Cash outlay per unit [a]				
$0	17%	21%	25%	24%
$1-20	55	46	49	43
$21-40	10	14	10	15
$41-100	11	10	10	13
$100-200	3	4	3	3
$200-1000	3	4	3	2
$1000+	(b)	1	(b)	(b)
	100%	100%	100%	100%
Mean	$55	$81	$39	$37
Median	$10	$11	$ 8	$10

Source: Derived from McDowell [C61], pp. 22-23, and U.S. Department of Housing and Urban Development [E165], p. 60. Includes repairs reported to housing allowance offices between January 1976 and June 1977.

a. Does not include value of unpaid labor.
b. Less than 1 percent.

most of the observations, the range of per unit outlays is considerably narrowed. The table indicates that this median ranged between $8 and $11.

Given the types of activities undertaken and the low levels of costs associated with them, it is perhaps not surprising that in many cases tenants in rental units undertook repair actions themselves rather than attempting to convince their landlords to undertake them. Table 8.3 indicates that in 38 to 47 percent of the rental units undergoing repairs after initially failing inspections, tenants did their own repair work, and, in an additional 10 to 12 percent of the cases, engaged the help of a friend.

Table 8.3

Who Performed Repairs on Units Failing Initial Inspection Which Were
Subsequently Repaired?

	Owner-Occupied Units		Rental Units	
Person Performing Repair	Green Bay	South Bend	Green Bay	South Bend
Occupant	66%	45%	47%	38%
Landlord	—	—	35	40
Commercial contractor	13	19	8	10
Friend of occupant	21	32	10	12
Other	—	4	—	—
Total	100%	100%	100%	100%

Source: McDowell [C61], p. 25.

Landlords undertook 35 to 40 percent of the repairs. Homeowners at both
sites largely undertook the work themselves, although they used contractors
at a higher rate than was true for rental units.

In a smaller but still significant number of cases, tenants also
absorbed the costs of repairs when some cost was involved. As table 8.4
indicates, about one fourth of tenants paid for their own repairs. Among
homeowners, almost all outlays for repairs were absorbed by the households themselves. In a small number of cases, homeowners took advantage
of government repair assistance programs in addition to applying for
housing allowances. Green Bay offered grants to homeowners whose
dwellings violated city housing codes. In addition, two repair handyman
services were provided by church and neighborhood groups in which
qualifying homeowners paid only for the materials necessary for repairs.
The use of other programs by allowance recipients was greater in South
Bend, probably because more programs were available there. The city of
South Bend operated five (and at one point as many as eight) different
grant and loan programs for repairs. Although the number of allowance
recipients taking advantage of these programs was relatively small, it
points to the potential linkage between housing allowance programs and
programs designed to assist directly in housing repair.

None of the costs referred to in tables 8.2 and 8.4 includes the value
of unpaid labor. Were such costs to be estimated and included, these
figures would, of course, be somewhat higher. For example, recent
estimates of the full cost of repairs to units failing inspection, including valuing unpaid labor, were made for repairs occurring over an

Table 8.4

Who Paid for Repairs on Units Failing Initial Inspection Which Were
Subsequently Repaired?

	Owner-Occupied Units		Rental Units	
Person Paying for Repair	Green Bay	South Bend	Green Bay	South Bend
Occupant	71%	65%	21%	28%
Landlord	—	—	43	37
Other	2	8	2	2
No cash outlay	27	27	34	33
Total	100%	100%	100%	100%

Source: McDowell [C61], p. 26.

18-month period in 1978 and 1979. The mean full cost for rental units
was $56 and $42 in Green Bay and South Bend, respectively. The comparable figures for homeowners are $111 and $60.[13] They still do not
constitute "major rehabilitation" or even "modest rehabilitation" under
definitions commonly in use. With the possible exception of the 1 percent
or so of households spending over $1,000 in repair actions, it is hard to
imagine that the occupants of these housing units felt substantially better
housed after the initial inspection and repair process than before. On the
other hand, minor repairs, such as eliminating the draft from windows by
caulking or installing weather stripping, can make a real difference in a
household's comfort and in some instances lower fuel bills. Low repair
outlays also mean that most of the units offered by would-be participants
for inspection were in good condition. Since upgrading a unit was only
one of the ways to qualify for program participation, there is no inference
here about the extent of housing improvement of participants generally.[14]

---

13. Communication from the Rand Corporation March 26, 1980; contributed labor
is valued at the minimum wage of $2.90 per hour. Also note that, based on evidence
from a special survey of landlords, Rand estimates that tenants fail to report about
half of the cost of all repairs on their dwellings. Finally, note that the figures given
in the text are for "required repairs," i.e., repairs made between a unit failing an inspection and subsequently passing. As such, it includes units failing initial and annual
inspections. During the year September 1977 to September 1978, the first 9 months of
the 18-month period to which the date in the text refers, units failing annual inspections and requalifying later constituted 44 percent of all units failing inspections and
requalifying, as calculated using the figures in tables 2.5 and 2.6 in Rand [E130] and
tables 2.4 and 2.5 in Rand [E129].

14. See chapter 6 for a discussion of housing consumption changes associated with
receiving allowances.

Table 8.5

For Units Which Fail Initial Inspection: Proportion of Failed Units
Subsequently Repaired as a Function of the Number of Defects
Identified at Initial Inspection

| | Proportion of Failed Units Subsequently Repaired | | | |
| | Owner-Occupied Units | | Rental Units | |
Number of Defects Identified During Initial Inspection	Green Bay	South Bend	Green Bay	South Bend
1	87%	88%	67%	73%
2	81	78	60	55
3	67	63	52	52
4+	46	51	31	32
Average	79%	79%	59%	57%

Source: McDowell [C61], p. 20.

Which Units Were Repaired?

In addition to considering the magnitude of repair actions undertaken
on units which are being repaired, it is important to investigate the
number and characteristics of units which fail initial program inspection
but then are never repaired and reinspected. Table 8.5 indicates for Green
Bay and South Bend the proportion of households whose unit fails
initial inspection who repaired those units and had them pass a subsequent
inspection. It indicates that the larger the number of defects requiring
repair which the inspection identified, the lower the probability that the
unit will receive repairs. For example, while 87 percent of Green Bay
howeowners facing one inspection-identified defect elected to repair their
homes, only 81 percent of the same group did so when they faced two
defects, only 67 percent did so when facing three defects, and only 46
percent did so in the face of four or more defects. While the number of
defects found in an inspection is not an ideal indicator of the general
state of repair of the house, it may be used as an approximate index. What
these data then suggest is that typically the units which were undergoing
repair are units which are in better general condition than are the units
which are going unrepaired. Seriously deficient housing units, which
would require more extensive and expensive modifications to meet program standards, generally are not affected by the housing allowance
program; if they are inspected and fail, their occupants decline to undertake repairs. On the other hand, units which are only marginally deficient,
with only a small number of defects each of which can be corrected

Table 8.6

Incidence of Substandard Housing and Proportion of Units Repaired in Response to Program Requirements in the Supply Sites through September 1979

	Renter		Owner	
	Green Bay	*South Bend*	*Green Bay*	*South Bend*
Total dwellings	15,502	21,070	34,705	58,601
Substandard dwellings				
Total	5,717	9,720	9,479	17,402
Inspected by the allowance program	4,616	6,570	1,621	3,772
Repaired through the allowance program	2,912	3,767	1,249	2,822
Percentage of all substandard units repaired through the program	51	39	13	16

Source: Communication from the Rand Corporation, March 26, 1980.

cheaply and easily, will be the ones where program-induced repairs follow initial inspections.

In focusing tightly on the actual types of repairs undertaken, it is possible to overlook the sheer volume of units repaired cumulatively through the program. The Rand Corporation has recently estimated that a majority of the rental housing defined as substandard by program criteria has been inspected under the program (table 8.6). Moreover, half of all substantial rental units have been repaired in Green Bay in order to qualify for the program; in South Bend, 39 percent have been repaired. While there is no assurance that these repaired units have been maintained at program standards, especially when their occupants leave the program, the impact on the housing quality in the sites is obviously substantial, when judged by application of the program's dwelling standard.

ONGOING HOUSING UNIT MAINTENANCE

While the most immediate effect of a housing allowance program on the housing stock is to induce repairs following intial inspection, it might not be the most important effect in the long run. Additional repairs and improvements may be promoted during the course of the program. Indeed, improved maintenance over the long term could make a fundamental difference in dwelling quality and neighborhood conditions. Annual housing improvement figures presented here are for approximately the first two years of program operations in each site. As such, they provide only a hint of the long-term effects. Ultimately, four years of data will be analyzed in the Supply Experiment, given a better picture of ongoing improvements. Even now, though, we know that there is a great deal of turnover among recipients, which means that the incentives provided by allowance payments for ongoing maintenance will, in general, be variable for individual dwellings.

Improvements over the year might be made in anticipation of the annual reinspection. Households would seek to forestall an interruption of their payments that might occur if they failed the annual reinspection and had to repair at that time. Or they might maintain their housing at a higher level because the inspection process has made them generally more conscious of housing defects and the need for their eradication. At the same time, by providing low-income households with somewhat enhanced purchasing power, housing allowances might provide funds to households eager to maintain their housing but previously unable to afford to do so; this latter effect may be particularly important for homeowners, especially elderly homeowners, for whom deferring home maintenance is sometimes a means of stretching limited incomes.

Because there is no control group in the Supply Experiment, most of the data presented here simply describe the actions of participants without reference to households' and landlords' normal activities. As such, they provide information on the maintenance process that has generally not been available heretofore. The final section presents some rough information on program effects on routine maintenance and repair activity.

Improvements Undertaken by Homeowners

Estimating the extent of annual repairs is more difficult for renters than for homeowners, since renters sometimes may be unaware of the improvements actually being made. This is particularly true for multifamily dwellings in which landlords might undertake repairs to the furnace or the roof, for example, without tenants' awareness. Therefore, this section considers improvements undertaken by homeowners in the Supply Experiment. A later section will consider the limited data thus far available on renter-occupied units—those provided by the tenants themselves.[15]

---

15. At the time of this report, data were not yet available on a special survey of housing allowance office clients' landlords, undertaken to determine repairs made in 1978. This information should provide an important key to the extent of annual repairs undertaken on allowance program housing units.

Table 8.7

Annual Repair Actions by Homeowners, Green Bay and South Bend

Repair Action	Percentage of all Improvements	Average Cost
Paint or repair ceilings, floors, walls	30%	$141
Repair major systems [a]	9	76
Repair foundation, roof	7	25
Paint or repair fence, accessory structure, porch	7	106
Install or replace ceiling, floor, or wall	5	314
Install or replace fixtures [b]	5	110
Install or replace major systems	3	454
Install or replace appliances [c]	3	194
Install or replace foundation or roof	3	452
Repair windows	3	53
Replace or install door	3	86
Replace or install windows	3	157
Other (no category more than 3%)	20	—
All actions	100%	$162
Total number of actions	6773	5417

Source: Derived from special tabulations provided by the Rand Corporation. Includes repairs reported to the housing allowance offices between January 1976 and June 1977. Cost figures are based on a reduced set of records because of missing data items.

a. Major systems include the furnace, heating system, plumbing system, and electrical system. Repairs to major systems include replacement and installation of electrical fixtures and outlets.

b. Fixtures include bathtubs, showers, sinks, and toilets.

c. Appliances include ranges, refrigerators, water heaters, and room heaters.

At the time of each annual reinspection in the Supply Experiment, data were collected on the types of improvements undertaken during the previous year. Table 8.7 lists the types of improvements undertaken, their frequency, and their average cost. As this table indicates, there are major differences between these activities and those reported in table 8.1 for the time period immediately following initial inspection failures. Noticeably absent from the annual repairs are installation of handrails and prying open of windows, which together accounted for about 38 percent of the repairs following unit failure at initial inspection. Picking up litter or broken glass and connecting appliances, often required to pass inspections, also do not constitute appreciable percentages of annual improvement activities. The most frequent activity undertaken during the year was painting and repairing ceilings, floors, and walls, which accounted for about 30 percent of all actions. This sort of painting and repairing also was undertaken after failing initial inspections, although at a lower rate (9 percent of homeowner activities). However, the painting and repairing activities undertaken as part of annual repairs were more substantial in scope than those done in order to pass inspections. The out-of-pocket costs for these activities during annual repairs averaged $141, almost $100 more than the average out-of-pocket costs for painting and repair activties undertaken subsequent to failing initial inspection.

The remainder of common annual improvement activities are fairly diverse. Repairs to major systems, foundations, roofs, fences, accessory structures, and porches constituted a greater percentage of annual improvements than activities undertaken after failing inspection. In each case, such activities cost from five to six times more than at the time of inspection, indicating again that annual repairs were probably more substantial in nature. Replacements constituted a greater percentage of annual improvements than of initial improvements (9 versus 20 percent). In some cases, these activities were expensive, particularly when they involved major systems such as the furnace, plumbing, or electrical system. In contrast, installations, which accounted for 41 percent of initial improvements, are only 13 percent of annual improvements. Overall, the out-of-pocket costs of improvements done during the year averaged $162 per improvement, with actions involving installations and replacements typically exceeding the costs associated with actions which are repairs.

It is also important to note that more than one third of the repairs made voluntarily by both owners and renters are on the dwelling's exterior.[16] This contrasts with about one fifth of repairs required to qualify a unit, either initially or after failing an annual inspection. Since external repairs improve the external appearance of the unit, they affect the views of others about the condition of the neighborhood and may help produce the upgrading of other properties.

Improvements per Unit

Another important indicator of ongoing maintenance activity is the total number of improvements undertaken per unit and the per unit total costs of the full set of improvements undertaken. In both Supply Experiment sites, as shown in table 8.8, approximately the same percentage of

---

16. Data are for the period January 1976 through June 1977. Special communication from the Rand Corporation, March 26, 1980. External items include dwelling roofs, walls, and foundations; and, if present, porches, eaves, gutters, drain spouts, sidewalks, handrails, steps, garages, accessory structures, fences, site grading, and accumulations of trash or garbage. Windows and doors are counted as interior items.

homeowners reported no activities over the course of a year: 27 percent in Green Bay and 26 percent in South Bend. Of homeowners who undertook some improvement, the distribution of number of actions per unit is roughly similar to the two sites. About one fifth of all homeowners participating in the Supply Experiment did one, two, and three repairs, respectively, and approximately one fifth did more than four repairs. The average number of improvements per dwelling, in dwellings where any actions were undertaken, was 2.6 at Green Bay and 2.7 at South Bend. These averages are higher than that reported in table 8.2 for actions undertaken following initial inspection, when the majority of homeowners completed one improvement activity in order to pass the standards.

The cash outlay per unit varies considerably, matching the variation in the number of repair actions. Because of this variation, several alternative statistics—averages, medians, and ranges in percentiles—are presented in table 8.8. The table indicates that 50 percent of all cases involved annual cash outlays of $105 or less in Green Bay and $125 or less in South Bend. As noted above, about one fourth of homeowners report spending no money at all on annual improvements. On the other hand, some homeowners obviously undertook major rehabilitation of their homes over the course of the year, with a maximum of approximately $10,000 spent by a few homeowners in both sites. The interquartile range (representing the 50 percent of the cases in the middle of the spectrum) itself has a considerable range—from $0 to $355 in Green Bay and from $0 to $412 in South Bend. The average outlays, influenced heavily by the few cases of major expenditures, are $324 and $347 for Green Bay and South Bend, respectively.[17] Average cash outlay figures for repaired units only, of course, are higher at both sites than are average figures which refer to all units, whether they undergo any repair action or not; total annual out-of-pocket repair expenditures for the former group averaged $437 in Green Bay and $467 in South Bend.

The overall picture created by these figures is one of wide variation in annual outlays for improvements to units by homeowners who participated in the Supply Experiment. Part of the reason for this variation is that improvement expenditures by an individual household are typically not constant over time. Some households spend a great deal on repairs and improvements in one year and little in the next. Households may "piggyback" several improvement actions together to reduce total costs or because

17. Estimated full costs, including nonpaid labor, for an 18-month period in 1978-1979, averaged $351 and $370 in Green Bay and South Bend. (Communication from the Rand Corporation, March 26, 1980.) However, since the data in the text are for 1976-1977, no direct statement about the value of contributed labor is possible.

Table 8.8

Housing Improvement Actions per Unit, Annual Voluntary Repairs:
Homeowners in Green Bay and South Bend

	Percentage of Units	
	Green Bay	South Bend
Number of actions per unit		
0	27%	26%
1	21	18
2	20	21
3	15	17
4	8	9
5+	9	9
	100%	100%
Mean (repaired units only)	2.6	2.7
Cash outlay per unit (all evaluated units)		
25th percentile	$ 0	$ 0
50th percentile (median)	105	125
75th percentile	355	412
100th percentile	10,000	10,088
Mean	$ 324	$ 347
Cash outlay per unit (repaired units only)		
Mean	$ 437	$ 467
Median	210	250

Source: McDowell [C61] pp. 45, 49. Based on repairs reported to the housing allowance offices between January 1796 and June 1977.

doing several together is more convenient. Clearly, such expenditures are not like rent or mortgage payment which are evenly distributed during the year.

Table 8.9 indicates that commercial contractors were used in many more cases for annual improvements than they were in the case of improvements made following initial inspection. In Green Bay, work on 30 percent of the units involved contractors, and in South Bend half did so; the corresponding figures for initial repairs were 13 percent and 19 percent, respectively. This larger number of contracted jobs is consistent with the observation that annual repairs were more substantial and more costly than were initial repairs. Similarly, table 8.10 indicates that, in contrast to repairs done at the time of inspection, only 2 percent of annual improvements were done for no cash outlay; when improvements were undertaken, they almost always were paid for by the homeowner.

Table 8.9

Who Performed Annual Improvements on Owner-Occupied Units?

	Green Bay	South Bend
Owner	52%	29%
Friend	18	21
Commercial contractor	30	50
Total	100%	100%

Source: McDowell [C57], p. 47.

Table 8.10

Who Paid for Annual Improvements on Owner-Occupied Units?

	Green Bay	South Bend
Owner	95%	95%
Other	3	3
No cash outlay	2	2
Total	100%	100%

Source: McDowell [C61], p. 49.

Renter-Reported Improvements

The same type of improvement information collected for homeowners was collected for renter households in the Supply Experiment, although, for reasons just cited, renter-provided information is likely to understate the true extent of repairs on renter-occupied units. In fact, very recent estimates, based on a special survey of clients' landlords, indicate that clients fail to report about half of the total cost on all repairs on their dwellings, apparently because they lack information about landlord-paid repairs.[18]

The information so far available, however, provides some insights into improvements to the rental stock. Table 8.11 provides the breakdown of renter-reported instances of repair actions undertaken during the year. Interestingly, the types of actions reported are very similar to those reported by homeowners in table 8.6. In fact, the type of action constituting the greatest percentage (38 percent) of all renter-reported actions—painting or repairing ceilings, floors and wall—constituted the largest per-

---

18. Communication from the Rand Corporation, March 26, 1980.

Table 8.11

Renter-Reported Annual Repair Actions, Green Bay and South Bend

Repair Action	Percentage of all Improvements	Average Cost
Paint or repair ceilings, floors, walls	38%	$ 53
Repair major systems [a]	9	87
Install or replace ceilings, floors, walls	6	173
Repair fixtures [b]	5	24
Repair foundation, roof	4	280
Install or replace appliances [c]	4	182
Install or replace fixtures	4	78
Paint or repair fence, accessory structure, porch	4	69
Repair windows	3	40
Replace or install door	3	74
Replace or install windows	3	125
Other (no category more than 3%)	17	—
All actions	100%	$ 106
Total number of actions	2575	1475

Source: Derived from special tabulations provided by the Rand Corporation. Includes repairs reported to the housing allowance offices between January 1976 and June 1977. Cost figures are based on a reduced set of records because of missing data items.

   a. Major systems include the furnace, heating system, plumbing system, and electrical system. Repairs to major systems include replacement and installation of electrical fixtures and outlets.

   b. Fixtures include bathtubs, showers, sinks, and toilets.

   c. Appliances include ranges, refrigerators, water heaters, and room heaters.

centage (30 percent) of actions reported by homeowners. Other actions high on the renter-reported list, such as repairs to major systems, installation or replacement of ceilings, floors, and walls, and repairs to foundations and roofs, were also high on the list of homeowner annual repair items. As with homeowners, renters list a large variety of repairs undertaken, and other than painting and repairing ceilings, floors, and walls, no other single action constituted more than 9 percent of all improvements.

Table 8.11 presents the average cost reported by renters for these repairs. In all cases except one—the repair of major systems—the expenditure data reported by renters are below those reported by homeowners for the same action. In the most frequent category—painting and repairing ceilings, floors, and walls—renter estimates were only one third of the estimates by homeowners ($53 compared to $141). This pattern tends again to make one question relying solely on renter-reported figures.

Table 8.12

Renter-Reported Annual Repair Actions per Unit, Green Bay and
South Bend

	Percentage of Units	
	Green Bay	*South Bend*
Number of actions per unit		
0	58%	57%
1	18	19
2	13	12
3	6	7
4+	5	5
	100%	100%
Mean (repaired units only)	2.0	2.0
Cash outlay per unit (all evaluated units)		
25th percentile	$ 0	$ 0
50th percentile (median)	0	0
75th percentile	46	65
100th percentile	10,500	20,123
Mean	88	116
Cash outlay per unit (repaired units only)		
Mean	$ 202	$ 269
Median	65	75

Source: See table 8.14.

Table 8.13

Who Performed Annual Improvements on Renter-Occupied Units?

	Green Bay	*South Bend*
Tenant	35%	34%
Landlord	35	28
Friend of tenant	7	12
Contractor	23	26
Total	100%	100%

Source: See table 8.14.

Further investigation of this issue must await information provided by
landlords.

Despite their limited value, tables 8.12, 8.13, and 8.14 provide break-
downs of information similar to those provided earlier for homeowners.
The average cash outlay per unit estimated by renters is $88 for Green
Bay and $116 for South Bend, compared to the $324 and $347 cited
earlier for homeowners in the respective sites. Lower means and medians

Table 8.14

Who Paid for Annual Improvements on Renter-Occupied Units?

	Green Bay	South Bend
Tenant	28%	46%
Landlorld	68	48
Other	1	3
No cash outlay	4	3
Total	100%	100%

Source: McDowell [C61] pp. 45, 47, 49. Based on renter-reported repairs provided to the housing allowance offices between January 1976 and June 1977.

for renters probably reflect the larger number of cases in which no repair actions are reported. In the case of renter-reported data, nearly three fifths of the cases in each site indicated no repair actions per unit. In the case of homeowners, it will be recalled, fewer than one third of the cases involved no actions undertaken during the year. Again, these differences may be due to underreporting by renters rather than lower levels of investment for renter-occupied units.

Table 8.13 indicates that a substantial proportion of the improvement actions—about one third—were undertaken by the tenants themselves. In an additional 7 percent of the cases in Green Bay and 12 percent in South Bend, tenants were helped by friends in completing the repairs. In a surprising number of cases, tenants paid for the annual improvements themselves. Table 8.14 indicates that this was particularly true for South Bend, where about 46 percent of the number of annual improvements are paid for by the tenants.[19] It is not clear from the data that are available whether the program induced a greater percentage of tenant-paid repairs than normally takes place.

The Impact of the Allowance Program

An important question is whether or not these annual repair data represent significant changes in the pattern of expenditures which would have occurred in the absence of the allowance program. Because there was no control group included in the Supply Experiment and because any observation is now limited to owner-occupied properties, a precise response to this question is not possible. To suggest at least an approximate answer

19. Less than 5 percent of the repairs were paid for jointly by tenants and landlords.

to that question, figure 8.2 compares the expenditures of low-income home-owners who participated in the Supply Experiment to a sample of all low-income households residing within standard metropolitan statistical areas in the North Central Census region of the United States. Only households with incomes below $7,500 are included in this comparison group, to approximate the income range of Supply Experiment eligibility.

The figure suggests that Supply Experiment homeowners may in fact spend more on annual repairs and improvements than do comparable low-income homeowners generally. For all dwellings evaluated, both mean expenditures and median expenditures are substantially higher for Green Bay and South Bend EHAP participants than for this comparison group. For example, median expenditures of $105 in Green Bay and $125 in South Bend substantially exceed the regional low-income household median of $19. The same pattern of higher expenditures within EHAP than in the comparison group also holds for data on expenditures per repaired dwelling, presented in the lower half of the figure.

Of course, these data do not prove conclusively that housing allowance recipients spent more on annual improvements than did other comparable households. The estimate in the latter case is a regional estimate, and Green Bay and South Bend households might be higher than the regional average. In addition, the higher figures for allowance recipients might be due to some form of self-selection into the program; those households electing to participate in the allowance program might have a higher pref-erence for housing and thus might spend more on annual improvements than the average household of the same income.

Despite these possibilities, this simple comparison suggests that allow-ance payments may have a favorable effect on annual expenditures for housing repairs and improvements. Further analysis which, it is to be hoped, will be performed on data from the Supply Experiment, may eventually refine the conclusion. In particular, analysis is needed to identify the mechanism by which this improved maintenance effect, if it really exists, is promoted by allowances. Does imposition of housing quality standards through annual inspections induce homeowners to better maintain their properties in order to remain eligible for allowance bene-fits? Alternatively, are the payments themselves the crucial element, pro-viding the purchasing power low-income households need to perform repairs that they had wanted to do but previously could not afford? Would these increased maintenance levels continue indefinitely in a permanent housing allowance program, or would they cease after a "backlog" of long-overdue repairs was completed? And, finally, since the only evidence available to date refers to homeowners, do similar patterns of increased maintenance apply to landlords' actions in relation to their rental units?

Figure 8.2

Cash Outlays for Annual Improvements: Supply Experiment Homeowner Participants Compared to Low-Income Homeowners in North Central States

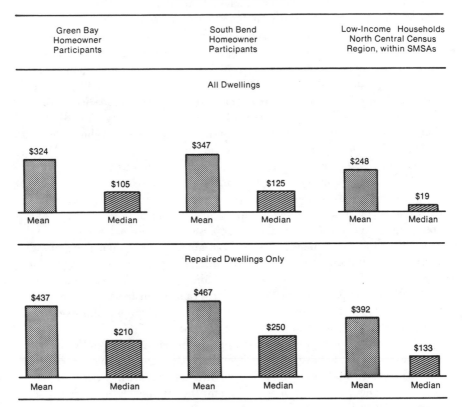

Green Bay Homeowner Participants	South Bend Homeowner Participants	Low-Income Households North Central Census Region, within SMSAs

All Dwellings

Repaired Dwellings Only

Sources: HAO records through June 1976 for Green Bay and December 1976 for South Bend. Census tabulations were run on residential alterations and repairs ("C50" data). "Low-income households" are those with incomes under $7500, to approximate eligibility level for Supply Experiment.

Analyses done to date for owner-occupants, mostly with data not from the Supply Experiment, suggest that the incremental income received through allowance payments would not be sufficient to induce the differentials between the Supply Experiment sites and the North Central Census region of the size reported above.[20] This in turn implies that inspections, or perhaps the belief on the part of participants that allowances "should be spent on housing," are the operative mechanisms inducing greater repair activity. Firm conclusions depend upon further analysis, some to be done with the full body of data from the Supply Experiment.

CONCLUSIONS

We began this chapter by presenting definitions of terms used to describe the nature and extent of housing repairs. We saw there that even such nonambitious terms as "modest rehabilitation" were conventionally defined to involve expenditures of at least several hundreds of dollars. Anything of smaller magnitude was referred to as maintenance or minor repairs, while terms implying substantial efforts, such as "major replacements" or "additions and alterations" typically were reserved for more extensive undertakings.

Using this as a reference for the initial effects of the housing allowance program on the units occupied by program recipients, we are clearly led to characterize these effects as the promotion of maintenance and minor repairs. We have seen that, in general, the housing units which were recruited into the program were those which either already met program quality standards at the time of initial inspection or could meet them after only minor actions such as installation of a stairway handrail or prying open a window that was painted shut. On average, fewer than two improvement actions were required to qualify units which failed initial inspection and subsequently passed, and the median total cash expenditure involved was about $10. While some of these actions induced by the allowance program requirements may have added at least a little to the quality of housing services enjoyed by the current residents of the units, their magnitude is too trivial to indicate any substantial alteration of the current condition or future longevity of the dwelling unit. They could not be considered rehabilitation or upgrading of the unit in even their most modest form.

The effect of the allowance program on the ongoing maintenance of

---

20. For evidence on this point see Mendelsohn [C69]; Helbers [H57]; Struyk and Soldo [C107], chapter 5.

housing units over time presents a more hopeful outcome, although the evidence on which we can base conclusions is incomplete. It appears fairly certain that housing allowances are associated with a higher level of annual maintenance activities among homeowner recipients than would occur in the absence of the program. However, we do not yet know the exact magnitude of this effect, nor the mechanisms by which it occurs, nor whether it extends to landlords of rental-occupancy units as well as to homeowners. If further research confirms the reality of this effect, however, it would indicate one important long-run benefit of an allowance program. If housing units currently in the existing stock and in reasonable condition can be prevented from deteriorating, the supply of housing available for low-income families may be substantially enhanced at modest cost.

CHAPTER 9

Communitywide Effects of Housing Allowances

Larry J. Ozanne and James P. Zais

THE PREMIER communitywide impact anticipated from implementation of a housing allowance program was inflation in the cost of housing, caused by a substantial infusion of housing demand from the subsidy payments. But other far-reaching effects were also thought possible: if allowances induced substantial upgrading of dwellings occupied by program participants, this might induce others—both landlords and homeowners—to undertake improvements and foster a broad revitalization of a neighborhood's physical plant; market intermediaries—among them, realtors, bankers, and contractors—might act to promote or thwart the program, depending on how they perceived it; the community at large might welcome or resist the notion of "welfare payments for housing" and, finally, there might be mass migrations of allowance recipients within the metropolitan area which would affect the stability of neighborhoods and community acceptance.

This chapter reviews the evidence available to date on each of these communitywide effects. The bulk of the material deals with the issues of program-induced inflation in the housing sector. After presenting and explaining these findings, evidence on the other issues is reviewed.

ALLOWANCES, SUPPLIER BEHAVIOR, AND INFLATION

This section addresses the question: Would a housing allowance program raise housing prices? This possibility was perhaps the major drawback mentioned for allowances in the preexperimental discussions of allow-

207

ances.[1] By now we know from the experiments that programs on the scale of those tested are likely to inflate rents little if at all for recipients and not at all for others. Early results from the Supply Experiment find that introduction of the program had no major immediate effect on marketwide rent inflation and little if any immediate effect on recipients' rent inflation.[2] Furthermore, we know from all three experiments that the allowance programs contributed only marginally to existing demands for housing.[3] Thus it is extremely unlikely that demand pressures in any sort of housing allowance program would ever be sufficient to heighten market rent inflation substantially.

Prior to the experimental findings, the question of price effects was of relatively great importance because analysis confidently assumed that allowances would unleash strong demand for housing but were uncertain about how landlords, builders, and other market participants would respond. If these suppliers responded primarily by raising prices, recipients would gain little from allowances, other consumers could be made worse off, and landlords or other suppliers would get most of the subsidy.

For some the concern that suppliers would primarily raise prices in response to allowances, stemmed from a belief that landlords had monopolistic or other exploitative powers to charge as much as their tenants could bear.[4] The landlords' power was felt to come from the isolation of many low-income tenants into narrow submarkets, by virtue of their race, poverty, welfare status, family composition, and the tenants' own lack of competence at shopping and negotiating for housing. For others, the concern was not that individual landlords were monopolists but that the marketwide supply of housing was so tight that the increased demand in the short run would lead to a rise in market rent levels that affected recipients and others alike.[5] Accelerated inflation in medical costs had begun about the same time Medicare and Medicaid were enacted, and some feared a similar sequence of events from enactment of an allowance program.[6] In the course of a few years, so this view held, the market could be expected to respond with additional output and the price pressure would be dissipated. In reaction to the latter view, it was frequently proposed that an allowance program be phased in slowly. However, a third and final set of concerns focused on more permanent market

---

1. See President's Committee on Urban Housing [P66], p. 71-291; U.S. Congress [P79]; de Leeuw [P12].
2. Barnett and Lowry [C8].
3. See chapters 4 and 6.
4. An expression of this concern appears in Freiden [P22], pp. 11-1*d*
5. The President's Committee on Housing [P66], pp. 71-72.
6. U.S. Congress [P79], p. 308.

effects. Some observers felt that higher output of services would lead to permanently higher prices through higher supply costs, that is, from higher land costs or production diseconomies.

The variety of these concerns revealed how little was known about how suppliers of housing respond to the demand for additional housing services. Only a few general statistics and a handful of studies were available at that time. For example. it was generally apparent that growing population and rising incomes from 1940 to 1970 had been accompanied by a large increase in suburban housing; the Census showed a steadily declining incidence of substandard housing over the same period; and the Consumer Price Index for housing had risen no faster than average prices. These patterns suggested that, in the long run at least, housing suppliers do respond flexibly to increases in demand and that price rises are therefore not inevitable. Supporting the general information, one research study had shown that the large expansions in new construction which occurred from year to year in response to changes in demand were accompanied by little effect on prices.[7] Optimistic as these pieces of information were, they dealt only with average national trends in the United States and focused mostly on the construction of new dwellings. Slum housing was still readily apparent in all metropolitan areas and still expanding in some. Even if new construction did respond well for upper- and middle-income households, the supply of housing services provided by landlords for low-income households could respond quite differently.

Knowledge about landlords in low-income neighborhoods was even scantier than knowledge about new construction and economywide trends. Two case studies of such landlords were completed in the 1960s, one for housing in Newark and the other in Baltimore.[8] The landlords in these studies hardly fit the "slumlord" stereotype, as they struggled with high costs, short lines of credit, and low rental income. From these studies and other information, it seemed that most landlords in low-income neighborhoods owned a small fraction of the units in any area and that entry by others into the business of owning and operating rental properties was easy and common. The underlying conditions for a competitive market appeared to be satisfied, and, consequently, monopoly restrictions on output suggested by some would not seem possible. On the other hand, two case studies are hardly definitive, given the diversity among U.S. metropolitan areas. Furthermore, even if monopoly power is unavailable to landlords, there may be other sources of market control, such as racial or economic segregation, lack of tenants' knowledge or bargaining strength, or, in the case of allowances, lack of concern about how allowance dollars are spent.

---

7. Muth [H99].
8. Sternlieb [C102]; Stegman [C101].

Finally, these studies lacked quantitative estimates of how much landlords would be able to raise rents in the face of general increased demand.

This limited information available about the behavior of landlords and other market suppliers presented a major obstacle to full assessment of housing allowances. Consequently, as interest in allowances grew, several studies were launched to find out how the supply of housing responds to increased demand. The Supply Experiment, with its detailed, metropolitanwide survey of landlords, tenants, howeowners, realtors, mortgage lenders, and others, is the most ambitious of these studies. Application of large-scale simulation models which incorporate suppliers' behavior has been another major effort, and there have also been additional research papers of the more traditional econometric type.

In this section, we review much of the research stimulated by the housing allowance question to summarize what has been learned about supply-side responses to increased demand. As of 1980, very little precise quantitative information has yet been established. Studies outside of the Supply Experiment have found existing data sources unyielding, and the Supply Experiment has found collection of high quality data much slower and more time consuming than originally thought.

Ironically, however, the original question concerning housing allowances has been answered without much information concerning housing suppliers. In EHAP, the basic assumption that an allowance program would greatly stimulate housing demand proved to be wrong; little additional demand was induced. Consequently, because suppliers have not faced a substantial increase in demand, marketwide housing prices and outputs have remained largely undisturbed. The original policy concern about runaway inflation of rents was thus rendered moot in terms of housing allowances themselves.

In spite of answering this housing allowance question, however, research has not quieted many of the more basic concerns about how suppliers respond to increases in demand were such an increase in demand to occur. How much would landlords raise prices in the short run? If prices rose, would the increase be permanent? How fast would additional housing services be forthcoming? Would prices of land, new structures, or wages rise because of the higher demand? These questions remain important because other programs may still focus sizable demand increases on small neighborhoods, because income transfer programs on a larger scale than those now operating may someday be considered, and because shifts in population and income themselves frequently cause sizable changes in housing demand within metropolitan markets. The following sections review what is known about supplier behavior, examine the results of the Supply Experiment carefully, and discuss the seeming contradictions between the conclusions of research and the experimental findings.

Basic Concepts

In going through studies on supply behavior it will be useful to refer to a few standardized concepts. The first of these is housing services—the composite flow of services such as warmth, shelter, and privacy that tenants normally receive from units operated by landlords. Landlords produce housing services from buildings, maintenance and management labor, utilities, and other inputs that they buy in related markets.[9] Rents, which represent tenant expenditures for a month's housing service, can be thought of as the product of a price per unit of housing service multiplied by the quantity of services received. A housing allowance program that raises rents because it increases the quantity of services would not be inflationary, but one which raised the price per unit of services without changing the quantity of services would be.

The second concept is the price elasticity of supply. It is defined as the percentage increase in output of housing services associated with a 1 percent increase in price. When large increases in output are provided with small increases in price, supply is said to be elastic or responsive. When large increases in price yield only small increases in output, then supply is inelastic or unresponsive. Much of the concern about the price effects of housing allowances can be expressed as concern about the degree of elasticity or inelasticity of the supply of housing services, and many researchers have tried to estimate one aspect or another of this elasticity. Some studies focus on the elasticity from existing individual dwellings; others look at entire metropolitan markets, which include the construction of new units. Some studies consider the short run, when there is insufficient time to build new units or to train additional labor, while others look at longer periods when both types of change are possible. Some studies look just at the supply elasticity for new buildings (for which better data are available), while others try to measure the elasticity of supply for the services actually exchanged between landlords and tenants.

Early Studies of Supply Responses

Several of these studies were forthcoming in the early 1970s in direct response to interest in housing allowances. The studies generally supported the concern that augmented demand would lead to higher prices, but the

---

9. Homeowners act as both tenants and landlords providing their own services.

price increases predicted were not always substantial. A study by de Leeuw and Ekanem focused on the permanent price effects of augmented demand.[10] By comparing rents and incomes among metropolitan areas, they concluded that a 1 percent increase in income leads to a .5 percent increase in rental prices. Their model assumed that markets were competitive; and since the difference among cities persist for long times, they concluded that these rent increases would be permanent. In other words, they found the long-run supply for housing services in competitive markets to be somewhat inelastic. The source of rising prices appeared to be diseconomies of scale in the output of services per dwelling rather than in producing additional dwellings.. Applying these results to allowance programs, de Leeuw and Ekanem concluded that an unrestricted allowance which raised incomes of eligible households by 10 percent would inflate rents for recipients by between 1 and 4 percent, depending on how well the market for recipients is integrated with or segmented from the rest of the market.

In a second study, de Leeuw and Ekanem tried to identify the short-run impacts of increased incomes on rents.[11] In particular, they wanted to see if augmented demands were likely to lead to short-run "overreactions" in rents which then would be moderated as supply expanded in the longer run. They studied the pattern of year to year price changes from the early 1950s to the late 1960s in the Boston, Detroit, San Francisco, and Washington metropolitan areas. Their findings were that increased incomes filter only slowly into increased rents. Households tended to be slow to translate increased income into expressed demands for housing, and landlords tended to be slow to raise rents in response to observed increases in demand. Thus, rents gradually rise to their long-run level over a few years rather than overshooting initially and then falling back over time. In tight markets, the pattern would be speeded up, and in loose markets it would be more protracted, but after about five years the same long-run position would be reached. If these marketwide findings were applicable to the moderate income sectors, then de Leeuw and Ekanem concluded that an unrestricted allowance subsidy would cause rents to rise gradually to their long-run levels rather than to overreach in the short run.

A different approach was taken by Bernard Frieden.[12] Instead of examining metropolitan housing markets, he used a survey of low- and moderate-income households across all metropolitan areas. He compared the housing conditions of welfare recipients to other low-income house-

10. de Leeuw and Ekanem [C13].
11. de Leeuw and Ekanem [C14].
12. Frieden [P22], pp. 11-14.

holds and found over half of the welfare recipients to be in substandard or overcrowded housing, compared to 34 to 43 percent of the other low-income households. Frieden suggested that welfare recipients may get less adequate housing for their incomes, in part because of monopoly power on the part of landlords and segregation of welfare recipients into a limited portion of the market.

These three studies examined different aspects of housing markets but express the common theme that augmenting housing demand will lead to higher prices. Thus, initial studies focusing directly on market effects of housing allowances supported the original concerns. Of course, these studies were hardly definitive. Only one of them dealt with allowance transfers to low-income households, and that one lacked a careful linking to rent effects. Furthermore, all the authors of these papers noted the limited nature of their finding and urged further study.

EHAP's Nonexperimental Studies

This brings us to the time, early in the 1970s, when HUD expressly established EHAP for a concerted effort to evaluate the housing allowance approach. The concern about rent inflation was reflected most prominently in the Supply Experiment to which EHAP allocated the majority of its research budget. But at the same time, EHAP provided separate support for nonexperimental research on the market effects of housing allowances. A large part of these funds went to support the development of urban housing market simulation models which held out the possibility of extending the experimental finding to various markets and different allowance programs.

The Supply Experiment has been described in detail in chapter 3 of this volume, but the simulation models need a short introduction. The Urban Institute's Housing Market Model (HMM) and the National Bureau of Economic Research's Urban Simulation Model (USM) both received support from EHAP and provided simulations of the market effect of housing allowance programs.[13] Both models describe changes over time in the demand for and supply of housing services within a metropolitan area. The models specify "model" households to represent the demand for housing. These model households are characterized by income, race, family type, and other attributes, and each has explicit preferences for housing, neighborhood amenities, and nonhousing consumption goods. When the models are applied to individual metropolitan areas these model households are specified to represent the income distribution, racial com-

---

13. For a complete description of HMM see de Leeuw and Struyk [C15]; for USM see Kain et al. [C43, C42]; Ingram et al. [C36].

position, and preferences of actual households in that city. HMM uses 35 to 45 model households to represent a metropolitan population while USM uses 70 to 80 thousand households. In both models, all households bid for housing services as though they were renters, although some are identified as homeowners in USM.

The supply side of metropolitan markets is characterized by model dwellings representing existing structures and units that could be created through new construction. Model dwellings are specified by their initial size, location, and other attributes. Housing services are produced from existing or new dwellings according to specified technologies for combining operating inputs (such as fuels or maintenance) and capital improvements. Rents are taken as exogenous to the model dwelling, and the output of services is set as that which maximizes profits for that dwelling. In applications to cities, each existing model dwelling represents the same number of actual dwellings as a model household represents actual households. For this reason, the number of existing model dwellings is of the same order of magnitude as the number of model households, and the difference between them represents population change over the period. All model dwellings are located in 1 of 4 to 6 geographic zones in HMM and 1 of 200 zones in USM. These zones are characterized by their access to employment, their wealth, and their racial composition, the latter two of which are determined by the solution procedures of the models themselves.

Another actor in the simulation models is government. Government can set rules for suppliers such as zoning laws. It can increase model households' incomes through welfare programs or decrease them through income taxation. In short, the scope for representing actual policies is very broad.

Given sets of model households, existing model dwellings, a new construction sector, and government, the models solve by determining which dwelling each household occupies, how much is paid in rent, what level of services is produced per dwelling, how many new dwellings are constructed, how big each one is, and how many existing dwellings are withdrawn from use or are left vacant. The solution procedures represent each household behaving to maximize its satisfaction and each dwelling owner behaving to maximize his profits. HMM uses a trial and error search for its market solution, and USM uses linear programming techniques. Each HMM solution represents changes over a 10-year period; each USM solution portrays year to year changes but is usually simulated for 7 consecutive years.

Development of HMM began in 1972, and by 1974 it had been calibrated for six metropolitan housing markets for the 1960-1970 decade—

Austin, Chicago, Durham, Pittsburgh, Portland (Oregon), and Washington, D.C. In 1976, it was calibrated to the two Supply Experiment sites. These eight sites represent a cross-section of American metropolitan areas in size, regional location, population growth rate, and racial composition. That the model has been able accurately to reproduce historic events in these markets therefore suggests it is a flexible tool for representing the broad range of U.S. urban housing markets. Development of USM began in 1968, and an early version was calibrated to Detroit. The present version is calibrated to the Pittsburgh and Chicago metropolitan areas.

Calibration of the models to specific cities includes the setting of several parameters which describe the behavior of model households, model dwellings, builders, and so on. Some parameters, particularly household demand parameters, are obtained by econometric estimation techniques. Other parameters are obtained by simulating the model with a variety of parameter values and selecting the values which best describe actual market outcomes for the city being calibrated. Both models have been calibrated over the 1960-1970 decade because of the availability of Census data at the beginning and end of the decade. This is particularly important for the setting of parameters by repeated simulations, since actual market outcomes are the criteria used in selecting best values.

For this chapter, the parameters describing suppliers' pricing and output decisions are most important. HMM uses repeated simulations to set the two major parameters describing an existing dwelling's supply of services decision. Calibration to the eight metropolitan areas has identified a range of reasonable values for this pair of parameters. In terms of supply elasticities, the pair implies values ranging from about 0.4 to 1.1.[14] The former implies that output rises a relatively unresponsive 4 percent when faced with a 10 percent increase in price; the latter implies a more responsive 11 percent in output for a 10 percent increase in price. Within this span, HMM find that most parameter values are about equally good at reproducing actual market outcomes. The divergence of values does, however, affect simulated predictions of program implementation. Consequently, in policy simulations HMM uses two sets of supply parameters, one describing relatively inelastic or unresponsive output changes, the other one describing more elastic or responsive output changes.

The supply side of USM is specified in considerably more detail than that of HMM. For example, landlords' responses are decomposed into three separate decisions: one on conversion of the basic structure into more or fewer dwelling units; one on the level of services to produce in the present year; and one on the level of maintenance and capital im-

---

14. de Leeuw and Struyk [C15], p. 94.

provement for future years. The greater detail means more parameters need to be set when calibrating the model. These parameters are set by a combination of traditional estimation, repeated simulations, and assumption. Because of the limited data for estimating so many parameters and because the present model has been calibrated to only two cities, little is known about the precision of the parameters currently in use.

Both HMM and USM have been used extensively to simulate the market effects of housing allowances. Ultimately, EHAP experimental evidence can be incorporated into the simulation models, but for now, the simulation models provide independent estimates of the effect of housing allowance programs.

Housing allowance programs have been simulated with HMM for the 1960-1970 decade in all eight of the metropolitan areas to which the model has been calibrated.[15] Allowances have also been simulated for the same decade in four prototypical cities designed to represent the major categories of all U.S. urban areas in terms of growth rates, racial proportions, household income distribution, and central city-suburban population shares.[16] Importantly, housing allowances have been simulated for the 1970-1980 as well as 1960-1970 decade in Green Bay and South Bend, the two Supply Experiment sites.[17]

The main allowance program simulated in all the cities has been of the minimum standard, housing-gap type with about one fifth of the metropolitan population eligible for the allowance program. Thus, in scale and in payment formula, it is similar to the main program field-tested in the EHAP experiments. The minimum housing quality standard has been represented in the model by a minimum quantity of housing services which households must consume in order to receive an allowance, and the standard was varied by household type to reflect the additional space required for larger households to meet minimum occupancy standards. In calibrating the model to actual markets, a majority of the eligible households appeared to be consuming below the standard in the absence of the program.

The simulated responses of model households to this program are remarkably consistent among all cities and for both decades. Participation rates are generally 70 percent or higher, except in Durham for 1960-1970 (36 percent) and Green Bay for 1970-1980 (57 percent). Those participating also tend to spend at least half of their allowance on increased housing expenditures. Thus, in the simulations, the allowances program stimulates

---

15. Ozanne [C82] ; Marshall [C67] ; Vanski [C117].
16. de Leeuw and Struyk [C15].
17. Vanski and Ozanne [C118].

a substantial additional demand for housing from the lowest income quintile of urban households.

The simulated supply responses to this demand vary considerably among markets, but there is a pattern to this variation which follows underlying market conditions. In slowly growing markets, HMM typically finds excess supplies of lower quality dwellings in the absence of an allowance program. This condition tends to depress rents below their replacement costs, discourages upgrading, and increases withdrawals (e.g., abandonments, conversions, demolitions). Introduction of an allowance program stimulates demand in this sector, prices recover, upgrading now becomes profitable, and fewer dwellings are withdrawn. In contrast, in rapidly growing markets, HMM usually finds strong demand for the lower quality stock even in the absence of an allowance program. Rents remain near their replacement costs throughout the market, most existing dwellings are upgraded as well as they can be, given upgrading costs relative to rents in other units, and additional construction is necessary to serve the demand of households even with quite modest incomes. Introduction of an allowance program does not push prices much higher under these conditions. Prices are already near replacement costs, and the additional demand must be satisfied by households "filtering up" to better quality units and by pushing more moderate-income households into additional newly built housing.

When inelastic, or unresponsive, supply parameters are used, the slow growth pattern is intensified in all cities. When elastic parameters are used, the fast growth patterns are more pronounced in all cities. Numerically, the 10-year price increases paid by allowance recipients in the slowly growing cities ranged between a high of 30 percent on average under the inelastic parameters and 15 percent on average with the elastic parameters. In the rapidly growing cities, recipients' prices rise as much as 15 percent on average with the inelastic parameters and as little as 5 percent on average with the elastic parameters. In sum, HMM finds that rent prices paid by allowance recipients tend to rise 15 to 30 percent in slowly growing cities and 5 to 15 percent in rapidly growing cities. Except in rapidly growing cities with elastic supply parameters, price increases for recipients average at least 15 percent and perhaps as much as double that percentage.

On the other hand, in the parts of the market which do not include allowance recipients, HMM simulations show insignificant price increases for higher-income sectors, including households with income close to the eligibility limit for the programs. The price increases stimulated by the program are confined to the lowest-income households who, by and large, participate in the program. Indeed, some low-income households who do not participate in the allowance program face price reductions, since low-income households with allowances move to higher quality sections of the market leaving an excesss supply of the worst quality housing.

The housing allowance programs simulated with USM have purposely been larger than those in the experiments and with HMM. Between one fourth and one third of all households have been made eligible, and close to 90 percent of eligible households were designated as participating. The reason for simulating this large jump in demand has been to highlight the patterns of supply responses rather than to estimate precisely their magnitude, and the extensive detail of USM has indeed shown an interesting pattern of responses. Average prices marketwide are scarcely changed, but this constant average masks an intricate pattern of substantial price increases in some submarkets and offsetting declines in others. In Pittsburgh, 20 percent of the dwellings experience simulated price increases of more than 10 percent while 22 percent experience declines of the same magnitude. The corresponding percentage for the Chicago allowance simulations are 19 percent and 24 percent, respectively.[18] USM breaks down this pattern of increases by building type, apartment sizes, and residential locations. New construction and withdrawals of existing units are stimulated by the allowance program as well. New construction rises by 14 percent in Pittsburgh and 23 percent in Chicago. Thus, USM portrays an allowance program as causing very substantial shifts in the pattern of housing demand among low-income households, a pattern which raises prices and stimulates construction of standard housing of certain types and in certain locations while also sharply reducing prices and the use of substandard housing in less desirable neighborhoods. This pattern, more than the marketwide price movement, is what USM identifies as the essential nature of the market's response.

Together, HMM and USM provide a substantial advance in the analysis of the market effects of housing allowances. Prior studies were either marketwide or national in their focus. Some dealt with new construction rather than rental housing services. Few explicitly modeled the determinants of rental service prices or dealt separately with low-income households. The two simulation models represent the low-income sector of urban housing markets in substantial detail as well as relate this sector to the rest of the market. Besides addressing price effects, they also show effects on consumption of housing services, on household location, on levels of new construction, on dwelling upgrading, and on many other factors.

In terms of price effects, our primary focus in this chapter, both models predict that an allowance program which enrolls from one fifth to

18. Kain et al. [C42], p. 4.

one third of the population is likely to raise price per unit of service for recipients by 10 percent or more. Both models also predict price declines and withdrawals of some dwellings that are too low quality to be profitably upgraded. Finally, both models predict that the price effects will be confined to the lower quality sector of the market; middle- and upper-income housing sectors are largely unaffected. HMM additionally finds that the magnitude of the price effects depends on the underlying conditions in a market. Prices are predicted to rise more in markets where they would otherwise be depressed and rise less where prices would normally be high enough for new construction.

A major weakness of the two models for evaluating the market effects of housing allowances is that their supply-side parameters lack precision, a defect which must be reflected by lack of precision in predicted price effects. HMM has been calibrated to enough markets to reveal this limitation and to suggest a range within which the answer should lie. Unfortunately, as reported above, this range is wide. USM lacks sufficient experience to even suggested an interval around its predictions. Clearly then, the predictions of both models would benefit greatly from improved estimates of landlords' responsiveness to shifts in household demands. Interestingly, better estimates of such responses for use in simulation modeling may be one of the most important long-run benefits from the Supply Experiment.

Lack of precision in HMM supply-side parameters stimulated two additional studies. One of these attempted to estimate the responsiveness of individual suppliers directly.[19] This study started from a linked sample of dwellings observed in both the 1960 and 1970 Census of Housing. It then tried to relate quality changes in the units over the decade to market conditions affecting the units. Quality changes recorded in the Census are major ones, such as adding a bathroom or central air conditioning, and omit less dramatic changes such as painting, replastering walls, or adding better appliances. Individual units were found to undergo these major improvements infrequently in response to price increases, suggesting that demands for higher quality would have to raise prices considerably before such upgrading occurred. The authors, however, felt that their findings were overly pessimistic because of statistical problems in the data and because less extensive upgrading could not be measured.

The second study tried to estimate marketwide responses to large shifts in demand to avoid the problems encountered in the first study.[20] This study was essentially an extension of an earlier study, already discussed, which examines the determinants of rent levels among metropolitan

19. Ozanne and Struyk [C83].
20. Ozanne and Thibodeau [C84].

areas.[21] Extensions to the original model include an analysis of house prices as well as rents and less reliance on *a priori* assumptions. It also used a new data source, the Annual Housing Survey. This study, like the earlier one, found that markets with higher household incomes have higher housing prices. This time, though, the higher price appeared to result from the effect of greater demand for housing services on land prices. However, this study also encountered several empirical problems which created doubt about the precise magnitude of its predicted price increase.

The studies just reported, from the earliest work by Muth on new construction through the simulation models and up to the recent cross-SMSA model, represent a relatively small body of research evidence. Furthermore, these studies have been plagued by a large number of statistical problems created by weak data. Nonetheless, the majority reach the conclusion that if a program stimulated the market demand for housing services, the response would include price increases as well as output improvements.[22]

EHAP's Experimental Evidence

Over the same period that the simulation and related studies were predicting price increases from allowance stimulated demands, the Supply Experiment began enrolling households and monitoring market responses in Green Bay and South Bend. A recent paper summarizes what has been learned so far about price effects from that experiment.[23] It reports rent changes over the first 33 months of program operation in Green Bay and 17 months of operation in South Bend.[24] It also presents preliminary analysis of program impacts on rent changes.

---

21. The earlier study described above is de Leeuw and Ekanem [C13].

22. The studies considered so far in this chapter have focused primarily on the responsiveness of the supply of housing service to increases in the demand for output. Studies of other aspects of housing supply have been carried out, but these are not easily related to the basic price question being addressed in this chapter. A large number of studies have focused on the determinants of new construction activity. (See Fredland and MacRae [C25].) A much smaller body of work has analyzed landlords' maintenance and investment decision making. (See Mayer [C68].) The new construction studies generally model the number of new units or value of new construction rather than housing services and frequently do not have separately identified supply equation (Follain [C23]). The landlord investment decision models have been largely theoretical and do not identify supply elasticities. (Mayer [C68] is an exception.)

23. Barnett and Lowry [C8].

24. Survey records in Green Bay cover 33 months of open enrollment and 6 months immediately preceding open enrollment. Survey records in South Bend cover 17 months of open enrollment plus the 4 preceding months. Program records in Green Bay cover 24 months of open enrollment and in South Bend cover 19 months. Barnett and Lowry [C8].

Table 9.1

Comparison of Contract Rent Increases: National, Regional, and Local,
1973-1977 [a]

Area	Average Annual Increase in Contract Rent [b] (%)				
	1973	*1974*	*1975*	*1976*	*1977* [c]
All U.S. cities	4.9	5.2	5.3	5.5	6.3
North Central cities, by size:					
Over 1,400,000	6.8	4.8	3.7	3.9	5.7
250,000-1,400,000	2.4	3.6	4.5	4.2	6.4
50,000-250,000	2.8	4.6	5.0	7.1	5.3
2,500-50,000	4.1	5.0	5.0	4.4	7.2
Green Bay		3.7	4.4	4.8	
South Bend			3.1		

Source: Barnett and Lowry [C8], table 8.

a. U.S. Bureau of Labor Statistics, *Monthly Labor Review,* various issues, and special tabulations for North Central cities; Green Bay and South Bend entries are averages of rent changes for each dwelling in a marketwide sample periodically resurveyed in each site.

b. Entries for the U.S. and North Central region are based on the BLS index of "residential rent," definitionally equivalent to contract rent. Changes are calculated from December to December.

c. Increase for December 1976 to September 1977, annualized.

The monitoring of rent changes relied on the periodic surveys of the occupants of dwellings in the permanent panel of dwellings, described in Appendix A. The survey records for each unit were linked to make unit-specific computations possible. The survey instrument elicited detailed information on expenditures for rent and for utilities, if paid for separately. From these data, changes in contract rents and utility payments were calculated. Moreover, estimates were made of the share of expenditures accounted for by changes in the price of utility services (e.g., dollars per kilowatt hour for electricity) and changes in consumption.[25]

The allowance program has not caused substantial marketwide rent inflation in its first years of operation. As shown in table 9.1, market contract rents rose less in the two experimental sites than did rents nationally or regionally. Furthermore, in both sites rents (exclusive of utilities) rose less rapidly than maintenance and operating costs, indicating that rental income declined relative to costs.[26] Table 9.2 divides total rents in Green Bay at four points in time between a shelter compo-

25. For a further description of these calculations, see Stucker [C103].
26. Barnett and Lowry [C8], p. 23.

Table 9.2

Components of Gross Rent Increase for Typical Dwelling: Green Bay, 1974-1977

Date or Period	Shelter Rent	Fuel and Utilities	Gross Rent
Typical Monthly Expense ($)			
January 1974	128.89	41.11	170.00
January 1975	131.03	49.70	180.73
January 1976	135.40	61.05	196.45
January 1977	141.44	70.69	212.13
Change in Expense (%)			
1974-1975	1.7	20.9	6.3
1975-1976	3.3	22.8	8.7
1976-1977	4.5	15.8	8.0
Annual average	3.2	19.8	7.7

Source: Barnett and Lowry [C8], table 6.
Note: Estimates are for a 5-room dwelling meeting program standards and renting for $170 (including fuel and utilities) in January 1974. Gross rent inflation was estimated from survey data for the years indicated; inflation in fuel and utility expenses was estimated from consumption norms and local rate schedules. Shelter rent inflation was derived as a residual.

nent and a fuel and utilities component. The figures document the dominance of the fuel and utilities component in determining rental increases the 1974-1977 period. A similar pattern was found in South Bend.

In the one submarket examined, Central South Bend, where over a fourth of all renters enrolled in the program, rents rose less rapidly than did rents in suburban areas; the program did not revive the generally more depressed submarket, at least during the first 17 months of operation. Finally, rents for recipients who stayed in their original units rose only 3 percent in Green Bay and 1 percent in South Bend.[27] While this appears to be slightly more than rent increases for the typical nonmover, it is still minimal, since average operating costs and average rents in the two sites both rose by more.

Substantial rent increases induced by the program are also unlikely to appear in future years. This seems to be the case even though the one study which analyzed market changes found that income changes probably take three to five years to be fully reflected in rents.[28] From this schedule, one would expect that some of the program adjustments are yet to occur in South Bend, which has been monitored for only a year and

27. Barnett and Lowry [C8], p. 31.
28. de Leeuw and Ekanem [C14].

a half of program operation. But even in this short a period, some notable market effects should have occurred if substantial rent increases were going to appear.

The clearest explanation for the lack of market rent inflation in the first years of program operation, and its unlikely later appearance, is that the allowance program itself is causing a very small increase in marketwide demand for housing. About a fifth of all households are estimated to be eligible for allowances in each site. Of these eligibles, 40 to 50 percent were receiving payments as of the second half of 1976. Furthermore, of these participating households, 76 percent in Green Bay and 70 percent in South Bend were occupying their preenrollment dwellings. Most of these units required only small improvements to meet standards, and for those that did, the median cost of meeting the standards was only $10.[29] Even among renters, who are faster to adjust than homeowners, the net increase in housing demand appears to be very limited. The small increase in demand for housing seen in the Supply Experiment is consistent with experience in the rest of EHAP, as reviewed in chapters 4 to 7.

Given that the allowance programs tested in EHAP provide little stimulus to the demand for housing, the absence of marked price responses is hardly surprising. Factors which might lead to price increases in a competitive market will not be operative. (Such inoperative factors include declines in vacancy rates for standard housing, increasing costs of upgrading substandard units, and shortages of materials or sites for additions to standard housing.) Rather, price increases would be forthcoming only if landlords held some monopolistic or other exploitative powers over tenants or if tenants treated allowances as less valuable than other income. The Supply Experiment, as noted earlier, has found no evidence of significant price increases paid by renter participants. Also, the Demand Experiment with its control group and treatment variations has found that landlords do not exercise such power extensively nor do tenants generally treat their allowances cavalierly.[30] Certainly one would not expect to find widespread power in the hands of landlords, since even in Green Bay and South Bend ownership of properties is widely diffused; and home purchase is a relatively available option even for lower-income households.

The observation of no substantial rent inflation effects from the program in either Green Bay or South Bend, coupled with the unlikelihood of any future effects, answers the main question addressed by the Supply

---

29. See Rand [E129], and chapter 9 of this book for more information on repair activity.

30. Kennedy and Merrill [E71].

Experiment at its inception: would there be significant price increase in response to a housing allowance program? The experiment has shown there will not be significant rent inflation.

What has not been learned from the Supply Experiment, but may still be observed, is how prices respond to substantial increases in the demand for housing.[31] This is clearly a secondary question for EHAP, since the allowance-generated demand increase turned out to be small. But, as noted, it continues to be of interest for other programs. The Supply Experiment should eventually be able to teach us much about the answer to this secondary question because the monitoring apparatus is set up to observe the market rather than the recipient or his landlord. Many factors contribute to total market demand shift besides the allowance program, so the experiment may yet find sufficient total demand stimulus during the course of its market monitoring to measure supply response. If so, the experiment could provide the precise estimates of landlord and market supply elasticities that have eluded the other studies discussed in this chapter.

An example of what can be learned from the Supply Experiment about the effects of general demand shifts appears in a recent paper by Rydell.[32] He observes from preexperimental data that rents in central

---

31. The Supply Experiment has not found out precisely how much of the small increase in demand has gone into higher prices and how much goes into increased service. This distinction may never be deduced because the magnitudes are so small and because there is no experimental control. The analysis of Barnett and Lowry [C8] illustrates these problems. The paper shows that the shelter component of rents is rising slower than operating costs in the sites and concludes, ". . . this is not what one would expect from demand-driven inflation" (p. 23). But rents might have been rising even more slowly in the absence of the program due to, say, more slowly rising capital costs. In fact, rents in the whole North Central region were rising less rapidly than were operating costs. If the gap between rents and operating costs is narrowing more slowly in the sites than elsewhere in the region, then this is what would be expected from greater demand inflation in the sites than elsewhere.

Another example of the difficulty in identifying small program effects occurs in the interpretation of rent movements over time. Rents in Green Bay are observed to start from a lower rate of inflation than rents elsewhere and accelerate during program years up toward the other rates (p. 26). The authors conclude that such a change is "a logical result if rent inflation in Brown County was driven by price increases in national factor markets" (p. 27). Of course, it is just as logical that if national factor markets are driving rent increases then all cities should show the same inflation rates throughout the three years observed. It is also just as logical that this minor acceleration in Green Bay is due to the allowance program or even to a statistical fluke (such as a less pronounced tendency for landlords in Green Bay to charge separately for utility payments than is occurring elsewhere). Given incomplete data and the absence of proper experiment controls, it is impossible to identify small program effects on rents.

32. Rydell [C93].

South Bend are only slightly below those in the rest of the site and in Green Bay. This is surprising, since central South Bend has been losing population and has a 13 percent vacancy rate, while the other two areas are gaining population and have a 6 percent and a 4 percent vacancy rate, respectively. Simulations with HMM predicted substantial rent discounts for lower quality South Bend units under these conditions.[33] The similarity of rents is especially surprising since rental property values in central South Bend are observed to be discounted by about a quarter from the values in the rest of the site and by about 50 percent from the values in Green Bay. Prompted by these observations, Rydell develops a theory of the short-run response of housing markets to demand shifts which is consistent with the observed rents and values. According to this theory, short-run adjustments in demand are reflected mainly by changes in vacancy rates rather than in monthly rent levels. Lower vacancy rates significantly raise landlord's revenues and profits, even though rents are largely unchanged; and this produces significant increases in the value of rental property. Using the preexperimental observations to estimate his model, Rydell then predicts that a demand increase in central South Bend allowance programs of 4 percent should raise rents by only 1 percent but raise rental property values by 20 percent. These predictions (and others by HMM described below) can be compared to future observations from the experiment. The work on which they are based definitely helps to improve our understanding of how markets respond to changes in demand.

The Experiments and the Simulation Models

The simulation models predicted substantial program-induced price effects from an allowance program, but the Supply Experiment shows these effects have not occurred. Clearly the models failed to predict market outcomes and need revision based on the experimental findings.

It is also clear that the models did not fail because of shortcomings in their representation of housing supply. As we already have noted, the supply sides of HMM and USM were thought to be their weakest parts, so failure there would not have been unexpected. The models failed because they did not predict the low participation rates or low earmarking effects of the allowances. That is, they overestimated the demand impact created by the allowance programs. Both models typically show participation rates of 70 percent or more, whereas 40 to 50 percent actually occurred. Both models showed most households needing substantial housing improvements

---

33. Vanski and Ozanne [C118].

in order to pass program standards, whereas few were far below standards in the experiments.[34]

Because the models predicted a surge in demand that did not materialize in the experiments, there still remains a great deal of uncertainty about how well the models represent supply responses. A conclusive but impractical way to investigate the accuracy of the models' supply sides would be to run a larger scale experiment like those simulated by the models. A less conclusive but more practical approach is to rerun the models, constraining them to represent the participation and earmarking rates of the experiments. If the predicted supply responses reflect actual market outcomes, then the supply sides of the models gain credence. Since the experimental shift in demand was so small, it would not require a finely tuned supply side to approximate market responses. Nevertheless, gross problems should be apparent.

Just such a test has been carried out with the HMM in simulations of the Green Bay and South Bend markets over the 1970-1980 decade.[35] Participation rates in the model were constrained to 43 percent in Green Bay and 50 percent in South Bend, reasonable approximations of equilibrium participation rates in the experiments. Program standards in the model were lowered so that two thirds of the dwellings in Green Bay and three fourths in South Bend pass them in the absence of the program. In the experiments, half passed standards in their preexperimental housing and another 40 percent passed with minor improvements.

HMM's constrained simulations of market effects appear to be close to those emerging from the Supply Experiment, but later observations from South Bend will be needed to certify this. The simulations predict that Green Bay recipients' 10-year rent inflation will run 2 to 4 percent while marketwide average rents will be unaffected.[36] This is consistent with the apparent findings reported for the site, that is, 2 to 3 percent increase for nonmover participants in the first 33 months and no marketwide effects.[37] The simulations for South Bend predict recipients' prices will rise 9 to 10 percent over a decade, some nonparticipants' prices will fall, and marketwide prices will be unaffected.[38] Nineteen months of program opera-

---

34. To some extent USM can be excused for overestimating the size of the allowance program since it consciously attempted to simulate a large program. But it cannot escape responsibility entirely, since it claimed that its simulations were relevant to the allowance program. USM would have to simulate a more representative program and show that it does reflect experimental outcomes to be entirely absolved of prediction error.

35. Vanski and Ozanne [C118]. In particular see pp. 47-66.

36. Vanski and Ozanne [C118], p. 62.

37. Barnett and Lowry [C8], pp. 33-34.

38. Vanski and Ozanne [C118], p. 62.

tion is too short a period to tell if site results will approach these predicted ones. So far there is an indication of a 1.7 percent effect on rents for nonmover participants, and there are indications of no effect on rents marketwide.[39] Rydell's previously mentioned analysis of the site suggests rents are not discounted much below replacement costs as predicted by the model but that house values are. It is possible that these house values could recover, thereby providing a degree of price increase which has not occurred in Green Bay.[40]

In conclusion, it is the assumptions used in the simulation models about changes in housing demand that the experiments have shown to be inadequate, not the supply sides. In fact the supply side of HMM may yet predict supply-side effects in both sites quite accurately. Clearly, the models can benefit from the lessons of the experiments on household responses to the allowance program. It should also be clear from the example of Rydell's paper that the models should benefit a great deal from future analyses of the experimental data on how landlords and markets respond to general shifts in demands. Incorporation of experimental findings into detailed models like HMM and USM probably represent the best hope of extending the basic behavioral findings of the experiments to other programs and to other markets.

OTHER COMMUNITY IMPACTS

So far, this chapter has considered what many believe to be the most important communitywide impact of housing allowances—potential increases in the price of housing in the market. The evidence above appears quite conclusive that the programs administered in the Supply Experiment had little impact on prices in the two communities in which it was tested.

Neighborhood Effects

Other impacts also deserve attention, and they too stem from fears or hopes for allowances held by various individuals and groups. This section considers three areas: (1) neighborhood effects, (2) responses by market intermediaries and indirect suppliers of housing, and (3) responses by community leaders, both governmental and nongovernmental. The experiences reported here relate chiefly to the Supply Experiment sites, although

---

39. Barnett and Lowry [C8], pp. 33-34.

40. HMM and analysis from the Supply Experiment concur that discounting does not exist in Green Bay.

information on community reactions to the site selection process in the other two experiments is also relevant.

One hope for housing allowances is that they would produce sufficient housing-related activities to arrest neighborhood deterioration or even to induce neighborhood upgrading in dilapidated low-income neighborhoods. In the Demand and Administrative Agency Experiments, such outcomes would not be expected, since these programs had limited enrollments representing only a fraction of households in a market and scattered throughout very large program areas. Expectations of neighborhood effects from the Supply Experiment, however, are more reasonable, since enrollment of households was not limited at these sites. The impact of neighborhoods here might be felt in two ways. First, through *mobility* patterns induced by the program, some neighborhoods might suffer loss of households and others might gain households at a scale which could measurably change the character of these neighborhoods. Secondly, through induced repair and improvement activities, the physical stock of housing in various neighborhoods might be upgraded both by the improvements made by allowance-participating households and by improvements by nonparticipating households in the neighborhood stimulated by the allowance-induced improvement activities of their neighbors. The evidence from the Supply Experiment (at least from its early years) is that neither effect was forthcoming.

For purposes of analysis, Green Bay and South Bend were divided by Rand Corporation staff into analytic districts of between 2,000 and 4,000 households, using boundaries based on similarity of units and environmental conditions. These districts were aggregates of neighborhoods—108 in Green Bay and 86 in South Bend—which had been defined in a similar way.[41] In the first two years of the program, the allowance program may have induced some moving from deteriorated residential areas to areas with better housing. In Green Bay, for example, the two most central districts lost households to districts further out. Still, the net moves of participants over a two-year period did not constitute more than 1.2 percent of all the households in either the originating district or the district of destination.[42]

In the case of South Bend, most of the enrollment, as well as moving by participants, has taken place in central South Bend. The area that lost the most enrollees is called "Core West," which has the worst housing and the highest crime rate in the city. Most households moved to adjacent areas, but it is not clear that any moves by EHAP households were pro-

---

41. See Ellikson [C19] for Green Bay neighborhood designations and Bala [C4] for South Bend.
42. Rand [E129], p. 129.

gram-induced. The Core West area was already experiencing decline, and nearly a sixth of its housing units were demolished without being replaced between 1970 and 1976.[43] As bad as conditions were, Core West only lost 53 of its 986 participating households, so the impact on the program for the area or for adjacent districts where households moved was not substantial.

Overall, the number of moves in the Supply Experiment has been low, and as a means of transforming neighborhoods, the program impact through moves is so small that it defies measurement.[44] What then of the impact of program-induced improvements to the housing stock? In chapter 8 it was demonstrated that the repairs undertaken to pass program standards were small, with a mean cash outlay per unit ranging from $37 to $81, depending on site and tenure. Many small repairs, such as replacing windows or painting porches, could improve the overall exterior appearance of the dwelling and thus induce neighbors to undertake improvements on their own. It has been estimated, however, that only about 30 percent of these initial repairs affect either the exterior or surrounding property.[45] In part, this is because health and safety considerations are paramount in the standards used in the Supply Experiment; a unit may pass the standards despite unattractive exteriors. The following example demonstrates this:

A 200-year-old dwelling with a new tar paper roof, plastic sheets in place of storm windows, a barren yard, and severely peeling paint could pass (housing allowance office) standards (if children under seven years of age did not occupy or frequently visit the dwelling). Most building materials are acceptable so long as they meet specified performance criteria. There are no building standards that apply to building age or to sparse landscaping. Peeling paint may reveal underlying structural damage; but if there is no structural damage, and if children are not present, paint of any color or condition will meet program standards.[46]

Thus, since most of the initial repairs were applied to the kitchen, bathroom, and other interior rooms, and since these repairs were small, it is not surprising that major neighborhood impacts were not felt.

The longer-term effects of repair behavior, however, cannot be easily dismissed. Expenditures for repairs are higher for participating households in central South Bend, for example, than they are for the fringe

43. Rand [E129], p. 129.
44. For a discussion of the role of mobility in improving housing conditions for participants, as opposed to having an impact on neighborhoods, see chapters 4 through 7.
45. McDowell [C61], p.24.
46. McDowell [C61], p. 6.

areas of the city or the suburbs.[47] With high participation rates and more expenditures per household concentrated in a few neighborhoods, thresholds might eventually be approached when nonparticipants will be induced to fix up their own dwellings in response to the repair behavior undertaken by participants.

Market Intermediaries and Indirect Suppliers

The individuals most directly involved in housing allowance programs are the households themselves—renters and owners—and, to some extent, landlords who rent units to participating households. The program is structured to place most of the burden of decision making on households seeking allowance payments. Sometimes, however, these households are dependent on services provided by market intermediaries and indirect suppliers of housing such as real estate brokers, property management firms, rental agents, mortgage lenders, insurance underwriters, home improvement contractors, and maintenance service firms. The role of such groups in housing markets differs, but their posture and attitude toward an allowance program might influence its results. Conversely, the policies of such groups might undergo changes resulting from the allowance program in their communities.

In Green Bay and South Bend, it was found that property management firms, rental agents, and maintenance firms were not important in either promoting or hindering the allowance program.[48] And given the lack of substantial rehabilitation associated with the program, home improvement contractors appear to have been very little affected. Home improvement loans were also rare. To the extent that the program has had an impact, it has been on the real estate brokers and financial institutions of South Bend. Mortgage banks have financed purchases of homes for allowance recipients in South Bend (as noted in chapter 6), provided that the Federal Housing Administration (FHA) insured the loan. Although allowance income was viewed favorably by the FHA, households with poor credit histories have been a problem.[49] In Green Bay, home purchases by allowance clients have been rare, so financial institutions have not been affected.

In sum, market intermediaries and indirect suppliers have not affected the program's operations, nor have they been affected by the program, be-

---

47. McDowell [C61], p. 68.
48. See White [C121] for a discussion of Green Bay. South Bend market intermediaries and indirect suppliers of housing are discussed in White [C122].
49. Rand [E129], p. 110.

cause the demand for housing was not greatly altered by the program at either Supply Experiment site.

In general, EHAP has found landlords cooperative in their attitude toward the program. One exception to this pattern occurred at the Jacksonville site of the Administrative Agency Experiment. Operating the program in this market proved particularly difficult, and unlike other AAE sites, Jacksonville did not initially come near to meeting its target of enrolled households. Indeed, a second enrollment period was required in order to compensate for this fact.

A number of program and market factors contributed to the problem. Jacksonville established what became effectively the most stringent housing standards in the AAE, adopting the entire city housing code as its standards and subcontracting enforcement of the standards to city code enforcers. Furthermore, Jacksonville is highly racially segregated, and its housing stock contains a high proportion of units which did not meet the standard; and when standard units were available at rents that enrollees could afford, landlords resisted the program because of objection to certain features, including the inspection of units. Landlords of substandard units felt that insufficient incentives were provided them to upgrade their units, since under EHAP rents were not guaranteed unless the unit was occupied by a program participant.

In the second enrollment period, a greater emphasis was placed by the agency on actively explaining the program to landlords. Although a higher proportion of enrollees succeeded in becoming recipients during this period, there is no evidence to suggest that a more positive attitude of landlords resulting from the agency's efforts contributed significantly to this. Apparently, enrollees in the second period lived in better housing and therefore were more likely to succeed.[50] Overall, the Jacksonville experience suggests that particularly severe housing market problems can affect the operation of housing allowance programs, and special measures may be needed to compensate for these circumstances.

Community Leaders

The attitudes and actions of community leaders can have an impact on a housing allowance program in two ways. Because by federal statute operation of EHAP required the approval by the government of the jurisdiction, community leaders could affect site selection through veto. Secondly, community leaders might attempt to influence the direction of the program once it was underway.

---

50. For a discussion of the Jacksonville second enrollment efforts, see Wolfe and Hamilton [C124].

In fact, site selection was a critical problem for EHAP because the program's designers wanted participation by all of the jurisdictions which make up a housing market. If this consent could be obtained, enrollees would be free to search for housing throughout a housing market, and the locational effects of housing allowances could thereby be tested. But it was exactly the unknown impact of locational dispersal which troubled a number of suburban jurisdictions who feared that black households would relocate into their areas. EHAP staff could not guarantee that this would not happen, leading several jurisdictions to decline participation.[51]

Even in the rather small-scale AAE and Demand Experiments, several jurisdictions resisted. Portions of two sites which in fact became AAE sites declined to participate—Rialto in the San Bernardino area and Peoria and Tazewell counties in the Peoria area. Holyoke in the Springfield area refused to participate in either the Demand Experiment or the AAE. (Springfield was selected as an AAE site, nevertheless.) Lack of local cooperation prevented site selection of two other cities—Syracuse, New York in the AAE and Saginaw, Michigan in the Supply Experiment.

The cooperation of area jurisdictions was particularly crucial to the Supply Experiment. All local governments in the Green Bay area, which is racially homogeneous, agreed to participate in the program. Saginaw, however, was lost as a site because of the fears of white suburban jurisdictions.[52] Ultimately, South Bend, Indiana, was chosen as a "slow-growth, high percentage black" site for the Supply Experiment, despite the fact that not all jurisdictions joined the program. Within 18 months of the program's beginning, however, opposition lessened and these jurisdictions voted to participate. By this time, it was clear that allowance subsidies were not inducing locational changes.

After program operations had begun, community leaders reacted on the basis of their expectations about what the program would do. Green Bay and South Bend offer contrasting pictures in this regard. In Green Bay there are few formal political organizations, and to the extent that there have been complaints about the program, they have been about the principle of giving government subsidies to households, not about the impact on special interest groups. South Bend, on the other hand, is a community with a large number of local organizations, and many of these

---

51. It should be noted that, despite the refusal of some jurisdictions to participate, the eventual EHAP geographic areas at each of the 12 sites succeeded in representing roughly the housing markets in these sites. For an argument that EHAP experience in this regard can be transferred to other HUD programs, see Heinberg [P31], pp. 244-245.

52. See Appendix B for a discussion of the site selection process in each of the experiments.

monitored the program's progress.[53] Leaders of minority organizations have attacked the direction of the program. A local NAACP official, for example, wanted a more positive desegregation policy tied to the program. An association of Hungarian immigrants raised the issue of confidentiality of records, because it did not trust the allowance agency's pledge in this regard.[54] It can safely be said, however, that these are exceptions rather than the rule. Lack of any persistent opposition on the part of community leaders seems to be attributable to the program sparking such low levels of housing-related changes, as discussed throughout this book.

---

53. Ellickson and Kanouse [C21], p. 22.
54. Wiewel [C119], p. 136.

CHAPTER 10

Administering Housing Allowances

James P. Zais

IN LARGE-SCALE evaluations of public programs, administrative questions are very often considered of secondary importance, and sometimes they are not explicitly addressed at all. This low-priority attention is unwise because program administration can have a major impact on both program outcomes and costs. As seen in chapter 3, the Experimental Housing Allowance Program recognized the importance of administrative issues by making them the central focus of one of its three major components—the Administrative Agency Experiment—as well as by considering administrative issues in the design and research agenda of the other two experiments. This chapter relies primarily on information from the AAE, although information from the other two experiments is also cited where applicable.

The broad questions to be addressed in this chapter are the following: (1) How feasible are housing allowances to administer? (2) What options exist for performing the administrative functions needed to implement an allowance program, and what are the outcomes associated with these options? (3) What are the administration costs incurred by a housing allowance program?

Before addressing these, however, it is important to understand the administrative framework for housing allowances as administered in EHAP, compared to other rental housing assistance programs. It is most efficient to begin by outlining the administrative responsibilities implicit in housing allowance programs. Allowances, unlike traditional housing programs, allow considerable independence to participating households to search for and find their own dwelling units and to handle housing-related problems. Hence, the administrative duties of the agency in an allowance program are quite different from those found in many other housing programs.

Although administrative details vary at the local level, figure 10.1 shows the broad relationships among agencies, landlords, and tenants in four housing programs, including allowances as structured in EHAP. For purposes of contrast, the table also shows the relationships inherent in private market transactions where no government program is involved. In conventional public housing, the housing unit is owned by a government agency, usually a housing authority. The agency essentially fulfills the role of the landlord, and tenants make rent payments to the agency according to agency rules, with tenant contributions rising with income. In the Section 23 program, on the other hand, the same local agencies lease privately owned housing units and then sublease them to low-income households.[1] Two separate contracts are involved: one between the agency and the landlord, another between the agency and the household. The household pays the agency an amount determined by the program formula, and the agency, in turn, pays the full contract rent to the landlord.

More recently, the Section 8 Lower-Income Rental Assistance Program for Existing Housing established a new pattern of relationships which placed more responsibility on the participating household. In this program, the government neither provides units nor leases them from private owners. Instead, households are expected to search for units themselves. When a unit has been found and certified as passing the program's standards, the agency enters into a housing assistance payments contract with the landlord. A lease is required between the tenant and the landlord, and rent is paid in two separate transactions: the household pays the landlord a share of the rent, and the agency pays the landlord the difference between the participant's contribution and the contract rent.

The allowance programs tested at all EHAP sites carry one step further the principle of allowing participating households to handle their own housing matters. Direct subsidy payments are made to households. No formal relationship exists between the agency and the landlord.[2] Thus, of all government housing programs, housing allowances come closest to the

---

1. The Section 23 leased housing program lasted from 1965 until early 1974, when it was replaced by the "revised Section 23 program," a program very similar to the Section 8 Lower Income Rental Assistance Program for Existing Housing. In 1974, Section 8 formally replaced the Section 23 program.

2. A lease between tenant and landlord was required in the Supply and Administrative Agency Experiments, primarily because Section 23 funds were used to fund payments to households in these two experiments and a lease was required in Section 23. The housing allowance concept, however, does not necessitate a lease between landlord and tenant, and none was therefore required in the Demand Experiment, in which subsidies were financed by research funds.

Figure 10.1

Contractual Relationships, Payments, and Certification of Eligibility in Four Housing Programs and in the Private Market

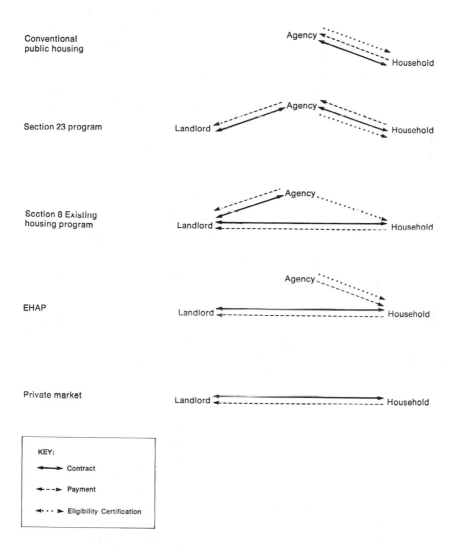

Adapted from Zais, Goedert, and Trutko [P95], p. 39.

essential relationship between tenant and landlord in the private market. The household is basically responsible for its own housing decisions, subject to meeting the program's dwelling quality standard.

Given this overall administrative framework, what are the major functions to be performed by agencies implementing allowance programs? The following discussion considers functions required to bring households into the program—called "intake" functions—as well as those required to deal with households once they begin to receive payments—called "maintenance" functions. In each case, this chapter reviews what has been learned from EHAP about the manner in which each function may be performed most effectively and efficiently. In the final section, the costs of administering a housing allowance are described; the cost associated with functions unique to housing allowances are separated from those which would be required under an unconstrained income transfer.

PERFORMING ADMINISTRATIVE FUNCTIONS

It will be recalled that housing allowances, unlike unconstrained transfer payments, require that enrollees live in standard housing.[3] Two functions discussed next, outreach and enrollment, would be necessary in any transfer program, constrained or not, while inspection of units is part of the program only because of its special housing focus. Client services, which in an allowance program help households in their attempts to locate and occupy standard units, are in some sense discretionary in any program; but they may be essential for achieving participation of some groups of households.

Outreach

Outreach is an intake function defined as the group of tasks related to informing the eligible population about the program. Although it is often called by other names (such as "public information service"), most programs which bestow benefits to households in the population require that some information be circulated on the availability of those benefits.

While outreach, at first glance, might be considered nothing more than a simple task involving advertising the free availability of a desired product, the function can be quite difficult. How outreach is conducted de-

---

3. As was explained in chapter 3, this rule was imposed on all recipients in the Supply Experiment and the Administrative Agency Experiment and for households in the five "housing gap-minimum standards" treatment cells in the Demand Experiment.

pends, in part, on the nature of the program being administered.[4] As we have seen in chapter 3, the public agencies selected to administer the Administrative Agency Experiment program in each of the AAE's eight sites were given a target number of households for participation. Under such circumstances, agencies had to try to maintain a balance in their out-reach efforts, encouraging enough households to apply and yet not raising unreasonably high expectations and frustration in the community. Supply Experiment administrators, on the other hand, faced the uncertainties im-plicit in an open enrollment program, in which all income-eligible house-holds could enroll in the program if they so chose. Outreach efforts in this case had to be timed carefully so that long waiting lists did not develop. Whether programs have limited entitlement or open enrollment, agencies had to gear their outreach to convey sufficient information so that primarily eligible households applied and large numbers of ineligible households did not. To the extent that an agency unnecessarily processes ineligible applications, administrative expenditures will be wasted and households disappointed.

Given these uncertainties, EHAP experience has confirmed that out-reach is one of the most difficult administrative functions to plan. Findings from the experiments, however, narrow the uncertainty about three ele-ments in an outreach program—the *audience* to be reached, the *media* to be used, and the *message* to be communicated.

In their limited enrollment programs, AAE agencies were charged with the task of enrolling groups in approximately the same proportions as their numbers in the eligible population. Although agencies generally achieved this goal, they found that some groups were harder to reach than others, an experience which was repeated in the other EHAP experi-ments.[5] In particular, proportionately fewer elderly households applied than existed in the eligible population.[6] The Supply Experiment programs experienced a somewhat more mixed pattern for the elderly. Elderly cou-ples, both renters and homeowners, were systematically underrepresented among applicants at both Green Bay and South Bend.[7] The single elderly

---

4. The door-to-door client recruitment procedures of the Demand Experiment were designed for research purposes only and are not considered typical of outreach in public programs. Following an initial survey, selected households individually were offered enrollment in one of the various programs tested in that experiment. Because this procedure is unlikely to be used in public programs, outreach in the Demand Ex-periment is not considered in this section.

5. For a comparison of eligibles and enrollees in the Administrative Agency Ex-periment, see Appendix A.

6. See MacMillan and Hamilton [C63], pp. 20-22.

7. See Rand [E129], p. 52. Higher rates for elderly singles than for elderly cou-ples also holds true in the AAE, but the differential was smaller. See MacMillan and Hamilton [C63], p. A-10.

did much better. In fact, single elderly persons represented one of the two largest groups of enrollees at both sites, the other group being single parents with children.

Single-headed households (usually female-headed) with children had the highest rates of enrollment throughout EHAP. When such households are already receiving other forms of government subsidies—typically public assistance or food stamps—their likelihood of enrolling in the allowance program was even higher.

A second pattern of underrepresentation exists for the "working poor" —nonelderly households who, although their family income is low, are in the labor market and are not receiving government grants or welfare income other than housing allowances. Such households are typically intact families with young children, and Supply Experiment evidence clearly indicates that households of this type are likely to have lower enrollment rates.[8]

A number of factors account for these differential enrollment rates, and many of them appear to be beyond the ability of agencies to control with their outreach program. Chapter 4, for example, suggests that the level of the subsidy offered to individual households is a factor strongly influencing participation. A special survey conducted at one site, however, suggests that part of the explanation for these patterns lies in the impact of outreach. As indicated in figure 10.2, at the site, elderly households were both less likely to hear about the program and less likely to apply even after they heard about it. As the figure indicates, less than half as many elderly as welfare or working poor households heard about the program. The latter two groups, on the other hand, were about equally aware of the program, but the welfare recipients applied at a much higher rate than the working poor. Thus, lower rates for the elderly—at least in Jacksonville—can be explained in part by lower levels of awareness. The pattern for the working poor requires some other explanation, perhaps related to the media used or the message conveyed in outreach. It might also be explained by the attitude of this group about accepting "welfare."

With respect to the types of media used, EHAP administrators at each of the sites chose a variety of vehicles. Free and paid advertising was used, including ads on television, on radio, and in newspapers. Pamphlets and brochures were printed and distributed, special presentations were made to community groups, and contacts were made with other social service agencies in the community to facilitate referrals. In both the AAE and the Supply Experiments, outreach efforts began as low-intensity efforts, as the agencies tried to get a sense of how many applications would be generated by outreach efforts. Almost always these efforts were followed by high-

8. Rand [E129], p. 53.

Figure 10.2

Awareness and Application by Demographic Groups, Jacksonville

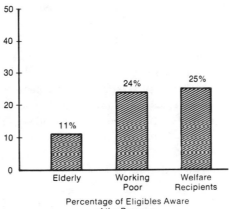

Percentage of Eligibles Aware
of the Program

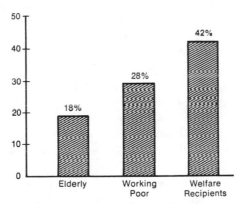

Percentage of Those Eligible and
Aware Who Applied

Source: Special survey of 1,417 eligible households in Jacksonville, Florida. For more detailed discussion, see MacMillan and Hamilton [C59], pp. 19-22.

intensity approaches because initial application levels were low. As outreach intensified, there was more reliance on professionally designed media campaigns.

Not surprisingly, the information sources cited by enrollees as the way they learned about the program differed consistently among demographic groups. Mass media campaigns, for example, were much more important for attracting the working poor, whereas welfare recipients most often found out about the program through referrals from social service agencies.[9] Clearly, many welfare recipients are already linked to information networks developed by other programs and can be reached in this relatively inexpensive way. As noted, some sites found that attracting the elderly population was a particular problem; and specially targeted approaches, such as presentations to elderly groups, were tried. The overall EHAP findings are unclear, however, concerning whether such targeted efforts improve the representation of the elderly in a program's enrolled population.[10]

The question of how the choice of media makes an impact on administrative costs can also be addressed, but only to a limited extent. The limitations are due to the fact that costs are calculated on a per recipient basis which only imperfectly captures other factors such as differences in the demographic composition in the eligible population and the degree of difficulty enrollees had in qualifying units for the program. There was considerable variation in the amount paid for advertising in the various media across the EHAP sites, but the use of professional advertising agencies or paid advertising on television and radio appears to have pushed up administrative costs. Table 10.1 shows the direct costs per recipient for outreach in each of the eight AAE and the two Supply Experiment sites. Tulsa's unusually high costs are a result of the use of a professional agency.[11] Overall, however, two facts seem clear. One is that there exists considerable variation in the direct costs of outreach across sites; and secondly, the choice of media advertising is a contributing factor to higher costs. A weaker relationship exists between the use of paid advertising and its overall effectiveness in attracting applicants, as demonstrated by the first and last columns in table 10.1.

EHAP also offers several lessons for the content or "message" of outreach. Although it was not always possible, most EHAP agencies strived to eliminate any possible "welfare image" from their outreach messages.

---

9. MacMillan and Hamilton [C63], p. 26, and Rand [E129], pp. 157-58.

10. MacMillan and Hamilton [C63], pp. 22-25.

11. Jacksonville did not use paid advertising, but its somewhat higher costs than Bismarck, San Bernardino, and Durham are probably due to special problems encountered in that site. For a discussion of these problems, see Wolfe et al. [C125].

Table 10.1

Use of Paid Advertising Campaign, Costs of Outreach, and Effectiveness of Media in EHAP Outreach

Administrative Agency Experiment	Direct Costs per Recipient	Use of Paid Advertising Campaign	Percentage of Applicants Hearing of Program through Media
Tulsa	$66	Yes	49%
Springfield	28	Yes	32
Peoria	15	Yes	40
Salem	15	Yes	28
Bismarck	8	No	31
San Bernardino	9	No	32
Jacksonville	15	No	31
Durham	3	No	31
Supply Experiment			
Green Bay	21	Yes	49
South Bend	37	Yes	51

Sources: U.S. Department of Housing and Urban Development [E164], p. 66; MacMillan and Hamilton [C63], p. A-20 and B-25; Rand [E127], p. 157.
Note: "Paid advertising campaign" is defined as the use of a professional advertising agency and/or paid radio and television advertising.

This was particularly the case in the Supply Experiment, and it appears that difficulties in enrolling the working poor in the Supply Experiment sites were far less pronounced than in other EHAP sites. Even so, advertising campaigns which promote programs to "give away government money" were criticized by others in the community at the Green Bay Supply Experiment site.[12]

Through their adjustments of outreach over time, some agencies learned that they could not get across as much information about the program as they would have liked. In general, simple messages seemed to work best, and complicated information on eligibility was difficult to transmit outside of face-to-face enrollment interviews. Agencies, of course, hoped that more precise information on eligibility would avoid the costs of processing applicants who were ultimately found ineligible. However, early campaigns in the Supply Experiment were later modified to project only the basic features of the program, encouraging those interested to call the housing allowance office for more information.[13]

---

12. Ellickson and Kanouse [C21], p. 26.
13. Rand [E127], p. 155.

Enrollment

Once households were induced to apply to the program, the agency was faced with a series of additional intake functions known as enrollment. The exact sequencing of steps involved in enrollment differs across local agencies in many public programs, and this was also true in EHAP. Sometimes initial eligibility screening was used to eliminate cases of obvious ineligibility and sometimes not. Some agencies engaged the client in an extensive face-to-face enrollment interview, while others accepted mail-in applications. Some agencies elicited detailed information from the applicant on household incomes, while others relied on later verification through third-party contacts (such as employers, bankers, or welfare agencies). Whatever way it proceeded, the enrollment process led to one of two results: (1) the household was declared eligible for program benefits and a benefit level was established by formula (pending completion of additional procedures for establishing that the household was occupying program-approved housing), or (2) the household was declared ineligible.

The most important enrollment task was the certification of income and household size. Both determined whether the household was eligible and what the size of payments would be. In recent years, there has been much public controversy about high "error rates" in various public assistance programs which have led to large numbers of ineligible households on the rolls of such programs and inaccurate payment levels for many who are eligible. Many suggestions for remedying this situation have focused attention on modifying the procedures used for certifying income and household size.[14]

Table 10.2 lists six general techniques often suggested for improving the certification of income in transfer programs. They include (1) a general increase in the extent to which verification is used; (2) employing selective case verification; (3) altering the frequency of eliciting information from clients or frequency of reverification; (4) altering the form of elicitation; (5) requiring mandatory agency/client contact; and (6) improving interagency exchanges of information on clients. The table indicates the major EHAP findings concerning the effectiveness of various certification procedures falling under each of these broad categories of reform.

The most straightforward of these reforms, and the one most frequently suggested, is the increased use of verification. Some public programs have accepted the self-declarations of participants or subjected these

---

14. For a fairly exhaustive compilation of the range of procedures possible regarding each element of the certification function, see Zais, Melton, and Berkman [E180].

Table 10.2

EHAP Findings concerning the Effectiveness of Alternative Eligibility
Certification Improvement Techniques

Technique	Findings	Experiment
General increase in extent of income variation	Third-party contacts and documentation detect significantly more income or income changes than self-declaration. Less substantial variation observed among verification methods than between verification and self-declaration.	AAE
	Requiring as much client documentation as possible, with undocumented entries subject to verification on sample basis, results in few income changes.	Supply
Selective case verification	Elderly participants less likely to have income changes. No other demographic group systematically less likely to have income changes.	AAE
	Clients with predominantly grant income less likely to have income changes than those with earned income. Clients with income from more than one source more likely to have income changes. Income changes closely related to changes in household size.	AAE Demand Supply
Frequency of elicitation, reverification	Elapsed time between elicitation and certification single most important factor explaining income changes. Quarterly recertification found more cost effective than yearly or monthly recertification.	AAE
Form of elicitation	Relatively small income changes when detailed elicitation used. Detailed elicitation and verification can be substituted for each other.	AAE
	Detailed initial interviews appear to elicit fairly complete and accurate information from clients.	Supply
Mandatory client contact	No findings	None
Interagency information exchange	No findings	None

Sources: Rand [E127]; Tebbets [C109]; Dickson [C16]; Hoaglin and Joseph [C33]; Zais, Melton, and Berkman [E180].

declarations to independent verification only on a spot check basis. A number of combinations of these techniques were used in the Administrative Agency Experiment agencies. One clear result from analysis of the effectiveness of these techniques is that verification through either documentation or third-party sources systematically uncovers more changes to the income information elicited from clients at application than any other technique. When income was verified using third-party sources, 65 percent of the cases incurred a change in income; when documentation was used, 61 percent of the cases resulted in changes. These figures contrast with the 35 percent of cases resulting in income changes when only client-provided information was used.[15]

Thus, the AAE experience established the superior effectiveness of verification over simply accepting the word of clients. What about the costs of these procedures? Administrative costs for third-party verification were estimated at $12 per case; documentary verification was estimated to cost $10 per case; and self-declaration $6.[16] Most often, the information on a particular client was certified using a combination of these methods; but in terms of both costs and effectiveness, there were smaller differences between third-party checks and documentation than between both these methods and self-declaration.

The Supply Experiment income certification procedure is a promising approach to this function and provides some insight into how documentation and third-party checks might be successfully used in combination. Under this approach, clients were responsible for providing as much documentation as they could. When the enrollment interview was scheduled, the client was given a list of the types of documentation to bring along. In fact, for each income source noted by the applicant, the interviewer requested documentation. If the client was unable to provide it, he was required to sign a form authorizing third-party checks of that item. Thus, all undocumented sources were potentially subject to third-party verification. However, only a sample was actually verified, with the probability that a particular case would be sampled depending on the extent to which other sources of income had been documented for that case. Four sampling categories are shown in table 10.3. The probability of being verified ranges from 10 percent—generally, when 50 percent or more of income is documented—to 100 percent—when less than 10 percent is documented. Quality control audit information indicates that this particular combination of documentation and third-party checks produces an accurate way to certify income. If the sample of third-party checks were not done, it is estimated that an average monthly overpayment of

---

15. Hamilton, Budding, and Holshouser [C31], p. 28.
16. Hamilton, Budding, and Holshouser [C31], p. 29.

Table 10.3

Sampling for Third Party Verification, Supply Experiment

Documentation Provided by Client	Percentage of Clients to be Verified
1. If client is able to document 50 percent or more of total household income from all sources of earned income greater than $2,000 per year and 50 percent or more of total assets. (If assets are within $1,000 of asset limit, all must be documented).	10
2. If client is able to document 10 percent or more but less than 50 percent of total household income; other asset requirements same as #1.	33⅓
3. If client documentation is insufficient to meet #1 or #2 specifications.	100
4. If client documentation is sufficient to meet #1 or #2 but interviewer judges that client gave unclear or conflicting responses.	100

Source: Tebbets [C109], pp. 13-14.

$7 would have resulted in Green Bay and $18 in South Bend. By employing third-party verification on a sample basis, $6 of the error was eliminated in Green Bay and $14 in South Bend.[17]

But are these savings worth the administrative costs involved in verification? There is no easy answer to this question since the figures cited only reflect *direct savings* and ignore the deterrent effects of verification. Restricting attention solely to direct savings, the Supply Experiment's system appears to cost more to administer than it saves, by about two dollars in Green Bay and by about two and one-half dollars in South Bend per enrollees verified.[18] Of course, how many deliberate errors would have been made by clients without the presence of a verification system can only be speculated.

Besides more extensive verification, reformers have also suggested selective verification for certain household types. Table 10.2 also indicates the major EHAP findings in this area. Throughout EHAP it was found that the elderly are less likely to have income changes once certified. No other group appears to be systematically as likely to have so few income changes. Additionally, in all three experiments, the composition of income was likely to influence whether verification would uncover changes. Clients with predominantly grant income and those with one

---

17. Tebbets [C109], p. x.
18. Rand [E127], pp. 168-170.

source of income were less likely to experience changes than those with wages or multiple sources of income.

A third general category of reform is to increase the frequency with which income information is elicited and/or verified. The importance of this type of reform is seen in the fact that within the AAE, the single most important variable associated with income changes was the length of time between application and certification of income.[19] Thus, if the backlog of cases awaiting certification can be reduced so that certification can more closely follow the time when enrollees volunteer their initial income information, income changes can be reduced. The best source of data on this question is the Demand Experiment which required that households mail in an updated monthly report on their income. However, analysis of this rich income-reporting data set in the Demand Experiment is not yet complete. Although monthly reporting may seem an undue burden on recipients, nearly all households reacted favorably to the monthly verification system in response to survey questions.[20] Forthcoming analysis should establish whether monthly reporting is cost effective. In part, of course, the answer will depend on the extent to which incomes fluctuate during the course of the year.[21]

As table 10.2 indicates, reformers have suggested several other techniques for increasing the accuracy of income verification systems. EHAP evidence is far less systematic here. Suggestions for improving the form of elicitation, the amount of mandatory agency/client contact, and the interagency exchange of income information were addressed in EHAP only on an impressionistic basis. In the variety of procedures used within the AAE, it did appear that relatively small income changes were produced when detailed elicitation was used. Thus, it is likely that there is a possibility of substitution between detailed elicitation and verification, and agencies can choose to do one or the other. In the experience of Supply Experiment staff, the detailed enrollment interviews just discussed seemed more reliable than forms completed by the applicants themselves, although the Supply Experiment did not include systematic variations in these procedures.

Table 10.4 indicates the relationship between the average costs of enrollment per recipient and the predominant method of income certification used. In very broad terms, that is, without controlling for differences in client characteristics, use of verification techniques was more costly than participant declaration. However, it is likely that the most cost-

---

19. Dickson [C16], p. 43.
20. Hoaglin and Joseph [C33], p. s-6.
21. See Jacobson [C37]. For a detailed discussion of the various issues regarding frequency of elicitation and verification, see Zais, Melton, and Berkman [E180].

Table 10.4

Costs of Enrollment per Recipient and Predominant Method of
Income Certification Used

Site	Costs of Enrollment per Recipient	Predominant Income Certification Method Used
Administrative Agency Experiment		
Tulsa	$45	Third party
Salem	42	Third party
Durham	40	Third party
Jacksonville	59	Mixed (participant declaration)
San Bernardino	31	Mixed (participant declaration)
Peoria	29	Mixed (third party)
Springfield	27	Participation declaration
Bismarck	26	Participation declaration
Supply Experiment		
Green Bay	57	Mixed (documentation)
South Bend	55	Mixed (documentation)

Note: "Third party" or "participant declaration" means that this method was used in more than 75 percent of cases. "Mixed" indicates that third-party documentaion or participant declaration was used in 50-75 percent of the cases, with other methods used in remaining cases. Method in parentheses indicates majority method used in mixed cases.

efficient system is some combination of accepting client declarations and verifying. Evidence from the experiments outlined above suggests several directions for such a system of selective verification.

Inspection

The inspection function is a set of activities involved in determining whether an enrollee's housing unit meets the program's standards. Of the functions considered so far, it is the first of the "housing-related" functions administered by the agencies. Outreach and enrollment would be required for subsidy programs of unconstrained payments and would also be a part of any other subsidy program which is income-conditioned.

With the exception of several treatment groups in the Demand Experiment, all households in EHAP were subject to a housing unit inspection.[22] The program standards applied differed across experiments as well

---

22. For a description of the exempt treatments, see chapter 3.

Table 10.5

Median Number of Inspections per Enrollee, AAE and Supply
Experiment Sites

Experiment and Site	Median Number of Inspections per Enrollee
Administrative Agency Experiment	
Bismarck	1.04
Durham	1.08
Jacksonville	.76
Peoria	.82
Salem	1.07
San Bernardino	1.11
Springfield	1.08
Tulsa	1.17
Supply Experiment	
Green Bay	1.40
South Bend	1.56

Sources: Derived from Rand [E127], p. 172; Budding et al. [C11], p. C-40.

as among the Administrative Agency Experiment sites.[23] All of the stand-ards, however, involved minimum physical and occupancy requirements.

Inspection, like certification of income, is both an intake and a mainte-nance function. As the former, it follows income-eligibility determination to establish whether income-eligible households are qualified to receive pay-ments because they live in standard units. Enrollees could nominate dwelling units for inspection in two ways: (1) by nominating their cur-rent dwelling, either before or after repairs to the unit; or, (2) by nomi-nating another dwelling to which they plan to move. If they chose the latter, enrollees were encouraged to request an inspection before moving, although this was not a requirement.

Before EHAP was undertaken, there were a number of fears about inspection which questioned the feasibility of this method of earmarking payments for housing. One fear was that enrollees in the program would nominate numerous dwellings for inspections, driving up administrative costs. In fact, this fear was not borne out, as demonstrated in table 10.5, which indicates that the highest median number of inspections per en-rollee among AAE and Supply Experiment sites was 1.6. The site median was 1.08 units. Apparently, enrollees did not recklessly nominate a large number of dwellings for inspection in their attempt to qualify for pay-ments.

---

23. The standards used in each experiment are described in Appendix C.

Besides fear about the number of inspections required, preexperimental estimates of the costs of professionally administered inspections suggested doubts about this approach. These cost estimates varied from about $30 per inspection to several hundred dollars.[24] Therefore, Administrative Agency Experiment agencies were encouraged to experiment with alternative procedures for inspecting units. The variations actually employed differed according to who did the inspection. Three types of inspectors were used: (1) professional code inspectors, (2) trained housing allowance agency staff, and (3) program participants themselves. Jacksonville subcontracted for city code inspectors. Durham, Peoria, Tulsa, and San Bernardino predominantly used trained agency staff. Springfield, Salem, and Bismarck relied mostly on participant inspections, frequently accompanied by agency spot checks. Both the Supply and Demand Experiments used trained agency staff.

Tables 10.6 and 10.7 provide information on the relative costs and effectiveness of these three approaches. Table 10.6 shows the result of an independent check by the evaluation contractor on the various types of inspections performed in the Administrative Agency Experiment. As the table indicates, the use of professional code inspectors was most likely to result in accurate inspections—87 percent of the cases falling into that category. Trained agency staff had a somewhat lower accuracy of 62 percent, and the independent inspection agreed with participant assessments in only 36 percent of the cases. Thus, the use of participant inspections greatly increases the chance that unacceptable units will get into the program.

At the same time, the average cost per inspection by professionals or agency staff was found to be about $32.[25] Training participants to use checklists for inspecting units and processing the information resulted in a cost of about $5 per inspection. Given different circumstances faced by agencies in various sites, however, one would expect the cost per recipient to vary; this is in fact the case, as shown by the figures in table 10.7. A definite relationship between choice of procedure and the resulting costs of administering the inspection function is evident in the table. The cost of professional code inspectors ranges from 2 to 15 times more than the use of participant inspections. Still, the outcome for professional or agency trained inspectors is on the lower end of preexperimental predictions.

Thus, there appears to be clear advantages to using inspectors rather

---

24. U.S. Department of Housing and Urban Development [E165], p. 70.

25. This figure is higher than those shown in table 10.7 because it is only for professionally made inspections while those in the table for the AAE are mixes of professionally made and other types of inspections.

Table 10.6

Accuracy of Various Types of Inspectors, Administrative
Agency Experiment

Inspector Type	Percentage of Units Accurately Assessed	Average cost per inspection
Professional code inspector	87% ⎫	$32
Trained agency staff	62 ⎬	
Program participant	36 ⎭	$ 5

Source: Budding et al. [C11], p. 13.
  Note: "Accurately assessed" means the inspector approximately identified units' deficiencies, as determined by an independent reinspection by the evaluation contractor in the experiment. Because of the limited number of cases involved, separate estimates were not available for professional inspectors and trained agency staff.

Table 10.7

Inspection Costs per Recipient and Predominant Inspection Method Used

Experiment and Site	Direct Costs per Recipient	Predominant Inspection Method Used
Administrative Agency Experiment		
Jacksonville	$30	Professional code inspectors
Tulsa	30	Trained agency staff
Durham	19	Trained agency staff
Peoria	15	Trained agency staff
San Bernardino	15	Trained agency staff
Springfield	8	Program participants
Bismarck	3	Program participants
Salem	2	Program participants
Supply Experiment		
Green Bay	24	Trained agency staff
South Bend	31	Trained agency staff

Sources: U.S. Department of Housing and Urban Development [E165], p. 66; Budding et al. [C11], pp. B-1 through B-6; Tebbets [C109], chapter 4.

than the participants themselves, although the differences between professional code enforcers and trained staff are small. Professional inspectors were found to record more detailed information and seemed to be more stringent in their inspections than were agency staffers. Comments written on inspection forms indicated that sometimes participants and agency staff lacked sufficient technical knowledge to recognize certain types of structural, electrical, and plumbing deficiencies. Agency staff also sometimes experienced a conflict in their role, particularly when the same staff members were used for inspecting units and for helping clients to qualify for payments. Agency staff were more likely than professional inspectors to take participant preferences, market conditions, and other factors into account. To prevent this type of "role conflict," the organizational structure of the allowance offices in the Supply Experiment organized performance of these functions into separate divisions, a solution which seems particularly feasible in a large-scale program.

In sum, the inspection function seems both more feasible and less costly than originally anticipated. EHAP provides valuable experience for application to other programs, particularly to the Section 8 Existing housing program, in which agencies face many of the same administrative functions found in the experiments.[26]

Client Services

A fourth major function in administering housing allowance programs was provision of client services, defined as those activities designed to help clients to attain standard housing and to keep clients qualified for payments. As such, it is a function both at intake and during maintenance. As seen in chapter 3, however, the concept of housing allowances and the provision of client services represent conflicting elements in program philosophy. Housing allowances embody notions of consumer freedom for clients to cope in the housing marketplace on their own. This general concept guided the development of the allowance programs at all EHAP sites. Yet there existed a feeling that some nonmonetary assistance needed to be provided, or at least made available for clients who want it. Equal opportunity assistance, for example, was mandated by law.

Table 10.8 lists the variety of services offered to enrollees at the 12 EHAP sites; it also gives a rough indication of the extensiveness of the services provided. The table indicates that the most consistently provided service took the form of information sessions on program rules, housing market information, and equal opportunity. All three experiments provided some of this type of service. In addition, the Administrative Agency Experiment sites provided a wider range of services, stemming from the general design feature of that experiment which allowed agencies to establish their own variations in procedures. Some agencies

26. For a discussion of the application of EHAP findings on inspection to the Section 8 Existing program, see Glatt [C26].

Table 10.8

Types and Intensity of Services Offered to Enrollees in the Twelve EHAP Sites

Services Offered	Administrative Agency Experiment								Demand Experiment		Supply Experiment	
	Tight Markets (≤7% Rental Vacancy Rate)				Loose Markets (>7% Rental Vacancy Rate)							
	Spring-field	Durham	Peoria	Jackson-ville	Tulsa	Salem	San Ber-nardino	Bismarck	Pitts-burgh	Phoenix	South Bend	Green Bay
Information Sessions												
Program	●	●	●	●	●	●	●	●	●	●	●	●
Housing	●	●	●	●	●	●	●	●	●	●	●	○
Equal Opportunity	●	◐	○	●	◐	◐	●	◐	●	●	◐	●
Telephone Information	●	○	○	◐	◐	◐	◐	○	●	●	●	◐
Discrimination Complaints	●	○	○	○	○	○	◐	○	◐	◐	◐	◐
Consumer Advocacy & Consciousness Raising	●						◐					
Lists of Available Units	◐	○	○	○	○	○	○	○	◐		◐	◐
Search Facilitation												
Transportation	○	●	○	●	◐	○	○	◐				
Childcare		◐		○			○	○				
Escort	○	●	○	○	●	○	○	○				
Phone calls		◐		○	●	○	○	○				

Move Facilitation
  Negotiation with landlords
  Security deposit
  Moving assistance
Referrals for Non-Housing Problems
Social Casework

|—No report that service was offered.
○—Minimal availability: no: effectively offered, offered only briefly, or offered only to a few enrollees.
◑—Offered across entire enrollment period but at a low intensity and/or not publicized.
●—Described, offered intens vely, and publicized or effectively required.

Source: Bernsten [H13], p. 8.

helped enrollees to search for housing by providing childcare, transportation, or escort services to units being considered. In some cases, moving assistance was also provided by the agency in the form of negotiating with the landlord, helping with the actual move, or providing a security deposit to be repaid on an installment basis.

The table shows that some agencies clearly did more than others. Springfield, for example, developed programs and presentations which approached a consumer advocacy and consciousness-raising mode. Durham developed a mode of operation consistent with the social casework tradition, including helping families with their nonhousing problems. In the Supply and Demand Experiments, services were more limited and controlled, restricted to information sessions, responses to inquiries, referrals, and equal opportunity services.

Analysis of the effects of these services proved to be more difficult than any of the other administrative functions in EHAP. Unlike inspection and income certification, which were done on a one-time basis, the interaction between agency and client involved in the services function was ongoing. Measurement of services provision proved to be fairly elusive because staff members found it difficult to record each of these interactions.

Despite these difficulties, two major studies of the effects of services have been performed, approaching the issue by using different perspectives on the measurement of services. One grouped the AAE agencies by the level of "responsive services" provided.[27] These services included assistance provided to individual households as needed, in contrast to the more formal services provided to all households, such as information sessions. The essential results of this analysis are given in table 10.9, with level of services provision defined at the site level. The percentage of enrollees succeeding in finding standard units (and qualifying for payments) was significantly affected by three factors—market conditions, race, and plans to move or stay in preprogram units.

In looser markets—defined in this analysis as markets with vacancy rates of more than 7 percent—the table indicates few differences in success rates, for movers as well as stayers, regardless of race and regardless of the level of services provided. The range of success is only 78 to 89 percent. More variation is evident in tighter markets, where the services provided appear to make a difference. Services appear to be more important to movers and to help to close the gap among households, bringing black and white success rates closer. These results suggest that a strategy of selective provision of services, perhaps based on market conditions and the

---

27. Holshouser et al. [C35].

Table 10.9

Success Rates for Enrollees Becoming Recipients under Various Service and Housing Market Conditions, by Race, in the Administrative Agency Experiment

Market Conditions[a]	Level of Services	Preenrollment Moving Plans				Totals
		To Move		To Stay		
		Black	White	Black	White	
Tighter	High (Springfield, Durham)	65% (290)[b]	63% (336)	77% (223)	77% (470)	70% (1,319)
	Low (Peoria, Jacksonville)	26% (219)	54% (389)	53% (92)	76% (552)	51% (1,252)
Looser	High (Tulsa)	82% (132)	84% (211)	84% (38)	88% (479)	86% (860)
	Low (Salem, San Bernardino, Bismarck)	78% (67)	81% (779)	85% (40)	89% (1,063)	85% (1,949)
Totals		47% (708)	69% (1,715)	71% (393)	84% (3,564)	71% (5,380)

Source: Holshouser et al. [C35], p. 22.
a. Tight markets are those with a rental vacancy rate of 7 percent or less.
b. Sample size in parentheses.

demographic makeup of the community, would be more cost effective than provision of the same services to all clients.

These findings must, however, be tempered by the presence of vast inconsistencies between agency reports of the services they provided (which formed the basis of the analysis just discussed) and participant reports on the amount of services delivered. A second analysis, therefore, developed various measures of actual service utilization, including minutes of agency/client interaction, use of housing lists provided by the agency, and the like.[28] Evidence was compiled from all three experiments on the effects of services.

In this analysis, information services were found to be used by a high proportion of those who shopped for a new unit; and, judging from survey responses, these services were highly valued by these households. Information services also made a difference to key program outcomes. Shoppers in Jacksonville, for example, who faced a strict housing standard and a difficult market, were clearly aided by information services. Information sessions were also found to be helpful to Demand Experiment households. Demand households were particularly helped when agencies provided information on where to look for new units within the sites. The hypothesis that those who used the services consisted mostly of shoppers who would have succeeded anyway was tested, with negative results. In fact, minority households who had a more difficult time searching were helped more by these services than were nonminority households.[29]

When the use of problem-responsive services was analyzed, far fewer households were found to actually use such services than used information services. In contrast to information services, most utilization of problem-responsive services was concentrated in a small number of households. Indeed, some agencies appear to have initiated some of these services in the absence of a clear need.[30] Furthermore, nothing in the analysis demonstrated a clear impact of such services on success in qualifying for payments, on changes in housing quality, or on satisfaction of households with their dwelling. The preponderance of the evidence, therefore, suggests that enrollees both wanted and used information services and held particularly positive feelings about information supplied by agencies which helped them find a standard unit. Other services—such as transportation and child care—appear to be premised on a traditional casework approach to program administration and often overstated the need to provide such services to households.

---

28. Bernsten [H13].
29. Bernsten [H13], p. 174.
30. Bernsten [H13], p. 217.

Table 10.10

Intensity of Client Service Delivery and Costs per Recipient

Site	Services Intensity Index (Rank)	Direct Costs per Recipient	
		Dollars	Rank
Durham	1	$40	4
Springfield	2	64	1
Jacksonville	3	59	2
Tulsa	4	45	3
San Bernardino	5	31	5
Bismarck	6.5	24	6
Salem	6.5	17	7
Peoria	8	10	8
South Bend	9	8	9
Green Bay	10	1	10
Spearman's rho (correlation between ranks) = .92			

Sources: Services intensity index is calculated by summing information provided in table 10.8, with values of 1, 2, or 3 depending on intensity
of services. Costs per recipient is from U.S. Department of Housing
and Urban Development [E165], p. 66.

Not surprisingly, the variation in administrative costs associated with client services was considerable across the EHAP sites. Table 10.10 shows the calculated direct costs per recipient of providing intake services, ranging from a low of $1 in Green Bay, which provided very little assistance beyond subsidy payments, to $64 in Springfield, which provided a wide range of services, as just discussed. For purposes of displaying the relationship between these cost figures and the intensity of services provision, an index was formed using the information provided in table 10.8. This index simply assigned ordinal values to each item in the table and summed the results. Sites were then ranked according to their services intensity index, and a rank order correlation between this index and the site ranking on cost was calculated to be .92.

In sum, the EHAP research on the effects of services can assist in the development of policy alternatives for administering housing allowance programs. The results suggest that services might best be provided in markets where households face real difficulties in finding standard units, such as markets with low vacancy rates. In addition, services which provide information on the market—especially where households might look for program-eligible units—appear to be more productive than other services which try to respond to a myriad of other household needs.

OVERALL ADMINISTRATIVE COSTS

The preceding section considered the four major administrative functions in housing allowance programs in terms of the costs and effectiveness of alternative procedures. EHAP experience has clearly narrowed the range of reasonable procedures for use in operating a program. For example, the evidence is quite clear that some form of professional inspection should be used for ascertaining whether dwellings pass program standards if program standards are to be reasonably effective. Likewise, it is clear that errors in income determination are far more likely where participant declarations are accepted without verification; and EHAP suggests some selective ways to verify incomes short of the costly approach of verifying all items.

Besides providing information on individual procedures, EHAP has produced important data on total administrative costs. Table 10.11, which uses roughly comparable cost definitions for all the experiments, demonstrates that overall costs varied considerably across EHAP sites. The coefficient of variation given for each function (in the final row of figures) provides an indication of cost variation across sites. Because of problems of allocating indirect costs to specific functions, the figures for individual functions include only direct costs; the total dollar figures for intake, maintenance, and all costs include both direct and indirect costs.

The figures indicate that costs were more likely to vary for outreach and client services than for enrollment, inspections, and payment operations.[31] These differences reflect the basic characteristics of the functions: enrollment, inspection, and payments operations can be highly routinized, and clearly defined goals can be specified for them. Outreach and services appear to be more open-ended and discretionary. On the basis of these observations, it may be reasonable for federal regulations to establish more detailed procedures for the administration of certification of income and inspection but to give local agencies wider discretion in the other functional areas. Another possibility is that for functions which may be cost effective in certain circumstances but not so in others (such as perhaps is true for the provision of client services), HUD would permit expenditure of funds when a local agency established the need for them.

With respect to intake functions, enrollment consumed the greatest percentage of direct costs. At the AAE sites, a median of 41 percent was spent on enrollment. However, even though the coefficient of variation for this function is lower than any other intake function, the percentage still

---

31. Payment operations included activities involved in calculating payments and sending out payments to households. Because agencies' procedures did not vary systematically in this function, this function is not analyzed here.

varied from 21 to 55 percent. Enrollment also constituted the greatest percentage of intake costs in the Supply Experiment. The major difference between the two experiments in intake was in the services function, which constituted a median of 33 percent in the AAE but only 4 percent in the Supply Experiment.

There were also major divergences among sites in the costs of maintenance functions. Again, the Supply Experiment spent very little on services, while this function constituted 48 percent of the AAE's direct cost of maintenance. The Supply Experiment's semiannual income recertification affected its cost for this function, with a median of 59 percent of all maintenance outlays going for recertification, compared to a median of 22 percent in the AAE, which recertified income only on an annual basis.

Total intake and maintenance costs, shown in columns (5) and (10) in table 10.11, include both direct costs and indirect costs. Combining these to establish the total administrative costs per recipient year requires some amortization of intake costs over the period participants stay in the program. The computations in the final column of table 10.11 assume that participants average two years in the program. Thus, total administrative costs per recipient year are equal to one half of the intake costs per new recipient added to the total maintenance costs per recipient year.[32] When computed this way, total annual administrative costs are seen to vary a great deal, from a high of $589 in the Jacksonville AAE site to a low of $209 in the Green Bay Supply Experiment site. The Supply Experiment median of $220 is $100 less than the AAE median, probably indicating a combination of the economies of scale that are possible by implementing a larger program over a longer period of time and the great attention given to efficient administration at the sites.

CONCLUSIONS ON ADMINISTRATIVE FEASIBILITY

As EHAP was launched, two questions about administrative feasibility were especially prominent: whether local agencies whose past activities had not involved housing to a large degree, as well as housing authorities, could successfully carry out all of the functions required to operate a housing allowance program, and whether, in particular, a physical housing

---

32. The estimate of two years average participation per recipient household is based on about five years of experience in South Bend. The cumulative total of households authorized for payments divided by the number terminated is .46. Owners stay in the program slightly longer than renters (.41 compared to .51). On the basis of these numbers, the two years assumption was used. See Housing Allowance Office, Inc. [F59].

Table 10.11

Total Administrative Costs per Recipient Year, Supply and AAE Sites
(1976 dollars)

| Site | Intake Functions (percentage distribution of direct costs) | | | | | Maintenance Functions (percentage distribution of direct costs) | | | | | |
	Out-reach (1)	Enroll-ment (2)	Inspec-tion (3)	Serv-ices (4)	Total Intake Costs [a] (5)	Pay-ment Opera-tions (6)	Recerti-fication (7)	Rein-spec-tion (8)	Serv-ices (9)	Total Mainte-nance Costs [a] (10)	Total Adminis-trative Costs [b] (11)
Administrative Agency Experiment											
Bismarck	13%	43%	5%	39%	$179	12%	39%	5%	45%	$235	$325
Durham	3	44	17	36	258	16	19	8	57	231	360
Jacksonville	7	53	13	26	534	25	15	6	53	322	589
Peoria	22	42	22	14	178	24	18	30	30	171	260
Salem	20	55	3	22	186	41	30	(c)	30	129	222
San Bernardino	8	50	14	28	271	29	37	7	27	178	314
Springfield	22	21	6	50	248	16	13	8	64	267	391
Tulsa	35	26	16	24	300	19	19	19	44	144	294

Median for eight sites	14%	41%	14%	33%	$253	18%	22%	10%	48%	$205	$320
Supply Experiment											
Green Bay	20%	55%	23%	1%	$189	14%	62%	22%	2%	$114	$209
South Bend	28	42	24	6	235	18	55	23	5	113	231
Median for two sites	25%	47%	24%	4%	$212	16%	59%	22%	3%	$114	$220
Coefficient of variation	.85	.53	.62	.73		.43	.55	.59	.91		

Source: U.S. Department of Housing and Urban Development [E164], p. 66. Totals for total administrative costs differ from this source because of difference in assumption on average duration of participation.

a. Per new recipient. Includes indirect costs.

b. Per amortized recipient year, based on assumption of two years average participation per recipient household.

c. Less than 0.5%.

standard could be imposed at reasonable administrative cost. The evidence from EHAP provides a strong affirmative response to both questions. All of the agencies, regardless of past experience, successfully implemented the program. As for inspections, the fears of a large number of units needing to be inspected for each enrollee and of the cost per inspection being high proved unfounded. Ultimately of course, the general feasibility of the program was proven by the launching of the Section 8 Existing program, which is administered by thousands of local agencies; and the lessons learned in EHAP were used in designing its administration.

PART V.

Broader
Perspectives

CHAPTER 11

Policy Implications: Moving from Research to Programs

Morton L. Isler

THE Experimental Housing Allowance Program provides much more than a test of a freestanding housing allowance. Many programs will benefit from the knowledge derived from EHAP. Consequently, the reader is forewarned that this chapter does not provide any simple or single policy prescription. The problems confronting urban and rural America are too complex for any single approach, and the rich set of EHAP results provides important insights for building a comprehensive approach to meeting housing and community development goals.

THE MULTIFACETED PROGRAM WORLD

In the United States today, individuals and localities are affected by numerous public programs. What implications do the results of the Experimental Housing Allowance Program have for these individuals and their communities?

Clearly, ongoing housing subsidy programs should benefit by the knowledge derived from EHAP; but other programs can benefit as well, especially programs concerned with community development. Housing investment is often a primary objective of local community development activities, and the Community Development Block Grant program has a large housing component. Indeed, the housing rehabilitation carried out under block grants now dwarfs that carried out with explicit housing appropriations.

Furthermore, perhaps over a third of the expenditures of the nation's public assistance and Social Security systems are spent in housing markets. EHAP findings can help those concerned with welfare reform to link public assistance and housing programs. The goals of welfare reform and of "decent housing in a suitable environment" are not mutually exclusive. In fact, they can be mutually supportive. Through a strategic combination of income support and housing and community development assistance, the nation can equitably distribute aid for those households in need and, at the same time, help conserve and develop our communities.

While governmental policies and programs have an effect on every community, the type of effect is not always the same because communities differ. Those formulating national housing and community development policies are increasingly cognizant of important differences among communities and housing markets. The price of housing available to lower-income groups may be less in one market than in another; decent housing may be in surplus in one market and in short supply in others. Such fundamental differences in housing market conditions should lead to a different mix of housing actions in different markets.[1]

Public policies and programs are also characterized by multiple goals. Rather than go through a litany of the numerous goals enunciated in the legislative process or promulgated by the executive branch, we would simply assert that these goals reflect concern with one or more of the following three types of benefits:[2]

1. *Benefits to individuals.* Public policies are concerned with the standard of living and the quality of life obtained by individuals. To some, this may simply be a question of the distribution of income; if the distribution were more equal, everyone would be able to afford a reasonable set of goods and services, including housing. Others are concerned with specific goods and services that the poor consume such as food, housing, and medical care. Both views include a concern with questions of equity and equality of opportunity in how a program treats individuals.

2. *Benefits to the community.* Other goals of public policy encompass benefits that are generally distributed throughout the community, or at least that are enjoyed by individuals other than the direct beneficiaries of a program. In housing programs, the improvement of a dwelling should not only benefit the occupant but the neighbors as well. Examples may be found in neighborhoods where programs of upgrading dwellings bolster the value of adjoining homes that remain

---

1. See Struyk, Marshall, and Ozanne [P78] for an analysis of how different program mixes fit various housing market conditions.

2. See Weicher [P87]; Levine [P46] for discussions of housing rationales and goals.

unimproved. Moreover, housing stock improvements should benefit future generations as well as current occupants.

3. *Benefits to the Housing Sector.* Political interest in the housing sector of the economy is exemplified by two concerns. First, smoothing out the fluctuations in new housing production is the concern of some who believe these cycles cause inefficiency in the homebuilding industry and lead to higher housing costs. Second, others wish to reduce housing market imperfections thought caused by the biased behavior of actors in local housing markets (realtors, landlords, repair contractors, etc.) in dealing with the poor. Concern with the housing sector is important in the nation's political processes, and EHAP findings should be reviewed from this perspective.

This chapter employs these three perspectives of benefits as a framework and suggests how findings from EHAP may be useful in policy making. The second section examines the outcomes of EHAP from the perspective of individual benefits and compares housing allowances with other housing programs. The relationship with income maintenance programs is also discussed in this section.

The third section treats the community benefits of housing allowances as observed in EHAP. Because EHAP has produced little information regarding community benefits at this point (pending completion of the Supply Experiment) and even less knowledge exists for other housing programs, interprogram comparisons of community benefits cannot be made. The third section also discusses the current laxity in housing code enforcement and suggests that a stepped-up program of housing code enforcement could drastically alter the effects of housing allowances.

This chapter's fourth section touches on the apparently small benefits to the housing sector of the allowance program. This section also compares the costs and production efficiency of new construction with programs using the existing stock.

Finally, the fifth section of the chapter brings these perspectives together and, given the findings of EHAP, describes how housing allowances fit in a mix of housing and community development programs. This section develops the logic for coordinating the Section 8 Existing housing program with community development activities and reviews EHAP findings as they pertain to the critical issue of extending eligibility for the Section 8 Existing housing program to homeowners.

BENEFITS TO INDIVIDUALS

Even though EHAP provides a rich set of data regarding benefits to individuals, relating these findings to government policies and programs is difficult because individuals in our society hold varying views on the proper role of government. For example, while there is surely widespread belief in "equal opportunity," individuals disagree on how equal opportunity should be defined. Should we be concerned with the equality of opportunity for participating in an educational program, for example, or should we be concerned with equality of outcomes? The same question can be raised as to what constitutes "equity."

Equitable treatment for individuals is a primary goal of public programs. The basic objectives of equity are to treat households in like circumstances alike and to provide greater benefits to households with fewer resources of their own. Probably nothing in this world is perfectly equitable, so it is more appropriate to speak of the relative equity of the outcomes of one action versus another rather than to expect perfect equity.

If one is concerned with equity of outcomes, the gateway to equitable treatment is program participation. As shown in chapter 4, about one third of the eligible households participated in the Demand Experiment's housing allowance programs. The participation rates for the unconstrained subsidies were about twice that of a housing constrained program. Therefore, from the viewpoint of the proportion of eligibles receiving benefits, the outcome of the housing-constrained allowance program was clearly less equitable than that of the unconstrained program.

On the other hand, the results might not look so bad to those concerned with equitable opportunity rather than equitable outcome, especially if they were sure that the lower participation rate of a housing-constrained program simply reflects the preferences of eligible households with respect to meeting the program's housing standard. Unfortunately, EHAP results to date are less than clear on the degree to which decisions not to participate reflected household choices or were promoted by the program's design or by supply conditions that constrained freedom of choice.

For example, large households (of seven or more persons) had a relatively low participation rate compared to smaller households. Besides a household preference not to participate in a government program, there are two explanations for this low participation rate. First, the benefits of participating may have been relatively smaller for large households than for smaller ones, given the amount each was offered. By not participating under this condition, the large households were only acting in their best interests: the benefits of participation did not outweigh the costs. In such a case, a change in the program's design, such as increasing the subsidy for that group relative to other groups, could make the program more equitable.

Second, large households face problems in the housing market that other households do not face—such as landlord discrimination or an absolute shortage of large dwellings. So, large households would require much larger increases in housing allowance benefits to overcome these problems. In this case, a program that deals directly with conditions of housing supply might treat large households more equitably. This suggests the importance of comparing housing allowances and other housing programs.

Housing Quality

The housing allowance Demand Experiment contrasted the quality of the housing occupied by individuals participating in its minimum standards treatment groups to the quality of housing in three other housing subsidy programs: Section 23 leased housing, conventional public housing, and Section 236 with rent supplements.[3] In 1975, a sample of participants in these programs in Pittsburgh and Phoenix were surveyed to obtain data comparable to that available for housing allowance recipients and for the EHAP control group who received no subsidies, referred to in this chapter as the "no program" group.

One yardstick of housing quality only includes measures of the dwelling's physical condition considered essential to the health and safety of the occupants or to the well-being of their neighbors. Two such measures are employed in table 11.1: the Demand Experiment's own minimum standards of housing quality and a more stringent version of these standards termed "high" minimum standards.[4]

The table shows the percentage of dwellings passing each standard for households participating in each of the four housing programs and for households receiving no assistance. Three results of these comparisons are especially significant. First, in every one of the four housing programs, a greater proportion of the participants lived in housing that met minimum standards than did households who were not in a program. However, differences were relatively slight between the proportions of Section 23 participants meeting standards and those not in a program, especially in Pittsburgh. The small quality differences between Section 23 and the "no

---

3. The study is reported in full in Mayo et al. [P53] and Mayo et al. [P54]. Both the conventional public housing and the Section 236 rent supplement units were newly constructed. All of the Section 236 projects and approximately one third of the Section 236 units within the projects sampled also involved additional rent supplements; hence the appellation "Section 236 with rent supplements."

4. The Demand Experiment's standards are described in Appendix C. Definitions for the set of high standards are given in Mayo et al. [P53]. "High" minimum standards are more stringent in the required condition of windows, ceilings, walls, floors, and roofs. While the Demand Experiment's minimum standards would fail these building components only when they needed replacement, the high minimum standards would fail them even if they only needed repair.

Table 11.1

Housing Unit Quality for Recipients of Housing Allowances: Selected
HUD Programs and Households without Assistance, 1975

	Percentage of Units Meeting Demand Experiment's Minimum Standards		Percentage of Units Meeting "High" Minimum Standards	
	Phoenix	*Pittsburgh*	*Phoenix*	*Pittsburgh*
Housing allowance (minimum standards)	86.5%	74.2%	43.8%	10.1%
Section 23-leased housing	48.3	33.0	30.3	6.4
Public housing	74.6	62.7	50.2	50.2
Section 236 with rent supplements	63.2	62.3	46.0	46.6
No program	35.8	28.7	20.1	10.7

Source: Mayo et al. [P53], pp. 126-127. Housing allowance households are
those under the housing gap-minimum standards treatment who were
active and receiving full payments at two years after enrollment in the
Demand Experiment. Households in other programs constituted a
sample of those participating in public housing, Section 23, and Section 236 in Allegheny (Pittsburgh) and Maricopa (Phoenix) counties.
The public housing sample was restricted to those in two subprograms
—conventional and turnkey I programs. The Section 23 sample was
restricted to those in units otherwise unsubsidized. The Section 236
sample was limited to projects which contained at least some rent
supplement units. "No program" households included control households in the Demand Experiment active after two years of enrollment.
These households received a nominal payment for reporting the same
information as allowance households, although they receive no subsidy.

program" group may reflect either this program's standards or the way
the standards were enforced. This latter possibility underlines the importance of administrative practices such as those discussed in chapter 10
and suggests that the quality results obtained in EHAP could differ from
those obtained by agencies typically operating a national program. Of the
four programs, housing allowances performed best in terms of the minimum standards of quality which, of course, were the program's own
standards.

Second, the quality of dwellings for all four programs and for the
"no program" group declines when judged according to the "high minimum" standards, and this decline is proportionately greatest for the housing allowance program. This finding supports the observation, made in
chapter 6 of this book, that allowance payments did induce changes in
housing consumption consistent with the program standards but that the

allowances did not significantly increase consumption of housing services in general.

Third, in most comparisons of the outcomes in the two sites shown in table 11.1, a higher proportion of Phoenix households than Pittsburgh households met the standards. The differences in the percentage of housing allowance recipients meeting the high minimum standards in the two cities is particularly striking. These outcomes probably reflect important differences between the two areas in housing market conditions—for example, dwelling quality, vacancy rates, and average rates of household mobility.

Finally, there are some caveats. Remember that the Demand Experiment quality standards do not address the total set of services provided by some housing programs. Public housing, for example, often provides recreation or social services not typically included in the housing package provided by the private market. Furthermore, housing quality and other attributes of housing programs vary among cities according to the quality of administration, and the programs in Pittsburgh and Phoenix may or may not be representative.

Neighborhood Quality: Income and Minority Concentration

In addition to concern about housing quality, public policy has been characterized by concern about the quality of neighborhoods in which recipients of housing assistance programs live. Table 11.2 provides some of the Demand Experiment's indicators of the neighborhood conditions of recipients under the four housing programs and the "no program" group. The indicators include physical condition of the buildings and streets in the neighborhood (as indicated by abandoned buildings or litter); quality of public services in the neighborhood; absence of crime; convenience of the location of schools, shopping, public services, and medical facilities; and proximity to places of employment.[5]

According to the indicators presented in the table, housing allowance participants did relatively well compared to the three other programs and the "no program" households.

Differences in metropolitan conditions show up in the neighborhood quality indicators, as they did in the housing quality measures. The market differences between Phoenix and Pittsburgh are clearest in the neighborhood conditions of the three comparison programs. Especially with regard to problems of abandoned buildings and litter, participants in Phoenix experienced better neighborhood conditions.

---

5. See Mayo et al. [P53] for the full results incorporating a larger number of measures and additional analyses. The measures presented in table 11.2 were chosen to reflect the general nature of Mayo's findings.

Table 11.2

Neighborhood Quality for Recipients of Housing Allowances: Selected HUD Programs and Households without Assistance, 1975

Indicators	Housing Allowances (minimum standards)		Section 23 Leased Housing		Public Housing		Section 236 with Rent Supplements		No Program	
	Phoenix	Pittsburgh	Phoenix	Pittsburgh	Phoenix	Pittsburgh	Phoenix	Pittsburgh	Phoenix	Pittsburgh
Percentage of households rated by housing evaluators to be in neighborhoods with abandoned buildings	5%	10%	1%	51%	1%	11%	0%	20%	3%	15%
Percentage of households rated by housing evaluators to be in neighborhoods with considerable or lots of litter	8%	14%	8%	39%	8%	23%	2%	16%	24%	14%

Mean participant [a] rating of neighborhood public services	4.4	4.1	3.7	2.7	3.3	3.5	3.9	3.2	3.9	3.7
Mean participant [a] rating of neighborhood crime problems	1.6	1.5	1.6	1.4	1.3	1.3	1.4	1.4	1.5	1.5
Percentage of households rating convenience to shopping good or fair	99%	88%	91%	80%	86%	62%	91%	75%	92%	88%
Participant estimate of mean minutes to work	17	20	22	24	24	26	17	24	17	21

Source: Based on data presented in Mayo et al. [P53], pp. 220, 222, and 224. For a description of the sample, see table 11.1.
a. Higher mean scores indicate more favorable participant ratings.

Also striking in table 11.2 is that, on 17 of 24 comparisons,[6] house-holds living in public housing or Section 236 with rent supplements fared worse than those in no programs at all. This finding probably reflects two disadvantages of the new construction programs: (a) their fixed invest-ment in a location which may suffer neighborhood decline after the project is completed, and (b) the difficulties of acquiring sites in better neighbor-hoods. In particular, many public housing projects were poorly located during the 1950s and 1960s, when there were substantial pressures on public housing for relocation that would help urban renewal.

Mayo and his colleagues also studied the degree to which participants in the four programs and the "no program" group were located in neigh-borhoods of low-income or minority concentration.[7] They found a "perhaps surprising degree of spatial dispersion under each program."[8] Of the four programs, only public housing seemed to increase the low-income concen-tration of participants. Housing allowance dwellings did tend to be more outside of areas of minority concentration than did dwellings in the three comparison programs in Pittsburgh and the public housing program in Phoenix. But these differences seemed to reflect the location of projects and the preparticipation location of participants in each program: "par-ticipants tended to be drawn from households that lived in or were likely to live in similar neighborhoods anyway."[9]

Remember that findings on neighborhood quality and on income and minority concentration contain implications not only for benefits to indi-viduals but also for benefits to communities. For example, providing sub-sidies to households to move to a different neighborhood may conflict with a goal of stimulating neighborhood preservation by encouraging house-holds to invest in their current residences.

Housing the "Neediest"

Another concern that characterizes housing programs is distributing bene-fits to particular groups, for example, the handicapped or the elderly with physical or mental impairments. EHAP did not make a special attempt to bring these groups into the experiments. On the other hand, new construc-tion programs often include dwellings that are specially built or modified to meet the requirements of these households. Other population subgroups are often cited in studies of housing "need" as requiring special attention because of their high incidence of housing problems. These subgroups in-

6. Twenty-four comparisons result from two programs being compared in two cities on six indicators.

7. Mayo et al. [P53], chapter 5.

8. Mayo et al. [P53], p. 188.

9. Ibid., p. 225.

clude households living in poverty, large households, and members of minority groups.

Table 11.3 presents data on how well the four housing programs, as administered in Phoenix and Pittsburgh, succeeded in serving these "special" groups. These data indicate that the Section 23 program seems relatively effective in reaching these groups, while Section 236 with some units having rent supplements performs least well; housing allowances and public housing occupy an intermediate position. In interpreting these results, keep in mind that within a broad housing strategy, different programs might well be targeted to different groups in the population; and when the treatment of each group is considered in the aggregate, each group might be fairly served.

Implications of EHAP for Other Public Programs: Income Maintenance

In this section, EHAP has been compared to other housing programs solely from the standpoint of benefits to individual households. In the next section we will examine EHAP's possible implications for developing communities and for benefiting the housing sector. But first, the program's broader implications for benefiting individual households are examined.

Findings presented earlier show housing allowance treatments were only moderately effective in encouraging recipients to use the allowance to consume more housing. To put it another way, allowances were used principally to reduce rent burdens. Reasoning which argues for housing allowances in terms of reducing rent burdens to recipient households must contend with the logical extrapolation of this idea—namely, that a system of cash benefits to these same households would provide even more effective general assistance to these persons in need than housing allowances would provide. The extra administrative costs of a special housing allowance program could be avoided and distributed as benefits instead. At the same time, a cash program would transfer income more equitably by avoiding the housing allowance's failure to serve many of the poorest households occupying the worst housing units. Unless there are benefits to the community or housing sector from housing allowances, the nation might be better off reallocating the resources that would be used for an allowance program to cash income assistance instead.

For the past 15 years, succeeding administrations have sought and failed to profoundly alter the welfare system. Arguments against cash income assistance to individuals tend to be political and administrative rather than economic;[10] and today even the staunchest advocates of an

---

10. See Isler [P35].

Table 11.3

Participation in Housing Allowances and Other HUD Programs, 1975

Indicator Percentage of Recipients	Housing Allowances (minimum standards)		Section 23 Leased Housing		Public Housing		Section 236 with Rent Supplements	
	Phoenix	*Pittsburgh*	*Phoenix*	*Pittsburgh*	*Phoenix*	*Pittsburgh*	*Phoenix*	*Pittsburgh*
At or below poverty [a]	42%	48%	75%	52%	81%	56%	38%	27%
In households headed by a minority	30%	21%	38%	93%	80%	61%	19%	63%
In households headed by an elderly person	25%	27%	45%	6%	21%	48%	37%	34%
In large family households	12%	14%	12%	72%	38%	16%	10%	8%

Source: Based on data presented in Mayo et al. [P53], p. 44. For a description of the sample see table 11.1.
a. U.S. Bureau of the Census definition of poverty.

improved welfare system seek incremental change rather than wholesale reform. Yet proposed changes in the system, advanced in 1978 (which did not pass Congress), would still have fallen far short of providing recipients with enough income to meet the cost of adequate housing (defined by EHAP-like standards) and still have money for basic necessities.[11] But ironically, the same years which have witnessed repeated defeat in Congress of proposals for expansion or "reform" of cash welfare programs have also witnessed explosive growth in the Food Stamp program, creation of new programs which provide supplemental nutrition to mothers and infants, and even creation of a program to assist the poor with fuel bills.[12]

Creation of a carefully designed welfare-housing allowance system might be the most equitable, economic way to assist individuals needing housing and other basic necessities. Since housing costs have a larger impact on regional differences in the cost of living than any other component, a jointly designed welfare-housing allowance system would be more efficient than welfare reform without regional cost differences. Housing subsidies could be set differently from place to place to reflect fair market rents, thereby adjusting the total set of income transfers to the local cost of living. Recent improvements in estimating local housing costs, such as fair market rents in the Section 8 program, support this possibility. The options for simultaneously administering housing and welfare programs range from completely separate administration to joint administration by a single agency—presumably the welfare agency. Greater administrative efficiency is the principal argument for joint administration; the principal argument against it is that housing goals might not be achieved under joint administration.[13] Whichever approach is chosen, the linkages between housing and welfare programs (e.g., how income from one program is treated in the other) must be designed carefully.[14]

BENEFITS TO THE COMMUNITY

In the introductory sections of chapter 8 and this chapter, we outlined some of the expectations of benefits to communities that might be derived

---

11. Khadduri, Lyall, and Struyk [P42]. Debate regarding this proposal did bring into focus how the benefit levels and program coverage of other income transfers relate to housing programs. It is obvious that monitoring of the interactions of housing programs with welfare should be established on a continuing basis.

12. See Bendick [P7].

13. This result depends on exactly how joint administration would be handled. For five different models of joint administration, see Zais and Trutko [E181] chapter 4.

14. Khadduri, Lyall, and Struyk [P42]; Lurie [P49]; Heinberg et al. [P32, P33].

from use of housing allowances. These objectives involve our nation's investment in its housing stock and in its neighborhoods and communities, capital investments whose role is to serve succeeding generations of residents. Will we have enough housing stock to serve tomorrow's generations as well as today's? What is the most efficient way of providing this level of service? Are we conserving our community investments, or are we wasting them? These are perspectives of those concerned with what we have broadly termed community benefits.

Community benefits are not, however, to be regarded as something apart from people. The perspective of community benefits reflects just as much a concern for people as does the perspective of individual benefits. But, as pointed out earlier, analyses of a program's direct benefits to individuals do not incorporate the program's value to others in the neighborhood, nor do they encompass the program's impact on the stream of services to future residents. This section discusses findings regarding these two important aspects of community benefits: neighborhood effects and potential benefits to future residents as represented by stock improvements.

Improving Neighborhoods

Of the three field operations, only the Supply Experiment provides direct information regarding neighborhood effects, and that analysis is still under way at this time (1980). Even if these findings were currently available, they could not be directly compared to the neighborhood effects of other housing programs, as was done for individual benefits. A comprehensive and methodologically sound analysis of the neighborhood effects of current housing programs does not exist.[15]

Consequently, we can only speculate about the neighborhood effects of housing allowances from bits and pieces of what we have learned so far from EHAP. Only gross generalizations are possible about the probable size of neighborhood effects (i.e., large or small), their location (widespread or local), and the kind of physical actions undertaken (improvement or maintenance).

The most important clue about the potential of neighborhood effects derives from the level of improvement of the dwellings occupied by recipients of housing allowances. Clearly, the greater the improvement of participants' dwellings, the more likely there will be spillover effects. Little

---

15. Some program evaluations are now under way, but they are of neighborhood (neighborhood housing services) or community (community development block grants) programs that involve housing activities, not of housing programs *per se*. The closest approximation to a community-benefits evaluation of a housing program is the ongoing analysis of the small Urban Homesteading program.

upgrading of participants' housing took place, however, although many maintenance and minor repair actions were undertaken on dwellings.

Many aspects of EHAP findings fit the pattern of behaviors related to low levels of housing improvement. Fundamental among them are the higher participation rates of households whose dwellings already met standards at time of enrollment as contrasted to households whose dwellings failed. In the Demand Experiment, those renters whose units failed were more likely to meet housing standards by moving rather than by upgrading. Homeowners in the Supply Experiment, on the other hand, were likely to upgrade their houses in order to participate; but the homeowners participated at a much lower rate than renters.

Chapter 8 describes the pattern of repair and maintenance activities by participants in EHAP. Noteworthy are the small number of actions initially undertaken and these were almost always limited to those necessary to meet housing requirements; the relatively minor nature of these actions; and the concentration of repairs in housing with relatively few deficiencies. Equally interesting is the continuing record of repair and maintenance activities for homeowners that is now emerging from later years of Supply Experiment data. These annual data suggest that a long-term allowance program would have a growing maintenance effect on the dwellings of participants compared to those of nonparticipants.

A second major clue to the possibility of neighborhood effects is the quality of the neighborhoods in which repaired dwellings are located. We would expect fewer spillover effects of repair activities in neighborhoods in the poorest condition, up to some threshold level of investment. In this regard, the Supply Experiment is showing that the poorest neighborhoods had the highest proportion of eligible households and the highest participation rates.[16] Because of these higher participation rates and because more repairs are required, repair expenditures in poor quality neighborhoods are higher.[17] If the repair activity attains some critical mass, spillovers will be achieved; otherwise, the only effect will be the improvement of individual units.

As a third clue, cumulative data from the two Supply sites show that repairs were extensive: a large percentage (50 percent in Green Bay) of substandard rental dwellings were improved at some time during the experiment. As a final clue, about a third of the expenditures for housing repairs and maintenance were spent on the exterior of the houses, an encouraging sign for neighborhood effects.

How do these somewhat conflicting clues add up? Pending analysis of the Supply Experiment data, our qualitative judgment is that large-scale

16. McDowell [C61] and Bala [C4].
17. McDowell [C61].

and clearly visible neighborhood effects are unlikely. The rather widespread undertaking of repairs in the rental stock, however, can be expected to improve the general level of housing maintenance in a number of neighborhoods in Green Bay and South Bend.

Improving the Housing Stock

While we can draw on a larger set of EHAP information regarding stock improvements than we could for neighborhood effects, we lack the knowledge to make comparisons of housing stock improvements with other housing programs. Clearly, new construction and rehabilitation programs build or improve dwellings; but their net addition to the housing stock has never been accurately gauged. To some extent, new subsidized housing substitutes for dwellings that would have been built anyway—albeit in different neighborhoods for different households—and to some extent it substitutes for the maintenance and improvement of existing stock. The limited research available suggests that these substitution effects do exist and that they may be substantial.

The first step in reviewing the effect of housing allowances on the housing stock is to take another look at participation. In many neighborhoods and for many dwellings, the level of housing expenditures is insufficient to support the maintenance and improvement of the housing stock. To a large extent the low expenditures are tied to the low incomes of residents. In this respect housing allowances were expected to help, and the relatively low overall participation rates observed in EHAP are a disappointment.

The second step in examining potential effects on housing stock is to determine whether participating households used allowances to increase housing consumption or to reduce rent burden. As chapter 6 describes, findings on this subject must be broken in two, depending on whether eligible households met quality standards at enrollment or whether they were required to move or upgrade dwellings before participating. For households who met the program's standards, allowances reduced their rent burden without an immediate increase in their consumption. Since they were already spending 43 to 51 percent of their income to acquire standard housing, this is not surprising.

For households who did not meet quality standards at enrollment but who eventually met standards in order to participate, the story is mixed. In both Phoenix and Pittsburgh, their housing *expenditures* increased significantly, but when the level of housing *services* that they received is examined, the results differed. In Phoenix the level of housing services improved significantly; in Pittsburgh they did not. Apparently, the Pittsburgh households used their subsidy to buy only relatively minor repairs or moved to housing that met program standards but otherwise was of similar quality.

The final step in analyzing the effect of the experiment on the housing stock is to examine the housing improvements, as described in chapter 8, that were made in response to the program's standards. Those improvements made initially to qualify units were generally minor, but those made in later years—at least for homeowners—appear significantly greater than what would have taken place otherwise (although final estimates of their extent must await future results from the Supply Experiment). As a result, the housing allowances may have a major effect of *preventing* deterioration, even though they do not restore buildings already deteriorated.

In summary, allowances alone will probably neither revive neighborhoods already in substantial decline nor cause large-scale improvement of deteriorated dwellings. Allowances, though, will certainly slow housing stock deterioration, and even though housing allowances will not provide all the community benefits sought in national policies, allowances can be beneficial in a "mix" of housing and community development programs.

Connections with Housing Code Enforcement

Since housing standards were a primary means of earmarking subsidies in the Experimental Housing Allowance Program, it is quite appropriate to explore the connections between housing allowances and enforcement of housing codes. Specific EHAP standards were based on housing codes, the same codes that most U.S. municipalities already have on their books. Yet, EHAP found that a majority of eligible households live in substandard, and therefore presumably illegal, housing. Clearly, housing codes are not being enforced.

Lax code enforcement is a characteristic of most U.S. cities. Housing codes are not comprehensively enforced for a combination of political, economic, and fiscal reasons. The political reasons have to do with the complaints of affected landlords and homeowners and the opposition of those who disagree with the principles of housing codes. The economic reason for lack of enforcement is equally important: where housing is occupied by the poor, stringent code enforcement would require spending more money than the poor (whether owners or renters) can afford and could lead to abandonment of low-cost dwellings.

With the introduction of housing allowances, stepped up enforcement of housing codes is a strong possibility. Control of enforcement is a local responsibility, not a federal one; and the availability of federal funds for housing allowances might be an opportunity for municipal officials to increase code enforcement. Indeed, advocates for the poor might even demand more stringent enforcement.

The housing allowance experiments did not test an allowance in an environment of widespread housing code enforcement. Eligible households could refuse to participate and continue to live in housing not meeting code standards. Owners who were not participants in the program were not required to meet standards. These options would be lost with the simultaneous introduction of entitlement allowances and programs of systematic enforcement of housing codes. In that circumstance, the principal EHAP findings could change substantially. Participation would be likely to increase, and with it, aggregate program costs. Changes in the housing stock, both improvement and abandonment, would probably become more dramatic. Price inflation might occur. On the other hand, per unit administrative costs of allowances should decrease because the enforcement of standards as part of the allowance program could be eliminated.

In addition to pointing out possible shifts in the outcomes of a universal housing allowance program coupled with code enforcement, consideration of independent housing code enforcement suggests two additional policy implications. First, when accompanied by general code enforcement, a housing allowance program loses its most significant source of distinction from general income maintenance. Putting it another way, the community benefits of a housing allowance might be achieved equally well by a general program of income maintenance accompanied by a comprehensive program of housing code enforcement. Second any "income approach" to housing and other problems of low income must take housing code enforcement into account. To some extent, additional transfer payments associated with "welfare reform" could be directed into the housing market by local enforcement of housing codes. Of course, whatever the benefits to the community, benefits to individuals might decline with the loss of freedom that consumers have to live in housing below code standards. How much housing code enforcement is in the public interest depends partly on just how much each housing standard does benefit individuals and communities.

BENEFITS TO THE HOUSING SECTOR

The vitality and stability of the homebuilding industry has long been a concern in the formation of national economic policy. Housing subsidy programs are expected as well to contribute to the well-being of institutions of housing finance and market intermediaries (real estate brokers, home improvement contractors). In the following paragraphs, EHAP's findings in regard to the homebuilding industry are discussed.

Costs and Efficiency

Would the additional housing demand generated by the introduction of housing allowances, directly or indirectly, result in new construction or major housing rehabilitation? While no one expected large new construction effects from EHAP's experimental programs, some policy makers hoped that major rehabilitation would occur. To date, there has been a negligible construction effect. However, the cumulative repair process emerging from the Supply Experiment may be large enough to be felt by the industry.

In examining a housing allowance, it is also logical to ask how its costs and efficiency compared to that of subsidy programs that directly involve new construction. This analysis was undertaken for Phoenix and Pittsburgh as part of the program comparisons study of the Demand Experiment. Two important measures of this aspect of the programs are provided in table 11.4.

The first pair of columns in the table compares the total mean annual cost for a two-bedroom unit provided through each of four programs in 1975. Total costs include those borne by the federal government, by local government, and by tenants themselves.[18] These cost figures do not standardize for differences in the level of services provided under the programs other than for dwelling unit size. The data show that a unit provided through either the public housing program or the Section 236 program with rent supplements is considerably more expensive than comparable units provided through either a housing allowance program or a Section 23 leased housing program. Units under the former two programs were 50 percent more expensive in Phoenix and more than 120 percent more costly in Pittsburgh than were units under housing allowances. The main reason for this cost difference is, of course, that both housing allowances and Section 23 operate by utilizing rental units from the existing stock of privately owned housing. They therefore avoid the expense of constructing new housing units which is inherent in both the public housing program and the Section 236 rent supplement program.

While the first set of columns in table 11.4 compares the cost of providing a two-bedroom unit under all four programs, the second set addresses the question of how "efficiently" each program provides housing services.[19] It presents the ratio of the total cost of providing the average housing unit and related services in a program to the estimated market

---

18. For a detailed description of how the comparisons were calculated, see Mayo et al. [P54].

19. The aspect of a program's efficiency is referred to by economists as "production efficiency."

Table 11.4

Cost and Efficiency of Housing Allowances and Other HUD Subsidy
Programs, 1975

	Mean Total Annual Cost for a Two-Bedroom Unit		Ratio of Mean Total Cost to Estimated Market Value	
	Phoenix	*Pittsburgh*	*Phoenix*	*Pittsburgh*
Housing allowances (minimum standards)	$2,361	$1,869	1.09	1.15
Section 23-leased	2,083	2,528	1.11	1.67
Public housing [1]	3,561	4,155	1.79	2.20
Section 236 [1]	3,571	4,136	1.47	2.01

Source: Mayo et. al., [P54], pp. 46, 136.
  1. These costs are for new additions to the stock, i.e., the estimated costs of dwellings built in 1975.

rent of standard quality units of the same unit-size mix as that of the actual program. A ratio of 1.0 indicates that a program is efficient, in the sense of paying no more for services than they are worth in the open market.[20]

Of the four programs examined in table 11.4, housing allowances, with ratios of 1.09 in Phoenix and 1.15 in Pittsburgh, come closest to the 1.0 benchmark. Furthermore, virtually the entire difference between these ratios and 1.0 can be accounted for by the administrative costs of the housing allowance program itself;[21] actual program expenditures to rent units consistently stayed at or below the market value of the units being rented.

Both the public housing program and the Section 236 rent supplement program incurred costs that substantially exceeded their estimated market value. The ratios for these two programs range from 1.47 (for Section 236 in Phoenix) to 2.20 (for public housing in Pittsburgh), indicating total expenditures from one and one half to more than twice what the housing was worth in the open market. Hence, housing allowances appear largely to fulfill the aspirations held prior to the experiments: housing allowances seem both significantly cheaper and more efficient than new construction.

---

20. The market values of units are estimated with the statistical technique of hedonic indexes; see Mayo et al. [P54], Appendix VI.

21. As discussed in chapter 10, administrative costs per participating household averaged about $275 per year in EHAP overall; in the Demand Experiment, whose data are used in the present calculations, they averaged $294.

This general conclusion should, however, be tempered by examining differences among housing markets. Table 11.4 shows that the relative inefficiency of the Section 236 rent supplement and public housing programs, compared to housing allowances, is substantially greater in Pittsburgh than in Phoenix. This result arises both from higher construction costs in Pittsburgh than in Phoenix and higher market rents in Phoenix than in Pittsburgh. Moreover, we only have data for two areas; in other housing markets, the relative cost and efficiency advantage of housing allowances over new construction may differ substantially.

Furthermore, just as comparative program performance may vary from market to market, so they may vary over time. The pattern of inflation experienced in the United States during the late 1970s has tended to reduce the cost effectiveness of new construction housing programs compared to programs which utilize the existing housing stock because the costs of new construction have inflated faster than rents. With the slowdown in the rate of new construction of multifamily housing in the last years of the 1970s and the erosion of tax advantages in rental housing, higher rents should be forthcoming. Hence the pendulum may swing to a position more favorable to new construction than is now the case.

Finally, the social science methods that were used in making these comparisons are still evolving. While these methods represent a substantial advance over what was available a decade ago, aspects of our current methods remain open to debate and future improvement. Whatever the uncertainty in methodology, however, the very large amount of the differences between the new and existing subsidy programs requires that these results be taken seriously.

Differences in costs and production efficiency have to be balanced against each program's benefits. Earlier, we compared housing allowances and new construction programs in terms of their direct benefits to individuals, and the differences did not support the new construction programs. Consequently, arguments for new construction have to be supported by the probability of benefits to the community and to the housing sector. Proponents of new production programs point to many such benefits; among them are positive neighborhood effects, the future value of the improvement of the housing stock, the importance of new construction as a symbol of community revitalization, alleviation of unemployment in the construction trades, and maintenance of an efficient homebuilding industry. But the size of these benefits to the community and the housing sector must be substantial in order to balance the large cost and production efficiency differentials observed in EHAP.

Defining benefits to the community and the housing sector derived from new construction programs will not be easy. Community and housing sector benefits are harder to measure than individual benefits, and a multi-city, multiyear analysis is required. The task must be undertaken, however, if the nation is to have a clear assessment of its various housing subsidy programs.

Effects on Market Intermediaries

As described in chapter 9, EHAP has caused little change in the role of real estate brokers, property management firms, rental agents, mortgage lenders, insurance underwriters, home improvement firms, and other market intermediaries to date. (The Supply Experiment may have more information on the subject in future reports.) Low mobility of recipients and absence of major improvements in the housing stock seem to be some reasons why changes in the roles of market intermediaries have not occurred.

FINDING THE PROGRAM MIX

This chapter has shown some linkages between the empirical results of EHAP and public policy. EHAP's implications regarding benefits to individuals, to community development, and to the housing sector have been described. Important differences in outcomes among programs and across housing markets were also noted. With regard to equity, for example, the housing allowance program tested must be given relatively higher marks compared to other housing programs and relatively lower marks compared to income maintenance. In two cities, new construction-related subsidies for low-income households provide somewhat higher quality housing to recipients than do allowances, but the differences in direct benefits do not appear large enough to justify the higher costs of new construction. Perhaps this finding is a result of inadequate measurement of the housing services provided; that remains to be seen.

Comparisons of various programs' benefits to community development and to the housing sector cannot be made based on existing data. So far, benefits to communities derived from the use of housing allowances have been limited to a stock maintenance effect, the magnitude of which must still be precisely defined in the Supply Experiment. The currently unmeasured community and housing sector benefits of new construction and major rehabilitation programs may be larger, but these benefits would have to be much larger than the benefits from allowances to justify their higher costs.

These findings must be tempered by a recognition of the differences among housing markets. EHAP clearly demonstrated that program benefits vary among markets.

EHAP AND SECTION 8

Finally, it is possible to take the concept of a housing allowance as tested in EHAP and determine the usefulness of EHAP's results for a contemporary public program—the Section 8 Existing housing program. Section 8 is the contemporary housing program that is most similar to the Experimental Housing Allowance Program.[22] Findings from EHAP are applied to two questions: (1) What are the ties between Section 8 Existing and community development activities? (2) Should eligibility for Section 8 Existing be extended to homeowners?

First, in applying EHAP findings to the Section 8 program, we assume no major change in the 1980s in the general condition of the economy, the levels of employment and income, the amount of new housing construction, and the size of regional population shifts—the vital determinants of housing market conditions. Second, we assume a large expansion of public assistance is not in the offing. Of course, a vast increase in welfare benefits would modify the requirements for housing subsidy programs, both in size and type.

Third, we assume continuation of the Section 8 program and more specifically, the Existing program. If the future annual funding of Section 8 Existing increases substantially, the findings of EHAP suggest one strategy for the use of these funds; if it remains at the current level or shrinks, a different strategy is suggested. Stepped-up funding for Section 8 Existing means less conflict and more progress toward simultaneous attainment of benefits both to individual households and to community development. Research on the Section 8 program and EHAP findings indicate that in many cities, if not most, recipients are located in many different neighborhoods. This pattern is consistent with the concept of freedom of choice for the individual;[23] however a pattern of widely dispersed recipients is less likely to generate desirable neighborhood effects. We cannot state with precision how much the incremental funding of Section 8 Existing would have to be increased to achieve sufficient en-

---

22. Differences between Section 8 Existing and the allowance concept are described in chapters 2 and 10 and in Zais, Goedert, and Trutko [P95].

23. There is anecdotal evidence that in some cities this pattern of dispersion is also a result of local political pressures to spread the benefits "fairly" to different constituencies. See "Fostering Community Development."

rollment to create improved neighborhoods. In chapter 1, we estimated that 6 million households would participate in an open enrollment program of the type underway in the Supply Experiment sites. At current funding levels of only 100 to 200 thousand units a year for Section 8 Existing, the nation will remain far from achieving "universal" entitlement during the 1980s.

Fostering Community Development

If universal entitlement will not be achieved, EHAP findings suggest that stronger linkages are needed between housing and community development programs in order to foster greater benefits to communities from housing subsidies. The challenge is to forge these links and yet minimize loss of consumer freedom and individual benefits.

If tradition were followed, housing subsidies and community development would be tied together directly by restricting the use of Section 8 Existing subsidies to households residing in defined areas. This targeting of the subsidy would be combined with intensive enforcement of housing codes in the neighborhood and with rehabilitation subsidies for dwellings that must be upgraded to meet standards. This approach is in the tradition of a series of programs created to concentrate resources in decaying neighborhoods. During the 1950s, such an approach developed as one component of the urban renewal programs; concentrated code enforcement (FACE) was created in the mid-1960s, the Model Cities program (whose roots, at least, were at the neighborhood level) in the late 1960s, and more recently, neighborhood strategy areas as part of the Community Development Block Grant (CDBG) program. Each initiative promised substantial neighborhood concentration of public resources with the expectation that private investment would follow.[24]

In the past this approach has not led to upgrading when local governments focused on neighborhoods holding little attraction for city residents. To avoid this problem, an option would let the mobility patterns of the Section 8 Existing program recipients and the investment patterns of their landlords decide on the target areas by restricting the use of the housing subsidies to areas where occupant subsidies seem to be having a neighborhood effect.[25] But although an improvement, this approach could

---

24. Many other programs and demonstrations involving lower levels of public investment could be mentioned. The principal example is the Neighborhood Housing Services program, now under the aegis of the Neighborhood Reinvestment Corporation, which provides a loan purchase pool, grants, and technical assistance to neighborhoods where a high private/public investment ratio appears feasible.

25. This strategy would have to take into account the participant selection procedures in the city to insure that locational decisions of recipients reflect their preferences and not racial, ethnic, or other forms of discrimination.

still allow bureaucratic misjudgment or political mischief to thwart individual freedom.

A better way out of the dilemma is to continue allowing complete freedom of choice for Section 8 Existing participants but to provide additional incentives to maintain and to attract households with high housing preferences to marginal but sound neighborhoods. Grants could be made in these neighborhoods, for example, to improve basic features of dwellings so that dwellings will meet standards imposed by housing codes. Community development block grants are now used in this way in some communities. Code enforcement could also be concentrated in these localities. To meet the impact of code enforcement, existing lower-income residents in the neighborhood could be given priority for Section 8 Existing without any stipulation, however, that the household must remain in the neighborhood.

Numerous EHAP findings support targeting additional incentives to particular neighborhoods where spillover effects might occur. Most important, EHAP shows that many low-income households have a high preference for housing but must spend a high proportion of their income to exercise that preference. Furthermore, EHAP shows that eligibles have a strong attachment to dwellings and neighborhoods. Finally, the benefits to community development of a housing allowance (still to be confirmed in the Supply Experiment) will probably be greatest in areas where maintenance, rather than extensive improvement, of the housing stock is appropriate; and these are areas with a concentration of high-housing-preference households who spend a high proportion of their income for housing. Setting and subsidizing a high housing standard in specific neighborhoods allows individuals to exercise and maintain a high housing preference.

In sum, EHAP findings suggest a strategy of targeting subsidies may be a good way to help individual households as well as neighborhoods. Targeting provides additional incentives to individuals who are already investing in their neighborhoods' housing [26] and attracts movers, who are looking for a better place to live, to these neighborhoods.

Making Homeowners Eligible for Section 8

One incentive for neighborhood improvement in conjunction with a demand-side subsidy might be a grant to the building owner to make im-

---

26. One might argue that either of these options will hinder integration, but we believe it can be shown that more economic and potentially racial integration would occur in the targeted neighborhoods than would occur without housing and community development assistance. This is an appropriate subject for further analysis of EHAP data.

provements to meet code standards. This "supply-side" action might be even more attractive if the owner were also the subsidy recipient, that is, an eligible homeowner. Present homowners are not eligible for Section 8 Existing subsidies although the possibility of making them eligible is continually debated.

The eligibility of homeowners for housing allowances was examined early in EHAP [27] and fortunately resulted in homeowners being deemed eligible to participate in the Supply Experiment.[28] EHAP's comparisons of the behavior of homeowners and landlords in housing programs futher bolsters the case for including homeowners in Section 8. For example, although data are still incomplete, participating homeowners seem to create more housing improvements than do landlords of participating renters. (See chapter 8.)

National data from the Annual Housing Survey and analysis of data from the Supply Experiment demonstrate that homeowners comprise nearly one half of households eligible for housing allowances.[29] Yet in EHAP the participation rate for homeowners was only two thirds of that for renters. In order to favorably affect neighborhoods, ways to increase that rate of participation must be found. On the other hand, participating homeowners tend to move less often than renters and tend to stay longer in the program, suggesting less fluctuation in income and more household stability. Such findings augur well for community development. Many homeowner eligibles are elderly, and the inclusion of homeowners would shift the mix of participating households toward the elderly.

Findings from EHAP make it possible to estimate benefits (as well as costs) that would occur by extending eligibility for Section 8 Existing to low-income elderly homeowners.[30]

Additionally, if homeowners were not excluded from Section 8, the program could be used to help low-income renters to purchase homes and fortify themselves against inflation. Even though from a total of 20,000 participants (in the Supply Experiment sites, as of September 1978) only 260 renters receiving housing allowances became homeowners,[31] such a result is not surprising given the level of housing allowance payment and the requirement for homeownership down payments. But, how many more renters would have become homeowners under alternate policies:

27. Drury et al. [P17].

28. Zais et al. [P95].

29. Zais et al. [P95]; Helbers [H57].

30. Struyk and Soldo [C107]. The plan they advance would base payments on operating costs (i.e., excluding mortgage costs) and would, therefore, be relatively cheap per household served.

31. Rand [E130].

higher payments, entitlement mortgage insurance, down payment subsidy, and so forth?

The twin questions of enabling low-income renters to become homeowners and enabling existing low-income homeowners to maintain their homes make the eligibility of homeowners to participate a critical issue. If community development is an important objective of housing programs, and if we are to provide incentives to concentrate demand and achieve neighborhood effects, then homeowners as well as renters in a community may have to be made eligible for housing subsidies.

FUTURE APPLICATIONS OF EHAP RESULTS

The foregoing section provides two examples of how linkages may be created between EHAP data and ongoing policy questions. These and many other applications are possible because EHAP represents a vast amount of primary data for use directly in policy and program analysis. HUD's Office of the Assistant Secretary of Policy Development and Research is already making these data more accessible. Such data can help to build effective responses to pressing issues in housing and community development.

The policy and program relevance of the results is limited severely by the lack of information regarding community and housing sector benefits of various housing programs. To some extent, this deficiency will be ameliorated by the forthcoming Supply Experiment results, but that experiment was not designed to evaluate new construction, major rehabilitation, and other housing programs. Analysis of the Experimental Housing Allowance Program demonstrates once again the critical need for measuring and understanding all the expected benefits of housing programs. Until the nation has comprehensive evaluations of housing programs— examining the programs' potentials for simultaneously meeting goals of community development, strengthening of individual households, and contributing to the vitality of the housing sector—public housing programs will be sorely tried in an increasingly analytical world.

CHAPTER 12

Social Experimentation and Policy Research

Raymond J. Struyk

S OCIAL experiments, carried out on a large scale with thousands of households and several years of observation, are a relatively new addition to the array of tools for social science research. The Experimental Housing Allowance Program was not the first of these experiments, having been preceded or paralleled by several studies of "negative income taxes," national health insurance, performance contracting for educational services, and supported work for the hard-to-employ.[1] But EHAP was the largest and, in many ways, the most complex. This chapter places EHAP within the context of some aspects of other social experiments and evaluates EHAP as an investment of social science research resources.

The following statement by Ferber and Hirsch from their survey of experiments defines a social experiment:

> [Social experimentation] seeks to measure the effects of changes in policy variables by applying these changes to human populations under conditions of controlled experimentation similar to that used in the physical and biological sciences. While controlled experiments in the physical sciences are usually designed to test the validity of an existing or proposed theory, social experiments seek to measure effects of new or potential social programs. Theory still plays a key role, particularly in the economic experiments, as the conceptual framework for the measurement of effects.[2]

Controlled experimentation requires a "normal" state against which to measure changes caused by altering the policy variables. By this criterion, as noted in chapter 2, only the Demand Experiment in EHAP meets

---

1. For an extensive list of social experiments, see Boruch [E22] and Ferber and Hirsch [E45].

2. Ferber and Hirsch [E45], pp. 1379-1380.

the definition; the Supply and Administrative Agency Experiments are more correctly classified as demonstrations. Economic theory especially guided the design of the Demand and Supply Experiments to insure that the data collected would be suitable for the planned empirical analysis. Previous empirical estimates provided a guide to expected outcomes and a base from which to evaluate outcomes. Further, each of the elements in EHAP centainly introduced policy changes into the existing environments. Overall, EHAP was conceived and executed as a social experiment, within the constraints imposed by its budget and by the types of issues being addressed.

By several measures—the number of participants, cost, and time of execution—EHAP was massive. Over 30,000 households received subsidy payments at the 12 sites in the course of the experiments. Table 12.1 catalogues the monetary resources invested by HUD in EHAP. They total $158 million, of which approximately $31 million were devoted to the Demand Experiment, $99 million went to the Supply Experiment, and $22 million were used for the Administrative Agency Experiment. Half of the total funds were for research. Eleven years will have elapsed between the 1970 congressional mandate to conduct the experiment and the scheduled 1981 completion of analysis for the Supply Experiment (the only remaining component of EHAP). By contrast, the first large-scale social experiment, the study of the effects of implementing a negative income tax welfare subsidy system in New Jersey and Pennsylvania, initially enrolled 1,216 families, cost $8 million, and was executed over a six-year period.[3] All four of the income maintenance experiments combined cost about $110 million, with 70 percent of the funds devoted to research.

The remainder of this chapter treats three aspects of EHAP as a social experiment. The first section examines two questions of great contemporary policy interest which were not thoroughly addressed in EHAP. Since these questions were also being discussed during the design of EHAP, we ask if the experiments could have done better in providing information on them. Secondly, lessons for designing future social experiments are drawn from the housing allowance experiments as they evolved. The last section addresses the question: Was EHAP worth the cost? Direct and indirect benefits of EHAP are considered along with some idea of the opportunity cost of the research funds involved.

ISSUES NOT ADDRESSED

Policy makers and analysts in the housing field are intensely inter-

3. Skidmore [E148].

Table 12.1

Total Cost of Experimental Housing Allowance Program

Experiment	Cost (in millions)				
	Payments to Households	Administrative Cost of Program operations	Research and Monitoring	Total	Percentage
Demand Experiment	$ 4	$ 2	$25	$ 31	19
Supply Experiment	40	18	41	99	63
Administrative Agency Experiment	10	3	9	22	14
Overall design and integrated analysis	0	0	7	7	4
Total	$53	$23	$82	$158	100
Percentage	34	15	51	100	

Source: U.S. Department of Housing and Urban Development; estimates as of April 1980.
Note: Totals may not add due to rounding.

ested in (1) the achievement of racial and social integration of residential areas and (2) the preservation of the existing housing stock, which fosters neighborhood preservation. In both areas housing allowances might be an especially effective vehicle of social policy. Could EHAP have produced more information in those areas without jeopardizing research on questions in the original charter?

Racial and Economic Integration

HUD's intense interest in the promotion of economic and racial integration has been highly visible during the Carter Administration. Such integration was singled out by Secretary Patricia Harris as an explicit departmental objective. Site selection standards for subsidized new construction and substantial rehabilitation projects have been tightened; advertisements of the availability of assisted housing units must have a strong component of affirmative action outreach. There are a dozen HUD-funded ongoing demonstrations to test ways of promoting integration through the use of Section 8 Existing resources, including the Gautreaux demonstration in Chicago.[4]

The Experimental Housing Allowance Program might have offered the opportunity to systematically test the effectiveness of alternative methods of assisting households to make "freedom of choice" more of a reality in choosing a residence in a housing allowance (or Section 8) program. The Demand and Administrative Agency Experiments provided some findings regarding integration; but the AAE lacks control groups, and the Demand Experiment lacks systematic variations in the search services provided.[5]

What might have been done? The bare outline of the experiment is clear. First, several levels of services to assist households needing help to find housing would be specified. These might range from (a) no assistance to (b) the provision of lists of available units, a certain fraction of which would be in neighborhoods of differing racial and/or economic compositions, to (c) offering to actually take households to units, again with the mix of units differing by key neighborhood characteristics. Both central city and suburban locations could be included.

---

4. For a description of the Gautreaux demonstration and initial findings, see U.S. Department of Housing and Urban Development [H124]. Unfortunately, the spate of demonstration activity lacks any comprehensive design so that it will not be possible to draw reliable conclusions about the effectiveness of alternative approaches.

5. Actually, in the Demand Experiment some households were offered information on housing while others were not. But the range of services was fairly narrow. See chapter 10 for a further description.

The Demand Experiment would have been the logical operation for carrying out this work.[6] The principal treatment groups would have been multiplied by a factor equal to the number of "integration treatments," including the no-special-services treatment. The principal housing allowance treatment groups to be included might well have been defined as the housing gap treatment plus the household receiving unconstrained payments.[7] If there were four integration assistance treatments, the number of participants required for the housing gap and unconstrained groups would rise from 777 to 3,108, an approximate doubling of the initial sample of 2,241 households still active at the end of the first two years of the experiment.

It is doubtful that a doubling of the sample size could have been tolerated within the constraints of a "thin sample" in the Demand Experiment required to be certain that the introduction of the limited allowance program would have had no market effects. Even if the larger sample could have been included, the ability to generalize findings in this area for two markets would still be questionable. Limited generalization and concern about an excessive number of participants would have required an expanded number of sites, and two or three integration assistance treatments would have to be tested in each site. This change would have fundamentally altered the character of the Demand Experiment.

With this much redesign, a different experiment would have emerged. Therefore, testing integration assistance in EHAP should not be viewed as an opportunity lost.

Stock and Neighborhood Preservation

EHAP offered little information about benefits to community development, that is, improvement and preservation of existing housing stock, that might be derived from housing allowances. The Supply Experiment, the part of EHAP in which such benefits might have been addressed, was intentionally directed away from these issues at the design stage by HUD.

Current discussions about how housing policies can enhance community development encompass four questions: (1) What is the extent of the long-term maintenance effects of housing allowances? (2) Does occupancy of a unit by a subsidized household for a limited time significantly affect the unit's depreciation trajectory? (3) Do allowance-induced improvements in some units contribute to the improvement of

---

6. The Supply Experiment is not a reasonable possibility since it was designed to test market effects of a freestanding program. "Steering" here would have made it impossible to obtain the answer to the fundamental questions.

7. In figure 3.2 these are cells 2 to 4 and 6 to 12.

nearby units and hence preserve neighborhoods? (4) Will the number of units withdrawn from the stock significantly decrease because of the operation of an open-enrollment allowance program in a market? Conceivably, the Supply Experiment could have been designed to address the first three questions.

What information was needed to address these three issues? For the questions about maintenance effects on units occupied by program participants (1 and 2), a panel of dwellings would have to be monitored over time. Careful records of expenditures for routine operations and investments would be essential, as would a full accounting of the tenancy, especially whether or not tenants were participants in an allowance program. The sample would have to be constructed to insure adequate samples of units occupied by participants for various lengths of time as well as those never occupied by participants. Tenant characteristics as well as their length of tenure would be important. It would be necessary to acquire detailed knowledge of how revenues and costs were effected, and as much information as possible on producer expectations and attitudes, which are key elements in the investment decision. Further, experimental payments would need to continue and the panel of units would have to be monitored over a very long time, perhaps 10-15 years, to determine long-term stock preservation effects.

To address the "contagion" effects of allowances (question 3), the sample just described would also have to be spatially specified. Two spatial sampling relations would be necessary. To capture the immediate contagion effect, units without participants must be sampled with varying proximity to units with participants. Furthermore, the spatial variation in the location of eligible households would have to be considered in drawing the design; neighborhoods with high eligibility rates could be, for example, sampled at a lower rate than others.

In some respects, the design of the Supply Experiment, as originally conceived, could with moderate changes have addressed the maintenance questions. Capturing the contagion effects would have required more fundamental restructuring. As noted in Appendix A, the strategy actually adopted was to sample structures and to follow a permanent panel of structures over time. Structures were sampled from 16 strata defined on the basis of tenure, placement in the rent or house value distribution, and urban versus rural location. The criterion chosen in designing the sample was the sampling reliability of estimates of the price elasticity of the supply of housing services, the parameter of primary interest in the Supply Experiment. It was envisioned that the sample of structures chosen would also yield the desired sample of households, that is, households occupying the dwelling in the structures. In fact, it was believed at the design stage in Green Bay that 939 of the 3,720 households living in monitored structures would be participants in the program; these estimates, in turn, were posited on participation rates of around 70 percent among the eligible households living in monitored dwelling units.[8] The sampling design had no explicit spatial dimension, but some concentration would be achieved given the geographic clustering of structures within each of the sampling strata.

If the design had required careful monitoring of the presence or absence of the program's participants in "permanent panel" dwellings, it could have addressed the questions concerning long-term maintenance effects and depreciation trajectory. However, this monitoring of participants was not included in the design, since landlords' responsiveness to price signals was the focus of the analysis. Furthermore, when participation rates turned out to be only about one third of those assumed in the sample design, the number of permanent panel structures occupied by participants was so small that it endangered analysis of these questions, following the original design.

As noted, to address the contagion question the design would have required an extremely complex sampling procedure and a massive expansion in the sample's size and in the Supply Experiment's cost. These expansions would undoubtedly have been refused by HUD, which was trying hard in the design stage to limit the size of the originally proposed sample.[9] In a revised design, a broad sampling strategy would probably have initially involved the permanent panel of units as originally conceived. Had design assumptions about participation proven correct, the permanent panel would have been supplemented by sampling units proximate to permanent panel units occupied by participants. If the low number of participants in permanent panel units that actually occurred had been detected quickly enough, the panel could have been augmented with units occupied by participants and their attendant "proximity units." The lag in discovering the low number of panel units with participants precluded taking this remedial action quickly enough, given the length of the monitoring period.

What are the possibilities today? The fourth wave of surveys of the permanent panel dwellings in Green Bay (conducted after three program years) found 217 dwellings occupied by households then receiving allowance payments. This is a number large enough to support some types of analysis; but as noted, to do the longitudinal analysis of primary interest one must have a continuous history of dwelling occupancy by participants over as long a period as possible. Although a longitudinal analysis of

---

8. Massell [E103], table 3, p. 13.
9. Massell [E103].

this type was not originally envisioned, this can be done by linking records from the administering agency (the housing allowance office in each city) on the location of program participants with the permanent panel dwelling records. This procedure establishes the long-term record and overcomes the problem of only having "snapshots" that occurs if permanent panel periodic survey records are relied upon exclusively. Depending on the exact spatial distribution of permanent panel dwellings not occupied by participants, limited analysis of contagion effects may also be possible. All of these analyses will certainly yield less information than if the experimental design had originally encompassed them, but valuable information may yet be forthcoming.

DESIGN LESSONS FOR FUTURE EXPERIMENTS

Design problems and corresponding corrective actions for new experimental enterprises have been gleaned from several ongoing and completed social experiments. Two additions to this growing body of knowledge are offered here: one having to do with contingency designs and the other focusing on the need for better estimates of the expected size of the shock being introduced into the system.[10] Interestingly, as manifested in EHAP, both these lessons stem from the experience with program participation.

The idea of a "contingency design" is simply that when designers are confronted with invincible ignorance about a key design parameter, the overall design should be so constructed so as to be able to shift the monitoring process if the best guess for this critical parameter turns out to be incorrect.[11] The design of the Supply Experiment, for example, was based on an assumption of high participation rates, rates approaching those of AFDC. In some ways, this was simply prudent. To be assured of adequate funds to operate the program, high estimates were warranted. But the monitoring apparatus was set up under the assumption of high participation rates and a high income elasticity of demand for housing services. The kind of monitoring desired changed as the program unfolded. One example of a possible shift was already noted, that is, adding participant-

10. Both of these points are anticipated to some degree in Hollister's excellent paper [E58].

11. Rivlin [E137] makes a related point in the context of experiments like the Supply Experiment, when she discusses the tension between researchers who seek to hold to an initial design and hence to avoid "contamination" and policy makers who want to extract as much information on as many key questions as possible (p. 351). The argument in the text is that the tension might be sharply reduced through advanced design of alternatives.

occupied units and, possibly, "proximate" units to the permanent panel. In fact, adjustments were made in monitoring program effects, mainly by eliminating some survey waves.

Ideally, primary and secondary research objectives would be defined at the outset in such cases. The initial design would be focused on the primary objectives, premised on the "best estimate" of the unknown key parameter; but it would be possible to shift to the secondary objectives with modest changes in the monitoring procedures if this estimate proved badly inaccurate.

Aside from having primary and secondary objectives that are sufficiently complementary, is it possible to be certain of the error in predicting the gross value of the key parameter quickly enough to permit shifting objectives? In the Supply Experiment, something approaching steady-state enrollment levels were not achieved until after two years of program operation. Allowing 6 months for confirmation, most of the monitoring period would have been lost. On the other hand, evidence of lower than expected rates was at hand within 12-18 months. But a shift in monitoring would still have been risky. If the monitoring period were 7 to 10 years, the shift would have made sense; and much additional information might have been derived from the experiment.

Another approach is to begin monitoring on a broad front to pursue both primary and secondary objectives. As the key parameter value becomes clear, part of the monitoring could be dropped. With this approach, it would not be necessary to delay beginning to achieve secondary objectives until after the parameter is identified. A disadvantage is high initial monitoring costs.

The case for such contingency designs, then, would seem stronger for experiments characterized by (a) gross uncertainty about one or two key parameters, (b) primary and secondary experimental goals having reasonably complementary data needs for analysis, and (c) an extended monitoring period. Given the massive costs of fielding many social experiments, it seems prudent to design them to maximize the amount of information they can yield with modest adjustments in the monitoring procedures.

The second "lesson" concerns better estimates of the net value of the inducement to households to join the experimental program. In the Demand Experiment of EHAP, this specifically meant defining the net value to the household of an allowance payment guaranteed for three years. For some households the cost of participating was simply that of signing up. For others, it entailed moving, possibly to a different neighborhood, to a dwelling which passed the program's housing standards; and, if the household felt uncertain of its ability to support higher rent payments after the conclusion of the experiment, costs of a second move (appropriately, discounted) must be added. Furthermore, the bulk of the benefits—an increased flow of housing services and more cash to spend on other goods and services—are received in future months or years.[12]

More generally, a low rate of participation is anticipated in any program that imposes a sizable cost on eligible households to participate, strings out the receipt of benefits over an extended and perhaps limited period, or offers a benefit that is modest in relation to base income. This phenomenon was probably not as thoroughly addressed at the design stage in EHAP as it could have been. This was partly because designers drew heavily on the experience of programs and experimental programs such as the income maintenance experiment, in which some important characteristics are the opposite of ones in EHAP.

Income maintenance is not the only example of a low entry cost and high benefit level program. An experimental housing program which required very little effort by the participant was the Prospective Insurance Payments (PIP) program under which HUD made mortgage payments to financial institutions for those mortgagors of HUD-insured homes who were experiencing what were judged as temporary reductions in incomes. The main cost to the household—repayment of the advances—was folded into a recast first mortgage and was spread many years into the future. High participation rates were found for mortgagors determined to be program eligible and who remained delinquent long enough to join the program.[13]

On the other hand, tax credits to owners of single-family homes for energy retrofitting may be less attractive to the household since it incurs the cost of installing insulation and/or storm doors and windows immediately but receives the majority of the benefits, reduced energy bills, in the future. Of course, the payback period depends on a large number of factors, especially the initial weatherization of the structures. Crude participation figures are consistent with the expected pattern in that proportionately fewer low-income households used the tax credit in 1978 than did those with incomes of over $10,000; about 8 percent of tax-return-filing households with incomes of $10,000 to $15,000 used the credit, compared with 3 percent of those with incomes under $10,000.[14] For lower-

---

12. This is discussed more completely in chapter 5.

13. On the other hand, very few delinquent mortgagors among those in the initial sample were found to be eligible for the program. And even among this small number, many who received a letter discussing possible "government assistance" were frightened or otherwise motivated into bringing their mortgages current. Hence, the overall impression is of low participation; but this is not the case.

14. These participation rates are for both homeowners and renters, although for practical purposes the program is only for homeowners. Since tax returns do not in-

compared to higher-income households, the cost of participation as a fraction of total resources is probably higher on average, and the rate at which they discount energy savings could also be higher; and this apparently more than offsets expected shorter payback periods in less well-weatherized units.

Yet another example is the Special Supplemental Food Program for Women, Infants, and Children (WIC), a nutrition supplementation activity for low-income pregnant and nursing mothers and young children. Under its provisions, persons judged to be "at nutritional risk" by medical or nutritional professionals due to low income and inadequate nutrition are eligible to receive free each month about $20 worth of high-protein, high-mineral, and high-vitamin foods. In addition, most participants receive routine medical care under the program. The value of perceived benefits may vary widely according to the understanding of the long-term health gains associated with the package of services. Nevertheless, there are real costs of participation in the form of visits to clinics. Sometimes such visits are necessary to pick up food packages; some agencies, however, deliver the food or provide vouchers usable at grocery stores. A modest evaluation of the program reached the conclusion that participation was sensitive to such costs:

> WIC participants—particularly those with lowest incomes—are sometimes prevented from participating by such barriers as lack of transportation, clinic hours during business hours only, and lack of child care.[15]

The broad point is clear: households rationally and carefully determine their net gains from participation before joining various programs. The experience with dozens of programs, demonstrations, and experiments fortifies this conclusion.[16] Still, the current structure of some of these programs suggests that the lesson has not been universally assimilated. The clarity of the experience from the Experimental Housing Allowance Program should be valuable in promulgating this observation and in achieving more careful assessment of the net benefit question at the design stage.

---

clude a question on tenure, it is not possible to be certain of tenure status for homeowners without mortgage debt or those taking the standard deduction. However, the broad pattern reported in the text would not be reversed under reasonable assumptions about the tenure distribution of tax-filing units by income class.

15. Bendick et al. [P8], p. 61; see also Bendick [P7, P12].

16. Rossi and Lyall [P67], p. 185, make this point explicitly in their review of the income maintenance experiment where they state that the adjustments households make in response to the policy change "are much smaller and more complex than researchers are generally inclined to think."

WAS EHAP WORTH THE COST?

The response to this question is in two parts, concerning (1) EHAP's success in responding to the issues that caused its implementation and (2) indirect benefits generated from the data or analyses developed by EHAP for questions outside its mandate. The benefits must be weighted against the opportunity cost of the research funds involved. These areas are now explored.

Direct Benefits

In assessing the "success" of the New Jersey Income Maintenance Experiment, Michael Barth and his colleagues use the following criteria which appear serviceable for judging EHAP as well:

● The central hypothesis should have compelling policy importance at the time the experiment was designed, with good reason to believe that this would continue.

● At the time of the experiment's design, there should be no cheaper or simpler way of obtaining the desired information.

● The experiment should be competently and honestly managed—including, of course, the analysis.

● The tracks of the experiment should allow other social scientists, in principle, to replicate the operations and other analysts, in fact, to replicate the econometrics.

● The results, however complex, should speak directly to the initial hypothesis.[17]

While on an overall basis EHAP gets high marks when judged by these criteria, some specific comments are in order.

The compelling and continuing policy importance of testing the market effects of an entitlement housing allowance program might be questioned. Was a universal program ever a real possibility? Even if it was, did it remain so after the Supply Experiment had been in the field for a year or two? While the possibility of an entitlement housing program was certainly soporific during the Carter Administration, it should not be counted out. In light of the continuing administration and congressional machinations about welfare reform and the relation between income transfers and housing, an entitlement program may again be advanced. Moreover, the willingness of the federal government to annually devote additional resources to the Section 8 Existing program in recent years—cumu-

17. Barth, Orr, and Palmer [P6], pp. 214-215.

latively on far less than an entitlement basis—may well have been possible only because of the lack of allowance-induced inflation experienced in the Supply Experiment sites.

Were there cheaper ways to obtain the information? The answer is a convincing "no." Although other less expensive approaches were available for estimating the income elasticity of the demand for housing, these procedures would have provided no information on the effects of earmarking on the housing consumption of participants or on rates of participation. As for market effects, no substitute was available. Indeed, the limitations of econometric and simulation models, reviewed in chapter 10, attest to this, as does the continuing skepticism of a few policy makers about the fact that the program did not cause inflation.

On the other hand, it seems that data acquisition was excessive; the instruments contained many questions which were ignored entirely or little used in the analysis. These tumid instruments, with their accordant greater interviewing, coding, key punching, and verification requirements, significantly increased costs and delayed analyses.

How clear a trail is being left by the experimenters? Our answer is conditional because of the modest extent of secondary data analysis completed as of this report. Supplemental analysis with data from the Demand Experiment by Cronin and by Quigley and Hanushek suggest these data are in good shape.[18] No data from the Supply Experiment have yet been available for such analysis. However, documentation of the data sets from the Supply Experiment which have been sent to HUD has been excellent. All of the EHAP data sets are to be widely disseminated by HUD, in part through a data bank which HUD is subsidizing.

Finally, have the results of EHAP spoken directly to the initial hypotheses? The answers listed in chapter 1 to the questions initially asked of EHAP indicate that the experiment "remained on target." Some doubt can occur about the robustness of some of the answers developed and whether all the results are definitive, especially concerning long-term effects of allowances on housing consumption. But the original issues certainly were addressed in depth; few extraneous issues received significant attention.

Indirect Benefits

EHAP has been credited by Aaron with producing "serendipitous findings," valuable findings outside of the experiment's original research objectives. Aaron summarizes the efficiency gains for housing programs based on EHAP as follows:

---

18. See Cronin [H22] to [H27]; Cronin [H29] to [H31]. Hanushek and Quigley [H51, H52, H55].

The housing allowance experiments have also produced information that has or can reduce administrative costs or incorrect payments sufficiently to pay for the experiments. At present, the elderly are recertified for eligibility biennially under existing programs. Based on experience from the housing experiments, it is estimated that annual recertification could save $12 million per year. Most of the savings comes from taking account of annual increases in social security payments one year sooner than occurs under present practices. From data developed in the experiments, it is estimated that payment of a credit to recipients of section 8 assistance equal to a fraction of the amount that actual rents are below estimated "fair market rents"—the highest rent that can be paid by tenants eligible for section 8 assistance—would save more than $50 million per year. HUD officials assert that data from the Administrative Agencies Experiment (AAE) induced them to set fees paid to local housing authorities for administering section 8 existing housing at 8½ percent of fair market rents rather than 10 percent or more that they would have paid based on data from other sources. Relative to a 10 percent fee, the 8½ percent fee reduces payments by HUD for administrative costs by $25 million per year. Again based on results from the AAE, HUD has introduced stricter methods than heretofore used in the section 8 program for the certification of tenant income. These methods are expected to reduce program costs $15 million per year.[19]

If all of the savings just enumerated were realized, the research component of EHAP would be financed with less than a year's savings.

Because the housing allowance program used in EHAP is similar but not identical in structure to the Section 8 Existing program, it has been possible to use EHAP findings to confront numerous aspects of Section 8 Existing. Questions about the Section 8 program debated within HUD using, in part, EHAP findings and data include the desirability of increasing the amount of housing improvement by making program participation contingent on living initially in substandard housing or on the household moving to another unit; alternative administrative practices to promote residential racial integration by participants; the gain in housing consumption achievable with removal of the fair market rent as the maximum rent the household can pay and still participate (a program feature not in EHAP allowance programs); and the need for and scope of an allowance type program with a somewhat higher rental schedule that would require a moderate amount of investment in a dwelling as a condition for a unit being used in the program.[20]

Besides these specific applications, the vast amount of information on basic behavioral relationships coming from EHAP can be widely applied.

---

19. Aaron [P1], pp. 48-49.
20. See Khadduri and Struyk [P43]; Olsen, Rasmussen, and Dick [P61].

EHAP findings on the differences in housing consumption induced by un-constrained cash grants compared with earmarked allowance payments were a critical element in the welfare reform debate in the summer of 1977.[21] The structure of some of HUD's initiatives to encourage racial in-tegration has been loosely based on EHAP findings on differences in search probability and methods of black and white households. Yet another ex-ample is the confirmatory evidence on the modesty of household response to moderate changes in incomes or the price of certain goods.

Beyond these findings, the general level of understanding about the functioning of housing markets has been significantly raised. One example is the importance of using vacancy durations in addition to vacancy rates in judging market conditions. Another is the knowledge about the opera-tion of the rental market: how many properties landlords own and manage, the way in which units are marketed, and the size of profit margins in various segments of the market.

Opportunity Cost

To discuss the opportunity cost of the $83 million of research funds re-quires that EHAP be placed in the context of HUD's research program of the past 10-12 years. The program came into its own during the tenure of Secretary George Romney, with the launching of Operation Breakthrough. Breakthrough, essentially a large-scale demonstration (about $100 million of federal funds) to apply advanced industrial methods to the residential construction industry to lower housing costs, catapulted the annual research budget from $10 million to $40 million. As Breakthrough wound down, EHAP funding requirements helped keep the research budget at high levels. With the conclusion of EHAP, the budget has settled back to about a $50 million level during the 1979-1981 fiscal years, a level about 2.2 times its level 12 years earlier after adjusting for inflation. It appears that EHAP resulted in a temporary expansion of the research budget, but there was certainly no tight relationship between EHAP and the total budget. Thus, there would likely have been some additional research monies avail-able in the absence of EHAP.

Besides Breakthrough and EHAP there was another very large proj-ect undertaken by the research office in the 1970s, the Public Housing Management Improvement Program (PHMIP). This was also a demonstra-tion, costing $25 million.[22] Both Breakthrough and PHMIP devoted only small shares of the available resources to evaluation. Hence, EHAP stands in contrast to the other very large research enterprises funded by HUD in

---

21. Khadduri, Lyall, and Struyk [P42].
22. For a description see Struyk [C106], chapter 8.

the extent of the evaluation carried out; in fact, almost all of payments to households in EHAP were from housing program appropriations.

The remainder of the HUD research budget falls into three categories: data acquisition, evaluation and demonstration/evaluation projects, and research studies. Data acquisition, including fielding the Annual Housing Survey, has been taking 20-30 percent of the total budget in recent years. Projects in the other two categories are typically small, averaging around $150,000 and taking 18 months to 2 years to complete. Sometimes these individual studies are part of a "research program," for example, lead base paint poisoning prevention; but these have generally been labels for a loose collection of activities rather than for a fully structured program. The exceptions are a handful of carefully structured evaluations and demonstrations with evaluations begun after 1975; prime examples are the demonstrations and evaluations of Neighborhood Housing Services and Urban Homesteading and evaluations of the CDBG and Section 8 programs.[23] These efforts are producing results used to improve program administration and to provide basic data for policy debates within the administration.

EHAP is unique in HUD's research program because of the size of data base it has generated for analysis of specific housing issues and in the long-term, high-level analytic resources concentrated on fundamental housing issues. The sustained nature of the intellectual effort seems key. Viewed in this light, EHAP can be credited with providing the basis for raising the quality of debate about many housing policy questions. Until the past few years, the opportunity cost of the funds was low; more recently, however, the cost has increased sharply for the marginal funds that would have been available in the absence of EHAP.

Summary

The potential exploitation of the EHAP findings and of the data based for secondary analysis is just beginning to be realized. With the use of the knowledge already acquired—to address both the specific objectives of EHAP and other policy questions—and with the prospect of even greater future use, the inescapable conclusion to us is that EHAP was a good investment yielding a high return on its cost.

---

23. This description fails to convey the real scope and diversity of the activities funded under the HUD research budget. The reader is encouraged to examine the documents sent to the Congress in support of the appropriations request for a more complete description. See, for example, the section on the Office of Policy Development and Research in U.S. Department of Housing and Urban Development [P83].

Data Collection in the Three Experiments

Chapter 3 described each of the three housing allowance experiments as operating programs, that is, as they were implemented by operating agencies and participated in by households. In contrast, this appendix describes these same experiments from the researcher's point of view, explaining how data were gathered on which the empirical findings presented throughout this book are based.

THE DEMAND EXPERIMENT

Figure A.1 provides a summary of the multiple sources from which research data were drawn in the Demand Experiment. Information was derived both from administrative records created in the course of program operations and from surveys conducted specifically for research purposes.

Household Data

Because household behavior was the primary focus in the Demand Experiment, most data collection centered there. The process began with a short, widely administered "screener survey" which was used to identify households to be included in the structured "baseline" survey interview. This second survey was administered to each allowance household prior to program enrollment. Topics covered included past housing occupancy; search and mobility behavior; program experience; current housing needs; and household demographic characteristics, employment experience, and income. This same interview, except the part covering past history and with

NOTE: Further information on data gathering and analysis in the Demand Experiment can be obtained from Abt Associates Inc. [E3, E9], pp. 5-20; [E38, E39, E40, E16].

Figure A.1

Data Collection in the Demand Experiment

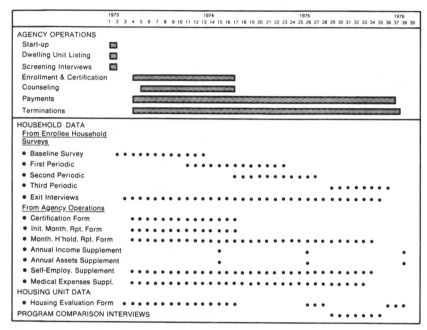

Source: Abt Associates, Inc. [E9, E11, E15]; Bakeman et al. [E18].

more detailed questions on mobility and search behavior added, was periodically repeated for households who went on to become program recipients, after 6 months, after 12 months, and after 24 months of receiving subsidy payments. A short exit interview was also administered to a sample of households whose enrollment terminated, including both those who had become recipients and those who never attained recipient status.

To receive each month's subsidy check, recipient households were required to submit monthly household report forms giving current information on household composition and income. While agencies used these forms to calculate the correct subsidy amount, these reports also formed records for research purposes. Similar dual roles were played by agency-required annual supplementary reports on households' incomes and assets and by special supplementary reports filed by self-employed households or those claiming large medical expenses on their income forms.

Households in the Demand Experiment's control group were also sub-jected to the same interviews and also were required to file monthly and other reports. To obtain their continuing cooperation, they were paid $25 for each periodic interview completed and $10 for each monthly report form filed. Households receiving allowance benefits were not paid for interviews.

Housing Unit Data

Information on the housing units occupied by program households—both recipients of benefits and control households—was also vital to Demand Experiment research. Each housing unit was inspected by a trained mem-ber of the Demand Experiment's staff, using a housing evaluation form containing over 100 items. This inspection was done for all allowance households on the same schedule as the household interviews. For house-holds in housing gap-minimum standards treatment groups, these inspec-tions served not only to gather data for research purposes but also to certify compliance with the program's minimum housing quality standards and therefore their eligibility for allowance benefits. For households in the minimum standards treatment group, an additional inspection was per-formed whenever the household moved or the household reapplied for a unit which had previously failed inspection and had subsequently been repaired.

Sample Size and Representativeness

In a study of household behavior, one important question is whether the households in the study sample accurately represent the general popula-tion to which the study's results are supposed to be relevant—in this case, those low-income households potentially involved in housing subsidy pro-grams. Many factors affect this representativeness, including the method by which the sample is initially selected, the rates at which households once selected refuse to cooperate, and the "rate of attrition" at which house-holds who cooperate with initial interviews become lost from the sample for subsequent interviews.

Tables A.1 and A.2 provide data with which we can examine such questions for the Demand Experiment in each of the two sites.[1] Using a simple t-test to determine significant differences in proportions, two com-parisons of representativeness have been made by contrasting the charac-

1. In the case of the Demand Experiment, another question of representativeness arises in considering how well households in Phoenix and Pittsburgh represent the set of households nationwide. This question is addressed in Appendix B.

Table A.1

Total Number and Demographic Characteristics of Household Sample, Phoenix

	Population Income-Eligible for Allowances, 1970[1]	Baseline Sample	Active at One Year	Active at Two Years
Number of Households	42,300	4073	1610	635
Race of Head of Household				
% Minority	21%	33%	38%	37%
% Nonminority	79	67	62	63
Total	100%	100%	100%	100%
Age of Head of Household				
Elderly ($\geq$65)	25%	15%	22%	25%
Nonelderly	75	85	78	75
Total	100%	100%	100%	100%
Sex of Head of Household				
Female	29%	35%	43%	44%
Male	71	65	57	56
Total	100%	100%	100%	100%
Number of Persons in Household				
1	18%	12%	15%	N.A.[2]
2	28	27	25	N.A.
3-4	33	40	36	N.A.
5 or more	21	22	24	N.A.
Total	100%	101%	100%	—
Gross Annual Household Income				
<$2,000	19%	12%	7%	N.A.
$2-2,999	11	12	16	N.A.
$3-4,999	27	22	29	N.A.
$5-6,999	23	21	27	N.A.
$7-9,999	18	22	13	N.A.
$10,000 or more	3	2	7	N.A.
Total	101%	101%	99%	—

Source: Wallace [H127], p. A129; Abt Associates, Inc. [E11], p. 36; Friedman and Weinberg [H38], p. A15.

1. Estimated using data from the 1970 Census of Population 1-in-100 user's tape.

2. N.A. = not available.

Table A.2

Total Number and Demographic Characteristics of Household Sample,
Pittsburgh

	Population Income-Eligible for Allowances, 1970 [1]	Baseline Sample	Active at One Year	Active at Two Years
Number of Households	56,900	4318	1635	525
Race of Head of Household				
% Minority	25%	23%	25%	23%
% Nonminority	75	77	75	77
Total	100%	100%	100%	100%
Age of Head of Household				
Elderly (≥65)	40% *	22%	26%	24%
Nonelderly	60	78	74	76
Total	100%	100%	100%	100%
Sex of Head of Household				
Female	47%	50%	61%	57%
Male	53	50	39	43
Total	100%	100%	100%	100%
Number of Persons in Household				
1	30% *	16%	18%	N.A. [2]
2	28	27	26	N.A.
3-4	26	37	37	N.A.
5 or more	17	20	19	N.A.
Total	101%	100%	100%	—
Gross Annual Household Income				
<$2,000	28%	9%	3%	N.A.
$2-2,999	17	18	17	N.A.
$3-4,999	29	30	42	N.A.
$5-6,999	22	20	23	N.A.
$7-9,999	4	17	12	N.A.
$10,000 or more	0	6	3	N.A.
Total	100%	100%	100%	—

Source: Wallace [H127], p. A-128; Abt Associates, Inc. [E11], p. 36; Friedman and Weinberg [H38], [H39], p. A15.

1. Estimated using data from the 1970 Census of Population 1-in-100 user's tape.

2. N.A. = not available.

* Significant difference between the eligible population and baseline sample, at .05 level or higher.

teristics of (a) those in the baseline sample versus those in the income-eligible population, and (b) those in the baseline sample versus those initial participants who were still participants at the end of the second year. No significant differences were found in Phoenix. In Pittsburgh, by contrast, the eligible population and baseline sample were found to differ in terms of household size distribution and the age of the head of household (elderly vs. nonelderly); but no differences were detected between baseline households and those active at the end of year two.[2]

Program Comparison Interviews

One of the special studies conducted within the Demand Experiment compared housing allowances against three other federal low-income housing subsidy programs: public housing (constructed since 1952), Section 23 leased housing, and Section 236 multifamily rental housing.[3] To support this research, interviews were conducted with over 1,200 households (491 in Phoenix and 722 in Pittsburgh) receiving benefits under one of the three comparison programs. These interviews involved questions drawn from the Demand Experiment's baseline and periodic household surveys and were conducted at approximately the same time as the Demand Experiment's third periodic survey. At the same time, the Demand Experiment's housing inspectors, using the experiment's housing evaluation form, evaluated a sample of the housing units occupied by interviewed households. These survey data were supplemented by cost data and other program materials obtained from HUD offices.

THE SUPPLY EXPERIMENT [4]

Because the primary research mandate in the Supply Experiment was to observe the effects of housing allowances on the housing market and the housing stock, the major research data base in the experiment tracked a sample of housing units over time, rather than a sample of households. Figure A. 2 indicates the sources from which information on these housing units and on other objects of research in the experiment were gathered. The figure refers specifically to Green Bay; data collection and program

---

2. Because of inflation, the test was not applied to incomes. Also note that the sample sizes for the Census data were used in making the t-tests, not the population sizes shown in the tables.

3. For further discussion of the methodology employed in this program comparison study, see Mayo et al. [P54], Appendix I and II.

4. Further information on data gathering and analysis in the Supply Experiment can be obtained from Levitt [E74, E75, E76].

operations in South Bend proceeded in a parallel fashion, but they started about six months later in South Bend than in Green Bay.

The Permanent Panel of Housing Units

The Supply Experiment's permanent panel of residential properties in Green Bay and South Bend was based on a probability sample of all residential properties at each site, as compiled from property tax records. Each property in the sample was assigned to one of 18 strata, based on whether it was a rental unit or owner-occupied, whether it was in a rural or urban location, its rent level or market value, the number of units in its building, and whether or not it was a rooming house or mobile home. Dwelling units were then sampled from these strata at different rates.

Once a unit was selected for inclusion in this panel, a chronological file of data was built for it by drawing information from two sources. The more important source was structured interviews (including unit evaluations) conducted with the owner of the unit, whether owner-occupant or landlord. In the case of rental units, a sample of interviews was also done with renters currently occupying the units. These interviews were first conducted prior to introduction of the allowance program at the site and then repeated annually for four years thereafter. They yielded information on the demographic, employment, housing histories, and income characteristics of current tenants; unit and building characteristics; residents' satisfaction with their unit, building, neighborhood, and landlords; and, for renters, the rent and utilities expenditures, or, for owners, cost data on operations, maintenance, mortgage, and insurance.

The second source of information was annual visual inspections of the exterior of units performed by agency staff. These inspections yielded information on major changes in property use and on the general condition of the building. Visual survey inspections were also conducted annually for each neighborhood to determine changes in land-use patterns, the type and condition of residential buildings, the availability of public facilities and services, and the general socioeconomic characteristics of the area.[5]

Tables A.3 and A.4 indicate the number of units, households, and landlords interviewed at baseline, permanently empaneled, and completing various waves of recurrent surveys during the first four years over which research data were collected at the two sites. There is no indication of the samples not being representative of the underlying populations.

---

5. Neighborhoods were defined based on public records and field observations. They each consisted of between 1,000 and 3,000 households and generally conformed to census tracts defined in the 1970 Census.

Figure A.2

Data Collection in the Supply Experiment, Green Bay

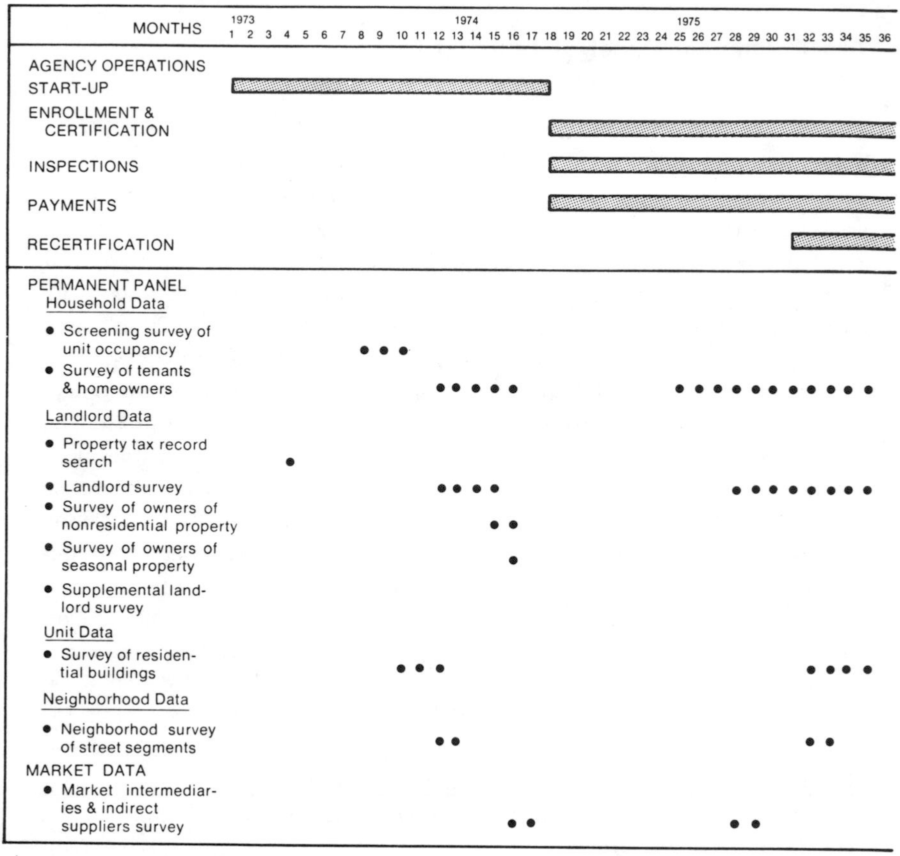

Data on Recipient Households and Their Housing

The panel of dwelling units just described was selected to represent all housing units in Green Bay and South Bend, not simply those participating in the allowance program. For units occupied by allowance recipients, more extensive unit condition information was available from detailed inspections done to determine eligibility for allowance payments; these inspections were performed at the time of enrollment, at the time of a move or repair after failing inspection, and annually thereafter.

In addition to information on the units occupied by allowance recipi-

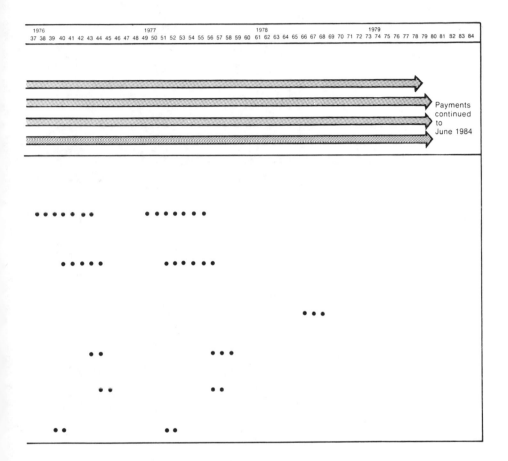

ents, data on the households themselves were provided by three major types of agency operating records: enrollment records, semiannual income recertification forms, and payment disbursement records. When merged, these sources provide extensive information on household income, demographic characteristics, housing choices, and the condition of their housing units. However, a serious problem arose because the overlap has been small between units in the longitudinal panel and units occupied by allowance program participants. In order to secure complete data on investments made to rental units occupied by allowance recipients, a supplemental survey of landlords concerning investments made in 1978 was undertaken

Table A.3

Percentage Distribution of Units at Baseline and over Time in Supply Experiment, Permanent Panel—Green Bay

Sample Stratification	Baseline Sample Completed April 1974				Second Wave Number Impaneled—December 1974				Third Wave October 1975-September 1976				Fourth Wave October 1976-September 1977			
			Households				Households				Households				Households	
	Units	Land-lords	Rent	Own	Units	Land-lords	Rent	Own	Units	Land-lords	Rent	Own	Units	Land-lords	Rent	Own
1. Urban Rental × Gross Rent × Size																
Lower Tercile:																
Single family	4.1	9.2	5.5	NA [1]	3.8	9.0	4.6	NA	3.8	8.8	4.4	NA	4.0	7.8	4.2	NA
2-4 units	11.0	14.6	14.2	NA	11.5	15.1	14.8	NA	11.3	15.4	14.9	NA	12.0	16.7	14.5	NA
5 + units	4.3	2.1	5.4	NA	4.4	2.4	5.2	NA	4.3	2.7	4.8	NA	4.1	2.2	4.5	NA
Middle Tercile:																
Single family	8.6	19.1	10.7	NA	8.4	17.3	9.7	NA	8.3	15.3	8.8	NA	7.9	15.3	7.8	NA
2-4 units	13.5	19.0	17.2	NA	14.9	19.1	19.5	NA	14.8	19.7	19.7	NA	15.7	19.7	20.1	NA
5 + units	13.6	6.1	17.9	NA	13.6	8.0	18.5	NA	14.1	8.3	18.5	NA	14.2	8.6	19.2	NA
Upper Tercile:																
Single family	3.3	7.3	4.4	NA	3.0	6.5	3.2	NA	3.1	5.6	5.6	NA	3.2	5.3	3.1	NA
2-4 units	4.0	6.0	5.2	NA	4.3	5.9	5.6	NA	4.3	6.1	5.9	NA	4.2	5.6	5.8	NA
5 + units	4.3	1.5	5.3	NA	4.3	2.1	5.6	NA	4.3	2.5	5.5	NA	4.1	2.3	5.5	NA

	1	2	3	4	5	6	7	8	9	10	11	12	13	14	15	16
2. Rural rental × Gross Rent																
Lower and middle tercile	6.5	10.9	8.3	NA	6.7	9.9	7.9	NA	6.8	9.8	7.6	NA	7.2	9.6	7.9	NA
Upper tercile	1.7	2.8	2.0	NA	1.9	2.7	2.2	NA	2.0	2.7	2.3	NA	1.9	3.1	2.2	NA
3. Urban Owner Occupied × Market Value																
Lower quartile	5.6	NA	NA	24.8	5.1	NA	NA	24.6	4.7	NA	NA	23.5	4.7	NA	NA	24.0
Second quartile	7.1	NA	NA	32.6	6.7	NA	NA	32.9	6.4	NA	NA	33.0	6.1	NA	NA	33.9
Third and fourth quartile	3.6	NA	NA	16.8	3.5	NA	NA	16.6	3.2	NA	NA	17.0	3.0	NA	NA	16.9
4. Rural Owner Occupied × Market Value																
Lower and second quartile	3.5	NA	NA	15.8	3.3	NA	NA	15.9	3.4	NA	NA	17.2	2.8	NA	NA	15.0
Third quartile	1.8	NA	NA	8.4	1.7	NA	NA	8.1	1.5	NA	NA	7.6	1.4	NA	NA	7.7
5. Other Residential Properties																
Rooming houses	2.1	1.2	2.5	NA	1.7	1.3	1.3	NA	1.8	1.3	1.4	NA	1.7	1.3	1.7	NA
Mobile home properties	1.4	0.2	1.8	1.8	1.3	0.6	1.4	1.7	1.8	0.8	1.8	1.3	2.0	0.8	2.0	1.9
Sample Size	2830	1269	2103	614	2632	1094	1883	529	2435	904	1687	460	2393	861	1685	413

Source: Proportions derived from tabulations made by Supply Experiment staff from household survey records, Site I, Waves 1 through 4. Includes only Rand sample housing units empaneled at baseline. Permanent stratum assigned to properties at baseline.

1. NA = not applicable.

Table A.4

Percentage Distribution of Units at Baseline and over Time in Supply Experiment, Permanent Panel—South Bend

Sampling Frame Stratification	Baseline Sample Completed April 1974		Households		Second Wave Number Impaneled— December 1974		Households		Third Wave October 1975- September 1976		Households		Fourth Wave October 1976- September 1977		Households	
	Units	Land-lords	Rent	Own	Units	Land-lords	Rent	Own	Units	Land-lords	Rent	Own	Units	Land-lords	Rent	Own
1. Urban Rental × Gross Rent × Size																
Lower Tercile:																
Single family	3.4	7.9	4.2	NA[1]	3.6	8.1	4.1	NA	3.2	7.8	3.8	NA	3.3	7.5	3.5	NA
2-4 units	14.2	15.0	17.9	NA	12.6	15.6	14.8	NA	13.9	16.3	17.0	NA	12.8	16.4	14.6	NA
5 + units	8.5	3.8	11.8	NA	9.3	3.2	11.4	NA	9.6	3.8	11.2	NA	9.7	3.2	12.0	NA
Middle Tercile:																
Single family	9.3	20.9	12.8	NA	9.1	21.1	11.1	NA	9.2	19.8	10.2	NA	8.7	19.1	9.5	NA
2-4 units	13.5	16.0	17.1	NA	13.8	16.0	15.7	NA	12.8	17.0	15.6	NA	13.2	16.2	16.3	NA
5 + units	4.7	2.4	6.1	NA	6.5	2.2	8.6	NA	6.2	2.4	8.1	NA	6.2	2.4	8.2	NA
Upper Tercile:																
Single family	7.3	12.5	10.5	NA	6.2	12.8	7.6	NA	5.6	11.1	6.6	NA	5.5	11.2	5.7	NA
2-4 units	3.5	4.6	3.9	NA	3.7	3.9	4.4	NA	3.7	4.3	4.6	NA	3.5	4.5	4.5	NA
5 + units	4.0	1.7	4.8	NA	6.0	2.1	8.6	NA	5.9	1.9	8.1	NA	6.8	1.7	9.5	NA

2. Rural Rental × Gross Rent																
Lower and middle tercile	4.5	9.7	6.1	NA	4.7	9.7	5.7	NA	5.3	8.8	5.8	NA	5.5	9.2	6.4	NA
Upper tercile	1.4	4.3	2.2	NA	1.9	3.5	2.1	NA	1.9	4.3	2.4	N.A	1.9	4.5	2.0	NA
3. Urban Owned Occupied × Market Value																
Lower quartile	6.6	NA	27.0		5.7	NA	28.3		5.5	NA	27.7		5.3	NA	27.2	
Second quartile	7.7	NA	31.6		6.5	NA	31.9		6.3	NA	33.1		6.4	NA	33.0	
Third and fourth quartile	3.4	NA	15.0		2.7	NA	14.3		2.4	NA	13.5		2.4	NA	13.5	
4. Rural Owner Occupied × Market Value																
Lower and second quartile	3.7	NA	15.4		3.0	NA	15.5		2.9	NA	16.4		3.0	NA	17.0	
Third quartile	2.5	NA	10.6		1.8	NA	10.1		1.6	NA	9.1		1.6	NA	9.1	
5. Other Residential Properties																
Rooming houses	0.3	0.1	0.2	NA	0.0	0.1	0.2	NA	0.2	0.1	1.0	NA	0.1	0.1	1.2	NA
Mobile home properties	1.5	0.8	2.1	0.4	2.9	0.9	3.6	0.0	3.7	0.6	3.8	0.2	3.9	1.3	4.6	0.3
Sample Size	2423	1404	1511	545	2369	914	1508	407	2489	927	1510	408	2412	823	1446	394

Source: Proportions derived from tabulations made by Supply Experiment staff from household survey records, Site II, Waves 1 though 4. Includes only Rand sample housing units empaneled at baseline. Permanent stratum assigned to properties at baseline.

1. NA = not applicable.

to complement repair information gathered from tenants. (Homeowner recipients report for themselves.) Because the household data comes from agency operating records, they cover only households who enroll in the allowance program; no comparable information is generally available on households who did not enroll in the program.

To overcome this lack of data on nonparticipating households, two steps were taken. First, at the outset of the experiment a "comparability sample" of households to be followed longitudinally at both sites was drawn. These data were to be used by The Urban Institute in performing some analyses similar to those ongoing in the Demand Experiment. (To date little use has been made of these data.) Second, in 1978 the Supply Experiment commissioned a special study of nonparticipating households in the experimental communities. These were households who had at some point enrolled in the program but for some reason left the program before beginning to receive payments.

Other Information Sources

Structured surveys were also conducted by research staff on two parts of the housing supplier community: local mortgage lending institutions and property insurance companies.

Rand also maintained research employees at each site to serve as on-site observers. Their products included detailed narrative descriptions of agency operations, as well as monitoring of press coverage of the allowance program.

THE ADMINISTRATIVE AGENCY EXPERIMENT [6]

Because agency operations were the central research interest in the Administrative Agency Experiment, the AAE collected more detailed information on agency staff, operations, and organization than did either of the other experiments. However, some information was also gathered on households and their dwellings, both through agency records and through special surveys. Figure A.3 presents a summary of data sources in the experiment.

One research technique which within EHAP was used most extensively in the AAE was that of on-site observers. These observers, members of the Abt staff with training in anthropological "participant observer" techniques, spent approximately one year in residence at each site. Their mission was to capture holistic aspects of the housing allowance experience

---

6. Further information on data gathering and analysis in the AAE can be obtained in Abt Associates, Inc. [E8, E13]; Comptroller General [E27].

Figure A.3

Data Collection in the Administrative Agency Experiment

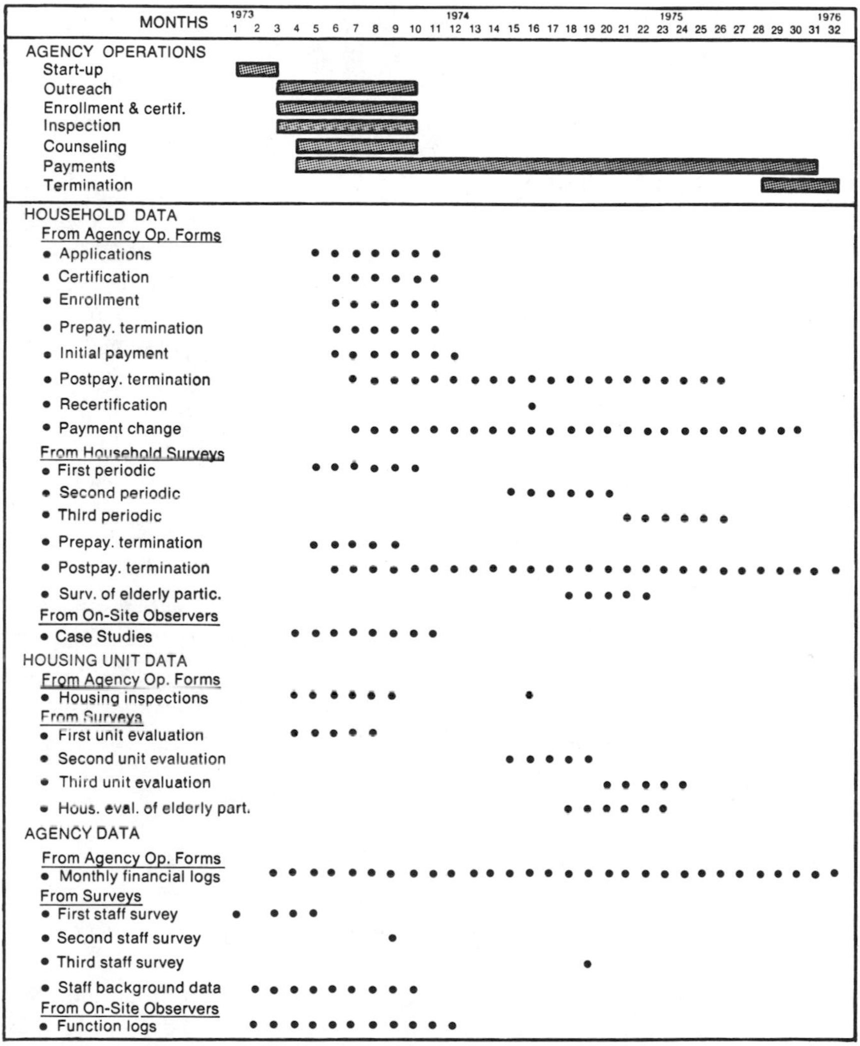

MONTHS	1973											1974												1975							1976
	1	2	3	4	5	6	7	8	9	10	11	12	13	14	15	16	17	18	19	20	21	22	23	24	25	26	27	28	29	30	31	32

AGENCY OPERATIONS
  Start-up
  Outreach
  Enrollment & certif.
  Inspection
  Counseling
  Payments
  Termination

HOUSEHOLD DATA
  From Agency Op. Forms
    • Applications
    • Certification
    • Enrollment
    • Prepay. termination
    • Initial payment
    • Postpay. termination
    • Recertification
    • Payment change
  From Household Surveys
    • First periodic
    • Second periodic
    • Third periodic
    • Prepay. termination
    • Postpay. termination
    • Surv. of elderly partic.
  From On-Site Observers
    • Case Studies

HOUSING UNIT DATA
  From Agency Op. Forms
    • Housing inspections
  From Surveys
    • First unit evaluation
    • Second unit evaluation
    • Third unit evaluation
    • Hous. eval. of elderly part.

AGENCY DATA
  From Agency Op. Forms
    • Monthly financial logs
  From Surveys
    • First staff survey
    • Second staff survey
    • Third staff survey
    • Staff background data
  From On-Site Observers
    • Function logs

Sources: Abt [E10]; Temple et al. [E150]; Benson and Kelly [E20]; Salem Housing Authority [E141].

which might be lost in the more formal statistical analyses which were the main methodology applied in all three experiments.[7] One major responsibility of these researchers was to write narrative descriptions and day-to-day "function logs" of program operations at the agency office. Another was to select several enrollee households as "case studies" and to follow their reactions to allowances over time through in-depth, unstructured interviews.[8] A third responsibility was to track general events in the communities in which allowances were operating.

Data on Agency Operations

Each of the eight operating agencies was required to submit monthly financial reporting forms to Abt Associates, detailing actual monthly administrative costs, estimated upcoming monthly costs, and actual contributed services and materials costs. These reporting forms were designed by Abt Associates to minimize the amount of additional reporting burdens on the agencies by incorporating the same cost categories required in other HUD reporting forms. In addition, agencies were required to submit monthly time reports which detailed the number of man-hours expended by staff members on each program function.

Abt also collected attitudinal and demographic data from staff members. Demographic data were collected at the beginning of the experiment from staff background forms. Attitudinal surveys were self-administered. Staff were asked to describe their jobs within the agency, to evaluate specific program functions and procedures, to describe staffing networks, and to characterize the attitudes toward program recipients held by themselves and their coworkers.

Data on Households and Their Dwelling Units

While households and their housing were not the central focus of the AAE, some data were nevertheless collected on them. As in the other two experiments, the twin sources of these data were agency operating records and special research surveys.

Eight agency operating forms were used to gather information about households. The application, certification, enrollment, and recertification forms contained demographic and occupancy data required to verify household eligibility for participation in the program. Initial payment and pay-

---

7. The on-site observer at the Bismarck AAE site reported his experiences in a book; see Trend [E152].

8. Appendix D to this book presents edited versions of four household narratives written by these observers.

ment change forms documented the amount of subsidy payments given a particular household and the type of unit occupied. Pre- and postpayment termination forms monitored household reasons for leaving the program prior to its completion.

Housing units were inspected at least twice during the program: at enrollment and during the recertification process. If a household moved after joining the program, the new unit also received an inspection. However, as chapter 3 describes, each of the eight agencies in the AAE selected both its own standards of housing quality and its own inspection methods. Therefore, the outcomes of these inspections are not strictly comparable across sites.

To supplement agency operations data in a standardized procedure across sites, Abt Associates conducted a number of structured surveys of households participating in the allowance program. Households were surveyed three times: at enrollment, about 6 months after enrollment, and finally about 16 months after enrollment. Additionally, for households leaving the program prior to its termination, exit interviews were conducted to assess the reasons for departure.

One group of households of special interest in the AAE were elderly households; a special survey of the elderly and special evaluation of their housing were conducted at all sites.[9]

Finally, we turn to the question of the representativeness of the households involved in the AAE compared with the population of eligible households. A goal from the outset of the experiment was to achieve a reasonable match between program applicants and the eligible population, and outreach efforts were designed with this objective in mind.[10] The data in table A.5 show the extent to which the goal was achieved across all eight sites combined. Several disparities between the two groups are recorded: the elderly and working poor are underrepresented compared to welfare recipients, and households headed by a nonminority person were underrepresented compared to those headed by a member of a minority. On the other hand, the two groups were similar in terms of the sex of the head of the household, household size, and household income.

CONCLUSIONS

Chapter 3 showed that each of the three experiments operated in significantly different ways from each other. Data collected to monitor pro-

---

9. The special report on the elderly's experience in the AAE is Wolfe et al. [C125].

10. The outreach efforts are outlined in chapter 10.

Table A.5

Representativeness of Applicants—Comparison of Selected Demographic Characteristics of the Eligible and Applicant Populations (AAE) [a]

Demographic Characteristics	Eligible Applicants	Eligible Population
Household Type		
Elderly	12%	32% [b]
Working poor	33	54 [b]
Welfare recipients	55	14 [b]
Head of House		
Male	33	45
Female	67	55
Minority Status of Household Head		
Minority	38	25 [b]
Nonminority	62	75 [b]
Income		
$0-1,999	24	33
$2,000-3,999	44	38
$4,000-5,999	24	24
$6,000+	8	5
Household Size		
1	16	23
2	25	29
3-4	36	30
5+	22	18
Number of cases	14,404	81,743

Source: Macmillan and Hamilton et al. [C63], table A3-1.
   a. Percentages may not add to 100 due to rounding.
   b. Proportions differ significantly between applicants and the eligible population at 5 percent level or greater.

gram operations and their outcomes, as described in this appendix, were collected in quite different ways as well. These differences both in program operations and data gathering procedures were motivated by differences in the research goals of the three experiments, and they were functional in promoting those goals. Nevertheless, awareness of these differences should caution the reader in comparing specific findings from the three experiments. Even apparently comparable numbers (e.g., "participation rates") reflect different situations and are measured in different ways. Therefore, what should be expected from the three experiments are consistent general findings but not identical, detailed numbers.

The Representativeness of EHAP Sites

Many of the conclusions in this report are stated in universal terms—that housing allowances do this or that, regardless of context. But recent housing research has clarified the diversity of housing market conditions from place to place in the nation and the strong influence which market conditions exercise on the effects of housing programs.[1] To what extent can EHAP results—based on 12 particular cities in the three experiments—support generalizations applicable to the nation as a whole?

This appendix discusses two topics relevant to assessing the degree to which EHAP findings can be generalized to other settings. The criteria and process used in selecting EHAP sites are discussed first. A discussion follows of how well these sites represent the housing market situation of the nation. The appendix concludes that while the 12 sites are not representative of the nation as a whole in a strict statistical sense, they do collectively represent a wide range of the circumstances in which housing allowances might have to operate. The only important exception is that the sites are predominantly middle-size cities and offer little opportunity to observe housing allowances in operation in either rural areas or in the nation's largest cities.

THE SITE SELECTION PROCESS [2]

Sites that offered widely varying circumstances on factors thought to have strong effects on housing allowance program outcomes were chosen for the experiments. Because the outcomes to be observed differed among the three experiments, the factors used in site selection also varied.

---

1. See Struyk [P77].
2. For further details concerning the site selection process, including references to documents from each experiment component, see Goedert [E49].

329

Demand Experiment

Because the primary focus of the Demand Experiment was the behavior of households, Demand Experiment sites were selected to meet criteria concerning population and market conditions considered to have the greatest influence on household responses. Standard Metropolitan Statistical Areas (SMSAs) were used in the selection process.

Certain types of SMSAs were excluded; for example, SMSAs with populations under 500,000 were eliminated because in small markets the additional demand for housing by allowance recipients might affect the cost of housing and thereby confound observation of household responses. SMSAs overlapping more than one state were excluded because of the administrative problems they would present. SMSAs lacking federal housing programs (recently completed public housing, Section 23 leased housing, and Section 236 projects) were excluded because part of the analysis proposed for the Demand Experiment involved comparing housing allowances with these programs. Finally, SMSAs with another major federal demonstration project or social experiment were eliminated because of potential interference between the studies.

After excluding these SMSAs, 31 potential sites remained. These sites were then examined to identify two sites with sufficient vacancies to insure that no inflationary impacts would be engendered by the experiment and which offered contrasting values on several key parameters. The most important of these parameters, and the corresponding values for the selected sites, Phoenix and Pittsburgh, are presented in table B.1. Phoenix represents a typical "new" Western city with rapid growth and a substantial Hispanic population. In contrast, Pittsburgh is a larger, older Northeastern city with a declining population and a substantial black community.

Supply Experiment

SMSAs were used as the unit of analysis in selecting the two Supply Experiment sites, and candidate SMSAs were eliminated in a multistage screening process.

The first stage examined two variables—the growth rate of the central city between 1960 and 1970 (an indicator of housing market conditions) and the percentage of blacks in the central city population (a factor viewed by the designers of the Supply Experiment as the most powerful sociocultural distinction in U.S. housing markets). This stage eliminated all SMSAs except those that were either "slow-growth, high percentage black" or "fast-growth, low percentage black," as judged by comparison of each site

Table B.1

Major Criteria Used in Selecting Demand Experiment Sites and Corresponding Values for Phoenix and Pittsburgh

Selection Criteria	Indicator	Phoenix SMSA	Pittsburgh SMSA
Sufficient vacancy rates to avoid inflationary impact	Rental vacancy rate in 1970	7.2 percent [c]	5.8 percent [b]
Contrasting population size	Population in 1970	967,522 [b]	2,401,245 [c]
Contrasting growth rate	Percentage change in population change in 1960 and 1970	45.8 percent [c]	−0.2 percent [a]
Contrasting locations	Census region	West	Northeast
Contrasting ethnic composition with sufficient minority population	Percentage of population minority 1970	17.9 percent [b] primarily Spanish-American	7.1 percent [a] black
Contrasting cost of housing	Median monthly gross rent	$121 [c]	$96 [a]

Source: Goedert [E49], p. 12; U.S. Bureau of the Census, [C111], pp. 548-579; U.S. Bureau of the Census [C113], vol. 1, pp. 333-353.

a. This value ranks in the lower third of the distribution of values for all SMSAs with populations over 500,000.
b. This value ranks in the middle third of the distribution of values for all SMSAs with populations over 500,000.
c. This value ranks in the upper third of the distribution of values for all SMSAs with populations over 500,000.

to the median values of these variables for the 231 SMSAs under consideration.

In the second stage, sites with any of several undesirable characteristics were eliminated. Potential sites were limited to those with populations
under 250,000 because of the cost of conducting an open-enrollment allowance program in a larger SMSA. On the other hand, SMSAs with populations under 100,000 were excluded because these sites would not be large
enough to permit analysis of submarkets. SMSAs with central cities whose
growth between 1960 and 1970 was attributed primarily to annexation
were excluded because increases in land area would not have the same
effect on the demand for housing as would increases due to in-migration
or births. SMSAs with interstate housing markets or without local housing
authorities[3] were eliminated because of administrative problems in operating an experiment under those conditions. This process reduced this set of
candidate metropolitan areas to 23.

For these candidate sites, a "suitability score" was computed based on
four central city characteristics: population growth rate, percentage black
population, percentage rental units in the housing stock, and rental vacancy
rate. Mean values were calculated separately for the set of 63 slow-growth,
high percentage black SMSAs and for the set of 64 fast-growth, low percentage black SMSAs. Each of the 23 SMSAs was given a score based on
how well its central city represented the typical (as described by the
mean) situation in its SMSA type.

Of the 23 SMSAs which reached the stage of having a suitability score
computed, 17 were subsequently eliminated for a variety of reasons such
as a shortage of suitable housing units, an inadequate local housing authority, or a large university or military population. Following extensive evaluation of the final list of six sites, Green Bay, Wisconsin was proposed as
the fast-growth, low percentage black site, and Saginaw, Michigan was
proposed as the slow-growth, high percentage black site.

While all local governments at the Green Bay site readily agreed to
participate in the program, serious delay occurred in negotiations with
some local jurisdictions surrounding the city of Saginaw. This delay was
due principally to fear on the part of local officials that the program would
promote black and other minority movement from the central city into
their primarily white suburban jurisdictions.[4] Therefore, the site selection
process was reopened to find an alternative slow-growth, high percentage

---

3. Since the Supply Experiment utilized Section 23 funds, all monies were chan-
neled through the local housing authority. Although the AAE also was funded through
Section 23, HUD contracted directly with the eight administrating agencies.

4. See Lowry and Repnau [E96].

black SMSA. To enlarge the field of possible sites, the maximum population criterion was increased from 250,000 to 350,000, and after further evaluation, South Bend, Indiana was selected. South Bend fulfilled all criteria used in the initial selection process, although compared to the original list of sites that reached the final screening, it had a relatively low suitability score.[5] Table B.2 shows the values of Green Bay and South Bend for the two primary criteria evaluated in selecting the Supply Experiment sites and for the other variables that formed the basis for the suitability scores.

While the two cities differ substantially in growth rate and presence of minorities, they share in common that they are in the upper Midwest region and that they are cities with extensive single-family owner-occupancy such as is more typical of small cities than of the central cities of the nation's major urban areas.

Administrative Agency Experiment

Since the AAE was designed primarily to provide information on different approaches to administering a housing allowance program, major emphasis in selecting the eight AAE sites was on agency characteristics. Four types of agencies were sought: local housing authorities, metropolitan area or county government agencies, state community development agencies, and county or state welfare agencies.

The selection process in the AAE was less structured than was the process for the other two experiments and relied as much on judgment and site visits as on quantitative indicators such as Census data. Each agency had to have a jurisdiction sufficiently large to encompass a local housing market. Other criteria included the interest of the agency and of local government bodies in participating in the program, the agency's demonstrated ability to operate housing programs, and an assessment of the overall feasibility of operating the AAE in the site. It was also considered important to provide a diverse group of sites. Geographical dispersion of sites across the nation was desired, as well as variation in total population size and in population and housing market characteristics such as racial composition, degree of urbanization, and the average quality of the housing stock. While variation in vacancy rates was also sought, sites with extremely high or low vacancy rates were considered less desirable.

---

5. Compared to the slow-growth, high percentage black SMSAs that reached the original final screening, South Bend had the second smallest percentage black and the smallest percentage of rental units in 1970. South Bend's growth rate and rental vacancy rate, however, fell within desirable limits.

Table B.2

Major Criteria Used in Selecting Supply Experiment Sites and Corresponding Values for Green Bay, South Bend, and All SMSAs

Criteria	Green Bay	Mean [a] of High-Growth, Low Percentage Black SMSAs	South Bend	Mean [a] of Low-Growth, High Percentage Black SMSAs	Median of All SMSAs
Population growth rate of central city, 1960-1970	39.6	31.2	—5.2	—6.0	6.9
Percentage black of central city population, 1970	0.1	5.2	14.1	32.6	10.8
Rental housing as a percentage of all year-around units in central city, 1970	33.9	41.2	27.5	53.3	42.0
Rental vacancy rate in central city, 1970	4.3	7.1	8.2	6.4	7.2

Source: Goedert [E49]; U.S. Bureau of the Census [C111].
a. Weighted by population.

Table B.3 presents information on the location and setting for each of the eight AAE sites.

WHAT DO THESE SITES REPRESENT?

As illustrated in the previous section, neither the sites within any of the three experiments nor the site of all three experiments combined were chosen as representative of the population of U.S. housing markets. Similarly, as chapter 3 indicates, individual households chosen for the allowance program within sites were not selected to generate a representative sample of the population of low-income U.S. households. Furthermore, even though 12 sites are large in a social experiment, that number is still small compared to the total number of U.S. housing markets. Therefore, there is no straightforward statistical basis for assessing the applicability of EHAP findings to other settings.[6]

Although the representativeness of the sites cannot be determined in a strict statistical sense, the 12 EHAP sites considered together do represent a wide variety of settings. The sites were scattered over nearly the entire country. Both declining older cities and dynamic young cities are included. EHAP was conducted in areas with high minority concentrations and segregated housing patterns as well as in areas with virtually no minorities. The sites include cities with both tight and loose housing markets, and the sites offer an opportunity to observe the effects of a housing allowance program in a wide variety of circumstances favorable and unfavorable to the effectiveness of allowance programs.

The sites, however, offer only limited variation on one potentially important influence on responses to a housing allowance program: population. Several of the EHAP sites encompass some peripheral rural territory, and the Bismarck, North Dakota AAE site encompasses substantial rural areas. Otherwise, EHAP is an "urban" experiment and offers little direct information on the effects of a housing allowance program in small towns and rural areas. Similarly, the sites cannot be said to represent directly the very largest urban areas of the country. Pittsburgh, the largest EHAP city, had an SMSA population in 1970 of 2.4 million and ranked eleventh in size among U.S. urbanized areas. However, in the Supply Experiment, where marketwide effects are the central issue, both sites are medium-sized cities in the same region of the country, and the larger site, South Bend, ranked only 120th in size among the nation's SMSA's in 1970. We have no direct evidence that EHAP findings, particularly those concerning mar-

---

6. For a more detailed discussion of the generalizability of EHAP findings, see Goedert [E49].

Table B.3

Selected Characteristics of Administrative Agency Experiment Sites

Site	Census Division	Population of Program Area	Area Description	Percentage of Families in Poverty (Census definition)	Percentage of Population Which is Minority	Percentage of Housing Stock Which is Rental	Percentage of Housing Stock Lacking Complete Plumbing	Rental Vacancy Rate (percentage)
Bismarck, North Dakota	West North Central	104,187	Small cities and towns with surrounding areas	11.8%	.8%	31.4%	5.9%	8.1%
Durham, North Carolina	South Atlantic	132,681	Medium-sized city with adjacent rural areas	14.0	37.6	53.0	2.9	6.0
Jacksonville, Florida	South Atlantic	545,900	Large metropolitan area	14.0	22.9	32.7	4.4	4.0
Peoria, Illinois	East North Central	196,865	Medium-sized city with nearby rural areas	5.9	6.3	30.9	3.0	4.5

Salem, Oregon	Pacific	186,658	Medium-sized city with adjacent growth area	7.9	1.7	37.3	1.5	7.2
San Bernardino, California	Pacific	547,258	Area of multiple medium-sized cities	9.8	23.0	36.4	.9	12.0
Springfield, Massachusetts	New England	472,917	Area of multiple medium-sized cities and towns	6.6	5.0	41.5	2.7	6.2
Tulsa, Oklahoma	West South Central	324,000	Large metropolitan area	9.0	12.5	33.0	1.9	13.6

Source: Adapted from Abt Associates, Inc. [E14].

ket reactions to an allowance program, would be repeated in large, decaying urban centers such as Detroit or Newark, which are the focus of much public policy concern.[7]

Thus, while the EHAP sites represent many types of urban areas, they offer findings for very large metropolitan areas only by extrapolation. In 1970, approximately 45 percent of the U.S. population residing in the urbanized portions of metropolitan areas lived in urbanized areas in the size range covered by the 11 largest EHAP sites (excluding Bismarck); only 5 percent of this population lived in urbanized areas smaller in population than Durham, the smallest of these 11 sites, with a population of about 100,000. Hence, about half of the population residing in urbanized areas lived in those larger than Pittsburgh.

Rural areas were covered only by Bismarck in the AAE and by the inclusion of the nonurbanized portions of some metropolitan areas in all of the experiments. The extent of coverage here is unclear. About one third of the rural population lives within metropolitan areas, but no analysis has been done of the extent to which households within SMSA rural areas included in the experiments are similar to all such households. Furthermore, the Bismarck site alone clearly provides only minimal representation of the rich variation in rural housing markets.[8]

Finally, the strict site representativeness question must ultimately be considered in light of the extent of the sensitivity of the results of the experiments to market conditions, including size. The less sensitive the results, the less emphasis need be placed on this question. As shown in chapters 4 through 10, the principal findings are remarkable robust.

---

7. As noted in chapter 2, EHAP's lack of direct observation of market effects in a major urban area was criticized by the U.S. General Accounting Office; see Comptroller General [E27].

8. See Drury et al. [P18].

Housing Quality Standards in the Experiments

This appendix describes the physical housing standards and occupancy requirements imposed in the three EHAP experiments as a condition for receiving allowance benefits.[1] It discusses the development of these standards and compares them across experiments. It also analyzes the stringency of EHAP's standards compared to housing quality requirements in other programs. The primary conclusions are that Demand Experiment standards are significantly more stringent than those applied in the Supply Experiment. However, no firm conclusions can be stated about the relative stringency of those two experiments' requirements in comparison to either the standards in the Administrative Agency Experiment or those in model housing codes, existing local codes, or ongoing federal housing programs.

PHYSICAL HOUSING STANDARDS

Demand Experiment

The Recommended Housing Maintenance and Occupancy Ordinance of the American Public Health Association (APHA), as revised in 1971, and The Urban Institute's modifications of it, served as the basic model for physical housing standards in the Demand Experiment.[2] The experiment's standards are identical to APHA's in some cases; for instance, they both specify that for a room to have adequate light, the window area must

---

1. As chapter 3 discussed, every household in the Supply Experiment and the Administrative Agency Experiment had to meet minimum housing requirements as a condition for receiving allowance benefits. In the Demand Experiment, only households in the housing gap-minimum standards treatment cells were subject to such requirements.

2. See American Public Health Association [C3] and Sherer et al. [E147].

equal at least 10 percent of the floor area. Other standards are modifications of the APHA requirements. For example, the APHA code requires inspection of how well plumbing facilities are installed, while the Demand Experiment's less stringent standards rate only the presence and working condition of plumbing.

The Demand Experiment's physical housing requirements involve the following components.

1. *Core rooms.* A living room, bathroom, and kitchen must be present.

2. *Bathroom facilities.* Private toilet facilities, a shower or tub with hot and cold running water, and a washbasin with hot and cold running water must be present and in working condition.

3. *Kitchen facilities.* A cooking stove or range, a refrigerator, and a kitchen sink with hot and cold running water must be present and in working condition.

4. *Light Fixtures and Outlets.* A ceiling or wall-type fixture must be present and working in the bathroom and kitchen. At least one electric outlet must be present and operable in the living room and kitchen. A working wall switch, pull-chain light switch, or additional electrical outlet must be present in the living room.

5. *Fire exits.* In buildings with three or more units, at least two exits from the dwelling unit must lead to safe and open space at ground level.[3]

6. *Heating equipment.* Adequate heating must be present. Unvented room heaters which burn gas, oil, or kerosene or heat provided mainly with portable electric room heaters are unacceptable.

7. *Room structure and surface.* In any room, ceiling or wall structure or surfaces which require replacement (such as those with severe bulging or leaning) are unacceptable.

8. *Floor structure and surface.* For all rooms, floor structure and surfaces requiring replacement (such as those with large holes or missing parts) are unacceptable.

9. *Roof structure.* Infirm roof structure is unacceptable (applied only to sections of the roof which are visible).

10. *Exterior walls.* Exterior wall structure or exterior wall surfaces needing replacement are unacceptable.

---

3. This requirement was modified in November 1973 to accept units judged safe even though they lacked a second exit. First-floor units then failed this requirement only if all their windows were barred or permanently shut, and upper floor units with one exit were acceptable if located in "fire-proof" buildings.

11. *Ceiling height.* For living room, bathroom, and kitchen, the ceiling must be seven feet or higher in at least one half the room area.

12. *Light and ventilation.* The unit must have a 10 percent ratio of window area to floor and at least one openable window in the living room, bathroom, and kitchen. If kitchen or bathroom has an adequate mechanical ventilation system in working condition, the requirement is met for that room.

Supply Experiment

The housing requirements of the Supply Experiment were developed after the Demand Experiment standards and relied heavily on a different national model code, the Building Officials of America Code (BOAC). Some emphasis was also placed on compatibility with the local housing codes in Supply Experiment sites, but only minor attention was given to consistency with the standards used in the Demand Experiment.

The components of the Supply Experiment standard are as follows: [4]

1. *Sanitation and Storage.* Heavy accumulations of litter or other debris in interior or exterior are unacceptable.

2. *Grading and Drainage.* Seepage into building or standing water is unacceptable.

3. *Trees and Plants.* Noxious plants or overgrowth causing blockage of natural light or normal access are unacceptable.

4. *Fences and Accessory Structures.* Severe structural defects around areas of normal human activity are unacceptable.

5. *Foundation.* Severe structural defects or penetrability by water are unacceptable.

6. *Stairs, Porches, and Railings.* Severe structural defects, broken and missing steps, or absence of a handrail for six or more consecutive steps, either interior or exterior, are unacceptable.

7. *Exterior walls.* Severe buckling, major holes or missing sections, or persistent moisture, dry rot, or insect damage are unacceptable.

8. *Roofs.* Sagging, buckling, or major holes or missing sections are unacceptable.

9. *Window Conditions.* Missing or broken panes or heavily rotted or damaged sashes are unacceptable.

10. *Doors and Hatchways.* Missing or broken doors between the exterior and the interior are unacceptable.

---

4. See Lowry [E99], pp. 13-16.

11. *Exits.* One exit from the unit and at least two safe exits from the building to the exterior are required.

12. *Room structure and surface.* Severe buckling, major holes or missing sections, or evidence of persistent moisture, dry rot, or insect damage in ceilings, floors, or walls are unacceptable.

13. *Floor structure and surface.* Severe buckling, noticeable movement under stress, major holes or missing sections, or evidence of persistent moisture, dry rot, or insect damage are unacceptable.

14. *Bathroom facilities.* A working flush toilet, a shower or tub with hot and cold running water, and a washbasin with hot and cold running water must be present and in working condition. Severely damaged fixtures or major leaks are unacceptable. The bathroom must have a permanent source of heat. The toilet and the bathtub or shower must have some form of enclosure to insure privacy.

15. *Kitchen facilities.* A cooking range with at least one burner and oven, a refrigerator, and a sink with hot and cold running water must be present and in working condition. Severely damaged facilities are unacceptable.

16. *Light fixtures and outlets.* The kitchen must have two properly installed electrical outlets or one outlet and a ceiling or wall light fixture with a switching device. The bathroom must have one outlet or a ceiling or wall fixture.

17. *Water Heater.* A functioning water heater and adequate hot water must be present. For the water heater, the following are unacceptable: gas leakage, danger of flooding, breaks or damage, a vent pipe seriously cracked or broken, improper venting for exhaust gases, or lack of a temperature and pressure valve.

18. *Plumbing System.* A plumbing system must be present and free of any condition in which clean water and waste are not distributed effectively between all fixtures in the unit to a public system or other disposal mechanism. Major cracks or broken pipes, improperly sealed joints, and deficiencies causing leakage are unacceptable.

19. *Heating System.* An acceptable primary source of heat must be present and free of any breakage or damage to the source of heat, ducts, or fixtures. A vent pipe seriously cracked or broken and unvented room heaters that burn gas, oil, or other flammable liquids are unacceptable.

20. *Electrical System.* An electrical system must be present and free of exposed, noninsulated, or frayed wires; improper connections, insulation, or grounding for any component of the system; overloading of capacity; and wires in or near standing water or other unsafe places.

21. *Ceiling Height.* The ceiling of the room in which the kitchen facilities are located must be at least 6'6" high over at least 35 square feet of room area.

22. *Light.* Sufficient light is required in the kitchen, either from natural or artificial sources, to permit normal domestic activities.

23. *Ventilation.* At least one openable window or other device that provides ventilation is required for the kitchen and the bathroom.

24. *Lead-Based Paint Hazards.*[5] Cracking, scaling, chipping, peeling, or loose paint on interior and exterior surfaces which possibly contain dangerous lead content are unacceptable if children under seven years of age reside in or frequently visit the dwelling.

Administrative Agency Experiment

In the Administrative Agency Experiment, responsibility for developing housing standards was delegated to the existing public agency which operated the program at each of the eight sites. The only provision was that standards be broadly consistent with those of the Section 23 rental assistance payments program whose funds financed payments to households.[6] The agencies relied heavily on codes already applied to housing in their areas, but only the Jacksonville agency adopted its city code in its entirety. As a result of this procedure, the checklists or inspection guidelines for the AAE varied considerably in length and detail, as well as in the level of quality specified as minimally acceptable.

Table C.1 indicates the topics covered by standards at each site, as well as the areas covered in the Section 23 program guidance. Coverage of a topic did not necessarily imply that a specific requirement was imposed or that a specific requirement stated in the written standard was actually enforced by the AAE agency. The list simply indicates the various items which were addressed in standards developed by local agencies under only broad federal guidelines.[7]

In their standards, all eight agencies included items about the structure of the building exterior and roof, interior walls, and floor or ceilings. All lists had items about the presence of an adequate kitchen, bathroom, and heating facilities, running water, bathroom ventilation, and electrical fixtures. A prohibition against lead paint, on the other hand, was specified in only four of the eight sites, and a private bathroom was required by only five agencies.

---

5. This requirement was imposed starting in January 1977.

6. See Abt Associates, Inc. [E5], pp. 4-95.

7. For a complete set of the agencies' inspection forms, see Budding et al. [C11].

Table C.1

Topics Addressed in Physical Housing Standards Developed by Agencies in the Administrative Agency Experiment

Item	Bis-marck	Durham	Jackson-ville	Peoria	Salem	San Bernar-dino	Spring-field	Tulsa	Section 23 Circular
Site									
Condition of yard		X	X		X			X	
Condition of streets, sidewalks		X			X				
Condition of driveway		X							
Parking space available		X							
Condition of outbuildings		X	X						
Neighborhood quality		X						X	
Access to public facilities		X							
Fences		X						X	
Proper drainage		X	X	X			X	X	

	C1	C2	C3	C4	C5	C6	C7	C8	C9
Exterior									
Generally structurally sound		X	X	X	X	X	X	X	X
Foundation	X	X	X	X	X	X	X	X	X
Exterior wall surfaces		X		X		X	X	X	X
—weather proofed		X		X		X	X	X	X
Roof structure		X	X	X	X	X	X	X	X
Roof surface		X	X	X	X	X	X	X	
Eaves and cornices					X		X		
Gutters								X	
Porches structurally sound		X	X			X	X	X	
Exterior steps		X	X			X	X	X	
Porch railing		X	X		X	X	X	X	
Handrails		X	X		X		X	X	
Chimney and flues	X			X					
Interior (structure and surfaces)									
Walls		X	X	X	X	X	X	X	X
Floors		X	X	X		X	X	X	X
Ceilings		X	X		X	X	X	X	X
Lead paint prohibited	X	X	X			X			
Walls afford privacy		X	X						
Interior stairs		X	X				X		
Handrails							X		

Table C.1—Continued

Topics Addressed in Physical Housing Standards Developed by Agencies in the Administrative Agency Experiment

Item	Bismarck	Durham	Jacksonville	Peoria	Salem	San Bernardino	Springfield	Tulsa	Section 23 Circular
Windows and Doors									
Private access and egress				X				X	X
Locking exterior doors				X				X	X
Doors sound, weathertight		X	X	X		X	X	X	•
Screen doors		X	X	X			X	X	
Windows, good condition		X	X	X		X	X	X	
Window screens		X	X	X		X		X	
Kitchen—Adequate									
Presence	X	X	X	X	X	X	X	X	X
Cold pressurized water	X	X	X	X	X	X	X	X	X
Hot pressurized water	X	X	X	X	X	X	X	X	
Sink	X	X	X	X	X	X	X	X	
—drain	X	X	X	X	X	X	X	X	
Stove and/or hook-up		X	X			X	X	X	X
Refrigerator and/or hook-up	X	X		X				X	X

Storage space

Counter-top

—nonporous surface

Floors of nonporous
material

Bathroom—Adequate

Presence

Private

Flush toilet

—adequate water

—connected to sewer

Sink

—cold pressurized water

—hot pressurized water

—drain

Nonporous walls

Nonporous floors

Plumbing—General

Hot water heater—present

Public or private water
supply

Sewer or septic tank

Table C.1—Continued

Topics Addressed in Physical Housing Standards Developed by Agencies in the Administrative Agency Experiment

Item	Bis-marck	Durham	Jackson-ville	Peoria	Salem	San Bernar-dino	Spring-field	Tulsa	Section 23 Circular
Plumbing—General, continued									
Hot water heater vented		X	X			X	X		
—pressure relief valve		X						X	
Plumbing fixtures properly installed		X			X	X	X	X	
Water pipes properly installed		X						X	
Waste pipes properly installed		X						X	
Heating									
Adequate central heat or spaceheaters	X	X	X	X	X	X	X	X	X
Space heaters properly vented	X			X	X	X	X	X	
Oil properly stored	X	X							

	1	2	3	4	5	6	7	8	9
Electrical—Adequacy									
Adequate service		X	X	X		X			X
Outlet and fixtures—									
all rooms		X							
Fixtures—bathroom		X	X	X	X	X	X	X	
—kitchen		X	X		X	X	X	X	
—laundry room			X	X	X		X	X	
—furnace room				X		X	X	X	
—public halls			X	X	X	X			
Wall switches		X						X	
No temporary wires		X		X	X				
No bare or exposed wires		X					X	X	
Outlet for air conditioning						X			X
Ventilation									
Windows = 10% of floor area	X	X	X	X	X	X	X	X	
Openable windows in habitable rooms	X	X	X	X		X		X	
Window and/or fan—bathroom	X	X	X	X	X	X	X	X	
Window and/or fan—kitchen	X	X	X	X		X	X		

Table C.1—Continued

Topics Addressed in Physical Housing Standards Developed by Agencies in the Administrative Agency Experiment

Item	Bis-marck	Durham	Jackson-ville	Peoria	Salem	San Bernar-dino	Spring-field	Tulsa	Section 23 Circular
Basement Rooms									
Floors and walls water and damp proof									
Windows = 10% of floor area				X			X		
Openable window or fan	X			X			X		
No obstruction less than 6 above floor				X					
No more than 4' below grade				X					
Health and Safety									
No dumps or junk yards	X						X		
No insects	X						X	X	
No rodents	X			X					

Adequate rodent proofing

No trash, garbage

Adequate garbage storage

Safe storage—drugs and poisons

Two exits

Public doors open from inside

No interruption of services

Conformance with fire codes

Amenities

Laundry and/or washer-dryer

Air conditioning

Wall-to-wall carpeting

Garbage disposal

Dishwasher

Source: Budding et al. [C11], p. A-44–A48.

Between four and seven agencies specified detailed items covering such aspects as building structure, floors, doors, windows, kitchen appliances, plumbing facilities, hot water heaters, and electrical systems. Items mentioned on three or fewer checklists concerned the condition of the yard and neighborhood, gutters, interior building condition, private access, kitchen counters, pressure relief valve on hot water heaters, drainage pipes, oil storage, electrical fixtures, basement condition, presence of rats or insects, closet space, and the presence of such amenities as dishwashers or full carpeting.

As table C.1 also indicates, the checklists varied considerably in length. At some sites, related items were included in a single question, while other checklists required that the same attributes be evaluated separately. For example, the Bismarck checklist required only a summary evaluation of the entire structure of the unit, including the floors, walls, roof, and foundation. In contrast, the Springfield form had 17 different questions about the exterior and interior structure and surfaces.

The physical housing standards applied by the Administrative Agency Experiment agencies also tended to vary over time. Unlike the Demand and Supply Experiments, where research contractors paid close attention to maintaining consistency in how standards were applied, standards in the AAE tended to change through the cumulative effect of judgments and decisions made by individual agency staff members. Furthermore, in six of the eight AAE agencies, the agencies themselves made conscious policy decisions to adjust their original standards. Both the conscious decisions and the informal adjustments by staff members tended to weaken the stringency of requirements.[8]

OCCUPANCY STANDARDS

Occupancy standards are statements of the minimum size of a housing unit which is acceptable for occupancy by a household with a certain size and composition.

In the Demand Experiment, only households whose units had to pass the physical standards had to satisfy the occupancy standards. The basic standard was that there could be no more than two persons for each "adequate" bedroom in the unit. A bedroom was considered adequate if it met four physical requirements:

1. The structure and surface of walls, ceilings, and floor in the room must not need replacement.

---

8. See Budding et al. [C11], pp. A-13 to A-29.

2. The window area in the room had to equal at least 10 percent of floor area, and at least one openable window or a working air conditioner had to be present.

3. The ceiling had to be at least seven feet in height across at least one half of the room's area.

4. Two or more working electrical outlets or one outlet and one wall or pull-chain switch for overhead light had to be present and working.

Households with more than seven persons were only required to occupy units with at least four bedrooms.

The Supply Experiment also required that there be no more than two persons per bedroom, and like the Demand Experiment, each bedroom was subjected to physical standards:

1. Seventy square feet or more of floor area.

2. Ceiling height of at least 6′6″ over at least 35 square feet of floor area.

3. Natural light from at least one window facing directly outdoors or onto a well-lighted sunporch.

4. Adequate ventilation from at least one openable window or mechanical device.

5. At least one properly installed and working electric convenience outlet.

6. Adequate heat from a source other than a portable electric heater.

7. Absence of special adaptations for use as a kitchen, bathroom, or utility room.

8. Rigid walls, secured in position from floor to ceiling, including a doorway with a door, curtain, or other screening device.

Seven of the eight agencies in the Administrative Agency Experiment specified an occupancy requirement. Table C.2 lists the types of occupancy requirements used at AAE sites. As the table indicates, a variety of standards were used, including various density and space requirements. It is important to note that household size was rarely verified by agencies in the AAE,[9] so the actual impact of these requirements is unknown.

EFFECTIVE STRINGENCY OF THE STANDARDS

Thus far, this appendix has described *written* standards. To assess the effective impact of such standards on participation, however, information

9. See Dickson [C16], Appendix C.

Table C.2

Occupancy Standards Adopted by Agencies in the Administrative Agency Experiment

Occupancy Requirement	Bismarck	Durham	Jacksonville	Peoria	Salem	San Bernardino	Springfield	Tulsa
One family per unit								X
Square feet per occupant		X	X	X		X	X	X
Number of occupants per habitable room								
Adequate headroom		X		X	X			X
Adequate room size		X		X	X	X		X
Separate access to bath				X				X
—bedrooms				X	X			X
4 sq. ft. closet space/occupant					X		X	

is required on the actual implementation of the standards. Written standards and their implementation together determine how stringent these facets that should be compared. One is how the standards compare if implemented in conformance with agency guidelines. The other is the extent to which application of the standard within an agency varied from agency guidelines, that is, quality control. Clearly, if within-agency variance is great enough, the first implementation comparison will be meaningless. These two topics are discussed in the following paragraphs.

Differences among Standards in the Three Experiments

A direct test was conducted in EHAP to compare the stringency of the standards in the Demand and Supply Experiments.[10] Teams of evaluators were formed consisting of one evaluator from a Demand Experiment site and one evaluator from a Supply Experiment site. These teams then assessed a common sample of housing units in each of the four sites of the Demand and Supply Experiments, with each unit being separately evaluated by both members of the teams and each evaluator applying the standards of his experiment. Three hundred and sixty-three units from the four sites were sampled.

It was found that 75 percent of the housing units failed the Demand Experiment standards as applied by Demand Experiment inspectors, compared to 60 percent that failed Supply Experiment standards as applied by Supply Experiment staff. When physical standards were examined separately from occupancy standards, 70 percent of the units failed Demand physical standards, while 55 percent failed the Supply standards. The largest proportion of the higher failure rate under Demand standards is attributable to the Demand Experiment's more stringent requirement for light and ventilation in bathrooms and kitchens.[11] Since, as detailed next, the Demand and Supply standards were rigorously adhered to throughout these experiments, the test described is an accurate comparison of the stringency of the two standards.

Because of the diversity in standards among the eight AAE sites, it is not possible to reach similar conclusions concerning the relative standards in the Administrative Agency Experiment compared to those in the Demand Experiment and the Supply Experiment. The two separate anal-

---

10. This test is described in Valenza [E170].

11. Other major differences between the two standards involved the condition of ceilings, walls, and floors; fixtures, outlets, and switches; and stairs, porches, and railings (where the Supply Experiment set higher requirements). See Valenza [E170], pp. 24-30.

yses of the stringency of Administrative Agency Experiment standards
even failed to agree on the relative rigor of the requirements among the
eight sites.[12]

Consistency in Standards Application

Rigorous quality control on inspections was practiced in both the Demand and Supply Experiments, beginning with thorough training of inspectors and proceeding through reinspections of a sample of units. In
the Demand Experiment, biases associated with individual inspectors
were sought through an analysis of variance of deficiencies found by inspectors. Random telephone contacts were made wtih households to check
on inspectors, and a random sample of 10 percent of all units were reinspected by supervisors.

Similar procedures were followed in the Supply Experiment, where
independent evaluations by supervisory personnel were conducted on a
5 percent sample of all inspections done by the regular evaluation staffs.
An analysis comparing the results of the original and supervisors' evaluations showed that less than 2 percent of the units inspected were misclass-
ified as "passing" or "failing" the program standard as a result of inspectors' errors.[13]

The practices in the Administrative Agency Experiment are quite a
different story. The individual agencies were freer to (and did) adopt
alternative standards and alternative methods of conducting the inspections—use of trained inspectors, members of agency staff without special-
ized training, and would-be participants themselves. Indeed, one major
set of findings from the AAE concerns the reliability of different types of
inspections.[14]

Clouding the situation even further, the majority of AAE agencies
modified the standards over time. Variations in the official standards not-
withstanding, there is ample evidence of staff members simply not applying the standards as the agency intended because they viewed some
aspect of the agency-adopted standard as unfair or inappropriate.[15] Both
these factors preclude careful analysis of inspection outcomes among the
AAE sites and between the AAE and the other experiments.

---

12. See Budding et al. [C11]; Bernsten [H13]. The studies did agree, however,
that the toughest standard existed in Jacksonville, which adopted the entire local housing code.

13. For a further description, see Tebbets [C109].

14. This is discussed further in chapter 10.

15. For a summary, see Hamilton [C30], pp. 70-114.

EHAP STANDARDS COMPARED TO STANDARDS IN OTHER PROGRAMS

It would also be useful to compare the standards used in the EHAP experiments to standards set forth in model codes, those used in ongoing housing programs, and those set forth in local housing codes. When attempts have been made to compare the written contents of such diverse sets of housing standards, however, the results of such comparisons are generally inconclusive. The EHAP experience itself clearly demonstrates that the number of items in a standard, which is one common way to compare written standards, is not a good indicator of stringency; the Supply Experiment standard included more items than the Demand Experiment standard, and yet implementation of the latter resulted in a higher failure rate. The effective stringency of the Demand Experiment standard was greater because of the impact of several critical items, and this is true of other codes as well.

That is not to suggest that comparisons of written standards can produce no insights. It is clear, for example, that standards that require not only the presence of certain systems but also that these systems be in working order, are more stringent than standards requiring only their presence. For example, the most important item in the Demand Experiment standard—light and ventilation—imposes a more lenient written standard than the national code upon which it is based because it requires only that a window be openable, while the APHA code specifies a minimum openable area. Still, in the absence of an actual test, it is difficult to know whether applying the national code's requirement would have made any significant difference in failure rates.

A similar situation arises in considering the relationship between allowance programs standards and local codes. The handrail requirement in the Supply Experiment, for example, differs from the local code standard in both Supply Experiment sites. Green Bay's local housing code is silent on the issue of handrails.. South Bend's requirement is that a handrail must be present for two or more consecutive steps, a requirement which is automatically more stringent than the Supply Experiment's requirement of a handrail in cases of six or more consecutive steps. It may be, however, that this distinction has little practical effect.

A particularly helpful comparison of stringency would be one that allowed comparison of EHAP standards to HUD's Section 8 Existing housing assistance payments program. However, the Section 8 program is similar to the AAE in that local public housing agencies are given considerable flexibility in selecting and enforcing their standards, subject only to a minimum level of "performance criteria" established by HUD. Because of the diversity of standards which has arisen in reaction to this local discretion, it is not possible to draw general conclusions concerning the relative stringency of EHAP standards and Section 8 requirements.

Case Studies of
Four Households

> Invariably, the rent supplements were fitted in
> with an array of other devices that make up the
> households' survival strategies.
>
> M. G. Trend [E152], p. 275

Federal social programs arrive at the local operating agency complete with statements of legislative intent, concepts of what they are intended to accomplish, and plans concerning whom they intend to enroll. The households who are targets of the program are bound by none of these goals, however, and they may be only dimly aware of them. Rather, households view the program from their own point of view—what it offers to them and requires of them—and they fit the program into the full set of circumstances in which they live. This appendix portrays the interrelatedness of the various decisions which a household must make regarding housing allowances with illustrations of the complex working out of those decisions in the lives of four households.

These case studies are selected from among those households whose experiences were recorded in detail by on-site observers at each site of the Administrative Agency Experiment.[1] The four cases illustrate several different types of housing decisions by allowance recipients: to stay in their preexperiment unit without repairs, to move to another unit, or to stay in their preexperiment unit with repairs. They also illustrate some of the diversity of allowance recipients in terms of age, ethnic background, and family circumstances. Lastly, because the cases are drawn from four different AAE sites, they illustrate some site-to-site differences in agency operating procedures.

---

1. In each case, names and other details were altered by the observers to preserve the privacy of the families.

THE HARTWICKS [2]

Gerald and Lydia Hartwick are an elderly couple residing in Tulsa, Oklahoma. They see themselves as members of "mainstream" American society who have recently met hard times because of high medical expenses, increased food prices, and the general state of the economy. Until his retirement three years ago, Gerald Hartwick had been steadily employed all his adult life, working as a chief timekeeper and field accountant for one construction company for more than 30 years. Together, he and his wife had created an attractive, stable home environment for their two sons and had provided them with college educations. Neither he nor Mrs. Hartwick would consider applying for welfare, food stamps, or public housing. The Hartwicks had always been able to manage on their own.

When the Hartwicks read a newspaper article about the housing allowance program in early September 1973, they did not think they would qualify. But they also felt that they needed assistance. They were living on an annual income of $3,254, a combination of Social Security benefits and a small retirement fund. Gerald's mother was ill, and he had her medical expenses to pay in addition to bills for a recent hospital stay by Lydia. Insurance took care of some of the bills, but for other expenses they had to use their savings, and money in their bank account had dwindled to practically nothing.

On the first day the application center opened, Gerald drove to the housing allowance program (HAP) office, at the local housing authority. Later he remembered proudly that he was the first one to sign up for the new program; and, unlike some of the people in the office, he had no trouble filling out the application form. The Hartwicks did not expect to be selected for the program and forgot about it until they received a card in the mail which said they had been selected.

Six weeks after they applied, the Hartwicks' counselor came to their house to enroll them. After hearing about the program and their rights and responsibilites under it, they signed the forms. As they remembered it, their counselor presented the information clearly, and they had few questions. She assured them that the program was intended to respond to the financial plight of people like themselves. By participating in the experiment, they were actually helping the government, she emphasized. This was an important point to the Hartwicks. They felt they needed the assistance, but they wanted to do something in return.

After some deliberation, the Hartwicks decided to remain in the house they were already renting. Consequently, the counselor returned to their home for the counseling session and inspection. This session

---

2. The following is an edited version of Muller [C71], pp. 165-175.

was short, as the Hartwicks felt they had all the information they needed. Both Gerald and Lydia went around with the counselor as she did the inspection. The house was in excellent condition, and all that was needed was a pressure release valve on the hot water heater, which the landlord immediately agreed to install.

Gerald Hartwick made the necessary contact with the landlord concerning the lease and inspection results. He saw no reason why he should rely on the counselor to do what he could easily do alone. The Hartwicks were surprised the landlord agreed so readily to the program, but they acknowledged that they had been good tenants and the landlord probably did not want to lose them. However, the landlord insisted on using his own lease, and the Hartwicks drove to the office of the landlord's attorney to sign it. A copy was later sent to the housing allowance office, where it was approved.

In the meantime, the counselor had submitted the necessary forms to the housing authority for payments initiation. On the first day of the following month, the Hartwicks received their first allowance check for $54. Gerald had a check for their portion of the rent ready. He signed the housing allowance check (a two party check made out to him and to the landlord) and sent both checks to the landlord. He repeated this process each month. Both he and Lydia said they didn't mind the two-party check, since it did not matter to them if the landlord knew they were receiving housing allowances. Gerald also said that he did not mind if their friends or neighbors knew about their participation in the program. The Hartwicks did not hide it, and it did not appear to make any difference in their relations with others.

The Hartwicks reported that they were glad they had decided to stay in the same house. It was conveniently located near the stores they had shopped in for years. They knew the area and had friends living nearby. They also felt it would have been too much trouble to move their furniture and belongings. They were not enthralled with the house because they did not own it, but they were satisfied with its condition. It had been repainted and remodeled just before they had moved in three years before.

Although the Hartwicks felt that their house met their needs, they were upset that the landlord had raised their rent when they told him they would be receiving a housing allowance. They had been paying $130 a month (plus utilities), but when they informed him of the program, the landlord told them he had been meaning to raise the rent to $140 because of an increase in property taxes. Their original lease was to have been renewed in March, but with the allowance payments they had to negotiate a new lease beginning in November at the $140 rate. The Hartwicks felt that the landlord "got us for $40" for the extra four months they paid the $10 increase. Gerald's first reaction to the rent increase was anger, and both of them questioned whether housing allowances would be worth the rent increase. In the end, however, they signed the new lease without comment. Later, Gerald confided that he had been afraid they would lose their payment if they moved; he subsequently learned from the counselor that moves were allowed.

After their initial enrollment visits, the Hartwicks had minimal contact with the agency during the first year. In July, Gerald called the agency to find out if the program was being affected when an article entitled "HAP No Answer Here" appeared in the newspaper.

During the summer, the Hartwicks began to talk about the annual recertification coming up in November. They were worried that their allowance payment might be reduced because Social Security benefits had been increased. Gerald also wanted to know if their allowance payments would be cut if he took a part-time job for 30 days to help pay their mounting doctors' bills. He did not have any specific job in mind but thought there was a chance of working at a golf course several days a week selling buckets of balls. Before he did anything, however, he wanted to check with the agency to see if it was all right.

When they talked about HAP, the Hartwicks appeared to be cautiously satisfied with their participation in the program. They were somewhat reserved because they felt their rent had been raised as a result of their allowance payment and they would not be able to pay the new rent once the program was over. At the same time, they acknowledged that their landlord might have raised their rent anyway. Gerald had also understood from the first newspaper ad that they might receive $80 or $90 in rent supplement. "If I had known the payment was going to be only $54, I probably wouldn't have gone down to the office."

Even with their anxieties about their economic situation, the Hartwicks were pleased with the few extra dollars that the housing allowance gave them each month. It was not a big help, but it was a help. Because they did not equate it with welfare, they felt they could participate in a housing allowance program. "That is just a rent supplement program, to help us with our rent," Mr. Hartwick stated. In this mind, he deserved this program because he had been a good citizen and had paid his taxes, and he felt that programs such as this were especially important for the elderly.

THE MICHAEL JACKSON FAMILY [3]

Michael Jackson, age 52, is the head of a large household that includes his wife Lenora, their four teen-age sons, and a granddaughter, Barbara.

---

3. The following is an edited version of White [C120], pp. 130-135.

Prior to the Jacksons' participation in EHAP, they lived in an isolated, all-black suburban housing tract north of the city of Fontana, near San Bernardino, California. The family occupied a cramped, cheaply built home with two small bedrooms for the boys and a master bedroom, which had been converted from other use, for the adults. Barbara slept in the living room on a convertible sofa. There was one small bathroom which required constant attention because the plumbing was not designed for use by so many people. The house was a one-story wood frame building with a fence around it. Little vegetation grew in the sand and rocky soil in the yard. The driveway was unpaved, and a number painted on the front of the house was the only thing that distinguished the Jacksons' house from all the others. The house leaked, and one window was covered only with plastic. There was little heat and no air conditioning. Lenore says she could never get the house clean, and when the hot desert winds blew in the ventilation system always seemed to fail. Michael summed up the situation by saying, "What do you expect for $70?"

In the neighborhood, a few homes were boarded up, and there were signs of vandalism in the area. The development had been built some 20 years ago by a developer who did not arrange for city sewer, trash, or other services. Garbage was collected by a private company, and each house had its own septic field. There were no sidewalks; streets were in poor repair, and there were few street lights. The nearest supermarket was four miles away, across the barren open spaces which surrounded the six-block tract.

When the family moved to Fontana, Michael was working as a maintenance man at a baseball park in Los Angeles, a job which required a 57-mile commute one-way from Fontana. Two years after moving, he went to work for San Bernardino county as a janitor. He likes the job and under their present plan can qualify for retirement in 19 years. He is the only employed member of the family, with annual earnings of $6800. In addition, he receives a small welfare grant to support his granddaughter.

In June of 1973, Michael saw an EHAP flyer in the county welfare office one night as he was cleaning and applied at the agency shortly afterward. In August, the Jackson family was selected for the EHAP program; they could now begin to look more realistically for a "real house" with the assurance of some additional money. At their enrollment conference in the Ontario office, the Jacksons' monthly housing allowance benefit was estimated at $95.

In September, Michael attended group and individual counseling. He remembers attending four sessions—which he called "school"—where he learned about leases and "getting things in black and white." Michael thinks the program will end when two years of monthly payments have elapsed, and this seems to have been an additional incentive to arrange a lease/option-to-buy agreement for a new house. He knows that the county runs EHAP, but he is unfamiliar with the linkage with the federal government. Termination from EHAP puzzles him, and he says that he asked about it but did not get a clear answer. He has few opinions about program requirements—he accepts these as rules over which he has no control. He feels that realtors' general unfamiliarity with EHAP has hindered his housing search but that the agency has treated him well. His counselor even told him of a likely place to rent. Although this lead did not work out, it left him with a positive impression of the agency's interest.

As soon as he was enrolled in EHAP, Michael knew he would have to move to a better quality unit in order to receive payments; his house in Fontana would never pass the agency inspection discussed in the group training session. He saw the move as an opportunity to leave the problem of the Fontana house behind, yet he was apprehensive about finding a replacement that would be decent and large enough to house his family. The Jacksons had very definite plans for the sort of house and neighborhood they should live in. They were looking for a three- or four-bedroom unit in a mixed neighborhood, closer to work. In many areas that Michael searched, the rents were too high, sometimes $250 to $300, or the quality was no better than the house he presently occupied. Michael read the daily newspaper classified sections and surveyed likely neighborhoods by car. After several weeks of frustrating and expensive searching, he began to wish the agency supplied housing rather than just the allowance—it was so difficult to find a place.

Once, when looking at a house in a mixed neighborhood, he was told that it had just been rented to someone else.. He suspects that he was discriminated against but did not report it to the agency; he felt that it would be too much trouble in light of the small results it would produce.

Aware that more than half of the house-hunting period had elapsed, the family grew increasingly anxious. Toward the end of October, however, Michael received a call from one of the realtors he had spoken with several months before. They had found a place, a four-bedroom house for which he could arrange a lease with an option to buy, renting for $225 per month. The new house is located in an integrated community within a predominantly black section of the city of San Bernardino. The house is a modest single-family suburban tract house built within the last 10 years. It has a small yard and is situated at the end of a quiet cul-de-sac. Michael and Lenora particularly noted that it had a separate bedroom for their granddaughter, a sewer hookup instead of a septic field, a two-car garage instead of none, a lawn, and central air conditioning and heat that served all rooms. In general, the house is much newer and larger than their Fontana house, and the neighborhood is far superior.

The sidewalks are well lit, and there are no signs of vandalism or abandonment.

It took Michael about one hour to do his own inspection of the new unit although he checked first with the agency to see if they were supposed to do it. Over the phone, their representative explained that Michael would be responsible for the inspection. "If you are satisfied, then the agency is satisfied," the representative said. "You have to live in it, so it's whatever you okay. If something is wrong with it, the agency won't issue a check until it is corrected. Participants should be completely satisfied before getting money from the agency." The house was in perfect shape, according to Michael, who inspected it about two weeks before the family moved in. Even the carpet was laid. Michael does not feel strongly one way or the other about the inspection other than that the checklist was difficult to understand. This was not to say that he did not look critically at the physical condition of the house; rather, the checklist and his own critical perceptions did not seem to mesh.

The entire Jackson family was extremely happy with the new house. It was a visible improvement over the Fontana house and probably any other house they have ever lived in. The kids were looking forward to a new high school and new friends and spent many hours making plans. Michael converted part of the garage into a room for the kids with a record player and some chairs, and the kids frequently had friends over. The two bathrooms, Lenora mentions, have made a world of difference, and the new place is much easier to keep clean.

The Jacksons have had little additional contact with the agency since they moved in. Checks have arrived on time. At the annual recertification, an agency staff member came to recertify their income and to reinspect the house. The house was in good condition, and there was no change in the family's income and consequently no change in payment.

Michael is concerned about his prospects for remaining in the house. He and his family did not want to lose it at the end of the two-year lease, yet the landlord has told him that he is interested in selling the house when the lease expires. If Michael cannot afford to buy it, the landlord will have to sell it to someone else. The Jacksons want to buy the house but cannot get the money needed for the down payment.

CARMEN RODRIGUEZ [4]

Carmen Rodriguez is a young Puerto Rican woman who supports her brother and her two young children by working at the Head Start program in Springfield, Massachusetts and by receiving Aid to Families with De-

4. The following is an edited version of Johannes [C39], pp. 118-121.

pendent Children. She came to New York City from Puerto Rico when she was 6 years old and moved to Springfield 15 years later when her family returned to Puerto Rico.

Carmen and her family had been living in a public housing project in Springfield's South End. The South End is regarded as the Italian neighborhood, but it is becoming a transitional neighborhood as the younger or more well-to-do families move to the suburbs. Although Carmen was somewhat embarrassed every time she had to give her address to someone and was occasionally upset by noise, vandalism, and interfering neighbors, she was not unhappy there. She had a comfortable, new apartment which cost her $38 a month, and she liked the neighborhood. However, to be eligible for EHAP allowance payments, Carmen had to move out of the housing project.

She looked for another apartment in the same area but could not find one there and even had difficulty finding one elsewhere. She was supporting a family of four on a gross annual income of $4,600, and a projected housing allowance payment of $82 did not bring most apartments into her price range. She estimated that she looked at 30 apartments, or at least tried to look at that many. Often landlords would not even show her a place. She thought that occurred when they heard her Spanish accent over the phone. Carmen felt she was being discriminated against, and it angered her.

Her program representative encouraged her to file a complaint—to help the rest of her people as well as herself—but she argued that she did not want to live where she was not wanted. She did eventually file a complaint, although nothing ever came of it, and the story is confused. The case was investigated, and no cause for discrimination was identified.

Most of the places she looked at were either too far from downtown, too expensive, or in very poor condition. Some of them would not rent to EHAP participants in any case, objecting either to the lease or to an inspection. Carmen felt that these excuses were coupled with a disinterest in her because she is single, Spanish, and a welfare recipient.

On the last day of Carmen's housing search period, she finally found a place. However, she has had nothing but trouble with the apartment since she signed the lease (which she did under the pretense of still being married, in order to avoid possible discrimination from this landlord, too). There were no kitchen cabinets and no refrigerator when Carmen moved in. In fact, she had delayed moving in order to give the landlord extra time to fix the apartment; her first allowance check was held up as a result. Because her name was not yet on the mailbox, she later had to go to the agency office to pick it up. She had not insisted on putting the repairs into the lease since she had previously known the landlord to be responsive to other tenants, but in this case he "dragged his feet" for months.

Carmen had been afraid that she would end up paying more for housing in her place than she had in the project. Although her new rent was only $75, she had to pay all her own utilities, and the heat loss was considerable in this old, six-family, wood-frame building. Fortunately, in spite of the heating oil shortage in New England that winter, her fuel costs did not increase. She kept the heat low, and her costs averaged $25 per month.

Carmen was not pleased with the apartment itself and had included a 30-day termination clause in her lease in anticipation of moving before another winter passed. She did enjoy the yard and nearby park. On the other hand, she did not like being on the North End of town; she had never wanted to live there, but it was all she could find at the last moment. The North End is a physically rundown "urban renewal" area which is now predominantly Puerto Rican.

Carmen is an ambitious, outward-looking young woman. She was in a job training program and is now working as an aide in a local community center and taking college courses in the evenings in hopes of becoming a professional counselor. Although she was actively involved in the Puerto Rican community, she preferred the cultural diversity and somewhat higher prestige of the South End to the isolation and ethnic identification of the North End. She and her children also missed their friends from the old neighborhood. Since she had a car, Carmen drove to the supermarket in the South End to shop, complaining that things were too expensive in the small shops in the North End.

After eight months on the housing allowance program, Carmen was not certain she had made the right choice in leaving the project. She wished that she had not had to decide on an apartment in such a short time. She had not attended any of the agency's optional group counseling sessions, nor did she plan to attend any future sessions. However, she felt that she had learned a lot from her program representative, particularly regarding legal rights and rental housing standards. She felt that the EHAP staff was more helpful than the staff of the welfare department and said, "At Welfare, all you can do is complain." She also appreciated the EHAP staff's respect for her privacy; she had been afraid that they would contact her estranged husband, but they never did. She felt that the program is better controlled than welfare since "they do review your eligibility, and they eventually have proof from the landlord that the money they give out is being used for rent."

Carmen's greatest criticism of the agency was that it was unable to assist people with finding apartments. She had used the agency housing list occasionally but found it unsatisfactory. "The places [on the list] were falling down, and most of them were in the black section. It's harder to get a black landlord to rent to you than anybody else." She pointed not only to her own experience but to those of several families she knows who had enrolled in the program but then dropped out because they could not find housing they could afford that was better than public housing. Carmen sometimes wishes she had done the same thing: "Not all the projects are bad . . . my apartment was nice, but it was noisy and there were too many kids and parents always fighting over the kids. There is really a nice project, though, on Pine Street . . . with not so many kids and more middle-aged people . . . it has more space and grass and some flowers. . . ."

Carmen was recertified in July 1974. She had increased her working hours at the community center, so her housing allowance was reduced. At the same time, she was planning to move to a four-room apartment back in the South End. A self-inspection form was completed satisfactorily for the new unit, but she never did move.

MAURICE AND LAURA FISK [5]

Maurice and Laura Fisk are a white couple in their early twenties and natives of Jacksonville, Florida. Both are high school graduates. Maurice had been working his way up in Jacksonville's major industries, starting as a welder and fitter in the shipyards and rising to the post of field service engineer for a construction company. He had been helping to construct a factory that would be used to build floating nuclear power plants, but in the autumn of 1974 he was laid off.

His wife, Laura, has lived through lean times before. This is her second marriage, the first having ended in divorce. She worked for several years and then married Maurice three years ago. A year later, the Fisks applied to the first enrollment effort in Jacksonville and were selected. However, they never enrolled. At that time, Laura says, "I was working hard, I was pregnant and having a nervous breakdown. My kids had decided to live with their father. I just couldn't get involved in anything else!"

During the winter of 1974-1975, Laura noticed housing allowance advertisements on the television and radio which said that the program was now taking "middle-income" people. She applied again, but the family income was over the federally established limit for participation. One month later, when Maurice was laid off, they applied to the program for a third time. When they applied, the Fisks listed unemployment compensation as the family's only income, and their allowance payment was computed at $86. They were selected at once and told they would receive payments of $150 until Maurice started receiving his unemployment checks.

At the enrollment meeting, the Fisks saw the taped audiovisual enrollment presentation and then met their service representative. She stressed

---

5. The following is an edited version of Wolfe and Hamilton [C124], pp. 346-349.

the need for quick action since the program was nearly filled, and the Fisks requested that the agency inspect the house they were living in as soon as possible. Their house is located in a newly developed subdivision to the south and west of Jacksonville's urban core. Most houses there are single-family, and most of the neighbors are middle-class and white.

Two days after the Fisks had enrolled, their house was inspected and failed. Screens and screen doors were missing or broken; the bathroom needed repair; electrical outlets and switches in a bedroom needed covers. The Fisks offered to make the repairs if their landlord would purchase the materials. The next day, the landlord bought a $30 screen door and other supplies, and Maurice set to work. Four days after the first inspection, the house passed the second inspection. This time a different inspector came. The Fisks say that the first inspector went through the house with a "fine-tooth comb" but that the second inspector said, "So what if there's a screen missing" and then passed the unit.

Although the landlord had agreed to the repairs, he was reluctant to sign the rental agreement, so the Fisks used the two-party check option as a selling point. They explained that if he signed the rental agreement, the checks from the agency could be made out to the tenant and landlord jointly. That way, the landlord would be assured of getting at least the amount of the payment each month. The landlord agreed, and the Fisks qualified for a payment. They did no other house hunting. Eleven days after the Fisks were selected, a payment was initiated for them.

While they were applying for the housing allowance program, the Fisks also applied for food stamps, not knowing that their allowance payment would affect how much they would have to pay for them. At first, they paid $31 for $154 worth of food stamps. After they reported the housing allowance payment to the food stamp office, the cost for $154 in stamps rose to $77—a difference of $46. Because their housing allowance payment was $86, the net gain to the Fisks from the allowance program was $40 a month.

The Fisks are satisfied with their housing allowance payment, although they feel they "can't live off it." They would like to move to a different house because they have been having more trouble with the landlord and because they would like to find something cheaper. They think that a family of four ought to be able to find a house renting for $150, but they cannot seem to find one. They have come to the conclusion that the rent standard on which their payment is based is too low, especially considering the high cost of utilities in Jacksonville. The amount they are paying for utilities has jumped recently because one of their water pipes leaks; their last water bill was $58. They have asked the landlord to repair the leak, but, they say, "He just screams at us" when they ask for any repairs to the house.

They said they never thought to contact the agency about the problems with their landlord. Instead, they are reading the paper every day, looking for a new unit.

It hurts Laura's pride to take the housing allowance. She feels that it is welfare and is ashamed of being a participant. Maurice feels it is tax money, saying, "When I work and make good money, they take lots out for taxes, and now I'm getting it back." He would like to be working again, and each week he checks for job openings at the employment office when he picks up his unemployment check. Laura feels that unemployment is welfare, too—and so are food stamps. However, she thinks that rent subsidies are a good alternative to public housing and says, "It's better for the kids to be in a house. I'm doing it for the kids." Whatever their feelings about accepting "welfare" payments, they are glad to have help. Laura says, "Without food stamps and the housing allowance, where would we be?"

Housing Allowances in Other Industrial Nations

Although their existence has played little role in U.S. consideration of housing allowances, similar programs have been adopted in other industrialized nations. Table E.1 presents some basic characteristics of current allowance programs in seven of these countries. The earliest program was initiated in Sweden in 1913, while the most recent one shown in the table was implemented in Great Britain in 1975.

An important characteristic the seven programs share is that they are viewed primarily as part of their nations' systems of income maintenance. In general, they were not implemented with the expectation that they would have major effects on the housing stock. This is reflected in the "housing quality standards" entries in the table which, for most of the seven programs, are either minimal or absent. Lack of housing standards probably also explains the comparatively low administrative costs estimated for the seven programs, compared to the EHAP experience.

Table E.1

Characteristics of Housing Allowances in Seven Industrial Nations

Characteristic	Sweden	France	Germany	Denmark	Netherlands	Norway	Great Britain
Year of Adoption	1913	1948	1965	1966	1970	1972	1975
Eligible of population	All households, subject to an income limit	Elderly, families receiving family allowances, both subject to an income limit	Elderly, families with children, subject to an income limit	Elderly, families with children, both subject to an income limit	All households, subject to an income limit	Elderly, disabled, families with children, subject to an income limit	All households, subject to an income limit
Tenure eligibility	Renters and home-owners	Renters and home-owners	Renters and home-owners	Renters only	Renters only	Renters and home-owners	Renters only
Recipients as a percentage of all households	42%	6%	7%	10%	8%	10%	1%

Housing quality standards	None	Unit must meet physical quality standards	None, but condition of unit affects amount of subsidy	Unit must meet physical quality standards	Unit must be less than 10 years old	Units must be less than 20 years old	None
Form of subsidy	Percentage of rent	Housing gap	Housing gap	Percentage of rent or housing gap, whichever leads to higher payments	Housing gap	Housing gap	Percentage of rent
Administrative cost (as a percentage of total program costs)	5%	12-15%	10%	3%	13%	N.A.	17%

Source: Abt Associates of Canada [P4]; Haanes-Olsen [P28]; Trutko, Hetzel, and Yates [E153]; Welfeld [P90]; and Wiewel [P91].
N.A. = not available.

References

1. PUBLIC POLICY AND HOUSING ALLOWANCES

P-1   Aaron, Henry J. "Policy Implications of the Housing Allowance Experiments: A Progress Report." In *Do Housing Allowances Work?* Edited by Katharine L. Bradbury and Anthony Downs. Washington, D.C.: The Brookings Institution, forthcoming 1981.

P-2   _____. *Shelter and Subsidies: Who Benefits from Federal Housing Policies?* Washington, D.C.: The Brookings Institution, 1972.

P-3   Aaron, Henry J. and von Furstenberg, George. "The Inefficiencies of Transfers In-kind: The Case of Housing Assistance." *Western Economic Journal* 9 (June 1971): 184-191.

P-4   Abt Associates of Canada. *Study of European Housing Allowance Programs.* Ottawa: Abt Associates, 1978.

P-5   Austin, David M. "Implications of the Experience with Shelter Component of Public Assistance for the Design of a National Housing Allowance." *Housing for the Seventies: Working Papers.* Washington, D.C.: U.S. Department of Housing and Urban Development, 1976.

P-6   Barth, M. C.; Orr, Larry L.; and Palmer, J. L. "Policy Implications: A Positive View." In *Work Incentives and Income Guarantees.* Edited by J. A. Pechman and P. M. Timpane. Washington, D.C.: The Brookings Institution, 1975.

P-7   Bendick, Marc, Jr. "WIC and the Paradox of In-kind Transfers." *Public Finance Quarterly* 6 (July 1978): 351-380.

P-8   Bendick, Marc, Jr., Campbell, Toby H., Bawden, D. Lee, and Jones, Melvin. *Toward Efficiency and Effectiveness in the WIC Delivery System.* Washington, D.C.: The Urban Institute, 1976.

P-9   Bendick, Marc, Jr., and Zais, James P. *Incomes and Housing: Lessons From Experiments With Housing Allowances.* URI 23900. Washington, D.C.: The Urban Institute, October 1978.

P-10 Carlton, Dennis W., and Ferreira, Joseph, Jr. "Selecting Subsidy Strategies for Housing Allowance Programs." *Journal of Urban Economics* 4 (July 1977): 221-247.

P-11 Conroy, Michael E., and Mayo, Stephen K. *Potential Migration Effects of a Direct Cash Assistance Program for Housing.* Cambridge, Massachusetts: Abt Associates, Inc., December 1974.

P-12 de Leeuw, Frank. *The Housing Allowance Approach.* Reprint 90-2100-3. Washington, D.C.: The Urban Institute, June 1971.

NOTE: PB numbers refer to catalog numbers in the collection of the National Technical Information Service (NTIS). HUD numbers refer to the HUD USER information system.

P-13 de Leeuw, Frank, and Leaman, Sam H. *The Section 23 Leasing Program.* URI 10087. U.S. Congress, Joint Economic Committee, 92nd Congress, 2nd Session, October 1972.

P-14 de Leeuw, Frank; Schnare, Ann B.; and Struyk, Raymond J. "Housing." In *The Urban Predicament.* Edited by William Gorham and Nathan Glazer. Washington, D.C.: The Urban Institute, 1976.

P-15 DeSalvo, Joseph S. "Housing Subsidies: Do We Know What We Are Doing?" *Policy Analysis* 2 (Winter 1976): 39-60.

P-16 Downs, Anthony. *Federal Housing Subsidies: How Are They Working?* Lexington: D.C. Heath, 1973.

P-17 Drury, Margaret J.; Fried, Harriet C.; Heinberg, John D.; and Kamm, Sylvan. *Direct Cash Assistance and Home Ownership: The Issues.* Working Paper 210-7. Washington, D.C.: The Urban Institute, July, 1974.

P-18 Drury, Margaret J.; Goedert, Jeanne E.; Fried, Harriet C.; Spohn-Peggy W.; and Taher, Grace M. *Housing Allowances in Rural America.* Working Paper 216-1. Washington, D.C.: The Urban Institute, 1974.

P-19 Drury, Margaret J.; Lee, Olson; Springer, Michael; and Yap, Lorene. *Lower Income Housing Assistance Program (Section 8) Nationwide Evaluation of the Existing Housing Program.* Washington, D.C.: U.S. Department of Housing and Urban Development, 1978. HUD 0000386.

P-20 Dubinsky, Robert; Grigsby, William G.; and Watson, Karen G. *Review of the Relationship Between the Housing Assistance Supply Experiment and Other Types of Assisted Housing Programs.* Working Note 9390-HUD. Santa Monica, California: The Rand Corporation, February 1976.

P-21 Eisenstadt, Karen; Gueron, Judith; and Lowry, Ira S. *Welfare Housing in New York City.* New York: New York City Rand Institute, 1972.

P-22 Frieden, Bernard J. *Improving Federal Housing Subsidies, Summary Report.* Working Paper No. 1. Cambridge, Massachusetts: Joint Center for Urban Studies, Spring 1971.

P-23 Friedman, Milton. *Capitalism and Freedom.* Chicago: The University of Chicago Press, 1962.

P-24 Gans, Herbert. "A Poor Man's Home is His Poorhouse." *New York Times Magazine* (March 3, 1974): 20-58.

P-25 Grigsby, William G. "The Housing Effects of a Guaranteed Annual Income." In *Housing and Economics: The American Dilemma.* Edited by Michael A. Stegman. Cambridge, Massachusetts: MIT Press, 1970.

P-26 _____. *Housing Markets and Public Policy.* Philadelphia: University of Pennsylvania Press, 1963.

P-27 Grigsby, William G., and Rosenberg, Louis. *Urban Housing Policy.* New York: APS Publications, Inc., 1975.

P-28 Haanes-Olsen, L. "Housing Allowances for Old Age Pensioners." *Social Security Bulletin* 37 (September 1974): 36-41.

P-29   Hanna, Sherman. "Housing Allowances in the Context of Governmental Social Welfare Programs." *Housing Educators Journal* 1 (1974) : 8-10.

P-30   Hartman, Chester and Keating, Dennis. "The Housing Allowance Delusion." *Social Policy* 4 (January/February 1974) : 31-37.

P-31   Heinberg, John D. "Housing Policy—Federal Objectives and the Local Role for Analysis." *Journal of Urban Analysis* 5 (1978).

P-32   Heinberg, John D.; Culbertson, Joanne; Drury, Margaret; and Zais, James P. *Integrating a Housing Allowance with the Welfare System: Further Analysis of Program-Linking Strategies and Joint Administration.* Working Paper 216-21. Washington, D.C.: The Urban Institute, November 1975. PB 249872. HUD 0050439.

P-33   Heinberg, John D.; Culbertson, Joanne; and Zais, James P. *The Missing Piece to the Puzzle? Housing Allowances and the Welfare System.* Working Paper 216-4. Washington, D.C.: The Urban Institute, December 1974.

P-34   Heinberg, John D.; Spohn, Peggy W.; and Taher, Grace M. *Housing Allowances in Kansas City and Wilmington: An Appraisal.* URI 11800. Washington, D.C.: The Urban Institute, May 1975.

P-35   Isler, Morton L. "The Goals of Housing Subsidy Programs." URI 10020. *Statement before the Committee on Banking and Currency.* U.S. House of Representatives, 92nd Congress, 1st Session, June 1971.

P-36   _____. *Thinking About Housing: A Policy Research Agenda.* Paper 60004. Washington, D.C.: The Urban Institute, 1970.

P-37   Isler, Morton L., and Agus, Robert E. *Direct Cash Assistance for Housing and Ongoing Community Development Programs.* Working Paper 216-12. Washington, D.C.: The Urban Institute, January 1975.

P-38   _____. *Housing Allowances and Existing Housing Regulations.* Working Paper 216-2. Washington, D.C.: The Urban Institute, January 1975.

P-39   Kain, John F. "Analysis of a Universal Housing Allowance Program." In *Do Housing Allowances Work?* Edited by Katharine L. Bradbury and Anthony Downs. Washington, D.C.: The Brookings Institution (forthcoming 1980).

P-40   Kain, John F., and Schafer, Robert. *Urban Housing Policies.* Cambridge, Massachusetts: Harvard University Department of City and Regional Planning, 1977.

P-41   Khadduri, Jill. "The Rent Reduction Credit Feature of the Section 8 Existing Housing Program." In *Occasional Papers in Housing and Community Affairs* 6 (December 1979) : 41-54.

P-42   Khadduri, Jill; Lyall, Katherine; and Struyk, Raymond J. "Welfare Reform and Housing Assistance: A National Policy Debate." *Journal of the American Institute of Planners* 44 (January 1978) : 2-12.

P-43   Khadduri, Jill, and Struyk, Raymond. "Improving Section 8 Rental Assistance: Translating Evaluation into Policy." *Evaluation Review* (forthcoming).

P-44 King, James R. *Proposals for Rent Subsidies in Historical Perspective.* Washington, D.C.: Congressional Research Service, 1965.

P-45 Kuh, Edwin. "A Basis for Welfare Reform." *The Public Interest* (Spring 1969) : 112-117.

P-46 Levine, Martin. *Federal Housing Policy: Current Programs and Recurring Issues.* Washington, D.C.: Congressional Budget Office, June 1978.

P-47 Linner, John, and Wright, Douglas. "The Housing Moratorium." *Planning* 39 (May 1974) : 23-25.

P-48 Lowry, Ira S. *Housing Assistance for Low-Income Urban Families: A Fresh Approach.* Paper 4645. Santa Monica, California: The Rand Corporation, May 1971.

P-49 Lurie, Irene (ed.). *Integrating Income Maintenance Programs.* New York: Academic Press, 1975.

P-50 MacDonald, Maurice. *Food Stamps and Income Maintenance.* New York: Academic Press, 1975.

P-51 Mayer, Neil. *Housing Occupancy Costs: Current Problems and Means to Relieve Them.* Working Paper 263-1. Washington, D.C.: The Urban Institute, June 1978.

P-52 Mayo, Stephen K. *Household Composition Effects and the Design of a Direct Cash Assistance Program for Housing.* Cambridge, Massachusetts: Abt Associates, Inc., February 1975.

P-53 Mayo, Stephen K.; Mansfield, Shirley; Warner, David; and Zwetchkenbaum, Richard. *Draft Report on Housing Allowances and Other Rental Housing Assistance Programs—A Comparison Based on Housing Allowance Demand Experiment, Part 1: Participation, Housing Consumption, Location and Satisfaction.* AAI No. 79-132. Cambridge, Massachusetts: Abt Associates, Inc., November 1979.

P-54 _____. *Draft Report on Housing Allowances and Other Rental Housing Assistance Programs—A Comparison Based on the Housing Allowance Demand Experiment, Part 2: Costs and Efficiency.* AAI No. 79-111. Cambridge: Massachusetts: Abt Associates, Inc., August 1979.

P-55 Moynihan, Daniel Patrick. "Toward a National Urban Policy." *The Public Interest* 17 (Fall 1969) : 3-20.

P-56 Muth, Richard F. *Cities and Housing.* Chicago: University of Chicago Press, 1969.

P-57 National Low Income Housing Coalition. *1981 Housing and Community Development Legislation.* Washington, D.C.: National Low-Income Housing Coalition, March 1980.

P-58 _____. *Remarks of Senator Edward W. Brooke, Chairperson, National Low Income Housing Coalition at Housing Economic Summit Conference, National Housing Center, November 7, 1979.* Washington, D.C.: National Low-Income Housing Coalition, March 1980.

P-59 Nourse, Hugh O. "Can We Design the Housing Allowance for Learning?" *American Real Estate and Urban Economics Journal* 4 (Spring 1976) : 97-104.

P-60 _____. "The Effect of a Negative Income Tax on the Number of Substandard Housing Units." *Land Economics* 4 (November 1970) : 435-446.

P-61 Olsen, Edgar O.; Rasmussen, David W.; and Dick, Eugen. "Section 8 Existing: A Program Evaluation and Policy Options." *Occasional Papers in Housing and Community Affairs* 6 (December 1979) : 1-32.

P-62 Orr, Larry. *The Welfare Economics of Housing the Poor.* Discussion Paper 3-69. Madison, Wisconsin: University of Wisconsin Institute for Research and Poverty, 1969.

P-63 Peabody, Malcolm E. "Housing Allowances, A New Way to House the Poor." *The New Republic* 170 (March 9, 1974) : 20-23.

P-64 Poirier, Dale J. "The Determinants of Home Buying." *The New Jersey Income Maintenance Experiment, Volume 3: Expenditures, Health, and Social Behavior; and the Quality of the Evidence.* Edited by Harold W. Watts and Albert Rees. New York: Academic Press, Inc., 1977.

P-65 Post, Marda, et al. *Eligibility in a Direct Cash Assistance Program.* Cambridge, Massachusetts: Abt Associates, Inc., August 1974.

P-66 President's Committee on Urban Housing. *A Decent Home, The Report of The President's Committee on Urban Housing.* Washington, D.C.: U.S. Government Printing Office, 1968.

P-67 Rossi, Peter H., and Lyall, Katherine C. *Reforming Public Welfare: A Critique of the Negative Income Tax Experiment.* New York: The Russell Sage Foundation, 1976.

P-68 Sadacca, Robert; Loux, Suzanne B.; Isler, Morton L.; and Drury, Margaret J. *Management Performance in Public Housing.* URI 61000. Washington, D.C.: The Urban Institute, January 1974.

P-69 Schafer, Robert. "Slum Formation, Race, and an Income Strategy." *Journal of the American Institute of Planners* 37 (September 1971) : 347-354.

P-70 Semer, Melton P.; Zimmerman, Julian H.; Foard, Ashley; and Frantz, John. "A Review of Federal Subsidized Housing Programs." In *Housing in the Seventies: Working Papers.* Washington, D.C.: U.S. Department of Housing and Urban Development, 1976.

P-71 Shaw, Jane. "Do Housing Allowances Work?" *House and Home* 45 (January 1974) : 8.

P-72 Smolensky, Eugene. "Public Housing or Income Supplements—The Economics of Housing for the Poor." *Journal of the American Institute of Planners* 34 (March 1968) : 94-101.

P-73 Solomon, Arthur P. "Housing Allowances and National Objectives." In *Housing in the Seventies: Working Papers.* Washington, D.C.: U.S. Department of Housing and Urban Development, 1976.

P-74 Solomon, Arthur P., et al. *A Comparison of Payment Formulas for a Direct Cash Assistance Program.* Cambridge, Massachusetts: Abt Associates, Inc., September 1974.

P-75 Solomon, Arthur P., and Fenton, Chester G. "The Nation's First Experi-

ence with Housing Allowances: The Kansas City Demonstration."
Land Economics 50 (August 1974): 213-223.

P-76   Struyk, Raymond J. "Government Activity to Foster Inner-city Residential Revitalization." In *Urban Housing*. San Francisco: Federal Home Loan Bank Board, December 1978.

P-77   ————. "The Need for Flexibility in Local Housing Policies." *Policy Analysis* 3 (Fall 1977): 471-483.

P-78   Struyk, Raymond J., Marshall, Sue A., and Ozanne, Larry J. *Housing Policies for the Urban Poor*. URI 23500. Washington, D.C.: The Urban Institute, 1978.

P-79   U.S. Congress, Joint Economic Committee. *Housing Subsidies and Housing Policies*. 92nd Congress. 2nd Session, 1973.

P-80   ————, Senate, Committee on Banking and Currency. *Bills Relating to Housing and Urban Development*. Hearings before the Subcommittee on Housing and Urban Affairs, Part I and II. Housing and Urban Development Legislation of 1970, United States Senate, 91st Congress, 2nd Session, 1970.

P-81   U.S. Department of Housing and Urban Development. *Housing in the Seventies: A Report of the National Housing Policy Review*. Washington, D.C.: U.S. Department of Housing and Urban Development, 1974.

P-82   ————. *Housing in the Seventies: Working Papers*. Washington, D.C.: U.S. Department of Housing and Urban Development, 1976.

P-83   ————. *Justification for 1980 Estimates*. Washington, D.C.: U.S. Department of Housing and Urban Development, 1979.

P-84   ————. *Lower Income Housing Assistance Program (Section 8): Interim Findings of Evaluation Research*. Washington, D.C.: U.S. Department of Housing and Urban Development, 1978. HUD 0000115.

P-85   ————. *Statistical Yearbook*. Washington, D.C.: U.S. Department of Housing and Urban Development, 1975.

P-86   Weaver, Robert C. "Housing Allowances." *Land Economics* 51 (August 1975): 206-211.

P-87   Weicher, John C. "The Rationales for Government Intervention in Housing, An Overview." In *Housing in the Seventies: Working Papers*. Washington, D.C.: U.S. Department of Housing and Urban Development, 1976.

P-88   ————. "Urban Housing Policy." In *Current Issues in Urban Economics*. Edited by Peter Mieszkowski and Mahlon Straszheim. Baltimore: Johns Hopkins University Press, 1979.

P-89   Welfeld, Irving H. "American Housing Policy: Perverse Programs by Prudent People." *The Public Interest* 98 (Summer 1977): 128-144.

P-90   ————. *European Housing Subsidy Systems, An American Perspective*. Washington, D.C.: U.S. Department of Housing and Urban Development, September 1972.

P-91   Wiewel, Wim. *Housing Allowances and the Dutch Rent Subsidy Pro-*

gram. Paper 5959. Santa Monica, California: The Rand Corporation, January 1979.

P-92 Woodfill, Barbara. *The Section 8 Housing Assistance Program: Notes on Eligibility and Benefits*. Working Note 8999-HUD. Santa Monica, California: The Rand Corporation, February 1975.

P-93 Woodridge, Judith. "Housing Consumption." In *The New Jersey Income Maintenance Experiment, Volume III: Expenditures, Health and Social Behavior; and the Quality of the Evidence*. Edited by Harold W. Watts and Albert Rees. New York: Academic Press, Inc., 1977.

P-94 Zais, James P. "Housing Allowances: Ongoing Experiments and Policy Options." In *The Politics of Housing in Older Urban Areas*. Edited by Robert E. Mendelsohn and Michael A. Quinn. New York: Praeger Publishers, 1976.

P-95 Zais, James P.; Goedert, Jeanne E.; and Trutko, John W. *Modifying Section 8: Implications from Experiments with Housing Allowances*. URI 24100. Washington, D.C.: The Urban Institute, January 1979.

2. THE EXPERIMENTAL HOUSING ALLOWANCE PROGRAM

E-1 Abt Associates, Inc. *Agency Program Manual (Administrative Agency Experiment)*. Cambridge, Massachusetts: Abt Associates, Inc., March 1973. PB 241992.

E-2 ———. *Alternative Methods of Computing the Cost of Standard Housing*. Cambridge, Massachusetts: Abt Associates, Inc., March 1973.

E-3 ———. *Evaluation Design of the Demand Experiment*. Cambridge, Massachusetts: Abt Associates, Inc., March 1973.

E-4 ———. *Evaluation Design: Executive Summary*. (Demand Experiment.) Cambridge, Massachusetts: Abt Associates, Inc., June 1973.

E-5 ———. *Evaluation Manual, Administrative Agency Experiment, Experimental Housing Allowance Program*. Cambridge, Massachusetts: Abt Associates, Inc., 1972.

E-6 ———. *Experimental Design and Analysis Plan of the Demand Experiment*. Cambridge, Massachusetts: Abt Associates, Inc., August 1973. PB 239507. HUD 0050516.

E-7 ———. *Experimental Design and Analysis Plan, Supplement A, Comparisons With Other Programs*. (Demand Experiment.) Cambridge, Massachusetts: Abt Associates, Inc., February 1974.

E-8 ———. *First Annual Report of the Administratitve Agency Experiment*. Cambridge, Massachusetts: Abt Associates, Inc., May 1974. PB 241545. HUD 0050059.

E-9 ———. *First Annual Report of the Demand Experiment*. Cambridge, Massachusetts: Abt Associates, Inc., March 1974. PB 239598. HUD 7501793.

E-10   _____. *Second Annual Report of the Administrative Agency Experiment.* Cambridge, Massachusetts: Abt Associates, Inc., December 1974. PB 241544. HUD 0050510.

E-11   _____. *Second Annual Report of the Demand Experiment.* Cambridge, Massachusetts: Abt Associates, Inc., February 1975. PB 241232.

E-12   _____. *Site Operating Procedures Handbook. (The Demand Experiment.)* Cambridge, Massachusetts: Abt Associates, Inc., April 1973.

E-13   _____. *Summary Evaluation Design, Demand Experiment, Experimental Housing Allowance Program.* Cambridge, Massachusetts: Abt Associates, Inc., June 1973. PB 241031. HUD 0050521.

E-14   _____. *Summary Evaluation Plan of the Administrative Agency Experiment.* Cambridge, Massachusetts: Abt Associates, Inc., January 1973.

E-15   _____. *Third Annual Report of the Demand Experiment.* Cambridge, Massachusetts: Abt Associates, Inc., October 1976. PB 261122. HUD 0050437.

E-16   _____. *Preliminary Working Paper on Policy Question Analysis.* AAI 73-158. Cambridge, Massachusetts: Abt Associates, Inc., December 1973.

E-17   Althauser, Robert P.; Grigsby, William G.; Campbell, Harrison, S.; and Lowry, Ira S. *Analysis Plan for Measuring Effects on Non-Recipients.* Working Note 8111-HUD. Santa Monica, California: The Rand Corporation, January 1973.

E-18   Bakeman, Helen E.; Kennedy, Stephen D.; and Wallace, James. *Fourth Annual Report of the Demand Experiment, Experimental Housing Allowance Program, January 1, 1976—December 31, 1976.* AAI 77-92. Cambridge, Massachusetts: Abt Associates, Inc., December 1977. PB 282828. HUD 0050442.

E-19   Beckham, Robert. "The Experimental Housing Allowance Program, An Old Idea Will Get a New Test in 1973." *Journal of Housing* (January 1973): 12-17.

E-20   Benson, Donita G., and Kelly, Bettye S. *Experimental Housing Allowance Program, Durham, North Carolina, Final Report.* Durham, North Carolina: Durham County Department of Social Services, December 1975. PB 249085. HUD 0050497.

E-21   Berry, Sandra H.; Relles, Daniel A.; and Seals, E. *Sample Selection Procedure for St. Joseph County, Indiana.* Working Note 8588-HUD. Santa Monica, California: The Rand Corporation, January 1974. PM 247669. HUD 7501938.

E-22   Boruch, Robert F. "On Common Contentions About Randomized Field Experiments." In *Experimental Testing of Public Policy.* Edited by R. F. Boruch and H. W. Riecken. Boulder, Colorado: Westview Press, 1975.

E-23   Buchanan, Garth and Heinberg, John D. *Housing Allowance Household*

Experiment Design: Part I—Summary and Overview. Working Paper 205-4. Washington, D.C.: The Urban Institute, May 1972.

E-24 Carlson, David B., and Heinberg, John D. *How Housing Allowances Work: Integrated Findings to Date from the Experimental Housing Allowance Program.* URI 21300. Washington, D.C.: The Urban Institute, February 1978.

E-25 Carter, Earl S. *Brown County Press Coverage of the Housing Allowance Program: December 1972-December 1974.* Working Note 9015-HUD. Santa Monica, California: The Rand Corporation, March 1975.

E-26 _____. *South Bend Press Coverage of the Housing Assistance Supply Experiment and the Allowance Program: January 1974-December 1974.* Working Note 9016-HUD. The Rand Corporation, March 1975.

E-27 Comptroller General of the United States. *An Assessment of the Department of Housing and Urban Development's Experimental Housing Allowance Program.* Washington, D.C.: U.S. General Accounting Office, March 1978. PB 278481.

E-28 _____. *Observations on Housing Allowances and the Experimental Housing Allowance Program.* Washington, D.C.: U.S. General Accounting Office, March 1974.

E-29 Corcoran, Timothy M. *The Effects of Nonresponse on Record Completion in a Panel of Residential Properties.* Working Note 8174-HUD. Santa Monica, California: The Rand Corporation, April 1973. PB 246403. HUD 0000781.

E-30 _____. *Sampling Non-residential Properties: Site I.* Working Note 8623-HUD. Santa Monica, California: The Rand Corporation, March 1974. PB 246400.

E-31 _____. *Selecting the Permanent Panel of Residential Properties, Site I.* Working Note 9575-HUD. Santa Monica, California: The Rand Corporation, April 1978.

E-32 _____. *Selecting the Permanent Panel of Residential Properties: Site II.* Working Note 9577-HUD. Santa Monica, California: The Rand Corporation, April 1977. PB 268877. HUD 0050440.

E-33 _____. *Survey Sample Design for Site I.* Working Note 8640-HUD. Santa Monica, California: The Rand Corporation, March 1974. PB 246402.

E-34 Corcoran, Timothy M.; Poggio, Eugene C.; and Repnau, Tiina. *Sample Design for the Housing Assistance Supply Experiment.* Working Note 8029-HUD. Santa Monica, California: The Rand Corporation, November 1972. PB 242270. HUD 7501644.

E-35 Culbertson, Joanne G., and Heinberg, John D. *Early Findings from the Experimental Housing Allowance Program and Estimates for a National Housing Allowance Program: A Comparative Analysis.* Working Paper 216-11. Washington, D.C.: The Urban Institute, May 1975.

E-36 de Leeuw, Frank; Leaman, Sam H.; and Blank, Helen. *The Design of a Housing Allowance.* URI 30005. Washington, D.C.: The Urban Institute, October 1970. HUD 0000794.

E-37 Department of Housing and Urban Development of the Consolidated City of Jacksonville, Florida. *Agency Final Report, Housing Allowance Program*. Jacksonville, Florida: Department of Housing and Urban Development, December 1975. PB 249123. HUD 0050493.

E-38 Design and Analysis Staff. *Analysis Plan for the Demand Experiment*. Cambridge, Massachusetts: Abt Associates, Inc., 1973.

E-39 _____. *Evaluation Design of the Demand Experiment*. Cambridge, Massachusetts: Abt Associates, Inc., 1973.

E-40 _____. *Variables in the Demand Experiment*. Cambridge, Massachusetts: Abt Associates, Inc., 1973.

E-41 Dodd, Colleen M.; Fujisaki, Misako C.; and Levitt, Gerald. *Data Management System for the Housing Assistance Supply Experiment*. Working Note 8054-HUD. Santa Monica, California: The Rand Corporation, November 1972. PB 247667.

E-42 Bradbury, Katharine L., and Downs, Anthony (editors). *Do Housing Allowances Work?* Washington, D.C.: The Brookings Institution, forthcoming 1981.

E-43 Dubinsky, Robert. *Collected Site Selection Documents: Housing Assistance Supply Experiment*. Working Note 8034-HUD. Santa Monica, California: The Rand Corporation, January 1973.

E-44 _____. *The Housing Allowance Program for the Supply Experiment: First Draft*. Working Note 8350-HUD. Santa Monica, California: The Rand Corporation, August 1973.

E-45 Ferber, Robert, and Hirsch, Werner T. "Social Experimentation and Economic Policy: A Survey." *Journal of Economic Literature* 16 (December 1978): 1379-1414.

E-46 Field Operations Staff. *Site Operating Procedures for Pittsburgh*. Cambridge, Massachusetts: Abt Associates, Inc., March 1973.

E-47 _____. *Site Specific Information—Phoenix*. Cambridge, Massachusetts: Abt Associates, Inc., March 1973.

E-48 _____. *Site Specific Information—Pittsburgh*. Cambridge, Massachusetts: Abt Associates, Inc., April 1973.

E-49 Goedert, Jeanne E. *Generalizing from the Experimental Housing Allowance Program: An Assessment of Site Characteristics*. URI 22900. Washington, D.C.: The Urban Institute, June 1978.

E-50 Goodman, John L., Jr., and Vogel, Mary. *The Process of Housing Choice: Conceptual Background and Research Plans*. Working Paper 216-7. Washington, D.C.: The Urban Institute, February 1975. PB 249875. HUD 0050402.

E-51 Gray, Kirk L. *Coming of Age in Policy Relevant Research*. Paper 5887. Santa Monica, California: The Rand Corporation, June 1977.

E-52 _____. *Using Anthropology in Policy-Relevant Research*. Paper 6150. Santa Monica, California: The Rand Corporation, June 1978.

E-53 _____. *Press Coverage of the Experimental Housing Allowance Program in Site I: January-June 1975*. Working Note 9307-HUD. Santa

Monica, California: The Rand Corporation, November 1975. PB 246749.

E-54 Greenwald, Alan F., and Lewis, David A. *The Housing Allowance Office: Functions and Procedures.* Working Notes 8209-HUD. Santa Monica, California: The Rand Corporation, March 1973.

E-55 Grigsby, William G.; Shanley, Michael G.; and White, Sammis B. *Market Intermediaries and Indirect Suppliers: Reconnaisance and Research Design for Site I.* Working Notes 8577-HUD. Santa Monica: The Rand Corporation.

E-56 _____. *Market Intermediaries and Indirect Suppliers: Reconnaissance and Research Design for Site II.* Working Notes 9026-HUD. Santa Monica, California: The Rand Corporation, May 1975. PB 266149. HUD 0050392.

E-57 Heinberg, John D. *The Transfer Cost of a Housing Allowance: Conceptual Issues and Benefit Patterns.* URI 30004. Washington, D.C.: The Urban Institute, May 1971.

E-58 Hollister, R. "The Role of Experimentation in Policy-decision Making." In *Experimental Testing of Public Policy.* Edited by R. F. Boruch and H. W. Riecken. Boulder, Colorado: Westview Press, 1975.

E-59 Housing Allowance Office, Inc. (Supply Experiment). *Monthly Status Report for the November, 1979 Reporting Period.* Santa Monica, California: The Rand Corporation, 1979.

E-60 Housing Assistance Supply Experiment Staff. *Completing the Supply Experiment.* Working Note 10223-HUD. Santa Monica, California: The Rand Corporation, June 1978. HUD 0000254.

E-61 _____. *Preliminary Description of Survey Instruments.* Working Note 7883-HUD. Santa Monica, California: The Rand Corporation, June 1972. PB 242032.

E-62 _____. *Proceedings of the General Design Review of the Housing Assistance Supply Experiment.* Working Note 8396-HUD. Santa Monica, California: The Rand Corporation, October 1973. PB 242273.

E-63 _____. *Site Selection for the Housing Assistance Supply Experiment: Stage I.* Working Note 7833-HUD. Santa Monica, California: The Rand Corporation, May 1972. PB 247665. HUD 7591939.

E-64 _____. *Site Selection for the Housing Assistance Supply Experiment: SMSAs Proposed for Site Visits (A Briefing).* Working Note 7907-HUD. Santa Monica, California: The Rand Corporation, August 1972.

E-65 _____. *Supplemental Design Papers for the Housing Assistance Supply Experiment.* Working Note 7982-HUD. Santa Monica, California: The Rand Corporation, July 1972.

E-66 Illinois Department of Local Government Affairs, Office of Housing and Buildings. *Experimental Housing Allowance Program: The Final Report.* Springfield, Illinois: Department of Community Affairs, February 1976. PB 266163. HUD 0050495.

E-67 Ingram, G. K.; Kain, John F.; and Ginn, J. R. *The Detroit Prototype of* the *NBER Urban Simulation Model.* New York: Columbia University Press, 1972.

E-68 Kain, John F. *Housing Policy Evaluation Research and Experimentation.* Policy Note P77-7. Cambridge, Massachusetts: Harvard University Department of City and Regional Planning, November 1977.

E-69 Katz, Arnold J., and Jackson, Wayne. "The Australian Housing Allowance Voucher Experiment: A Venture in Social Policy Development." *Social and Economic Administration* 12 (Winter 1978): 197-208.

E-70 Kellerman, Carol, and Rosen, George. *Special Report on Six Administrative Agency Plans.* Cambridge, Massachusetts: Abt Associates, Inc., January 1973.

E-71 Kennedy, Stephen D., and Merrill, Sally. *The Use of Hedonic Indices to Distinguish Changes in Housing and Housing Expenditures: Evidence from the Housing Allowance Demand Experiment.* Cambridge, Massachusetts: Abt Associates, Inc.

E-72 Kershaw, David, and Fair, Jerilyn. *The New Jersey Income Maintenance Experiment, Volume 1: Operations, Surveys and Administration.* New York: Academic Press, 1976.

E-73 Levine, R. A. *Failure Mode Analysis for the Housing Allowance Program.* Working Note 7895-HUD. Santa Monica: The Rand Corporation, July 1972.

E-74 Levitt, Gerald., (ed.). *Baseline Data Systems Design, Implementation and Operation Report.* Working Note 8611-HUD. Santa Monica, California: The Rand Corporation, March 1974. PB 246746.

E-75 _____. *Data Management System: Part I, Fieldwork Data and Data Transfer Specifications.* Working Note 7885-HUD. Santa Monica, California: The Rand Corporation, July 1972. PB 242030.

E-76 _____. *Data Management System: Part II, The Management of Data for Analysis.* Working Note 7953-HUD. Santa Monica, California: The Rand Corporation, August 1972. PB 247666.

E-77 Lewis, David B. *Phase II Price Controls and the Housing Assistance Supply Experiment.* Working Note 7888-HUD. Santa Monica, California: The Rand Corporation, July 1972.

E-78 Lewis, David B.; Greenwald, Alan F.; and Lowry, Ira S. *The Experimental Housing Allowance Program.* Working Note 8171-HUD. Santa Monica, California: The Rand Corporation, February 1973.

E-79 Lowry, Ira S. *Analysis Plan for Measuring Supply Responsiveness.* Working Note 8110-HUD. Santa Monica, California: The Rand Corporation, January 1973.

E-80 _____. *Are Further Survey Cycles Needed in Site I?* Working Note 9541-HUD. Santa Monica, California: The Rand Corporation, July 1976.

E-81 _____. *Early Findings from the Housing Assistance Supply Experiments.* Paper 6075. Santa Monica, California: The Rand Corporation, 1978.

E-82 _____. *Equity and Housing Objectives in Homeowner Assistance.* Working Note 8715-HUD. Santa Monica, California: The Rand Corporation, June 1974. PB 242034. HUD 0050072.

E-83 _____. *The Experimental Housing Allowance Program: An Update of Section III of the General Design Report.* Working Note 9070-HUD. Santa Monica, California: The Rand Corporation, November 1973.

E-84 _____. *Funding Homeowner Assistance in the Supply Experiment: Problems and Prospects.* Working Note 8489-HUD. Santa Monica, California: The Rand Corporation, November 1973.

E-85 _____. (ed.). *General Design Report: First Draft.* Working Note 8198-HUD. Santa Monica, California: The Rand Corporation, May 1973. PB 242033. HUD 0050076.

E-86 _____. *General Design Report: Supplement.* Working Note 8364. Santa Monica, California: The Rand Corporation, August 1973. PB 242031. HUD 0050077.

E-87 _____. *Generalizing from the Supply Experiment.* Working Note 8124-HUD. Santa Monica, California: The Rand Corporation, January 1973.

E-88 _____. *The Housing Assistance Supply Experiment: Tensions in Design and Implementation.* Paper 5302. Santa Monica, California: The Rand Corporation, September 1974.

E-89 _____. *Indexing the Cost of Producing Housing Services: Site II.* Santa Monica, California: The Rand Corporation, July 1976. PB 266149. HUD 0050392.

E-90 _____. *Introduction and Overview: An Update of Sections I and II of the General Design Report.* Working Note 9098-HUD. Santa Monica, California: The Rand Corporation, May 1975. HUD 0000599.

E-91 _____. *Monitoring the Experiment: An Update of Section IV of the General Design Report.* Working Note 9051-HUD. Santa Monica, California: The Rand Corporation, April 1975. HUD 0000597.

E-92 _____. *Preliminary Design for the Housing Assistance Supply Experiment.* Working Note 7866-HUD. Santa Monica, California: The Rand Corporation, June 1972.

E-93 _____. *A Topical Guide to HASE Research.* N-1215-HUD. Santa Monica California: The Rand Corporation, June 1979. HUD 0000820.

E-94 Lowry, Ira S.; Campbell, Harison S.; and Palmatier, M. A. *Monitoring the Supply Experiment.* Working Note 8243-HUD. Santa Monica, California: The Rand Corporation, April 1973.

E-95 Lowry, Ira S.; Ott, N. Mack; and Noland, C. W. *Housing Allowances and Household Behavior.* Working Note 8028-HUD. Santa Monica, California: The Rand Corporation, January 1973. PB 242029. HUD 0050071.

E-96 Lowry, Ira S., and Repnau, Tiina. *Is Saginaw County An Acceptable Site for the Housing Assistance Supply Experiment?* Working Note 8548-HUD. Santa Monica, California: The Rand Corporation, January 1974.

E-97   Lowry, Ira S.; Rydell, Peter C.; and de Ferranti, David M. *Testing the Supply Response to Housing Allowances: An Experimental Design.* Working Note 7711-HUD. Santa Monica, California: The Rand Corporation, December 1971.

E-98   Lowry, Ira E.; Woodfill, Barbara; and Repnau, Tiina. *Program Size and Cost for Site I: New Data from the Screener Survey.* Working Note 8547-HUD. Santa Monica, California: The Rand Corporation, December 1973. PB 246405.

E-99   _____. *Program Standards for Site I.* Working Note 8574-HUD. Santa Monica, California: The Rand Corporation, January 1974. PB 242036. HUD 0050111.

E-100   Lowry, Ira S.; Woodfill, Barbara; and Dade, Marsha A. *Program Standards for Site II.* Working Note 8974-HUD. Santa Monica, California: The Rand Corporation, 1975. PB 242035. HUD 0050112.

E-101   Massachusetts Department of Community Affairs. *Final Report, Massachusetts Experimental Housing Allowance Program.* Springfield, Massachusetts: Department of Community Affairs, 1977. PB 266194. HUD 0050485.

E-102   Massell, Adele P. *Compensating for Landlord Nonresponse in the Housing Assistance Supply Experiment.* Working Note 8268-HUD. Santa Monica, California: The Rand Corporation, June 1973. PB 242251.

E-103   _____. *The Role of Household Survey Data in the Supply Experiment.* Working Note 8218-HUD. Santa Monica, California: The Rand Corporation, March 1973. PB 242272. HUD 7501642.

E-104   Mathematica Policy Research. *Plans for an Analysis of Housing Data from the Seattle-Denver Income Maintenance Experiment.* Denver, Colorado: Mathematica Policy Research, 1976.

E-105   Melton, C. Reid. *Data Sources for the Integrated Analysis.* Working Paper 216-8. Washington, D.C.: The Urban Institute, February 1975. PB 249870. HUD 0050401.

E-106   Mieszkowski, Peter, and Straszheim, Mahlon., (eds.). *Current Issues in Urban Economics.* Baltimore: John Hopkins University Press, 1979.

E-107   Mulford, J. E.; Carter, G. M.; and Ellickson, Phyllis L. *Eligibility and Participation Research Plan for the Housing Assistance Supply Experiment.* Working Note 10328-HUD. Santa Monica, California: The Rand Corporation, October 1978. HUD 0000792.

E-108   Noland, Charles W. *Hedonic Indexes for St. Joseph County.* Working Draft 218-HUD. Santa Monica, California: The Rand Corporation, September 1979.

E-109   Noland, Charles W., and Lowry, Ira S. *Adjusting for Regional and Local Price Changes.* Working Note 8220-HUD. Santa Monica, California: The Rand Corporation, March 1973.

E-110   Noland, Charles W., and Shea, Michael. *Site Evaluation: Clark County, Ohio.* Working Note 8575-HUD. Santa Monica, California: The Rand Corporation, February 1974.

E-111 _____. *Site Evaluation: St. Joseph County, Indiana.* Working Note 8576-HUD. Santa Monica, California: The Rand Corporation, January 1974.

E-112 O'Nell, N., and Shanley, Michael. *Monitoring the Housing Allowance Program in St. Joseph County, Indiana: September 1974 to March 1975.* Working Note 9724-HUD. Santa Monica, California: The Rand Corporation, December 1977. PB 277717. HUD 0050079.

E-113 _____. *Monitoring the Housing Allowance Program in St. Joseph County, Indiana: April to August 1975.* Working Note 9725-HUD. Santa Monica, California: The Rand Corporation, December 1977. PB 277718. HUD 0050080.

E-114 _____. *Monitoring the Housing Allowance Program in St. Joseph County, Indiana: September to December 1975.* Working Note 9726-HUD. Santa Monica, California: The Rand Corporation, December 1977. PB 277719. HUD 0050081.

E-115 _____. *Monitoring the Housing Allowance Program in St. Joseph County Indiana: January to June 1976.* Working Note 9727-HUD. Santa Monica, California: The Rand Corporation, December 1977. PB 277720. HUD 0050082.

E-116 O'Nell, N. and Wiewel, Wim. *Monitoring the Housing Allowance Program in St. Joseph County, Indiana: July-September 1976.* Working Note 9728-HUD. Santa Monica, California: The Rand Corporation, December 1977. PB 277721. HUD 0050083.

E-117 _____. *Monitoring the Housing Allowance Program in St. Joseph County, Indiana: October-December 1976.* Working Note 10086-HUD. Santa Monica, California: The Rand Corporation, January 1979. HUD 0000596.

E-118 Ott, N. Mack. *Funding Housing Allowances for Homeowners Under Section 235.* Working Note 8025-HUD. Santa Monica, California: The Rand Corporation, 1972.

E-119 Ozanne, Larry J. *Integrating the Supply Experiment and the Housing Market Model.* Washington, D.C.: The Urban Institute, July 1975. PB 249873.

E-120 Ozanne, Larry J.; Andrews, Marcellus; and Malpezzi, Stephen. "The Efficacy of Hedonic Estimation with the Annual Housing Survey: Evidence from the Demand Experiment." In *Proceedings from the HUD Conference on Housing Choices of Low-Income Households.* Washington, D.C.: U.S. Department of Housing and Urban Development, forthcoming.

E-121 Phlips, Louis. "A Dynamic Version of the Linear Expenditure Model." *Review of Economics and Statistics* (November 1972): 450-458.

E-122 Poggio, Eugene C. *Preliminary Description of Sample Selection Procedures.* Working Note 8101-HUD. Santa Monica, California: The Rand Corporation, January 1973.

E-123 _____. *Sample Selection Procedures for Site I.* Working Note 8201-

HUD. Santa Monica, California: The Rand Corporation, March 1973. PB 242271. HUD 7501643.

E-124 _____. *Selecting the Baseline Sample of Residential Properties: Site I.* Working Note 8645-HUD. Santa Monica, California: The Rand Corporation, March 1977. PB 266159. HUD 0050359.

E-125 Power, Margaret et al. *Program Information, Equal Opportunity and Associated Services.* Cambridge, Massachusetts: Abt Associates, Inc., September 1974.

E-126 The Rand Corporation. *First Annual Report of the Housing Assistance Supply Experiment.* R-1659-HUD. Santa Monica, California: The Rand Corporation, October 1974. PB 241701. HUD 0000114.

E-127 _____. *Second Annual Report of the Housing Assistance Supply Experiment.* R-1959-HUD. Santa Monica, California: The Rand Corporation, May 1976. PB 266244. HUD 0050399.

E-128 _____. *Third Annual Report of the Housing Assistance Supply Experiment.* R-2151-HUD. Santa Monica, California: The Rand Corporation, February 1977. PB 266245. HUD 0050398.

E-129 _____. *Fourth Annual Report of the Housing Assistance Supply Experiment.* Rand 2302-HUD. Santa Monica, California: The Rand Corporation, May 1978. HUD 0000242.

E-130 _____. *Fifth Annual Report of the Housing Assistance Supply Experiment.* R-2434-HUD. Santa Monica, California: The Rand Corporation, June 1979. HUD 0000975.

E-131 _____. *Sixth Annual Report of the Housing Assistance Supply Experiment.* R-2544-HUD. Santa Monica, California: The Rand Corporation, May 1980.

E-132 _____. *Proceedings of the General Design Review of the Housing Assistance Supply Experiment.* Working Note 8396-HUD. Santa Monica, California: The Rand Corporation, October 1973. PB 242273. HUD 7501641.

E-133 Relles, Daniel A. *Selecting the Baseline Sample of Residential Properties: Site II.* Working Note 9027-HUD. Santa Monica, California: The Rand Corporation, October 1975. PB 266148. HUD 0050393.

E-134 _____. *Using Weights to Estimate Population Parameters from Survey Records.* Working Note 10095-HUD. Santa Monica, California: The Rand Corporation, April 1978.

E-135 Repnau, Tiina. *Characteristics of Residential Baseline Survey Samples for Site I.* Working Note 8682-HUD. Santa Monica, California: The Rand Corporation, May 1974. PB 266143. HUD 0050315.

E-136 Repnau, Tiina, and Woodfill, Barbara. *Additional Estimates of Enrollment and Allowance Payments under a National Housing Allowance Program.* Working Note 8167-HUD. Santa Monica, California: The Rand Corporation, March 1973. HUD 0000169.

E-137 Rivlin, Alice. "How Can Experiments Be More Useful?" *American Economic Review* 64 (May 1974), pp. 346-354.

E-138 Rogson, M. M. *Documentation in Social Science Experiments.* Paper 5494-1. Santa Monica, California: The Rand Corporation, January 1976.

E-158 _____. *Integrated Analysis of the Experimental Housing Allowance Rental Residential Property: Brown County, Wisconsin, 1973, and St. Joseph County, Indiana, 1974.* Working Draft 229-HUD. Santa Monica, California: The Rand Corporation, June 1979.

E-140 Rydell, C. Peter, and Stanton, Richard E. *A Plan for Analyzing Non-Response Bias: Survey of Landlords, Baseline, Site I.* Working Note 9211-HUD. Santa Monica, California: The Rand Corporation. August 1975. PB 245736.

E-141 Salem Housing Authority. *Experimental Housing Allowance Program, Final Report.* Salem, Oregon: Housing Authority of the City of Salem, January 1976. PB 249930. HUD 0050492.

E-142 San Bernardino Experimental Housing Allowance Program Administrative Agency. *Experimental Housing Allowance, Final Report.* San Bernardino, California: EHAP Administrative Agency, October 1976. PB 249112. HUD 0050524.

E-143 Sepanik, Ronald J. *The TRIM Projection Capability: A Report on the Validation of the Housing Allowance Data Base.* Working Paper 216-33. Washington, D.C.: The Urban Institute, March 1977.

E-144 _____. *Variations of Selection Design Elements for Housing Allowances: Simulations Using the TRIM Model.* Washington, D.C.: The Urban Institute, August 1975. PB 249869.

E-145 Sepanik, Ronald J.; Hendricks, Gary; and Heinberg, John D. *Simulations of National Housing Allowances: An Application of the TRIM Model.* Working Paper 216-13. Washington, D.C.: The Urban Institute.

E-146 Shanley, Michael. *Monitoring the Housing Allowance Program in St. Joseph County, Indiana: July to September 1974.* Working Note 9723-HUD. Santa Monica, California: The Rand Corporation, December 1977. PB 277716. HUD 0050078.

E-147 Sherer, Sam; Thomas, Cynthia; and Brand, Spencer. *Measurement and Operations, Memorandum for the Housing Allowance Experiment.* Working Paper 205-8. Washington, D.C.: The Urban Institute, 1972.

E-148 Skidmore, Felicity. "Operational Design of the Experiment." In *Work Incentives and Income Guarantees.* Edited by Joseph A. Pechman and P. Michael Timpane. Washington, D.C.: The Brookings Institution, 1975.

E-149 Social Services Board of North Dakota. *Final Report of the North Dakota Experimental Housing Allowance Project.* Bismarck, North Dakota: Social Service Board of North Dakota, April 1976. HUD 0050486.

E-150 Temple, Frederick T.; Holshouser, William L., Jr.; Trend, M. G.; Budding, David; and Ernst, Mireille L. *Administrative Agency Experiment Evaluation, Experimental Housing Allowance Program, Third Annual Report, October 1974-October 1975.* Cambridge, Massachusetts: Abt Associates, Inc., August 1976. PB 265648. HUD 0050283.

E-151 Thomas, Cynthia, and King, Thomas. *Housing Allowance Household Experiment Design: Part 3, Response Measures and Scaling Approaches.* Working Paper 205-3. Washington, D.C.: The Urban Institute, June 1972.

E-152 Trend, M. G. *Housing Allowances for the Poor: A Social Experiment.* Boulder: Westview Press, 1978.

E-153 Trutko, John; Hetzel, Otto J.; and Yates, A. David. *A Comparison of the Experimental Housing Allowance Program and Great Britain's Rent Allowance Program.* URI 22500. Washington, D.C.: The Urban Institute, April 1978.

E-154 Tulsa Housing Authority. *Experimental Housing Allowance Program Final Report.* Tulsa, Oklahoma: Tulsa Housing Authority, October 1975.

E-155 The Urban Institute. *The Experimental Housing Allowance Program: Second Year Report.* Working Paper 210-6. Washington, D.C.: The Urban Institute, September 1974. PB 249915. HUD 0050496.

E-156 _____. *Integrated Analysis of the Experimental Housing Allowance Program.* Working Paper 210-3. Washington, D.C.: The Urban Institute, November 1973. PB 249914. HUD 0050503.

E-157 _____. *Integrated Analysis of the Experimental Housing Allowance Program, Supplement.* Working Paper 210-4. Washington, D.C.: The Urban Institute, December 1973. PB 249868. HUD 0050503.

E-157 _____. *Integrated Analysis of the Experimental Housing Allowance Program, Third Year Report.* Working Paper 216-16. Washington, D.C.: The Urban Institute, June 1975. PB 249775.

E-159 _____. *Integrated Analysis of the Experimental Housing Allowance Program, Fourth Year Report.* Working Paper 216-32. Washington, D.C.: The Urban Institute, January 1977. PB 249914. HUD 0050509.

E-160 _____. *Integrated Analysis of the Experimental Housing Allowance Program: Fifth Year Report.* Working Paper 249-7. Washington, D.C.: The Urban Institute, March 1978.

E-161 _____. *Integrated Analysis of the Experimental Housing Allowance Program: Sixth Year Report.* Working Paper 249-14. Washington, D.C.: The Urban Institute, October 1978.

E-162 _____. *Integrated Design and Evaluation of the Experimental Housing Allowance Program: First Year Report.* Working Paper 210-2. Washington. D.C.: The Urban Institute, May 1973. PB 249867. HUD 0050525.

E-163 U.S. Department of Housing and Urban Development. *Administrative Agency Experiment Conference, Experimental Housing Allowance Program, Final Report.* Washington, D.C.: U.S. Department of Housing and Urban Development, November 1973. PB 241549. HUD 0050118.

E-164 _____. *Experimental Housing Allowance Program: Initial Impressions and Findings, Interim Report.* Washington, D.C.: U.S. Department of Housing and Urban Development, April 1975. PB 245815. HUD 0050118.

E-165 _____. *Experimental Housing Allowance Program: A 1979 Report of Findings.* Washington, D.C.: U.S. Department of Housing and Urban Development, April 1979. HUD 0000672.

E-166 _____. *First Annual Report of the Experimental Housing Allowance Program.* Washington, D.C.: U.S. Department of Housing and Urban Development, May 1973. PB 241490. HUD 0000166.

E-167 _____. *Housing Allowances: The 1976 Report to Congress.* Washington, D.C.: U.S. Department of Housing and Urban Development, February 1976. PB 263656. HUD 0050005.

E-168 _____. *Second Annual Report on the Experimental Housing Allowance Program.* Washington, D.C.: U.S. Department of Housing and Urban Development, June 1974. PB 244218. HUD 7591934.

E-169 _____. *A Summary Report of Current Findings from the Experimental Housing Allowance Program.* Washington, D.C.: U.S. Department of Housing and Urban Development, April 1978. HUD 0000179.

E-170 Valenza, Joseph J. *Program Housing Standards in the Experimental Housing Allowance Program: Analyzing Differences in the Demand and Supply Experiments.* URI 19300. Washington, D.C.: The Urban Institute, July 1977.

E-171 Vidal, Avis. *Draft Report on the Search Behavior of Black Households in Pittsburgh in the Housing Allowance Demand Experiment.* Cambridge, Massachusetts: Abt Associates, Inc., July 1978.

E-172 Wallace, James E., et al. *Selected Program Statistics Relating to Special Issues.* Cambridge, Massachusetts: Abt Associates, Inc., August 1975.

E-173 Watts, Harold. "Critique of EHAP Design and Lessons from EHAP Concerning Social Experimentation." In *Proceedings of the Brookings Conference on the Experimental Housing Allowance Program.* Edited by Anthony Downs. Washington. D.C.: The Brookings Institution (forthcoming 1981).

E-174 Wiewel, Wim, and O'Nell, N. *Monitoring the Housing Allowance Program in St. Joseph County, Indiana: January-March 1977.* Working Note 10139-HUD. Santa Monica, California: The Rand Corporation, February 1979. HUD 0000376.

E-175 Woodfill, Barbara. *Preliminary Estimates of Enrollment Rates and Allowance Costs.* Working Note 7901-HUD. Santa Monica, California: The Rand Corporation, July 1972.

E-176 Woodfill, Barbara, and Repnau, T. *Estimates of Eligibility and Allowance Entitlement Under Alternative Housing Allowance Programs.* Working Note 7974-HUD. Santa Monica, California: The Rand Corporation, September 1972.

E-177 Woodfill, Barbara; Repnau, T.; and Lowry, Ira E. *Estimates of Eligibility, Enrollment and Allowance Payments in Green Bay and Saginaw: 1974 and 1979.* Working Note 8439-HUD. Santa Monica, California: The Rand Corporation, September 1973.

E-178 Zais, James P. *Explaining Household Response Differences: Some Preliminary Considerations.* Working Paper 216-14. Washington, D.C.: The Urban Institute, May 1975.

E-179 Zais, James P.; Heinberg, John D.; and Drury, Margaret J. *Experimental Testing of Housing Allowances: Evidence of Program Feasibility and Other Preliminary Findings.* Working Paper 216-24. Washington, D.C.: The Urban Institute, February 1976.

E-180 Zais, James P.; Melton, C. Reid; and Berkman, Mark P. *A Framework for the Analysis of Income Accounting Systems in EHAP.* Working Paper 216-17. Washington, D.C.: The Urban Institute, July 1975. PB 249871.

E-181 Zais, James P., and Trutko, John W. *Integrated Analysis of Administration of Housing Allowance Programs.* Working Paper 215-31. Washington, D.C.: The Urban Institute, September 1976. HUD 0050400.

3. HOUSEHOLD RESPONSES TO ALLOWANCES

H-1 Abt Associates, Inc. *Working Paper on Early Findings: Demand Experiment, Experimental Housing Allowance Program.* Cambridge, Massachusetts: Abt Associates, Inc., January 1975. PB 242003. HUD 7501927.

H-2 Adams, John. "Directional Bias in Intra-Urban Migration." *Economic Geography* 45 (October 1969): 302-23.

H-3 Alonzo, William. *Location and Land Use.* Cambridge: Harvard University Press, 1964.

H-4 Apgar, William C., Jr., and Kain, John F. "Effects of Housing Allowances in the Pittsburgh Housing Market." *Progress Report on the Development of the NBER Urban Simulation Model and Interim Analysis of Housing Allowance Programs.* Edited by John F. Kain. New York: National Bureau of Economic Research, December 1974.

H-5 Atkinson, Reilly; Hamilton, William; and Myers, Dowell. *Draft Report on Racial/Ethnic Concentration in the Housing Allowance Demand Experiment.* Cambridge, Massachusetts: Abt Associates, Inc., January 1979.

H-6 Atkinson, Reilly, and Phipps, Anthony. *Locational Choice, Part II: Neighborhood Change in the Housing Allowance Demand Experiment.* Cambridge, Massachusetts: Abt Associates, Inc., August 1977. PB 274158.

H-7 Austin, Margery, and MacRae, Duncan C. *Estimating Demand for Owner-Occupied Housing Subject to the Income Tax.* Working Paper 116-08. Washington, D.C.: The Urban Institute, 1979.

H-8 Bakeman, Helen. *Draft Report on the Effectiveness of the Housing Information Program in the Housing Allowance Demand Experiment.* Cambridge, Massachusetts: Abt Associates, Inc., February 1979.

H-9   Bakeman, Helen E.; Dalto, Carol Ann; and White, Charles S. *Minimum Standards Requirements in the Housing Allowance Demand Experiment.* Cambridge, Massachusetts: Abt Associates, Inc. (forthcoming).

H-10   Barrett, Frank A. *Residential Search Behavior.* Geographic Monograph Number 1. Toronto: York University-Atkinson College, 1973.

H-11   Barton, David, and Olsen, Edgar. *The Benefits and Costs of Public Housing in New York.* Discussion Paper 372-76. Madison, Wisconsin: Institute for Research on Poverty, 1976.

H-12   Bendick, Marc, Jr. "Failure to Enroll in Public Assistance Programs." *Social Work* 25 (July 1980): 268-274.

H-13   Bernsten, Elizabeth. *Services in Support of Housing Search: How Necessary and Effective in the Experimental Housing Allowance Program.* Contract Report 249-34. Washington, D.C.: The Urban Institute, 1980.

II-14   Brown, Douglas. "Estimating the Price and Income Elasticity of Demand for Urban Housing." Paper presented at the Southern Regional Science Association Meetings, Atlanta, 1975.

H-15   Brown, Lawrence, and Holmes, John. "Intra-urban Migrant Lifelines: A Spatial View." *Demography* 8 (February 1971): 103-23.

H 16   _____. "Search Behavior in an Intra-Urban Migration Context: A Spatial Perspective." *Environment and Planning* 3 (1971): 307-326.

H-17   Brown, Lawrence, and Longbrake, David B. "Migration Flows in Intra-Urban Space: Place Utility Considerations." *Annals of the Association of Urban Geographers* 60 (June 1970): 368-384.

H-18   Budding, David W. *Draft Report on Housing Deprivation Among Enrollees in the Housing Allowance Demand Experiment.* Cambridge, Massachusetts: Abt Associates, Inc., November 1978.

H-19   Carliner, G. "Income Elasticity of Housing Demand." *Review of Economics and Statistics.* (November 1973): 528-532.

H-20   Clark, W. A. V., and Cadwallader, Martin. "Location Stress and Residential Mobility." *Environment and Behavior* 5 (March 1973): 29-41.

H-21   _____. "Residential Preferences: An Alternative View of Intra-Urban Space." *Environment and Planning* 6 (November/December 1973): 693-704.

H-22   Cronin, Francis J. *An Economic Analysis of Intra-Urban Search and Mobility Using Alternative Benefit Measures.* Working Paper 249-24. Washington, D.C.: The Urban Institute, April 1979.

H-23   _____. *The Efficiency of Demand-Oriented Housing Programs.* Working Paper 249-35. Washington, D.C.: The Urban Institute, November 1979.

H-24   _____. *Estimation of Dynamic Linear Expenditure Functions for Housing.* Working Paper 249-32. Washington, D.C.: The Urban Institute, September 1979.

H-25   _____. *The Housing Demand of Low-Income Households.* Working Paper 249-25. Washington, D.C.: The Urban Institute, August 1979.

H-26 _____. *How Low-Income Households Search for Housing: Preliminary Findings on Racial Differences.* Working Paper 249-20. Washington, D.C.: The Urban Institute, March 1979.

H-27 _____. *Intra-Urban Household Mobility: The Search Process.* Working Paper 249-16. Washington, D.C.: The Urban Institute, 1978.

H-28 _____. *Search, Mobility and Locational Choice: Preliminary Findings from the Experimental Housing Allowance Program.* Working Paper 249-11. Washington, D.C.: The Urban Institute, October 1978.

H-29 _____. *Search and Residential Mobility: Part I. Economic Models of the Decision to Search and Move Among Low-Income Households.* Working Paper 249-27. Washington, D.C.: The Urban Institute, November 1979.

H-30 _____. *Search and Residential Mobility: Part II. Strategies and Outcomes for Relocation Among Low-Income Households.* Washington, D.C.: The Urban Institute (forthcoming 1980).

H-31 _____. *The Household's Decision to Accept or Reject a Conditional Transfer Offer.* Working Paper 1510-2. Washington, D.C.: The Urban Institute, 1980.

H-32 de Leeuw, Frank. "The Demand for Housing: A Review of Cross-Section Evidence." *Review of Economics and Statistics* 53 (February 1971): 1-10.

H-33 De Salvo, Joseph. "Benefits and Costs of New York's Middle-Income Housing Program." *Journal of Political Economy* 83 (1975): 71-85.

H-34 Dusenberry, J. S., and Kistin, H. "The Role of Demand in the Economic Structure." *Studies in the Structure of the American Economy.* Edited by Wassily Leontif. New York: Oxford University Press, 1953.

H-35 Fenton, Chester. "The Permanent Income Hypothesis, Source of Income and the Demand for Rental Housing." In *Analysis of Selected Census and Welfare Program Data to Determine Relationships of Household Characteristics and Administrative Welfare Policies to a Direct Housing Assistance Program.* Cambridge, Massachusetts: Joint Center for Urban Studies, 1974.

H-36 Feins, Judith D., and White, Charles S., Jr. *The Ratio of Shelter Expenditures to Income: Definitional Issues, Current Patterns, and Historical Trends.* Cambridge, Massachusetts: Abt Associates, Inc.

H-37 Friedman, Joseph, and Kennedy, Stephen D. *Housing Expenditures and Quality, Part II: Report on Housing Expenditures Under a Housing Gap Housing Allowance.* Cambridge, Massachusetts: Abt Associates, Inc., May 1977. PB 271895. HUD 0050215.

H-38 Friedman, Joseph, and Weinberg, Daniel. *Draft Report on the Demand for Rental Housing: Evidence from a Percent of Rent Housing Allowance.* Cambridge, Massachusetts: Abt Associates, Inc., 1978.

H-39 _____. *Draft Report on Housing Consumption under a Constrained Income Transfer: Evidence from a Housing Gap Housing Allowance.* Cambridge, Massachusetts: Abt Associates, Inc., April 1979.

H-40 Goedert, Jeanne E. *Earmarking Housing Allowances: The Tradeoff Between Housing Consumption and Program Participation.* Working Paper 249-19. Washington, D.C.: The Urban Institute, September 1979.

H-41 Goedert, Jeanne E.; Ozanne, Larry J.; and Tinney, Robert W. *Development of Hedonic Regressions for Measuring Housing Quality.* Working Paper 216-20. Washington, D.C.: The Urban Institute, August 1975.

H-42 Goodman, John L., Jr. "Causes and Indicators of Housing Quality." *Social Indicators Research* 5 (1978): 195-210.

H-43 _____. *Chronic Movers: Who? Where? Why?* Working Paper 249-8. Washington, D.C.: The Urban Institute, March 1978.

H-44 _____. *Housing Allowances and Local Area Variation in Residential Mobility.* Working Paper 216-25. Washington, D.C.: The Urban Institute, June 1976.

H-45 _____. *Housing Allowances and Residential Mobility: An Interim Report.* Working Paper 249-1. Washington, D.C.: The Urban Institute, October 1976.

H-46 _____. "Housing Consumption Disequilibrium and Local Residential Mobility." *Environment and Planning A* 8 (December 1976): 855-874.

H-47 _____. "Housing Information and Optimal Housing Search." (Memorandum). Washington, D.C.: The Urban Institute, October 1975.

H-48 _____. "The Housing Search Process: A Theoretical Framework." (Memorandum). Washington, D.C.: The Urban Institute, November 1974.

H-49 _____. *Measuring and Interpreting Housing Change in the Experimental Housing Allowance Program.* Working Paper 249-4. Washington, D.C.: The Urban Institute, March 1978.

H-50 Goodman, John L., Jr., and Vogel, Mary. *The Process of Housing Choice: Conceptual Background and Research Plans.* Washington, D.C.: The Urban Institute, 1975. PB 249875. HUD 0050402.

H-51 Hanushek, Eric A., and Quigley, John M. "Dynamics of the Housing Market: A Stock Adjustment Model of Housing Consumption." *Journal of Urban Economics* (January 1979): 90-111.

H-52 _____. "An Explicit Model of Intra-Metropolitan Mobility." *Land Economics* 54 (November 1978): 411-429.

H-53 _____. "On the Relationship Between Complex Public Subsidies and Complex Human Behavior." In *Do Housing Allowances Work?* Edited by Katharine L. Bradbury and Anthony Downs. Washington, D.C.: The Brookings Institution (forthcoming 1981).

H-54 Hartman, Chester, and Keating, Dennis. "The Housing Allowance Delusion." *Social Policy* 4 (January/February): 31-37.

H-55 Hanushek, Eric, and Quigley, John M. "What is the Price Elasticity of Housing Demand?" Paper presented at the Econometric Society Meetings, Chicago, Illinois, August 1978.

H-56 Hayakawa, Hiroaki, and Venieris, Yiannis. "Consumer Interdependence via Reference Groups." *Journal of Political Economy* 85 (June 1977): 599-615.

H-57 Helbers, Lawrence. *Estimated Effects of Increased Income on Homeowner Repair Expenditures.* Rand Note 1192-HUD. Santa Monica, California: The Rand Corporation, November 1979.

H-58 _____. *Measuring Homeowner Needs for Housing Assistance.* Working Note 9079-HUD. Santa Monica, California: The Rand Corporation, February 1978. PB 278316.

H-59 Hicks, J. R. *A Revision of Demand Theory.* Oxford: Clarendon Press, 1956.

H-60 Holshouser, William L., Jr. *Supportive Services in the Administrative Agency Experiment.* Cambridge, Massachusetts: Abt Associates, Inc., February 1977.

H-61 Houthakker, H. S. "The Present State of Consumption Theory." *Econometrica* 29 (1961).

H-62 Houthakker, H. S., and Taylor, L. D. *Consumer Demand in the United States.* Cambridge: Harvard University Press, 1970.

H-63 Kennedy, Stephen D.; Kumar, R. Krishna; and Weisbrod, Glen. *Report on Participation under a Housing Gap Form of Housing Allowance.* Cambridge, Massachusetts: Abt Associates, Inc., May 1977.

H-64 Kennedy, Stephen D., and MacMillan, Jean. *Draft Report on Participation Under Alternative Housing Allowance Programs: Evidence from the HADE.* AAI No. 79-120. Cambridge, Massachusetts: Abt Associates, Inc., October 1979.

H-65 Kozimor, L. W. *Eligibility and Enrollment in the Housing Allowance Program: Brown and St. Joseph Counties through Year 2.* Working Note 9816-HUD. Santa Monica, California: The Rand Corporation, August 1978.

H-66 Lamar, B. W., and Lowry, Ira S. *Client Responses to Housing Requirements: The First Two Years.* Working Note 9814-HUD. Santa Monica, California: The Rand Corporation, February 1979.

H-67 Lee, Tong Hun. "Demand for Housing: Cross Section Analysis." *The Review of Economics and Statistics* (May 1963): 190-196.

H-68 _____. "Housing and Permanent Income: Tests Based on Three Year Reinterview Survey." *Review of Economics and Statistics* (November 1968): 480-490.

H-69 _____. "The Stock Demand Elasticities of Non-Farm Housing." *The Review of Economics and Statistics* (February 1964): 82-89.

H-70 Lee, Tong Hun, and Kong, C. M. "Elasticities and Housing Demand." *Southern Economics Journal* (October 1977): 298-305.

H-71 Leser, C. E. V. "Commodity Group Expenditure Functions for the United Kingdom, 1948-1957." *Econometrica* 29 (1961): 24-32.

H-72 Li, Mingche M. "An Analysis of Housing Consumption with Implications for the Design of a Housing Allowance Program." In *Analysis of Selected Census and Welfare Program Data to Determine the Relations of Household Characteristics and Administrative Welfare Policies to a Direct Housing Assistance Program.* Cambridge, Massachusetts: Joint Center for Urban Studies, 1973.

H-73   McCarthy, Kevin F. *The Household Life Cycle and Housing Choices.* Paper 5565. Santa Monica, California: The Rand Corporation, January 1976. HUD 0000590.

H-74   _____. *Housing Choices and Residential Mobility in Site I at Baseline.* Working Note 9029-HUD. Santa Monica, California: The Rand Corporation, August 1976. PB 266168. HUD 0050341.

H-75   _____.*Housing Choices and Residential Mobility in Site II at Baseline.* Working Note 9737-HUD. Santa Monica, California: The Rand Corporation, September 1977. PB 277629. HUD 005088.

H-76   _____. *Housing Search and Mobility.* R-2451-HUD. Santa Monica, California: The Rand Corporation, September 1979. HUD 0000953.

H-77   MacLennan, Duncan. "Information, Space and the Measurement of Housing Preferences and Demand." *Scottish Journal of Political Economy.* (June 1977): 97-115.

H-78   MacMillan, Jean. *Applicant Characteristics and Outreach Methods.* Cambridge, Massachusetts: Abt Associates, Inc., April 1976.

H-79   _____. "The Decision to Move—Evidence from the Demand Experiment." In *Do Housing Allowances Work?* Edited by Katharine L. Bradbury and Anthony Downs. Washington, D.C.: The Brookings Institution, forthcoming 1981.

H-80   _____. *Draft Report on Mobility in the Housing Allowance Demand Experiment.* Cambridge, Massachusetts: Abt Associates, Inc., 1978.

H-81   _____. *Report on Mobility in the Housing Allowance Demand Experiment.* Cambridge, Massachusetts: Abt Associates, Inc. (forthcoming).

H-82   Maisel, Sherman J.; Burnham, J,; and Austin, J. "The Demand for Housing: A Comment." *The Review of Economics and Statistics* (1971): 410-413.

H-83   Maisel, Sherman J., and Winnick, L. "Family Housing Expenditures: Elusive Laws and Intrusive Variances." *Proceedings of the Conference on Consumption and Savings.* Philadelphia: University of Pennsylvania Press, 1960.

H-84   Marshall, Alfred. *Principles of Economics.* London: MacMillan Co., 1952.

H-85   Massell, Adele P.; Barnett, C. Lance; and Stucker, James P. *Two Years of Housing Allowances: Income and Housing Expenditure.* Santa Monica, California: The Rand Corporation (forthcoming 1980).

H-86   Mayo, Stephen K. *Housing Expenditures and Quality, Part I: Report on Housing Expenditures under a Percent of Rent Housing Allowance.* Cambridge, Massachusetts: Abt Associates, Inc., January 1977. PB 265833.

H-87   _____. *Theory and Estimation in the Economics of Housing Demand.* Cambridge, Massachusetts: Abt Associates, Inc., 1978.

H-88   Menchik, Mark D. *Residential Mobility of Housing Allowance Recipients.* Note 1144-HUD. Santa Monica, California: The Rand Corporation, October 1979.

H-89   Merrill, Sally R. *Housing Expenditures and Quality, Part III, Report on Hedonic Indices as a Measure of Housing Quality.* Cambridge, Massachusetts: Abt Associates, Inc., December 1977.

H-90   _____. *Hedonic Indices as a Measure of Housing Quality.* Cambridge, Massachusetts: Abt Associates, Inc., December 1977.

H-91   Merrill, Sally R., and Joseph, Catherine A. *Draft Report on Housing Improvements and Upgrading in the Housing Allowance Demand Experiment.* Cambridge, Massachusetts: Abt Associates, Inc., February 1979.

H-92   Merrill, Sally R., and Kennedy, Stephen D. *Report on the Application of Estimated Hedonic Indices to the Measurement of Shopping Behavior.* Cambridge, Massachusetts: Abt Associates, Inc. (forthcoming).

H-93   Morton, Walter. *Housing Taxation.* Madison: University of Wisconsin Press, 1955.

H-94   Mulford, John E. *The Income Elasticity of Housing Demand.* R-2449-HUD. Santa Monica, California: The Rand Corporation, July 1979.

H-95   Murray, Michael. *Benefits to Participants and Non-participants in a Housing Allowance Program.* Working Paper 216-10. Washington, D.C.: The Urban Institute, April 1975.

H-96   _____. "The Distribution of Tenant Benefits in Public Housing." *Econometrica* 43 (July 1975): 771-788.

H-97   _____. *Housing Allowances and the Demand for Public Housing: An Exploratory Analysis.* Working Paper 216-5. Washington, D.C.: The Urban Institute, December 1974.

H-98   Muth, Richard F. "The Demand for Non-farm Housing." In *The Demand for Durable Goods.* Edited by A. Harberger. Chicago: University of Chicago Press, 1960.

H-99   _____. "The Derived Demand for Urban Residential Land." *Urban Studies* (1971): 243-254.

H-100 _____. "The Stock Demand Elasticities for Non-Farm Housing: Comment." *The Review of Economics and Statistics* (November 1975): 447-449.

H-101 Napior, David, and Phipps, Anthony. *Subjective Assessment of Neighborhoods.* Cambridge, Massachusetts: Abt Associates, Inc., 1979.

H-102 Ohls, James C., and Thomas, Cynthia. *The Effects of the Seattle and Denver Income Maintenance Experiments on Housing Consumption, Ownership and Mobility.* Denver, Colorado: Mathematica Policy Research, Inc., 1979.

H-103 Paldam, Martin. "What is Known About the Demand for Housing." *Swedish Journal of Economics* (1979): 130-148.

H-104 Phlips, Louis. *Applied Consumption Analysis.* Amsterdam: North-Holland, 1974.

H-105 Polinsky, A. M. "The Demand for Housing: A Study in Specification and Grouping." *Econometrica* (1977): 447-461.

H-106 Polinsky, A. M., and Ellwood, David. "An Empirical Reconciliation of Micro and Grouped Estimates of the Demand for Housing." *The Review of Economics and Statistics* (1979) : 199-205.

H-107 Pollak, Robert A., and Wales, Terance. "Estimation of Complete Demand Systems from Household Budget Data: The Linear and Quadratic Expenditure Systems." *American Economic Review* 68 (June 1978) : 348-359.

H-108 Quigley, John M., and Weinberg, Daniel H. "Intra-urban Residential Mobility: A Review and Synthesis." *International Regional Science Review.* (Fall 1977) : 41-66.

H-109 Reid, Margaret. *Housing and Income.* Chicago: University of Chicago Press, 1962.

H-110 Roistacher, Elizabeth. "Housing and Home Ownership." In *Five Thousand American Families, Patterns of Economic Progress: Volume II.* Edited by James N. Morgan. Ann Arbor: University of Michigan Institute for Social Research, 1974.

H-111 Rossi, Peter. "Mobility and Search Behavior Implications of EHAP." In *Do Housing Allowances Work?* Edited by Katharine L. Bradbury and Anthony Downs. Washington, D.C.: The Brookings Institution (forthcoming 1981).

H-112 Rydell, C. Peter; Mulford, J. E.; and Kozimor, L. W. *Dynamics of Participation in a Housing Allowance Program.* Working Notes 10200-HUD. Santa Monica, California: The Rand Corporation, June 1978. HUD 000236.

H-113 _____. *Participation Rates in Government Transfer Programs: Application to Housing Allowances.* Paper 6187. Santa Monica, California: The Rand Corporation, January 1979. HUD 0000943.

H-114 Shanley, Michael G., and Hotchkiss, Charles M. *How Low Income Renters Buy Homes.* N-1208-HUD. Santa Monica, California: The Rand Corporation, September 1979.

H-115 Speare, Alden. "Residential Satisfaction as an Intervening Variable in Residential Mobility." *Demography* (May 1974) : 173-188.

H-116 Speare, Alden; Goldstein, Sidney; and Frey, William H. *Residential Mobility, Migration and Metropolitan Change.* Cambridge: Ballinger, 1974.

H-117 Stigler, George J. "The Early History of Empirical Studies of Consumer Behavior." *Journal of Political Economy* (April 1954) : 95-113.

H-118 Straszheim, Mahlon R. "Estimation of the Demand for Urban Housing Services from Household Interview Data." *Review of Economics and Statistics* (February 1973) : 1-8.

H-119 _____. "Participation in the Experimental Housing Allowance Program." In *Do Housing Allowances Work?* Edited by Katharine L. Bradbury and Anthony Downs. Washington, D.C.: The Brookings Institution (forthcoming 1981).

H-120 Struyk, Raymond J. "The Housing Expense Burden of Households Headed by the Elderly." *The Gerontologist* 17 (April 1977) : 130-139.

H-121 _____. "The Housing Situation of Elderly Americans." *The Gerontologist* 17 (October 1977): 447-452.

H-122 Squire, Anne D. *Unit Maintenance and Tenant Satisfaction: Some Results From the Experimental Housing Allowance Program.* Working Paper 249-36. Washington, D.C.: The Urban Institute, November 1979.

H-123 Uhler, Russell. "The Demand for Housing: An Inverse Probability Approach." *The Review of Economics and Statistics* (1968): 129-134.

H-124 U.S. Department of Housing and Urban Development, Office of Policy Development. *The Gautreaux Housing Demonstration: An Evaluation of Its Impact on Participating Households.* Washington, D.C.: U.S. Department of Housing and Urban Development, 1979.

H-125 _____. *Proceedings of the HUD Conference on Housing Choices of Low-Income Households.* Washington, D.C.: U.S. Department of Housing and Urban Development (forthcoming 1981).

H-126 Vidal, Avis. *Draft Report on the Search Behavior of Black Households in Pittsburgh in the Housing Allowance Demand Experiment.* Cambridge, Massachusetts: Abt Associates, Inc., July 1978.

H-127 Wallace, James. *Preliminary Findings from the Experimental Housing Allowance Demand Experiment.* Cambridge, Massachusetts: Abt Associates, Inc., March 1978.

H-128 Weinberg, Daniel; Atkinson, Reilly; Vidal, Avis; Wallace, James E.; and Weisbrod, Glen. *Draft Report on Locational Choice, Part I: Search and Mobility in the Housing Allowance Demand Experiment.* Cambridge, Massachusetts: Abt Associates, Inc., August 1977. PB 273308. HUD 0050422.

H-129 Weinberg, Daniel; Friedman, Joseph; and Mayo, Stephen K. "A Disequilibrium Model of Housing Search and Residential Mobility." *Proceedings of the HUD Conference on Housing Choices of Low-Income Households.* Washington, D.C.: U.S. Department of Housing and Urban Development (forthcoming 1981).

H-130 Weiserbs, D. *More About Dynamic Demand Systems.* Working Paper 7312. Louvain: Institute des Science Economiques, 1973.

H-131 Wienk, Ronald E.; Reid, Clifford E.; Simonson, John C.; and Eggers, Frederick J. *Measuring Racial Discrimination in American Housing Markets: The Housing Market Practices Survey.* Washington, D.C.: U.S. Department of Housing and Urban Development, April 1979.

H-132 Wilkinson, R. K. "The Income Elasticity of Demand for Housing." *Oxford Economic Papers* (1973): 361-377.

H-133 Winger, Alan R. "Housing and Income." *Western Economic Journal* (June 1968): 226-232.

H-134 Winnick, Louis. "Housing: Has There Been a Downward Shift in Consumer Preferences?" *Quarterly Journal of Economics* (1955).

H-135 Wolpert, Julian. "Behavioral Aspects of the Decision to Migrate." *Papers of the Regional Science Association* 15 (1965): 159-169.

H-136 _____. "Migration as an Adjustment to Environmental Stress." *Journal of Social Issues* 22 (October 1966): 92-102.

4. COMMUNITY, MARKET, AND AGENCY ISSUES

C-1 Abt Associates, Inc. *Administrative Costs of Alternative Procedures: A Compendium of Analyses of Direct Costs in the Administrative Agency Experiment.* Cambridge, Massachusetts: Abt Associates, Inc., March 1977. PB 265656. HUD 0050282.

C-2 _____. *Draft Report on the Administration of a Housing Allowance Program: The Enrollment Process; Volume III: Appendices.* Cambridge, Massachusetts: Abt Associates, Inc., January 1975.

C-3 American Public Health Association. *Housing: Basic Health Principles and Recommended Ordinance, 1973.* Washington, D.C.: American Public Health Association, 1973.

C-4 Bala, John E. *Neighborhoods in St. Joseph County, Indiana.* Working Note 1205-HUD. Santa Monica, California: The Rand Corporation, September 1979.

C-5 Barnett, C. Lance. *Expected and Actual Effects of Housing Allowances on Housing Prices.* Paper 6184. Santa Monica, California: The Rand Corporation, January 1979.

C-6 _____. *Using Hedonic Indexes to Measure Housing Quality.* Rand 2450-HUD. Santa Monica, California: The Rand Corporation, October 1979.

C-7 _____. *Using Hedonic Indexes to Measure Supply Response to Housing Allowances.* Working Note 8686-HUD. Santa Monica, California: The Rand Corporation, August 1976. PB 266180. HUD 0050361.

C-8 Barnett, C. Lance, and Lowry, Ira S. *How Housing Allowances Affect Housing Prices.* Rand 2452-HUD. Santa Monica, California: The Rand Corporation, September 1979.

C-9 Birch, David W., et al. *The Behavioral Foundations of Neighborhood Change.* Washington, D.C.: U.S. Department of Housing and Urban Development, January 1979. HUD 0000514.

C-10 Brown, Raymond, and Heiland, Cynthia. *Special Report on Eight Administrative Agency Plans.* Cambridge, Massachusetts: Abt Associates, Inc., August 1973.

C-11 Budding, David W., et al. *Inspection: Implementing Housing Quality Requirements in the Administrative Agency Experiment.* Cambridge, Massachusetts: Abt Associates, Inc., February 1977. PB 266095.

C-12 Courant, Paul. "Racial Prejudice in a Model of the Urban Housing Market." *Journal of Urban Economics* 5 (July 1978).

C-13 de Leeuw, Frank, and Ekanem, Nkanta F. "The Supply of Rental Housing." *American Economic Review.* Volume LXI (December 1971): 806-817.

C-14 _____. "Time Lags in the Rental Housing Market." *Urban Studies.* 10 (February 1973): 39-68.

C-15 de Leeuw, Frank, and Struyk, Raymond J. *The Web of Urban Housing: Analyzing Policy with a Market Simulation.* URI 12900. Washington, D.C.: The Urban Institute, 1975. PB 249898.

C-16 Dickson, Donald S., et al. *Certification: Determining Eligibility and Setting Payment Levels in the Administrative Agency Experiment.* Cambridge, Massachusetts: Abt Associates, Inc., March 1977. PB 265695. HUD 0050388.

C-17 Dildine, L. L., and Massey, F. A. "Dynamic Model of Private Incentives to Housing Maintenance." *Southern Economic Journal* 40 (April 1974) : 631-639.

C-18 Eisenstadt, Karen M. *Factors Affecting Maintenance and Operating Costs in Private Renter Housing.* New York City: New York City Rand Institute, August 1972.

C-19 Ellickson, Bryan C. *Neighborhoods in Brown County.* Working Note 8468-HUD. Santa Monica, California: The Rand Corporation, November 1973. PB 246748. HUD 7501949.

C-20 Ellickson, Phyllis L. *Public Knowledge and Evaluation of Housing Allowances: St. Joseph County, Indiana, 1975.* R-2190-HUD. Santa Monica California: The Rand Corporation, February 1978. HUD 0000378.

C-21 Ellickson, Phyllis L., and Kanouse, David E. *How the Public Views Housing Allowances.* Paper 5960. Santa Monica, California: The Rand Corporation, August 1978.

C-22 _____. *Public Perceptions of Housing Allowances: The First Two Years.* Working Note 9817-HUD. Santa Monica, California: The Rand Corporation, January 1978. PB 278319. HUD 0050110.

C-23 Follain, James R., Jr. "The Price Elasticity of the Long-run Supply of New Housing Construction." *Land Economics* 55 (May 1979) : 190-199.

C-24 Follain, James R., Jr.; Katz, Jane; and Struyk, Raymond J. "Programmatic Options to Encourage Homeownership." In *Occasional Papers in Housing and Community Affairs.* Washington, D.C.: U.S. Department of Housing and Urban Development, 1978.

C-25 Fredland, J. Eric, and MacRae, C. Duncan. *Econometric Models of the Housing Sector, A Policy Oriented Survey.* Working Paper 250-1-1. Washington, D.C.: The Urban Institute, August 1978.

C-26 Glatt, Evelyn. *Potential Problems in the Quality of Housing of Participants in the Section 8 Existing Housing Program.* Washington, D.C.: U.S. Department of Housing and Urban Development, June 1978.

C-27 Goedert, Jeanne E., and Goodman, John L., Jr. *Indicators of the Quality of U.S. Housing.* URI 20200. Washington, D.C.: The Urban Institute, September 1977.

C-28 Grebler, Leo T. *Housing Market Behavior in a Declining Area.* New York: Columbia, 1952.

C-29 Grieson, Robert. "The Supply of Urban Housing." *American Economic Review* (August 1971) : 389-405.

C-30 Hamilton, William L. *A Social Experiment in Program Administration: The Housing Allowance Administrative Agency Experiment.* Cambridge: Abt Books, 1979.

C-31   Hamilton, William L.; Budding, David W.; and Holshouser, William L., Jr. *Administrative Procedures in a Housing Allowance Program: The Administrative Agency Experiment.* Cambridge, Massachusetts: Abt Associates, Inc., March 1977. PB 265635. HUD 0050284.

C-32   Hirsch, Werner Z. *Law and Economics, An Introductory Analysis.* New York: Academic Press, Inc., 1979.

C-33   Hoaglin, David C., and Joseph, Catherine A. *Draft Report on Income Reporting and Verification in the Housing Allowance Demand Experiment.* Cambridge, Massachusetts: Abt Associates, Inc., April 1978.

C-34   Holshouser, William L., Jr. *Report on Selected Aspects of the Jacksonville Housing Allowance Experiment.* Cambridge, Massachusetts, Abt Associates, Inc., 1976. PB 265654. HUD 0050390.

C-35   Holshouser, William L., Jr., et al. *Supportive Services in the Administrative Agency Experiment.* Cambridge, Massachusetts: Abt Associates, Inc., February 1977. PB 265655. HUD 0050404.

C-36   Ingram, Gregory K.; Leonard, Herman B.; and Schafer, Robert. *Simulation of the Market Effects of Housing Allowances, Volume III, Development of the Supply Sector of the NBER Urban Simulation Model.* New York: National Bureau of Economic Research, September 1976.

C-37   Jacobson, Alvin L. *Draft Report on Income Accounting Periods.* Cambridge, Massachusetts: Abt Associates, Inc. (forthcoming).

C-38   James, Franklin J. *Back to the City: An Appraisal of Housing Reinvestment and Population Change in Urban America.* Working Paper 0241-01. Washington, D.C.: The Urban Institute, 1977.

C-39   Johannes, Adell. "Site Focused Documentation, Springfield, Massachusetts, Experimental Housing Allowance Program." Unpublished material from the Administrative Agency Experiment, Abt Associates, Inc., 1976.

C-40   Kain, John F., and Apgar, William C. *Analysis of the Market Effects of Housing Allowances.* Discussion Paper D76-3. Cambridge, Massachusetts: Harvard University Department of City and Regional Planning, October 1976.

C-41   _____. *Simulation of Housing Market Dynamics and Evaluation of Housing Allowances.* Discussion Paper D77-7. Cambridge, Massachusetts: Harvard University Department of City and Regional Planning, June 1977.

C-42   _____. *Simulation of the Market Effects of Housing Allowances, Volume II, Baseline and Policy Simulation for Pittsburgh and Chicago.* New York: National Bureau of Economic Research, January 1977. PB 278364. HUD 0050420.

C-43   Kain, John F.; Apgar, William C., Jr.; and Ginn, J. Royce. *Simulation of the Market Effects of Housing Allowances, Volume I, Description of the NBER Urban Simulation Model.* New York: National Bureau of Economic Research, Inc., August 1976.

C-44   Kain, John F., and Quigley, John M. *Housing Markets and Racial Dis-*

crimination: A Microeconomic Analysis. New York: National Bureau of Economic Research, Inc., 1976.

C-45   Kanouse, David E. *Landlord Knowledge and Evaluation of Housing Allowances: St. Joseph County, Indiana, 1975.* Santa Monica, California: The Rand Corporation (forthcoming 1980).

C-46   Kanouse, David E., and Ellickson, Phyllis L. *Public Perceptions of Housing Allowances.* R-2259-HUD. Santa Monica, California: The Rand Corporation, September 1979. HUD 0000985.

C-47   Kershaw, David, and Williams, Roberton. "Administrative Lessons of the Experimental Housing Allowance Program." In *Do Housing Allowances Work?* Edited by Katharine L. Bradbury and Anthony Downs. Washington, D.C.: The Brookings Institution (forthcoming 1981).

C-48   Kingsley, G. Thomas. *Allowance Program Administration: Interim Findings.* Working Draft 275-HUD. Santa Monica, California: The Rand Corporation, November 1979.

C-49   Kingsley, G. Thomas, and Schlegel, Priscilla. *Analyzing Allowance Program Administrative Costs: Account Structures and Methodology.* Working Draft 274-HUD. Santa Monica, California: The Rand Corporation, August 1979.

C-50   Kozimor, Lawrence W., and Lowry, Ira S. *Estimating the Standard Cost of Adequate Housing.* Santa Monica, California: The Rand Corporation, February 1973.

C-51   Kozimor, Lawrence W., and Lowry, Ira S. *Public Housing and Housing Allowances in South Bend, 1975-76.* Working Note 9714-HUD. Santa Monica, California: The Rand Corporation, February 1977.

C-52   Leaman, Sam H. *Estimated Administrative Cost of a National Housing Allowance.* Working Paper 112-17. Washington, D.C.: The Urban Institute, February 1971.

C-53   Lewis, David B., and Lowry, Ira S. *Estimating the Standard Cost of Adequate Housing.* Working Note 8105-HUD. Santa Monica, California: The Rand Corporation, February 1973. PB 274668. HUD 7591938.

C-54   Lowry, Ira S. *Accounting for Supply Responses.* Working Note 8134-HUD. Santa Monica, California: The Rand Corporation, February 1973.

C-55   _____. "Filtering and Housing Standards." *Land Economics* 36 (November 1960): 362-370.

C-56   _____. *The Housing Assistance Supply Experiment: An Overview.* Paper 5567. Santa Monica, California: The Rand Corporation, January 1976.

C-57   _____. *Inflation in the Standard Cost of Adequate Housing: Site I, 1973-76.* Working Note 9430-HUD. Santa Monica, California: The Rand Corporation, March 1976. HUD 0000381.

C-58   _____. *An Overview of the Housing Assistance Supply Experiment.* Paper 5976. Santa Monica, California: The Rand Corporation, September 1977.

C-59   Lowry, Ira S., and Barnett, C. Lance. "How Housing Allowances Affect

Housing Prices." *Proceedings of HUD Conference on Housing Choices of Low-Income Households.* Washington, D.C.: U.S. Department of Housing and Urban Development (forthcoming 1980).

C-60 Lowry, Ira S.; Rydell, Peter C.; and de Ferranti, David M. *A Dynamic Model of the Production Function for Housing Services.* Working Note 8133-HUD. Santa Monica, California: The Rand Corporation, February 1973.

C-61 McDowell, James L. *Housing Allowances and Home Improvements: Early Findings.* N-1198-HUD. Santa Monica, California: The Rand Corporation, September 1979. HUD 0000967.

C-62 _____. *Housing Repair and Improvement in Response to a Housing Allowance Program.* Paper 6076. Santa Monica, California: The Rand Corporation, May 1978.

C-63 MacMillan, Jean; Hamilton, William L., et al. *Outreach: Generating Applications in the Administrative Agency Experiment.* Cambridge, Massachusetts: Abt Associates, Inc., February 1977. PB 265683. HUD 0050391.

C-64 Maloy, Charles H.; Ernst, Ulrich; Murray, Paul; and LeBlanc, Alice. *The Administrative Cost Simulation Model: A Methodology for Projecting Administrative Costs of a Housing Allowance Agency, Volume I.* Cambridge, Massachusetts: Abt Associates, Inc., March 1977.

C-65 _____. *The Administrative Cost Simulation Model: A Methodology for Projecting Administrative Costs of a Housing Allowance Agency, Volume II.* Cambridge, Massachusetts: Abt Associates, Inc., March 1977.

C-66 Maloy, Charles M.; Madden, Patrick, Jr.; Budding, David W.; and Hamilton, William L. *Administrative Costs in a Housing Allowance Program: Two-Year Costs in the Administrative Agency Experiment.* Cambridge, Massachusetts: Abt Associates, Inc., February 1977. PB 265675. HUD 0050312.

C-67 Marshall, Sue. *The Urban Institute Housing Model: Application to South Bend, Indiana.* Working Paper 216-26. Washington, D.C.: The Urban Institute, June 1976.

C-68 Mayer, Neil Stephen. "Determinants of Landlord Housing Rehabilitation Decisions." Ph.D. dissertation, University of California, Berkeley, 1978.

C-69 Mendelsohn, R. "Empirical Evidence on Home Improvements." *Journal of Urban Economics* 4 (1977): 459-468.

C-70 Mills, Edwin, and Sullivan, Arthur. "Market Effects of the Experimental Housing Allowance Program." In *Do Housing Allowances Work?* Edited by Katharine L. Bradbury and Anthony Downs. Washington, D.C.: The Brookings Institution (forthcoming 1981).

C-71 Muller, Jessica. "Site Focused Data Documentation, Tulsa, Oklahoma, Experimental Housing Allowance Program, Volume I." Unpublished material from the Administrative Agency Experiment, Abt Associates, Inc., 1976.

C-72 Myers, Dorwell. "Housing Allowances, Submarket Relationships and the Filtering Process." *Urban Affairs Quarterly* 1 (1975) : 214-240.

C-73 Neels, Kevin. *Housing Market Response to the Energy Crisis.* Working Draft 387-HUD. Santa Monica, California: The Rand Corporation, November 1979.

C-74 Noland, Charles W. *Indexing the Cost of Producing Housing Services in Site I, 1973-1975.* Working Note 9979-HUD. Santa Monica, California: The Rand Corporation, June 1978. HUD 0000260.

C-75 _____. *Indexing the Cost of Producing Housing Services in Site II, 1974-1975.* Working Note 9980-HUD. Santa Monica, California: The Rand Corporation, May 1978. HUD 0000233.

C-76 _____. *Indexing the Cost of Producing Housing Services: Site I, 1973.* Working Draft 9022-HUD. Santa Monica, California: The Rand Corporation, January 1977. PB 266251. HUD 0050498.

C-77 _____. *Indexing the Cost of Producing Housing Services: Site I, 1973-1974.* Working Note 9735-HUD. Santa Monica, California: The Rand Corporation, April 1977. PB 268867. HUD 0050499.

C-78 _____. *Indexing the Cost of Producing Housing Services: Site II, 1974.* Working Note 9736-HUD. Santa Monica, California: The Rand Corporation, May 1977. PB 270654. HUD 270654.

C-79 Owen, Michael S., and Struyk, Raymond J. *Market Effects of New Construction Subsidy Housing Allowance Programs.* Working Paper 221-4. Washington, D.C.: The Urban Institute, April 1975.

C-80 Ozanne, Larry J. *Estimates of the Inflationary Effects of Housing Allowances for 39 Metropolitan Areas.* Washington, D.C.: The Urban Institute, forthcoming.

C-81 _____. *Housing Allowances in Combination with New Construction and Rehabilitation Subsidies.* Working Paper 221-9. Washington, D.C.: The Urban Institute, August 1975.

C-82 _____. *Simulations of Housing Allowances Policies for U.S. Cities: 1960-1970.* Working Paper 216-3. Washington, D.C.: The Urban Institute, December 1974.

C-83 Ozanne, Larry J., and Struyk, Raymond J. *Housing from the Existing Stock: Comparative, Economic Analyses of Owner-Occupants and Landlords.* Paper 221-10. Washington, D.C.: The Urban Institute, May 1976.

C-84 Ozanne, Larry J., and Thibodeau, Thomas. *Market Effects of Housing Allowance Demand Shifts and the Price of Housing.* Working Paper 249-37. Washington, D.C.: The Urban Institute, January 1980.

C-85 Perry, Wayne D. *How Housing Allowance Programs Affect Housing Markets.* Working Draft 401-HUD. Santa Monica, California: The Rand Corporation, October 1979.

C-86 Pollock, Richard. "Supply of Residential Construction: A Cross-section

Examination of Recent Housing Market Behavior." *Land Economics* (February 1973) : 63-66.

C-87 Porter, David O. "Where is the Administration in the Administrative Agency Experiment? A Critique of 'Administrative Lessons of the Experimental Housing Allowance Programs' by Kershaw and Williams." In *Do Housing Allowances Work?* Edited by Katharine L. Bradbury and Anthony Downs. Washington, D.C.: The Brookings Institution (forthcoming 1981).

C-88 Rydell, Peter C. *Effects of Market Conditions on Prices and Profits of Rental Housing.* Paper 6008. Santa Monica, California: The Rand Corporation, September 1977. HUD 0000589.

C-89 _____. *Factors Affecting Maintenance and Operating Costs in Federal Public Housing Projects.* New York: New York City Rand Institute, December 1970.

C-90 _____. *Market Versus Regulation Methods of Preventing Price Increases in Housing Assistance Programs.* Working Draft 414-HUD. Santa Monica, California: The Rand Corporation, November 1979.

C-91 _____. *Measuring the Supply Response to Housing Allowances.* Paper 5564. Santa Monica, California: The Rand Corporation, January 1976.

C-92 _____. *Rental Housing in Site I: Characteristics of the Capital Stock at Baseline.* Working Note 8978-HUD. Santa Monica, California: The Rand Corporaiton, August 1975. PB 245853. HUD 0050049.

C-93 _____. *The Shortrun Response of Housing Markets to Demand Shifts.* Rand 2453-HUD. Santa Monica, California: The Rand Corporation, September 1979.

C-94 _____. *Vacancy Duration and Housing Market Condition.* Working Note 10074-HUD. Santa Monica, California: The Rand Corporation, January 1978. PB 277540. HUD 0050461.

C-95 Rydell, Peter C., and Friedman, J. *Rental Housing in Site I: Market Structure and Conditions at Baseline.* Working Note 8980-HUD. Santa Monica, California: The Rand Corporation, April 1975. PB 246747. HUD 7501945.

C-96 Schnare, Ann B. *Housing in Black and White: Patterns of Segregation in American Housing Markets.* Working Paper 246-4. Washington, D.C.: The Urban Institute, December 1977.

C-97 Schnare, Ann B., and Struyk, Raymond J. "An Analysis of Ghetto Housing Prices Over Time." In *Residential Location and Urban Housing Markets.* Edited by Gregory K. Ingram. Cambridge, Massachusetts: Ballinger Publishing Company, 1977.

C-98 Smith, Barton. "The Supply of Urban Housing." *Quarterly Journal of Economics.* (August 1976) : 389-405.

C-99 Smith, Rodney T. *Welfare Reform and Housing Assistance.* Rand 2333-HUD. Santa Monica, California: The Rand Corporation, September 1979.

C-100 Springer, Michael. *Enforcing Housing Quality Standards: Some Find-*

ings from the Experimental Housing Allowance Program. Working
Paper 249-10. Washington, D.C.: The Urban Institute, June 1978.

C-101 Stegman, Michael. *Housing Investment in the Inner City.* Cambridge:
MIT Press, 1972.

C-102 Sternlieb, George. *The Tenement Landlord.* New Brunswick: State University at Rutgers Urban Studies Center, 1969.

C-103 Stucker, James P. *Rent Inflation in Brown County, Wisconsin: 1973-78.*
Working Note 10073-HUD. Santa Monica, California: The Rand Corporation, August 1978. HUD 0000506.

C-104 _____. *Rent Inflation in St. Joseph County, Indiana: 1974-77.* Working Note 9734-HUD. Santa Monica, California: The Rand Corporation, September 1977. PB 277541. HUD 0050085.

C-105 Stucker, Jennifer. "The Importance of Income Verification in the Section
8 Housing Assistance Payments Program." *Occasional Papers in Housing and Community Affairs* 6 (December 1979) : 32-40.

C-106 Struyk, Raymond J. *A New System for Public Housing: Salvaging a
National Resource.* Washington, D.C.: The Urban Institute, 1980.

C-107 Struyk, Raymond J., and Soldo, Beth J. *Improving the Elderly's Housing.*
Cambridge: Ballinger Publishing Company, Inc., 1980.

C-108 Sweeney, James L. "Housing Unit Maintenance and the Mode of Tenure." *Journal of Economic Theory* 8 (June 1974) : 111-138.

C-109 Tebbets, Paul E. *Controlling Errors in Allowance Program Administration.* Working Note 1145-HUD. Santa Monica, California: The Rand
Corporation, August 1979. HUD 0000965.

C-110 Thomas, Cynthia. "Mobility in the Seattle and Denver Income Maintenance Experiments." *Proceedings from the HUD Conference on Housing Choices of Low-Income Households.* Washington, D.C.: U.S. Department of Housing and Urban Development (forthcoming 1981).

C-111 U.S. Bureau of the Census. *City and County Data Book: 1972.* Washington, D.C.: U.S. Government Printing Office, 1973.

C-112 _____. *Residential Alterations and Repairs, Annual 1977.* Washington, D.C.: U.S. Government Printing Office, May 1978.

C-113 _____. *U.S. Census of Housing: 1970 Housing Characteristics for
States, Cities and Counties, Volume I.* Washington, D.C.: U.S. Government Printing Office, 1971.

C-114 U.S. Department of Housing and Urban Development. *Home Improvement Financing.* Washington, D.C.: U.S. Department of Housing and
Urban Development, September 1977. HUD 0000818.

C-115 _____. *Proceedings of the HUD Conference on Housing Choices of
Low-Income Households.* Washington, D.C.: U.S. Department of Housing and Urban Development (forthcoming 1981).

C-116 _____. *The Section 8 Moderate Rehabilitation Program: An Application Guide.* Washington, D.C.: U.S. Department of Housing and Urban
Development, August 1979.

C-117 Vanski, Jean E. *The Urban Institute Housing Model: Application to*

Green Bay, Wisconsin. Working Paper 216-17. Washington, D.C.: The Urban Institute, June 1976.

C-118 Vanski, Jean E., and Ozanne, Larry J. *Simulating the Housing Allowance Program in Green Bay and South Bend: A Comparison of the Urban Institute Housing Model and the Supply Experiment.* URI 23800. Washington, D.C.: The Urban Institute, October 1978.

C-119 Wiewel, Wim. *Hungarian-Americans in St. Joseph County, Indiana: Implications of Ethnicity for Social Policy.* Paper 6225. Santa Monica, California: The Rand Corporation, March 1979.

C-120 White, Charles S. "Site Focused Data Documentation, San Bernardino, California, Experimental Housing Allowance Program, Volume I." Unpublished material from the Administrative Agency Experiment, Abt Associates, Inc., 1976.

C-121 White, Sammis B. *Market Intermediaries and Indirect Suppliers: First Year Report for Site I.* Working Note 9400-HUD. Santa Monica, California: The Rand Corporation, September 1976. PB 266141. HUD 0050523.

C-122 _____. *Market Intermediaries and Indirect Suppliers: First Year Report for Site II.* Working Note 9020-HUD. Santa Monica, California: The Rand Corporation, August 1977. PB 271638.

C-123 Winger, Alan R. "Some Internal Determinants of Upkeep Spending by Urban Homeowners." *Land Economics* 49 (November 1973): 474-479.

C-124 Wolfe, Marian F., and Hamilton, William L. *Jacksonville: Administering a Housing Allowance Program in a Difficult Environment.* Cambridge, Massachusetts: Abt Associates, Inc., February 1977. PB 264673.

C-125 Wolfe, Marian F.; Hamilton, William L.; Trend, M. G.; and Wild, Bradford S. *Elderly Participants in the Administrative Agency Experiment.* Cambridge, Massachusetts: Abt Associates, Inc., March 1977. PB 265685. HUD 0050349.

Index